Palgrave Advances in Bioeconomy: Economics and Policies

Series Editor
Justus Wesseler
Agricultural Economics and Rural Policy Group
Wageningen University
Wageningen, The Netherlands

This series addresses recent trends in the emerging field of the bioeconomy, with a focus on the implications for economics and policy. The range of topics covered includes the policy environment and related legal issues affecting the development of the bioeconomy; how to measure the contribution of the bioeconomy to sustainable economic development and the circular economy; understanding its impact on regional, and in particular rural, development; generation of economic opportunities to reduce urban migration; integration into and development of new supply chains for the bioeconomy; and strategies and opportunities for cascading utilisation of bio-based products. The series' publications will be relevant for students, researchers and policymakers eager to keep up-to-date with these developments for their own research and field of work.

Dalia Vidickienė • Rita Lankauskienė
Rasa Melnikienė
Živilė Gedminaitė-Raudonė
Paweł Chmieliński
Vitalija Simonaitytė • Goda Lukoseviciute

Human Settlement in the Service Economy Era

An Evolutionary Perspective

palgrave
macmillan

Dalia Vidickienė
Lithuanian Centre for Social Sciences
Vilnius, Lithuania

Rita Lankauskienė
Lithuanian Centre for Social Sciences
Vilnius, Lithuania

Rasa Melnikienė
Lithuanian Centre for Social Sciences
Vilnius, Lithuania

Živilė Gedminaitė-Raudonė
Lithuanian Centre for Social Sciences
Vilnius, Lithuania

Paweł Chmieliński
Polish Academy of Sciences
Warsaw, Poland

Vitalija Simonaitytė
Lithuanian Centre for Social Sciences
Vilnius, Lithuania

Goda Lukoseviciute
Luxembourg Institute
of Socio-Economic Research
Esch-sur-Alzette, Luxembourg

ISSN 2524-5848 ISSN 2524-5856 (electronic)
Palgrave Advances in Bioeconomy: Economics and Policies
ISBN 978-3-032-19389-6 ISBN 978-3-032-19390-2 (eBook)
https://doi.org/10.1007/978-3-032-19390-2

This Palgrave Macmillan imprint is published by the registered company Springer Nature Switzerland AG.
The registered company address is: Gewerbestrasse 11, 6330 Cham, Switzerland

Praise for *Human Settlement in the Service Economy Era*

"An excellent scientific explanation of the service economy on the background of human settlements, its historic and contemporary evolution and organisation. On the example of a broad variety of real cases various development strategies are clearly compared and conclusions are drawn in the way of detecting valuable symbiosis for the design of future sustainable settlements."

—Klaus Wagner, *Federal Institute of Agricultural Economics, Rural and Mountain Research, Vienna, Austria.*

"The evolutionary approach in social sciences is widely recognised as one of the most vital and promising perspectives, often inspiring transdisciplinary insights that enrich all disciplines involved. *Human Settlement in the Service Economy Era: An Evolutionary Perspective* represents both a holistic and evolutionary view, making this volume an engaging and potentially influential contribution to economics, sociology, economic geography, and environmental studies. Grounded in strong theoretical foundations – particularly the holistic Theory of Qualitative Structure and its derived strategies – the book offers a compelling discussion of evolutionary changes such as servitization and their implications for post-urban, post-industrial, and post-capitalist settlements – including their economies, lifestyles, cultures, and ecologies. From a policy perspective, it provides valuable insights into the urgently needed debate on the future developmental goals of human settlements. Altogether, this book stands as an important resource not only for researchers and students but also for policymakers."

—Katarzyna Leśniewska-Napierała & Tomasz Napierała, *Institute of Urban Geography, Tourism Studies, and Geoinformation, Faculty of Geographical Sciences, University of Lodz, Poland*

Human Settlement in the Service Economy Era: An Evolutionary Perspective collates and distils the latest thinking on how human settlements are changing in the post-industrial era. Reflecting shifts in work patterns, social dynamics and sustainability, the authors highlight symbiosis as a dominant theme throughout these and other patterns driving changes to human habitation, particularly in Europe. This book is an important guide to understanding human settlement in the 21st century.

—Jonny Hanson, PhD, *Queen's University Belfast, Northern Ireland*

Competing Interests The authors have no competing interests to declare that are relevant to the content of this manuscript.

About the Book

The book outlines the original theoretical background to the major socio-economic drivers of human settlement evolution throughout history, based on the Theory of Qualitative Structure. It is argued here that the rise of a post-industrial service-based economy works as a catalyst for cardinal changes in current lifestyles and requires the creation of a new vision for human settlement organization. In the same way that the transition from an agrarian to an industrial economic system has historically led to urbanization through the creation of manufacturing jobs that attracted people to cities and transformed their daily practices, the transition to a post-industrial service economy is leading to significant qualitative changes in lifestyles because of new forms of work organization. Innovative service-oriented business models based on the concept of servitization of manufacturing and farming, which are increasingly being used as an alternative to the industrial "take-make-dispose" business model, require substantial organizational changes in the planning and design of future settlements. The examination of the human settlement as a whole entity and analysis of its qualitative structure enabled the design of an evolutionary framework that explains how any human settlement can be gradually evolved through the implementation of six generic strategies. The framework reveals the evolutionary dynamics and logic hidden within the highly complex system of human settlements, providing us with a unique set of tools to understand better the general organizational patterns that emerge in human settlements. Case studies help link theory to the practical world, demonstrating a range of settlement designs and development strategies oriented to post-industrial realities. Findings from both theory and practice outline the general vision of settlements in the Service Economy Era and provide actionable insights for eco-communities and policymakers on how to exit the Anthropocene and enter the Symbiocene.

Contents

List of Figures

CHAPTER 1

Introduction: Service Economy as a Driver for a New Vision of the Human Settlement

Dalia Vidickienė

Human settlements are the foundation of human existence, shaping how we live, work, and interact with one another and the environment. Throughout history, settlements have served as sanctuaries where people build lives, secure resources, and cultivate connections. Everything that happens in human society is reflected in human settlements in an integrated way.

The global landscape of human settlement has undergone significant transformations throughout history. The last radical transformation in the organization of the human settlement system was related to the shift from the agrarian to the industrial settlement model. As noted by Taft (2018), since the Industrial Revolution, cities and industry have grown together. During the industrial era, cities were a preferred place to live, and the term 'urban development' was used as a synonym for the term 'development of human settlements'.

Urbanization has thus far been considered an inevitable paradigm, as cities are referred to as the centres of economic growth, opportunity, prosperity, innovation, and social and cultural interaction (Paddison, 2001; Michalina et al., 2021). However, the current urban conditions are drawing attention to the need to mitigate ongoing urbanization processes. Increased pollution, extended commuting, unbridled land use, precarious

D. Vidickienė et al., *Human Settlement in the Service Economy Era*, Palgrave Advances in Bioeconomy: Economics and Policies,
https://doi.org/10.1007/978-3-032-19390-2_1

settlements, and other negative impacts of urban population growth have progressively reduced the advantages of urban living. Urban development is now questioned by the widespread use of new technologies, the implementation of green and circular economies, and the urgent need to mitigate climate change, for which large urban agglomerations also have responsibility (Motta et al., 2022). All of this led us to reflect on whether existing urban development models remain valid in this profoundly changed context and to seek a new approach capable of overcoming the current shortcomings and the aforementioned negative impacts.

Over the past few decades, two discourses on the future of the human settlement system have emerged in response to growing environmental, economic, and social challenges. The discourses can be defined as a group of ideas and a patterned way of thinking based on the belief that the current urban development strategy should be (1) revised or (2) fundamentally changed.

The first discourse is based on the belief that the industrial system is the best and the only way forward for human development. It operates within the framework based on the binary of industrial versus post-industrial. The term 'post-industrial' is often used synonymously with economic decline, stagnation, and marginalization, which, in turn, has resulted in stigmatizing representations and depictions of those places deemed post-industrial (Luger & Schwarze, 2024).

Another synonym for the term 'post-industrial' for the advocates of the first discourse is 'deindustrialisation'. They describe deindustrialization as the decline of a nation's or region's industrial capacity, which emerged as a significant process in many advanced economies starting in the mid-twentieth century. This shift was characterized by a reduction of employment in manufacturing as a share of total employment and a corresponding increase in the service sector. The supporters of the first discourse regard deindustrialization with alarm and suspect that the growth in the number of people employed in the service sector is primarily related to the lack of jobs in the manufacturing sector and the expansion of the bureaucratic apparatus. They believe that countries or regions where the service sector will be developed more than the manufacturing sector may experience economic stagnation or at least slower economic growth. This point of view associates 'real' economic growth only with the increase in the production of manufactured goods; as in the early stages of industrialization, the productivity of most activities in the service sector was significantly lower than in manufacturing and industrialized agriculture. According to the first discourse, the process of deindustrialization is not a natural consequence of overproduction due to high productivity of many global industries, such as automobiles, electronics, and textiles, but rather a process during which countries and cities fail to ensure their economic growth and competitiveness (Alderson, 1999; Rowthorn & Coutts, 2004; Pike, 2019).

Urban sciences mainly analyse the deindustrialization processes in the context of geographical political economy. The primary escalating theme in urban studies is the transfer of manufacturing firms from highly developed countries to developing countries, as many large cities face significant challenges when industrial giants close their factories. As people and places suffering from structural economic change have registered disaffection with the political-economic system across both the global North and South, the supporters of the first discourse emphasize that deindustrialization disrupts the expected development path (Pike, 2022). Coping with deindustrialization for them means dealing with a two-steps-forward, one-step-back development trajectory that pulls people and places into a cycle of wins and losses, rather than onto a progressive upward curve (Doussard et al., 2009; Hackworth, 2019; Clark, 2022).

The proponents of the first discourse are trying to find an answer to the question: 'How to overcome the negative effects of the industrial system while retaining the same basic structure and ways of functioning?' In their opinion, it is possible to avoid or mitigate the negative effects of industrial mode emerging at the maturity stage of its life cycle through a combination of sustainable development programmes with technological innovations leading to the rise of 'smart cities' that leverage technologies like artificial intelligence, the Internet of Things, and big data to enhance transportation, energy management, and other aspects of urban life. The concept of Sustainable Development serves as a basis for global and local policies and initiatives and is referred to as a key tool for reconciliation between economic development, quality of social life, and natural environment. Urban sustainability studies have sought to clarify each dimension of sustainability by providing extensive lists of sustainability assessment indicators and recommendations on how to enhance sustainability through innovative technological and architectural solutions, as well as governance practices.

The environmental dimension received the most attention as the industrial economic system induced an unprecedented scale of environmental crisis. However, the proposed management initiatives addressing the environmental dimension of sustainability often fail, as the top-down approach to environmental crises has created a gap between rhetoric and action, frequently leading to greenwashing practices. Greenwashing is observed at all spheres and levels, including corporate (de Freitas Netto et al., 2020) and governmental (Ben Mahjoub, 2025). Greenwashing strategies in urban development have evolved from corporate greening in the past to the development of green urban utopias nowadays, which serve to mainstream corporations involved in 'business as usual' market interests (Sze, 2015; Schuetze & Chelleri, 2016). The tensions between sustainability and greenwashing are also discussed in the last decade's critiques on eco-cities, which are presented as laboratories where complex partnerships of private corporations and public entities test the latest design principles and technologies for the future so-called green and sustainable (or zero-emission) cities (Shwayri, 2013; Yu, 2014). Key criticisms include the tendency for eco-city projects to be techno-centric and market-driven, potentially neglecting social and democratic aspects of urban life. Urban planning experts argue that many top-down 'eco-city' projects do little to benefit nature beyond planting a few trees, while others inflict serious harm on the local environment and divert vast non-renewable resources to ambitious plans that often fail to materialize (Nugent, 2023). Case studies also reveal various critical insights for urban development concerning the current sustainability fallacy of mega-projects, related to top-down, technocratic densification, and greening practices (Marshall, 2000; Schuetze & Chelleri, 2016). The latest research findings indicate that urban renaissance, enabling sustainability principles, requires integrated, small-scale, incremental, and adaptive (stepwise) urban planning and design processes that go well beyond general strategies following the so-called green growth paradigm (Schuetze & Chelleri, 2016).

Based on the belief that the industrial system has no alternatives, a significant share of public financial resources is allocated to maintain the sustainability of the industrial mode. 2025 marks the 10th anniversary of the adoption of the Sustainable Development Goals (SDGs) and the 10th edition of the Sustainable Development Report (SDR). Prepared by the SDSN's SDG Transformation Center, the SDR reviews progress made each year on the SDGs since their adoption by the 193 UN member states. According to the last report, the SDGs are far off track (Sachs et al., 2025). At the global level, none of the 17 goals are currently on course to be achieved by 2030. Most UN member states have made significant progress only in achieving targets related to 1) mortality among children under five and neonates (SDG 3), and 2) the expansion of digital industrialization to ensure access to basic services and infrastructure, including mobile broadband (SDG 9), access to electricity (SDG 7), and internet usage (SDG 9).

Poor achievements raise a question: May the exhaustion of the sustainability framework finally open the intellectual and political space for a big push beyond the established socio-economic order? Supporters of the second discourse answer this question in the negative. In their opinion, the main reason for poor progress is that sustainability, by definition, is an insufficient framework to capture the myriad issues and solutions required to make a world more liveable for future generations. Costanza and Patten noted (1995, p. 193) that 'the basic idea of sustainability is quite straightforward: a sustainable system is one which survives or persists... Sustainability, at its base, always concerns temporality, and in particular, longevity'. While many well-intentioned actions occur within the sustainable development framework and can make a difference, the concept itself limits our ability to change and improve over time, and there is a need to go beyond the framework of sustainability (Blühdorn, 2016; Foster, 2018; Schurig & Turan, 2022; Takkinen, 2025).

The advocates of the second discourse argue that the concept of sustainability should be expanded to a more complex worldview that offers an evolutionary approach. From an evolutionary point of view, we should strive for more than just 'sustainability'. Sustainability can be defined as the ability or capacity of something to be maintained or to sustain itself over time. However, the evolution of humanity and human habitats is a continuous process; if the evolution of a particular settlement stops, conditions are created that would lead to its decline and eventual demise. *According to the proponents of the second discourse, the feasibility of pursuing an industrial way of economic and social development should be brought into question.* The evolutionary approach encourages us to ask the questions: Is the industrial mode of production and lifestyle a culmination of human civilization? Is there no more advanced economic development trajectory?

In the late twentieth century, doubts about the industrial paradigm as the most progressive development trajectory were growing, and academic literature often began to use a large number of terms with the prefix 'post'. They relate not only to the term 'post-industrial', which refers to the stage of economic and social development following industrialization. The critical reassessment and recognition of the limitations and shortcomings of earlier concepts developed during the industrial era, such as post-modernism, post-capitalism, post-fordism, post-humanism, and post-anthropocentrism, are widespread in the socioeconomic sciences. Doubts also arise about the main strategies of socio-economic development applied during the industrial era, as expressed through the terms 'post-growth' and 'post-productive'. In urban development literature, discussions on a 'post-rural' (Hopkins, 1998; Murdoch & Pratt, 1993; Brunori, 2006; Battaglia et al., 2015; Conn, 2024) and 'post-urban' world have also emerged (Westlund, 2014, 2018; Westlund & Haas, 2018; de Olde & Oosterlynck, 2022; Westlund & Borseková, 2025).

The prefix 'post' comes from the Latin word 'post', which means 'after' or 'beyond'. It refers to a change, a departure, or an evolution from what came before. When connected with a specific concept or paradigm, 'post-' usually refers to critical reflection or a response to the ideas and practices associated with that concept. The widespread use of the prefix 'post' testifies that many of the core attitudes prevailing in today's society are being challenged. Each new or repeatable use of terms with the prefix 'post' is a sign that it is not enough to make some improvements within the framework of the industrial paradigm. Growing critics of all major socio-economic conceptions of the industrial era indicate that humanity's development should enter a new cycle of its socio-economic evolution, leading to the fundamental transformation of the industrial lifestyle.

Over several centuries, humanity's evolution has been viewed through technological paradigm shifts, often referred to as revolutions. However, the evolutionary approach to the socio-economic paradigm encourages us to identify and understand changes over more extended periods. From the perspective of the human settlement system organization, the most influential forces on the worldwide landscape of human settlement have been the Agrarian and Industrial Revolutions. Both revolutions led to fundamental transformations of the dominant socio-economic paradigm, dramatically reshaping human settlements. The Agrarian Revolution encouraged a shift from the Hunter-Gatherer Lifestyle to the Farmer's lifestyle, leading to the establishment of permanent settlements instead of mobile camps. The Industrial Revolution spurred urbanization, leading to the growth of cities as manufacturing plants attracted large numbers of workers from rural areas.

As a result of the Industrial Revolution, society for a long time was divided into two distinct worlds—urban and rural. Employees of manufacturing plants have lived in company towns and cities, as dictated by the laws of industrial society, and the livelihood and lifestyle of rural area inhabitants have continued to depend on agriculture. The line between urban and rural lifestyles, however, became blurred because of the mass industrialization of agriculture. Contrary to urban dwellers' belief that industrialization of agricultural activities is a long-gone phenomenon, the authors studying the economic history of agriculture claim that the mass industrialization (often referred to as 'modernization') of agriculture began only after the Second World War (Federico, 2005; LaVerne, 2012; Martín-Retortillo & Pinilla, 2012). Until then, agricultural machinery was used on a large scale only on farms specializing in grain production in the Great Plains and Pacific regions of North America and in the Soviet Union. Due to the massive introduction of mechanization, electrification, irrigation, and chemicalization processes following the Second World War, the agricultural sector in the developed industrial (northern) countries has undergone a real revolution (Harwood, 1990; Clunies-Ross & Hildyard, 2013). Industrialized agriculture has essentially transformed farms into factories, requiring inputs such as synthetic fertilizers, chemical pesticides, large amounts of irrigation water, and fossil fuels to produce crops and livestock through mechanized production methods. The farmers began to depend on money, rather than land, to feed themselves. The production mode became the same as that applied in industry: mechanization and segmentation of work, specialization of output, and standardization of product. Agriculture had become capital-intensive, and farmers' capital and credit needs were growing at record paces. Farmers' business success had become heavily dependent on external factors, such as the situation in the manufacturing sector and the markets.

After the mass industrialization of agriculture, agricultural production has lost all its autonomy in the major industrialized nations. Traditional farms have been absorbed or obliterated by larger units and have become an integral part of industrial production and consumption. All the infrastructure of the countryside became a part of the urban fabric. Villages and small cities became dependencies, partial colonies of the metropolis. It led to the total urbanization through the 'homogenization of built environments, visual landscapes, and popular tastes and fashions' (Soja, 2011, p. 683).

The transformation processes in the lifestyles and livelihoods of rural inhabitants occurred incredibly rapidly after the Industrial Revolution in agriculture. Over several decades, the lifestyle in villages began to resemble that of residents in towns and small cities. Employment in the agricultural sector declined drastically in rural regions (Bryden & Bollman,

2000). For example, in 1990, employment in agriculture in predominantly rural regions as a percentage of total employment was 5.9% in the US, 10.3% in the UK, and 10.8% in France (OECD, 1996).

Typical peasant life in agricultural villages has also been organized according to the rules of manufacturing enterprises. The urban–rural dichotomy has terminated, and a synthesis has emerged in which neither the city nor the countryside is what they were before the mass industrialization of agriculture. The society has become 'completely urbanized' (Westlund, 2018).

In the twenty-first century, a complex interplay of new factors is again reshaping the way we inhabit our planet and could serve as a logical precursor to the next revolution, which is beginning a new big evolutionary cycle in all socioeconomic systems. Advocates of the second discourse believe that following earlier agrarian and industrial 'revolutions', post-industrialism suggested yet another revolution that would again transform how societies were organized (Hoey, 2015).

The main obstacle to applying the new socioeconomic development paradigm is that the essentiality of the term 'post-industrial' has long been misunderstood and underdeveloped. It is insufficient to declare that humanity has entered a new era; understanding the key differences between industrial and post-industrial societies is necessary. To understand the essence of the new post-industrial era, attempts have been made to find a name that best describes its main direction of socio-economic development. Various names were proposed for an emerging cycle of evolution: 'information', 'knowledge', 'organized', 'platform', 'network', 'conventional', 'programmable', experience', 'dream' society, etc. Scholars have developed special theories to argue their concepts.

For several decades, the essence of the new paradigm was shaped by the proponents of the first discourse. They examine the current stage of development within the framework of Kondratiev's long cycles of technological change (Barnett, 2016) and suggest that it has emerged as the next technological revolution, entailing a period of economic growth. As the Fourth Industrial Revolution enabled society to enter the Age of Information and Telecommunications, it was named the 'information society', where the usage, creation, distribution, manipulation, and integration of information are significant activities (Duff, 2014). In their opinion, in a socio-economic context, it means a shift from societies where physical resources and manual labour were primary to ones where information, knowledge, and digital technologies play a central role in all aspects of life. 'Information society' and 'knowledge society' became the most popular names, and they were widely used not only in academic literature but also in public administration and business management.

The proponents of the second discourse argue that the shift to post-industrial society is a broader process in which non-technological innovations play a key role. The post-industrial paradigm is emerging as a set of responses to the old industrialization paradigm through several paradigm innovations that require radical changes in our thinking and behaviour. 'Paradigm innovations are changes in the underlying mental models which frame what the organization does' (Bessant & Tidd, 2007, p. 13). Not all of them are well understood. However, most scholars agree that a holistic view of the differences between industrial and post-industrial paradigms should be based on the transition from producing and providing products as goods to service delivery, with very few firms directly manufacturing any goods. Although the role of the service sector was emphasized from the outset (see Bell, 1973), the real difference between the mental and organizational models of industrial and post-industrial economic systems became evident only in the last decade of the twentieth century with the concept of servitization. After several decades of criticism on the service-oriented nature of the post-industrial economic system, evidence has emerged that manufacturing firms are servitizing—either adding services to or integrating services into their core products. Servitization leads to the end of service as we know it.

The concept of servitization begins with the premise that companies must offer the function of the product, rather than the product itself. Industrial companies that manufacture technically complex machines and equipment, whose exploitation and repair require specialized high-tech skills, were among the first to apply various business models based on the 'Product plus service' system. They began to provide services by financing, exploiting, maintaining, and updating their own or other manufacturers' products installed in the production process. Various service-driven business models are applied. For example, Rolls-Royce, a manufacturer of jet aircraft engines, earns an increasing share of its revenue with the TotalCare® service package. With this service package, engines are rented to airlines. Rolls-Royce offers 'power by the hour', allowing customers to use aircraft engines and receive services like maintenance without actually owning them. The company leases the functionality of its engines, applying a 'pay-per-hour' payment system, and providing comprehensive maintenance services for its products to ensure that the engines operate flawlessly (Ng et al., 2012). A similar example of a service replacing a product-selling approach can be paint suppliers to automotive original equipment manufacturers (OEMs). Instead of selling paint and being paid per litre supplied, they are now often engaged to run the OEM's paint line and be paid per automobile painted (Spring & Araujo, 2009). Another manufacturing company often cited as an example of successful servitization is Xerox. At the first stage of servitization, the Xerox company transformed itself from a copier manufacturer into a document copying service provider (White et al., 1999). Later, it began offering advanced services. A firm initially known for photocopiers, Xerox now positions itself as an enterprise for business processes and management. Today, over half of Xerox's business comes from services. In recent years, Xerox has branched out to offer document publishing and production services, document management, and business process outsourcing. Examples of services in practice include providing Hertz with learning solutions, including curriculum content, administration, and learner support services. On the Xerox blog, the process Xerox has gone through is described as the essence of servitization: 'utilizing technology to offer services tightly coupled with existing products'.

Economic studies indicate that service processes in manufacturing companies are continually expanding. At the end of the last decade of the twentieth century, the income of manufacturing companies from providing services was 10–30% higher than the income from selling new products (Wise & Baumgartner, 1999). On average, the income of manufacturing companies from the provision of services accounted for 25% of their total income (Koudal, 2006). Recently, the pace of servitization of manufacturing companies has exceeded all expectations. The market for servitization has been growing exponentially, yielding significantly higher profit margins on services than on products sold by manufacturing firms (Probst et al., 2016). The number of manufacturers adding services to their offerings is rising, with recent evidence indicating that the proportion reaches up to two-thirds of manufacturing firms in developed economies (Crozet & Milet, 2017).

Farmers are also adopting various 'Product plus service' systems. Most farming servitization projects emerge when a farm that operates according to an industrial product-oriented business model faces serious business challenges. When the efforts to construct portfolios of agricultural products with a tolerable level of risk are unsuccessful, many farms decide to combine agricultural activities with the provision of services that are less risky and more profitable than agriculture. Instead of supplying agricultural products to a mass, anonymous, and unpredictable food market, entrepreneurial farmers are building their customer base through a combination of producing agricultural products and providing services (Vidickienė et al., 2024).

Adding services to agricultural products is becoming the standard organic food supply model (Lankauskienė et al., 2022; Vidickienė et al., 2023; Vidickienė & Lankauskienė, 2025). Many farms respond to growing consumer demands for fresh, locally produced food by delivering products directly to customers' workplaces or homes. Some farmers extend the service component and implement harvest-to-order or grow-to-order systems, thereby diversifying their food offerings to meet the specific needs of their clients. Servitization is a practical approach to overcoming barriers to farm development in specialized farms that derive all their income from a single product type and are more susceptible to economic risks. When a farm faces problems with low prices and profitability due to its primary product choice, it is time to consider a service-oriented business model. Some farmers, unwilling to change their specialization in a particular crop or animal, begin to use agricultural products as a major input for providing services rather than selling them as agricultural commodities. For example, horse breeding farms use unsold horses to provide riding or healing services. Some small farmers are even starting to organize most of their farm operations as a service business. They provide educational, entertainment, and transformative tourism services at the farm, where visitors learn how to apply special agroecological farming methods, take care of fruit trees or honeybees, bake pancakes or bread, preserve legumes, etc. (Lankauskienė et al., 2023).

At the current stage of servitization research, it becomes clear that the penetration of services through service-driven business models encourages paradigm change in the evolution of the global socioeconomic system. In this context, the term 'servitization' can be used as an analogy to the term 'industrialization'. Like industrialization is understood as the mass penetration of manufacturing technologies and business organization across all areas of the economy and social life, servitization is understood as the penetration of service elements into all areas of human life through innovative service-driven business models.

The servitization phenomenon includes all types of non-technological innovations (organizational, marketing, and social innovations) and explains how they work as a unified whole. The shift to servitization does not mean that the availability of service business extensions using technologies is ignored. For example, new digital technologies enable companies to create new revenue streams by charging for digital services that were previously not offered and help internationalize their revenue streams, reducing their dependence on home-market sales (Paschou et al., 2020; Gebauer et al., 2021; Kolagar et al., 2022; Vendrell-Herrero et al., 2024). However, many manufacturers are focusing too much on technology in their quest to drive service growth through digital servitization and, consequently, are often failing to attain the desired outcomes (Tronvoll et al., 2020).

Servitization is changing the very basics of humanity's organizational mode. As a result of servitization, the socioeconomic industrial system is evolving into a more complex phenomenon strongly dependent on intangible resources and oriented towards a service logic-based view of value creation, which differs significantly from value creation in manufacturing.

First, successful transitioning from a product-driven to a service-driven business model requires turning from technological to non-technological drivers of development. Consequently, the industrial patterns of thought about services in the traditional sense, which equate services with intangible goods, must be changed by service-dominant logic, which emphasizes other success factors than the conventional linear economic model of manufacturing 'take-transform-sell-consume/discard'.

Secondly, in a service economy, each stage of the service cycle should be seamlessly integrated, and each business function should be part of a coherent whole. This feature of the service-driven business model requires examining and designing all strategies according to a holistic approach. The biggest challenge is breaking down the barriers between the traditional structural blocks of the organizational models.

Third, competition should be replaced by the pursuit of symbiosis among participants in the business ecosystem. Transitioning from producing and selling products to 'Product plus service' systems means that a part of the new value is created by the customer rather than the service provider. The degree to which the service customer is involved in new value creation may vary, but it is becoming increasingly prevalent. The shift to a service-driven business model necessitates the establishment of a new kind of relationship, one that emphasizes value co-creation for the mutual benefit of all parties involved. Successfully entering servitization trajectories is impossible without shifting the focus from competitive and exploitative behaviour to building collaborative and synergistic relationships based on a symbiotic approach.

All the mentioned differences between industrial goods-oriented and service-driven business models led to radical qualitative changes in social life, fundamentally transforming the character of social structures, relationships, and cultural norms.

A rising post-industrial society gives rise to a post-urban world. Urban dwellers in the developed world have lived by the laws of industrial society for several centuries. Due to a new paradigm in the business sphere, new complexities and challenges have emerged, necessitating a fresh perspective to address them. As the development of cities is intertwined with the development of the manufacturing and industrial economy and society, we can suggest that growing servitization and deindustrialization processes should be an important factor encouraging the revision of the traditional city design, adapted to the needs of the working class. However, little research effort is being expended to assess the systemic impacts of a global socio-economic paradigm change on livelihoods and lifestyles. The literature is relatively silent on how rural and urban territories benefit from the increasing shift of local entrepreneurs from product-driven to innovative service-driven business models and how servitization processes impact consumption and transform the lifestyle and vision of high-quality human settlements formed in the industrial era.

The monograph presents a perspective that emphasizes the key difference between implementing innovations in industrial and service-based socioeconomic systems, which can be referred to as *shifting focus from technological to non-technological innovations.* To create an innovative vision of human settlement within the framework of service-driven post-industrial society, we must understand how paradigm innovations in the business sphere impact livelihoods and lifestyles, and where a fundamental shift is necessary in the strategic management of the global human settlement system. Reorganization of human settlements according to the livelihoods and lifestyles in the Service Economy Era requires more than the implementation of some green technology innovations. Successful innovators are not focused on new technologies, but rather on new ways of organizing, managing, or delivering value, as servitization brings groundbreaking changes to all spheres of human life. Service-driven business models transform consumption practices and markets, requiring the rethinking of existing processes, structures, and household models.

The monograph offers an original approach to human settlement research. It is based on an innovative theoretical background—the Qualitative Structure method, which enables examination of the global human settlement system through 1) holistic and 2) evolutionary approaches.

Holistic approach vs. *disciplinarity.* The disciplinary approach is a key obstacle to identifying paradigm differences and adopting human settlements to a new era, as most discussions in the context of 'post-urban' and 'post-industrial' still occur within the frameworks of separate disciplines. Nearly everything that happens to people takes place in settlements, and discussions on a new vision of high-quality human settlements should be based on a holistic view. According to Barbara Ward (1976, p. 125), we should examine the global human experience not in all its 'minute particulars' but in the close web of interdependence that holds it all together and largely determines the impact of each separate part. The book seeks to replace a disciplinary approach with an analysis of the human settlement as a whole entity. The Qualitative Structure theory serves as a reconciliation of various disciplines and research streams, offering an integrated agenda in the research of human settlements.

Evolution vs. *replacement.* According to the evolutionary approach, the prefix 'post' represents a subsequent stage of evolution that goes beyond a particular concept, movement, or era. It suggests a departure from the past, exploring new perspectives, theories, or practices that emerge after the previous phase. The transition from the agrarian stage to the industrial stage did not eliminate the importance of the agricultural sector. Similarly, the transition to the post-industrial stage does not mean that industry becomes irrelevant; rather, it signifies a shift from a dominating position. All the accumulated experience is incorporated into the new stage and, after being adapted to the new conditions, continues to be used. For this reason, the transition to a post-industrial service-based society is gradual, and in many countries, it is not easy to define a clear chronology of the transition. The concept of qualitative structure is based on the evolutionary approach, which is particularly relevant for studying human settlements during a shift from the industrial to the post-industrial stage of society's development. It explains the evolutionary nature of society's transition from one stage to another, pointing out that the new stage does not negate the previous one but complements it with new elements, shifting the emphasis. The Qualitative Structure method helps to avoid confrontation between innovators and proponents of the industrial mode of production, as the evolutionary approach emphasizes that all previous methods are not discarded. After a critical assessment of their strengths and weaknesses, the best features of these methods continue to be used in combination with new methods.

The main body of the monograph consists of three parts. The first part of the monograph is devoted to the theory of human settlement evolution. The first chapter discusses key challenges to understanding the complexity of modern cities in a holistic manner, providing an overview of the state of the art in research on human settlements as a whole and an evolving entity. The following chapters present the Qualitative Structure theory (Kalinauskas, 1991; Kalinauskas & Reinin, 1995; Vidickienė, 2013; Melnikienė & Vidickienė, 2019; Vidickienė et al., 2023) and explain how to apply it for understanding human settlement phenomena from a holistic and evolutionary perspective. The qualitative structure theory is a response to the increasing specialization and eclecticism in scientific inquiry into human settlements, as offered by various academic disciplines. The concept of the qualitative structure provides a genuine way to define human settlement as a whole entity and design guidelines for its stage-by-stage evolutionary pathway through the framework of six generic strategies.

The second part of the monograph highlights the significant role of large-scale cycles in shaping the evolution of the global human settlement system. It emphasizes the impact of livelihoods on the organization of the human settlement system through the lens of the Qualitative Structure method, which focuses on the relational perspective and reflects a holistic worldview with a cyclical, historical temporal orientation. The process of evolution is examined over a long period of time, during which, according to proponents of socio-economic evolutionary theory, human civilization underwent three big cycles of evolution, known as Hunter-Gatherer, Agrarian, and Industrial Eras, and entered the post-industrial Service Economy Era. The cycles are defined according to the dominant economic activity and examined, focusing on the big picture and essential characteristics of each era. Such an approach enables us to understand the evolution of human settlements holistically, where each new big cycle does not negate the previous one, but only makes it more complex. This knowledge is most crucial for understanding how the post-industrial economy affects the changes in livelihoods and lifestyles of the industrial era.

The third part of the monograph, which consists of Chaps. 4, 5, 6, 7 and 8, presents case studies that link theory to the practical world by demonstrating a range of settlement designs and their evolutionary path through the implementation of strategies based on the framework designed according to the Qualitative Structure theory. It consists of the case studies that illustrate, step by step, the evolutionary path in the design of post-industrial human settlements, from the pilot projects of ecovillages oriented towards a symbiosis between humans and the natural environment to complex strategies for organizing living in a manner different from urban planning and social infrastructure models developed during the industrial era.

Chapter 4 explores the evolving landscape of post-industrial human settlements, which are designed to transcend traditional divides between urban and rural life, work and leisure, and humans and nature. Rather than being mere lifestyle alternatives, the settlements discussed—including Understenshöjden in Sweden, Amatciems in Latvia, and Kardokai in Lithuania—function as experimental prototypes of a new paradigm in human habitation. They offer grounded insights into how ecovillages are initiated and grown, how governance and design choices reflect shifting values in post-industrial societies, and what it means to live relationally within one's environment. Through a critical examination of eco-settlements that embody innovation and extensive growth strategies, the chapter interrogates how pilot projects redefine place, infrastructure, and inhabitation by embracing ecological responsiveness, socio-spatial fluidity, and symbiotic human–nature relationships. As the chapter reveals, these emerging forms of settlement are not only reshaping physical landscapes but also signalling a more profound cultural shift toward integrated, place-based, and regenerative models of living.

Chapter 5 explores the intensification strategy in eco-settlement development as a critical phase following extensive physical expansion. While early growth focuses on environmentally conscious infrastructures—such as renewable energy, water management, and waste systems—long-term viability depends on cultivating robust social infrastructures. The intensification strategy shifts attention to the creation of 'living infrastructure' that integrates housing and other built arrangements with education, governance, and cultural life to sustain community cohesion and ecological values. Drawing on three case studies, the chapter illustrates practical applications of this strategy. Kardokai Nature School in Lithuania demonstrates how value-based, holistic education strengthens community resilience and attracts families seeking meaningful alternatives to conventional schooling. Sociocracy in ecovillages exemplifies participatory governance models that enhance trust, shared responsibility, and collective decision-making. The Resonancia Community in Spain serves as a laboratory of experiential living, providing flexible, nomadic infrastructures that foster creativity and a sense of belonging. Together, these cases illustrate how intensification strategy fosters deeper socio-ecological integration, positioning ecovillages as hubs of innovation and resilience for post-industrial societies.

Chapter 6 explores the evolution of human settlements from industrial specialization toward service-oriented, ecologically integrated communities. Unlike the industrial era, where settlements were built around dominant industries, post-industrial ecovillages specialize in service-oriented lifestyles that prioritize shared values, ecological stewardship, and cultural identity. Central to this transformation is Ecocracy (Symbiocracy), a governance approach that integrates physical, social, and spiritual dimensions of life, emphasizing reciprocity, cooperation, and interdependence between humans and ecosystems. Ecovillages embody these principles by fostering transformative services—initiatives that create lasting positive change in well-being for individuals, communities, and the environment. Rather than relying on expensive infrastructure, they cultivate 'intangible infrastructure' through culture, education, and collective governance. Processes of enculturation and socialization are redefined to instil ecological literacy, empathy toward non-human life, and cooperative values, aligning with post-humanist ethics and supporting the emergence of the Symbiocene, an era of reciprocal flourishing between human and more-than-human worlds. Three case studies illustrate these ideas: Tamera (Portugal), focusing on peace education and ecological restoration; Quinta do Coelho Azul (Portugal), specializing in permaculture education and regenerative living; and Rožkalni (Latvia), promoting therapeutic living and social inclusion. Together, these intentional communities demonstrate how specialization strategies can operationalize Ecocracy, offering scalable models for sustainable, inclusive, and symbiotic settlements.

Chapter 7 explores the ways of reorganizing human settlements according to post-anthropocentric and post-urban thinking through the diversification of place functions. It argues that while 'tabula rasa' settlements on empty land allow for the direct inscription of post-industrial values into desirable spatial form and main infrastructure facilities, the regeneration of existing cities and villages is equally feasible when guided by new cultural paradigms and ecological imperatives. Building on the insights of the Transition Towns and Ecovillage movements, the chapter analyses diversification as a multifaceted strategic tool capable of dissolving the inherited urban–rural binaries. Drawing on three case studies, the analysis illustrates how place-based initiatives enact post-industrial imaginaries in practice. In Druskininkai, Lithuania, diversification unfolds through regenerative health services, climate-neutral mobility, and biophilic governance, embedding Symbiocene infrastructures across the settlement fabric. The transformation of Smiltynė settlement in Lithuania demonstrates complementarity, layering health services, ecology, and cultural heritage within a UNESCO-protected landscape to create a multifunctional attractiveness of the place. The Local Action Group 'Green Neighbourhood' in Poland exemplifies how peri-urban communities can reorganize within post-anthropocentric and post-urban paradigms by integrating Smart Village initiatives, ecological stewardship, and participatory governance. Together, these cases demonstrate that diversification of place functions fosters resilience, inclusivity, and multispecies justice, offering a pluriversal framework for reorganizing human settlements in accordance with the needs of the post-industrial era.

Chapter 8 explores collaboration strategies for developing eco-settlements. The case study of the Global Ecovillage Network (GEN) is used to reveal collaborative activities that contribute to the successful establishment of new settlements and the transformation of existing ones, focusing on an innovative lifestyle in the service economy. Analysing the evolution of the ecovillage movement, GEN collaborations were examined as a unique case of coordinated self-regulation among settlements. This reveals how innovative organizations have used collaboration strategies from the outset to overcome difficulties in implementing lower-level strategies. Since the inception of the ecovillage movement, GEN has evolved into a collaborative platform that has helped ecovillages to achieve their strategic goals. The study highlights the collaboration tools that have enabled GEN to become an open ecosystem for the creation and implementation of innovation, based on open networking, multi-actor partnerships, and symbiotic relationships between network participants. The GEN experience offers a valuable model for the development of other open innovation systems for collaboration of settlements around the world.

In summary, the third part of the monograph contributes to a deeper understanding of how the shift to a service-driven economic system is shaping the vision of human settlements in Europe and what strategic transformations in attitudes, cultural and social relationships, and the built environment are occurring.

The final chapter of the monograph presents an overview of the main findings of the research that examined the evolution of human settlements from the perspective of radical change in the global economic system in the context of predominant livelihoods and lifestyles. Drawing on cross-disciplinary literature and case studies on the application of various strategies, designed according to the Qualitative Structure theory, it highlights how a shift from industrial to service-based livelihoods gives rise to new lifestyles and initiates a new 'big cycle' in the evolution of the human settlement system. Findings from both theory and practice outline the general vision of settlements in the Service Economy Era based on the symbiotic approach and provide actionable insights for eco-communities and policymakers on how to exit the Anthropocene and enter the Symbiocene.

Bibliography

Alderson, A. S. (1999). Explaining deindustrialization: Globalization, failure, or success? *American Sociological Review, 64*(5), 701–721.

Barnett, V. (2016). *Kondratiev and the dynamics of economic development: Long cycles and industrial growth in historical context.* Springer.

Battaglia, M., Certoma, C., & Frey, M. (2015). Rethinking attractiveness. The transformation of tangible and intangible factors in post-rural areas. *UNISCAPE-En Route, 1*(2), 211–218.

Bell, D. (1973). *The coming of post-industrial society.* Basic Books.

Ben Mahjoub, L. (2025). Greenwashing practices and ESG reporting: An international review. *International Journal of Sociology and Social Policy, 45*(1/2), 173–188.

Bessant, J., & Tidd, J. (2007). *Innovation and entrepreneurship.* John Wiley & Sons.

Blühdorn, I. (2016). Sustainability—post-sustainability—unsustainability. In T. Gabrielson, C. Hall, J. M. Meyer, & D. Schlosberg (Eds.), *The Oxford handbook of environmental political theory* (pp. 259–273). Oxford University Press. https://doi.org/10.1093/oxfordhb/9780199685271.013.39

Brunori, G. (2006). Post-rural processes in wealthy rural areas: Hybrid networks and symbolic capital. In *Between the local and the global* (pp. 121–145). Emerald Group Publishing Limited.

Bryden, J., & Bollman, R. (2000). Rural employment in industrialised countries★. *Agricultural Economics, 22*(2), 185–197. https://doi.org/10.1111/j.1574-0862.2000.tb00017.x

Clark, J. (2022). Reframing deindustrialization. *International Journal of Urban Sciences, 26*(1), 29–35.

Clunies-Ross, T., & Hildyard, N. (2013). *The politics of industrial agriculture.* Routledge.
Conn, S. (2024). Sub-urban or post-rural: Suburban development as a two-way street in the mid-twentieth century. *Journal of American Studies, 58*(1), 124–142.
Costanza, R., & Patten, B. C. (1995). Defining and predicting sustainability. *Ecological Economics, 15*(3), 193–196.
Crozet, M., & Milet, E. (2017). Should everybody be in services? The effect of servitization on manufacturing firm performance. *Journal of Economics & Management Strategy, 26*(4), 820–841. https://doi.org/10.1111/jems.12211
de Freitas Netto, S. V., Sobral, M. F. F., Ribeiro, A. R. B., & Soares, G. R. D. L. (2020). Concepts and forms of greenwashing: A systematic review. *Environmental Sciences Europe, 32*(1), 19.
de Olde, C., & Oosterlynck, S. (2022). 'The countryside starts here': How the urban-rural divide continues to matter in post-urban Flanders. *European Urban and Regional Studies, 29*(3), 281–296.
Doussard, M., Peck, J., & Theodore, N. (2009). After deindustrialization: Uneven growth and economic inequality in "postindustrial" Chicago. *Economic Geography, 85*(2), 183–207.
Duff, A. S. (2014). *Information society. International Encyclopedia of the Social & Behavioral Sciences (Second Edition)* (pp. 83–89). https://doi.org/10.1016/B978-0-08-097086-8.95017-7
Federico, G. (2005). *Feeding the world: An economic history of agriculture, 1800–2000.* Princeton University Press.
Foster, J. (2018). *Post-sustainability: Tragedy and transformation.* Routledge.
Gebauer, H., Paiola, M., Saccani, N., & Rapaccini, M. (2021). Digital servitization: Crossing the perspectives of digitization and servitization. *Industrial Marketing Management, 93*, 382–388.
Hackworth, J. (2019). Manufacturing decline. In *How racism and the conservative movement crush the American Rust Belt.* Columbia University Press.
Harwood, R. R. (1990). A history of sustainable agriculture. In C. A. Edwards (Ed.), *Sustainable agricultural systems* (pp. 3–19). CRC press.
Hoey, B. A. (2015). Postindustrial societies. In J. Wright (Ed.), *International encyclopedia of the Social & Behavioral Sciences* (2nd ed., pp. 663–669). Elsevier.
Hopkins, J. (1998). Signs of the post-rural: Marketing myths of a symbolic countryside. *Geografiska Annaler: Series B, Human Geography, 80*(2), 65–81.
Kalinauskas, I. N. (1991). *Najedine s mirom.* Oktiabrj.
Kalinauskas, I. N., & Reinin, G. P. (1995, December). Method of qualitative structures (MQS). Moscow aviation institute information. *Bulletin, Issue 4.*
Kolagar, M., Reim, W., Parida, V., & Sjödin, D. (2022). Digital servitization strategies for SME internationalization: The interplay between digital service maturity and ecosystem involvement. *Journal of Service Management, 33*(1), 143–162.

Koudal, P. (2006). The service revolution in global manufacturing industries. *Deloitte Research, 2*, 1–22.

Lankauskienė, R., Melnikienė, R., Simonaitytė, V., Gedminaitė-Raudonė, Ž., & Vidickienė, D. (2023). Case studies of farming servitization with different motivations. In *Rural transformation through Servitization: A qualitative structure approach* (pp. 91–169). Springer International Publishing.

Lankauskienė, R., Vidickienė, D., & Gedminaitė-Raudonė, Ž. (2022). Evolution of short food supply chain theory and practice: Two-sided networks and platforms. *Energies, 15*(3), 1137.

LaVerne, E. S. (2012). *History of rural electrification and farm wiring issues.* USDA, Agricultural Research Service.

Luger, J., & Schwarze, T. (2024). Leaving post-industrial urban studies behind? *Dialogues in Urban Research, 2*(2), 188–209. https://doi.org/10.1177/27541258241230058

Marshall, T. (2000). Urban planning and governance: Is there a Barcelona model? *International Planning Studies, 5*(3), 299–319.

Martín-Retortillo, M., & Pinilla, V. (2012). Why did agricultural labour productivity not converge in Europe from 1950 to 2005? EHES working papers in economic history, no. 25, European historical economics society, pp. 1–40.

Melnikienė, R., & Vidickienė, D. (2019). Evaluation of the Lithuanian agricultural policy based on the analysis of qualitative structure. *Public Policy and Administration, 18*(1), 52–67.

Michalina, D., Mederly, P., Diefenbacher, H., & Held, B. (2021). Sustainable urban development: A review of urban sustainability indicator frameworks. *Sustainability, 13*(16), 9348. https://doi.org/10.3390/su13169348

Motta, P., Jaime, C., & Escobar, F. S. (2022). Transformation of Urban–Rural Relationships in the Context of Global Challenges. *The International Journal of Social Quality, 12*(2), 25–50. https://doi.org/10.3167/IJSQ.2022.120203

Murdoch, J., & Pratt, A. C. (1993). Rural studies: Modernism, postmodernism and the 'post-rural'. *Journal of Rural Studies, 9*(4), 411–427.

Ng, I., Parry, G., Smith, L., Maull, R., & Briscoe, G. (2012). Transitioning from a goods-dominant to a service-dominant logic: Visualising the value proposition of Rolls-Royce. *Journal of Service Management, 23*(3), 416–439.

Nugent, C. (2023). So-called 'green' cities promise a climate-friendly utopia. The reality is a lot messier. *Time.* https://time.com/6278511/green-new-cities-climate/

OECD. (1996). *Territorial indicators of employment: Focusing on rural development.* OECD.

Paddison, R. (2001). *Handbook of Urban Studies.* SAGE Publications Ltd. https://doi.org/10.4135/9781848608375

Paschou, T., Rapaccini, M., Adrodegari, F., & Saccani, N. (2020). Digital servitization in manufacturing: A systematic literature review and research agenda. *Industrial Marketing Management, 89*, 278–292.
Pike, A. (2019). De-industrialisation. In A. Kobayashi et al. (Eds.), *International encyclopedia of human geography*. Elsevier.
Pike, A. (2022). Coping with deindustrialization in the global north and south. *International Journal of Urban Sciences, 26*(1), 1–22.
Probst, L., Frideres, L., Cambier, B., Ankeraa, J., & Lide, L. (2016). Servitisation: Service and predictive maintenance contracts. Business innovation observatory, European Union. Contract No 190/PP/ENT/CIP/12/C/N03C01.
Rowthorn, R., & Coutts, K. (2004). De-industrialisation and the balance of payments in advanced economies. *Cambridge Journal of Economics, 28*(5), 767–790.
Sachs, J. D., Lafortune, G., Fuller, G., & Iablonovski, G. (2025). Financing sustainable development to 2030 and mid-century. Sustainable Development Report, 2025.
Schuetze, T., & Chelleri, L. (2016). Urban sustainability versus green-washing—Fallacy and reality of urban regeneration in downtown Seoul. *Sustainability, 8*(1), 33. https://doi.org/10.3390/su8010033
Schurig, S., & Turan, K. (2022). The concept of a 'regenerative city': How to turn cities into regenerative systems. *Journal of Urban Regeneration & Renewal, 15*(2), 161–175.
Shwayri, S. T. (2013). A model Korean ubiquitous eco-city? The politics of making Songdo. *Journal of Urban Technology, 20*(1), 39–55.
Soja, E. W. (2011). Regional urbanization and the end of the metropolis era. In G. Bridge & S. Watson (Eds.), *The new Blackwell companion to the city* (pp. 679–689). Wiley-Blackwell. https://doi.org/10.1002/9781444395105.ch59
Spring, M., & Araujo, L. (2009). Service, services and products: Rethinking operations strategy. *International Journal of Operations & Production Management, 29*(5), 444–467.
Sze, J. (2015). *Fantasy islands: Chinese dreams and ecological fears in an age of climate crisis*. University of California Press.
Taft, C. (2018, June 25). Deindustrialization and the Postindustrial City, 1950–present. Oxford Research Encyclopedia of American History. Retrieved August 21, 2025, from https://oxfordre.com/americanhistory/view/10.1093/acrefore/9780199329175.001.0001/acrefore-9780199329175-e-574
Takkinen, P. (2025). Post-sustainability: A hermeneutic literature review. *The Anthropocene Review*. https://doi.org/10.1177/20530196251339474
Tronvoll, B., Sklyar, A., Sörhammar, D., & Kowalkowski, C. (2020). Transformational shifts through digital servitization. *Industrial Marketing Management, 89*, 293–305.

Vendrell-Herrero, F., Para-González, L., Mascaraque-Ramírez, C., & Freixanet, J. (2024). The order of the factors matters: How digital transformation and servitization integrate more efficiently. *International Journal of Production Economics, 271*, 109228. https://doi.org/10.1016/j.ijpe.2024.109228

Vidickienė, D. (2013). Evolution of the manufacturer's strategic thinking based on the qualitative structure method. Working paper no. 13-1, Naujos ekonomikos institutas.

Vidickienė, D., & Lankauskienė, R. (2025). Sustainability through the prism of innovative service-oriented business model in farming. *Discover Sustainability, 6*(1), 286.

Vidickienė, D., Lankauskienė, R., Melnikienė, R., Gedminaitė-Raudonė, Ž., & Simonaitytė, V. (2024). *Rural transformation through Servitization*. Springer Books.

Vidickienė, D., Simonaitytė, V., Lankauskienė, R., & Gedminaitė-Raudonė, Ž. (2023). Servitization of farming: A new approach to local food systems building. *European Countryside, 15*(1), 1–17.

Ward, B. (1976). The home of man: What nations and the international must do. *Habitat International, 1*(2), 125–132.

Westlund, H. (2014). Urban futures in planning, policy and regional science: Are we entering a post-urban world? *Built Environment, 40*(4), 447–457.

Westlund, H. (2018). Urban-rural relations in the post-urban world. In T. Haas, H. Westlund (Eds.) *In the post-urban world: Innovative transformations in Global City regions*, (pp. 70–81). Routledge.

Westlund, H., & Haas, T. (2018). In the post-urban world: An introduction. In T. Haas, H. Westlund (Eds.) *In the post-urban world: Innovative transformations in Global City regions*, (pp. 1–12). Routledge.

Westlund, H., & Borseková, K. (2025). The post-urban hypothesis. *Global Challenges & Regional Science, 1*, 100005. https://doi.org/10.1016/j.gcrs.2025.100005

White, A., Stoughton, M., & Feng, L. (1999). *Servicizing: The quiet transition to extended producer responsibility*. Technical Report, Tellus Institute.

Wise, R., & Baumgartner, P. (1999). Go downstream: The new profit imperative in manufacturing. *Harvard Business Review, 77*(5), 133–141.

Yu, L. (2014). Low carbon eco-city: New approach for Chinese urbanisation. *Habitat International, 44*, 102–110.

CHAPTER 2

Theory of Human Settlement Evolution

Dalia Vidickienė

State of the Art in Research on Human Settlements as a Whole and Evolving Entity

The term 'human settlement' lacks a widely agreed-upon definition and is frequently used in academic and professional literature. In general terms, we can define settlement as any form of human habitation. Depending on the period of settlement development and the focus of analysis, various synonyms are preferred to describe human settlements, including camp, village, colony, hamlet, fort, town, city, population, collective, and community. However, when it comes to defining the human settlement system, which encompasses various forms of settlements, for their development purposes, it is challenging to provide a clear-cut definition.

A key reason for the increasing problems of general definition relating to all forms of human settlement is that contemporary ways of living and working create an enormous diversity of lifestyles. In the twenty-first century, human settlements are highly complex systems, and to cope with this complexity, they are analysed and managed through various prisms. Numerous characteristics of settlements are considered essential to determine their quality, including size, shape, functionality, specialization according to the main economic or social activity, role in the regional or ecological system, development, etc. For example, according to the size criteria, the complexity of a settlement may range from a single dwelling

D. Vidickienė et al., *Human Settlement in the Service Economy Era*, Palgrave Advances in Bioeconomy: Economics and Policies, https://doi.org/10.1007/978-3-032-19390-2_2

to the largest of cities with surrounding urbanized areas. According to the main economic activity, the complexity of a human settlement may vary from a village dependent on agriculture or natural resource extraction to a city with a diverse job market, including various sectors, companies, and career paths to choose from.

Seeking a better understanding of human settlement characteristics, scientific inquiry simplifies their complexity through the disciplinary extension of knowledge. Contemporary human settlement is a research object for many disciplines and sub-disciplines, including geography, architecture, archaeology, sociology, statistics, and economics. Over the years, the concept of human settlements has been broadened as each discipline added new characteristics as important aspects of their quality. For instance, the environmental implications of rapid urbanization have encouraged a search for knowledge on urbanization and environmental linkages (Bai et al., 2017), and ecological research has become an essential part of human settlements studies in the twenty-first century.

The process of differentiation and specialization in academic research on human settlements continues to evolve with the emergence of new disciplines. It helps understand specific aspects and nuances of human settlement development; however, in many cases, logics that have become the foundational rationalities of different academic disciplines operate within different regimes of constructing the rational and methods of knowledge production. They may make valid insights, but may also be, at times, fundamentally incommensurable (Keith et al., 2020). For example, architecture operates through a rationality informed significantly by aesthetics, land use planning operates through a rationality informed by a synchronic understanding of city metabolism, and economics operates through a cognitive logic of utility optimization.

The high complexity of modern human settlements requires a non-reductionist approach, where the perspectives of different disciplines are not considered mutually exclusive (Næss, 2015). A growing consensus is emerging that the field can make progress through interdisciplinary and transdisciplinary approaches. For example, over the last two decades, the 'New Urban Science' has rapidly emerged as an enticing way to apply digital tools and techniques to some of the most challenging issues faced by cities. Proponents of the New Urban Science emphasize urban data analytics and modelling as a means to develop novel insights into how cities function (Karvonen et al., 2021). Interdisciplinary integration can help arrive at valid knowledge, but it still lacks a holistic approach, as integration mainly occurs within the framework of traditional scientific discipline classifications. For example, the academic fields known as 'urban studies' and 'rural studies' emerged. However, they represent an eclectic collection of key disciplines related to urban or rural development, primarily including geography, statistics, sociology, and urban planning (Taylor et al., 2006). An integrating theory that holistically examines the phenomenon of human settlement is lacking.

The effort to employ an interdisciplinary approach in a more systematic way presents human settlement science, also known as ekistics. It was proposed by Greek architect and urban planner Constantinos Doxiadis (Doxiadis, 1968, 1970), inspired by the advantages of the matrix organizational structure. The interest in matrix organizational structure in strategic management emerged in the mid-twentieth century, primarily in the US aerospace industry, as a response to the growing complexity of large, multi-faceted projects. According to management science, the matrix organizational structure enables efficient resource allocation, facilitates cross-functional collaboration, and allows for the simultaneous management of multiple, complex projects (Knight, 1976). The matrix boasts many traits necessary for managing global organizations (Bartlett & Ghoshal, 1998; Galbraith, 1994), encourages innovation and fast actions, and speeds information to those who know how to use it (Sy et al., 2005).

The efforts of ekistics to systematically explore human settlements are also based on matrix thinking, where ideas are not just linear but exist within a web of related concepts. The grid proposed by Doxiadis (1968) is a 5x5 matrix that links five sciences (economics, cultural disciplines, social sciences, political sciences, and technological disciplines) with five elements (nature, man, society, shells, and networks). Created by Doxiadis as a new thinking tool for constructive action in human settlement development, the ekistics enabled all the advantages of the matrix method to be exploited. Ekistics has had a significant influence on academic circles, inspiring many scholars to further explore the science of human settlements (Liu et al., 2023). However, we still lack a holistic approach to human settlement as the proposed matrix structure splits management into two streams based on dualistic thinking, which is a primary obstacle to seeing the whole picture of the research object.

The Western mind is highly trained in dualistic thinking, a concept that traces back to the ancient Greeks. It refers to the tendency to divide the world and our experiences into dichotomous categories, such as good-bad, big-small, cold-warm, black-white, heaven-earth, etc. The dualistic mind is essentially binary, operating in an either/or thinking mode. This type of thinking simplifies the complexity of reality and can have profound implications for how we perceive, process, and act in the world around us. Scientific inquiry into human settlements is usually also based on dualistic thinking. The development of human settlements is discussed in the context of traditional binaries such as individual/communal, physical/social, endogenous/exogenous, strength/weakness, material/non-material culture, etc. The central specific dichotomies in the field of human settlement research and development are presented between (1) rural and urban settlements, (2) the built and natural environments, and (3) human and non-human habitats.

The first dichotomy is related to the conventional approach to the roles of cities and villages in society. The industrial economic system created a situation in which cities became centres of economic activity, innovation, and cultural exchange, offering a wider range of opportunities and services due to their size and density. Consequently, the research on general laws of human settlement progress is based on urban studies. Contemporary rural settlements are often characterized by a higher prevalence of poverty compared to cities and are typically examined in the context of overall rural development. The global rural development inquiry focuses on agricultural and environmental issues, as well as the health and poverty of rural residents. The quantitative analysis of literature related to rural human settlements from 1999 to 2023 (see the literature review by Liu et al., 2023) reveals that the keyword that appears most frequently is health. There is a relatively limited number of studies on improving the rural human settlement environment through rural economic and cultural development. To some extent, this is because some scholars who studied rural economy and culture fail to incorporate their studies into the context of the science of human settlement environments. The rural economy is studied from the perspective of a single discipline, such as economics. There are also only a few studies on the rural human settlement environment that focus on improving infrastructure facilities, such as rural roads, electricity, and flood control. The problems of rural settlement infrastructure regeneration are considered to be the same as those in cities and are not typically introduced as an essential part of rural development research.

Before the mass industrialization of the agricultural sector following the Second World War, urban and rural communities were detached from their neighbours. However, in the twenty-first century, transportation innovations, ICT technologies, and the growing service sector have changed the situation (Tandoh-Offin, 2010). Due to the growing urban agglomerations, it is often impossible to distinguish between rural and urban settlements today. Even in the economically less-developed regions of the global South, the distinctive characteristics of city and countryside are becoming blurred (Borsdorf & Stadel, 2015).

The blurring of the line between urban and rural settlements is discussed in academic literature (Pateman, 2011; Wandl et al., 2014; Dymitrow & Stenseke, 2016; Hugo, 2017; Westlund, 2018; Yang et al., 2021; Delgado-Viñas & Gómez-Moreno, 2022), but scholars examine this phenomenon primarily through the lens of separate disciplines. For example, many scholars explore new challenges to spatial planning (Herlin, 2004; Scott et al., 2013; Seto et al., 2014; Savini et al., 2022) and land use (Doernberg & Weith, 2021; Van Vliet et al., 2020; Yuzhe et al., 2022).

The growing complexity and dynamism of rural-urban interactions raise new challenges to regional development (Dabson, 2019; Li et al., 2022) as, in the late period of urbanization, urban development problems are often caused by problems inherent to rural areas, and vice versa (Fang, 2022). Many regional studies have identified the limitations of a simple urban–rural dichotomy in accurately representing the actual situation of human settlements (Wandl et al., 2014; Shaw et al., 2020; Cyriac & Firoz, 2022; Li et al., 2023). However, research on the complementarity and integration of rural and urban settlement characteristics, viewed through the lens of the rural-urban continuum, remains limited and focuses primarily on the urban 'problematique' and its benefits (Motta et al., 2022).

In the twenty-first century, the post-industrial reality continues to narrow the gap between urban and rural areas, as radical changes in the global socio-economic system have led to an increase in rural and urban interdependence (Tandoh-Offin, 2010; Brown & Cromartie, 2017). The development of service-based business models and information and communication technologies bridges the gap in access to information, education, and economic opportunities between urban and rural inhabitants, fostering remote work and telework. Servitization of farming presents new opportunities for rural inhabitants to align their interests with lifestyle business and build close relationships with an urban population (Vidickienė et al., 2024). As communities are now linked in a web of interrelated networks, rather than relying solely on commuting, the quality of cultural and social life for rural residents is also improved. The development of tourism and recreation services in the countryside, which are growing in popularity, serves as a marketing tool to change the opinion of urban residents on the best place to live. Consequently, service economy-driven transformations require developing a holistic concept of human settlement, which considers its rural or urban characteristics as secondary-level indicators.

The second dichotomy between built and natural environments is also firmly rooted in urban development, as the industrial era led to the prosperity of urban built environments. (The built environment refers to man-made structures and landscapes, whereas the natural environment encompasses the world's natural features, including climate, ecosystems, and biodiversity.) As the natural environment has traditionally been contrasted with the urban environment, this dichotomy is often discussed in the context of the natural environment over the urban environment (Karmanov & Hamel, 2008; Scharper & Leman-Stefanovic, 2012; Choudhry et al., 2015). Both types of environments significantly influence the quality of life, but urban studies have long concentrated on the built environment. The point of view that the built environment must be understood to intertwine with the natural environment emerged only in the last few decades, when urban environments were found to lack the beneficial restorative properties of nature (Bartuska, 2007). However, the incentive for integrating the traditional concerns of city planning for the future of the built environment with improvements in our use of natural resources is driven and examined mainly from the perspective of human health and well-being (de Roo & Miller, 2017).

The third dichotomy between human and non-human habitats is closely linked with the second one but represents a more abstracted worldview. Over the last few decades, dualistic thinking in urban development has been significantly influenced by ideas from environmental social movements. As sociologists Dunlap and Catton pointed out (1983), an ecological perspective is a fruitful way of viewing the relations between societal and environmental phenomena and a means of integrating work on both built and natural environments. In the industrial era, humans and nature have been considered as two distinct systems, based on the way of thinking that holds human culture and nonhuman nature to be radically different ontological spheres (Hawkins, 2006). Such a division entails developing human settlements and non-human habitats as separate tasks. A spatial ordering in constructed spaces and the urban fabric designates humans as the default, singular user in this scene. Most urban planners design spaces focusing on humans' needs, comfort, and health. Non-human habitats are usually discussed separately or overlooked. From an academic perspective, the long-standing dichotomy between human and non-human habitats is related to the division of sciences into social and natural sciences, which are generally considered to be entirely different fields of knowledge. The concept of socio-ecosystems allows a more integrated approach, in which humans and nature are recognized as interdependent. However, this new perspective does not necessarily eliminate a hierarchy of humans over nature (Boulangeat et al., 2022). To inspire new possibilities for building settlements that consider not only humans but also other species, we must adopt a new way of thinking, one that is willing to question our binary conceptions. Human–nature integration versus dualism can offer insight into the advantages and limitations of various perspectives.

All three mentioned dichotomies are significant obstacles to creating a better future according to the rules of post-industrial society. We need new concepts for holistic thinking about human life, concepts that are not compromised by the long and ancient tradition of dualism (Cimatti, 2016). According to post-industrialists, it is essential to critically review current urban development principles and discard many urban development paradigms developed during the industrial era. Uncovering the social, physical, and economic forces that drive cities demands interdisciplinary scholarship that crosses social sciences, natural sciences, and the humanities (Keith et al., 2020).

The Qualitative Structure of a Human Settlement

Traditional dualistic thinking is not the only way to understand the world. Recognizing the complexity and diversity of human settlements, we should question the use of binary conceptions as a single way for their governance. Moreover, in the twenty-first century, the boundaries between the key dual mental constructions used to examine and develop human settlements are becoming increasingly blurred. It means that the dualistic, either-or mentality that underlies the science of the industrial era faces serious challenges and cannot be applied as a universal thinking tool.

One of the most helpful concepts for avoiding dualistic thinking in human settlement development is the Qualitative Structure Approach. This concept enables a comprehensive, transdisciplinary approach that helps compensate for the limitations and distortions inherent in using the viewpoints of a single discipline. The theory of qualitative structure empowers the exploration of a human settlement as a whole entity, without relying on key dichotomies rooted in human settlement system research, mentioned in the Section "State of the Art in Research on Human Settlements as a Whole and Evolving Entity".

The concept of the Qualitative Structure was proposed for the academic community in the early 1990s by Igor Kalinauskas as an innovative tool in behavioural psychology. Later, the Method of Qualitative Structure was successfully applied to analyse various whole entities in different fields of science, such as psychology, economics, management, sociology, and philosophy (Lobanova, 2003; Shmakov & Egorov, 2007; Vidickienė & Melnikienė, 2014; Melnikienė & Vidickienė, 2019; Vidickienė et al., 2019, 2023, 2024).

The concept of the Qualitative Structure is based on the assumption that 'each object exists through its quality and is viewed as something disconnected from other objects. At the same time, quality expresses the general features of an object that characterize the entire class of similar objects' (Kalinauskas, 1991, p. 89). Compared to the systemic approach, the qualitative structure approach is a step towards a better understanding of holistic thinking because the concept of qualitative structure highlights the difference between the object-system and the object-whole in particular. Kalinauskas emphasized that most systems can continue to exist even if a structural element is removed. In contrast, the qualitative structure of an object as a whole entity should be defined so that removing any structural element would destroy the object.

The Method of Qualitative Structure considers how to avoid the dichotomy between the traditional conceptualization of holistic and reductionistic approaches. Similar to the conventional structural analysis of a system using the reductionist approach, the analysis of qualitative structure requires defining key components of the whole. However, the components should be defined in a special way (Kalinauskas, 1991; Kalinauskas & Reinin, 1995; Vidickienė, 2023a). The analysis of the qualitative structure of any research object requires synchronic operation between three components of a whole entity and their relationships. This approach enables us to manage the complexity of human settlement by shifting from a dualistic to a three-dimensional perspective.

According to the theory of qualitative structure, the whole entity resides in a three-dimensional continuum. The dimensions are (1) the organizational construction, (2) functioning, and (3) the communication with the external environment. The dimensions are standard for any whole entity. A point of coordination connects them by maintaining wholeness (Fig. 2.1).

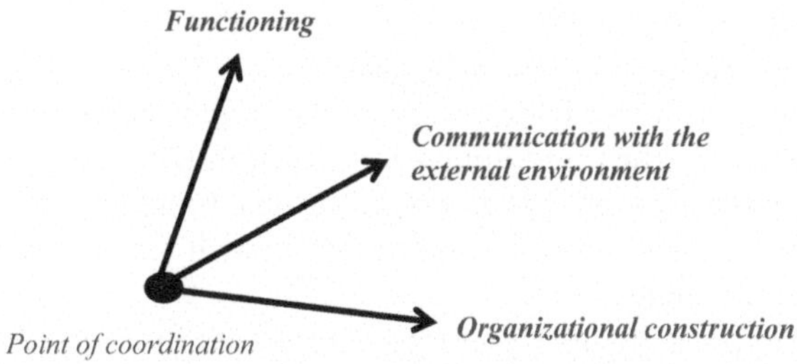

Fig. 2.1 Dimensions of the whole entity. (Source: Vidickienė, 2023a)

The identification and analysis of qualitative structure is a challenging process. Compared with traditional structural analysis, it has several specific characteristics.

First, identifying the qualitative structure of a whole entity demands a high level of abstraction. The concept of the qualitative structure is based on the assumption that quality expresses the general features of an object that characterize the entire class of similar subjects (Kalinauskas, 1991, p. 89). This means that the identified components of the qualitative structure of an analysed object should be appropriate for any representative of the entire class of similar objects. In our case, the qualitative structure of human settlement should be appropriate for all types of human settlements. The main challenge is to detach from the geographical and cultural specificities and historical context that offer a range of settlement forms and sizes. It means that it does not matter whether a human settlement is a homestead, a village, or a big city. According to the theory of qualitative structure, they all should have the same components of qualitative structure.

Second, in contrast to the conventional structural analysis of a system according to the systemic approach, which allows a different number of components, the qualitative structure analysis requires defining a finite set of three components. Compared to the systemic approach, the qualitative structure approach is a step towards a better understanding of holistic thinking because the concept of qualitative structure highlights the difference between the object-system and the object-whole in particular. Kalinauskas emphasized that most systems can continue to exist even if a structural element is removed. In contrast, the qualitative structure of an object as a whole entity should be defined in such a way that the removal of any structural element would destroy the object. Analysing the qualitative structure of a whole entity requires identifying structural components that exist throughout its lifespan.

Third, the set of three basic components should represent the tools of self-management in the three-dimensional continuum; that is, each identified component can be used as an organizational tool in the dimensions of organizational construction, communication with the external environment, and functioning.

Finally, the components should be determined in a special way, based on three-dimensional thinking. The qualitative structure should be presented in terms of an integral triadic pattern where no one component can operate alone; they should be fundamentally interdependent and mutually enabling.

In practice, identifying the three components when analysing the qualitative structure of any whole entity involves choosing names for the components using contemporary terminology. Multidisciplinary research in the field of human settlement studies makes this task particularly challenging, as modern human settlements and their components are defined through various prisms and terms. The terms often describe the same aspect or object, but multiple words can be used to highlight specific aspects or nuances of a concept within a particular context. The task is to find the terms that remain consistent across representatives of any human settlement. The suggestion for identifying the structural components of a human settlement in the current development of socio-economic terminology is the following:

> *The quality of the human settlement as a whole entity manifests itself through three components as tools for managing its quality: 1) inhabitants, 2) place, and 3) infrastructure.*

Component A. Inhabitants. To define a human settlement as a whole entity, it should have inhabitants. No settlement can be considered as functioning if no one lives there.

Throughout history, many settlements have been deserted in all parts of the world for various reasons (war, epidemic, famine, climate change, economic depressions, environmental destruction, deliberate clearances, etc.). Once-thriving spots, these villages, towns, and cities remain forgotten and neglected, ultimately destroyed by nature. Some depopulated settlements represent valuable bio-cultural heritage and can serve as tourist attractions, particularly those that preserve period-specific architecture.

However, they do not function as a usual human habitat. Consequently, a human settlement can only be considered viable and evolving if it has inhabitants.

Component B. *Place.* Many authors define human settlements as places where people live and sometimes work. A new settlement is started if a group of people is willing to live in a new area. To establish a settlement, people must find a suitable place. Despite an extraordinary variety of human settlements, they have been established in places that meet at least the minimum requirements of inhabitants to have a livelihood, shelter, and interaction with the environment.

The creation of a new settlement is a process of opening up and settling an area previously uninhabited by people. The possibility of using the territory as a place to live is a precondition for the existence of a settlement. In geography, this process is also known as occupancy. Therefore, we can say that one of the basic components of any settlement is a place.

The term 'place' involves more than 'space', a term often used in urban development literature. The distinction between 'space' and 'place' is not merely a philosophical debate; it lies at the core of creating environments that function as places for living. While 'space' refers to a physical location devoid of any inherent meaning except for its geometric dimensions, 'place' is considered a multidimensional, subjective, human-defined location. In the context of human settlements, the inhabitants create a place from space. In strategic management of human settlements, space is a neutral, measurable area, while a place is a modified space that has been imbued with experiences, emotions, memories, and social context, transforming it from a mere location into something unique and meaningful.

Component C. Infrastructure. The characteristics of the place, shaped by the natural environment, are complemented by the inhabitants with the physical facilities and organizational structures necessary for the better functioning of the settlement. They include the built environment, which refers to human-made or transformed natural resources (residential and business buildings, roads, power supplies, rest and communication zones, etc.), and the basic services and spatial-social arrangements designed to support and connect inhabitants' activities and way of life. The best contemporary term to define all people-made arrangements that allow the smooth flow of an economy's day-to-day activities and enhance the people's standard of living is 'infrastructure'. At a conceptual level, the term 'infrastructure' is useful precisely because it is about the background structures and systems that facilitate human activities and enable social, economic, cultural, and political life to happen. Currently, many people associate the term infrastructure with industrial facilities designed by technical specialists. However, infrastructures must not be understood solely as man-made functional objects; they also circulate aesthetic and affective atmospheres, including utopian visions of progress, modernity, and freedom (Zebrowski & Sage, 2017). To define the qualitative structure of the settlement as a whole entity, we should use a broad understanding of the settlement's infrastructure, which brings together built, natural, and social components providing public services essential to enabling, enhancing, or sustaining living conditions for inhabitants. It includes all essential systems and facilities a human settlement uses to support inhabitants' daily routines that enable them to be in action and participate in community life.

The three basic components suggested meet the following essential qualitative structure analysis requirements:

- All three components—inhabitants, place, and infrastructure—are necessary for a human settlement's wholeness. If a human settlement loses even one component, it ceases to exist as a representative of human settlements with the ability to evolve its quality.
- The structural components mentioned above exist throughout human settlements' lifespans. Regardless of constant changes in the local and global environment and the settlement itself, a living human settlement always has all three basic components.
- The components characterize the entire class of similar objects—human settlements. It does not matter their location, physical site, size, form, specific functions, key role in the region, population density, historical period, etc. They refer to the total of various human settlements.
- Each component can be used as an organizational tool in any of the three dimensions of the qualitative structure.

The three defined components of a human settlement can take different forms. Along with cultural, technological, and regional differences, the understanding of a suitable place for settlement, its basic infrastructure facilities, and the principles of residential community formation can differ substantially.

The 'big picture' of how three components are used as strategic organizational tools and their role in the evolution of human settlement provides a framework of six general strategies built according to the qualitative structure theory.

How Human Settlements Evolve: A Framework of Six General Strategies

The evolution of human settlements is a dynamic process of spatial and temporal adaptability that reflects the wisdom of creating a high-quality living environment. Throughout history, human settlements have been scattered in many sizes, shapes, and social-spatial arrangements. To provide helpful inspiration for new settlement planning and traditional settlement activation and utilization, it is not sufficient to analyse the differences between ancient and contemporary living environments. To manage the process of a settlement's quality growth, it is necessary to understand the factors that determine it.

Academic literature examines the transformation of ***human settlements*** from ancient homesteads to modern cities, primarily focusing on general cultural and socio-economic factors; however, little is known about the internal forces that create and reorganize them. Studies mainly present settlements as passive outcomes of environmental and societal changes on Earth (Marconcini et al., 2019). Moreover, the changes are usually given as random, circumstance-driven events, that is, things that happen by chance. Only a few authors analyse the changing characteristics of human settlements as path-dependent evolutionary processes. Even fewer studies are devoted to the causes of evolutionary changes in the organization processes of human settlements resulting from intentional organization policy actions.

The author of the Qualitative Structures Approach, Igor Kalinauskas, focused his research on identifying a static picture of the whole; however, any object-whole changes during its lifetime. To apply the qualitative structure method to the analysis of evolutionary pathways, theoretical insights of Kalinauskas have been developed. Further investigation into the manifestations and changes in the quality of different economic agents led to the development of an evolutionary framework for strategic management, which explains the evolutionary pathway of a whole entity. The framework suggests how the three basic components of the qualitative structure can be linked and explains how changing their role in a three-dimensional continuum helps to increase the quality of a phenomenon chosen for evolutionary analysis. Frameworks for analysis of producer evolution (Vidickienė, 2013), development of rural policy (Vidickienė & Melnikienė, 2014), examination of farming strategies (Melnikienė & Vidickienė, 2019), servitization of farming (Vidickienė et al., 2019, 2021; Vidickienė, 2023b), territorial servitization of rural regions (Vidickienė, 2023c), and evolution of networks (Vidickienė, 2023d) were developed. The logic of the evolutionary framework can also be applied to examine the evolution of human settlements.

The qualitative structure theory helps develop theoretical and practical guidelines that suggest new ways of thinking about evolutionary processes in human settlement systems. The theory explains how three basic settlement components and their interactions can be a source of generative processes that, stage by stage, increase the complexity and quality of the settlement.

The following principles must be considered to understand human settlement transformations along the evolutionary path.

Each combination of components has a special incentive to maintain or increase the achieved organizational quality and generates different

Principle 1. According to the theory of qualitative structure, the whole entity resides in a three-dimensional continuum. This means that the quality of human settlement should also be analysed as an object residing in a three-dimensional continuum.

Principle 2. Human settlement evolves due to changes in three components: A, B, and C. As was described in the Section "The Qualitative Structure of a Human Settlement", a human settlement as a whole entity has the following three basic components:

1. Component A. Inhabitants.
2. Component B. Place.
3. Component C. Infrastructure.

The three basic components mentioned are used as organizational tools.

Principle 3. All three components represent the forces responsible for the quality of the whole entity. They can play three different roles in the changes of the whole entity, including the role of:

- Active force
- Passive force
- Limiting force

The three mentioned forces work together. The active force is responsible for organizing actions that change the passive force, improving the quality of a settlement. The limiting force is responsible for communication with the external environment and defines the settlement's potential to evolve. It can be characterized as a threshold to generate positive synergy between three components.

Principle 4. According to the Theory of Qualitative Structure, a human settlement has the potential to use each of the three basic components mentioned as organizational tools in any dimension of the qualitative structure. Depending on the dimension in which the component is used, it has a different mission in creating and sustaining the quality of the settlement. The component, which is used in the dimension of organizational construction, becomes an active force. The settlement realizes the organizational process through changes in the quality and quantity of this component. Another component is used for the settlement's communication with the external environment and serves as a limiting force. The synergy between active and limiting forces modifies the third component. This component is a passive force. Its quality demonstrates a result of the settlement's functioning (Fig. 2.2).

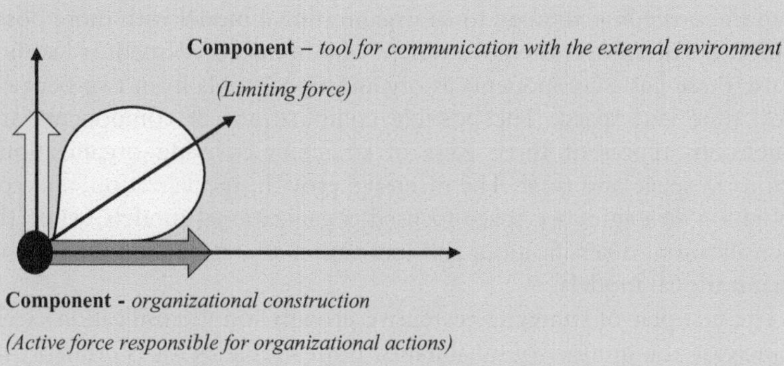

Fig. 2.2 Qualitative structure of the whole entity. (Source: Vidickienė, 2023a)

synergetic effects. Moving to the next combination, a human settlement increases in complexity and evolves its organizational quality by adding new knowledge and skills on how to manage the settlement.

There are six possible combinations of the three components of human settlement (place, infrastructure, and inhabitants) with three dimensions of qualitative structure (organizational construction, communication with the external environment, and result of functioning). Each combination could be defined as a particular organizational strategy. According to the main goal of the strategy, they were referred to as:

1. Extensive growth strategy
2. Intensification strategy
3. Specialization strategy
4. Diversification strategy
5. Collaboration strategy
6. Innovation strategy.

The six strategies mentioned create an evolutionary framework based on the Qualitative Structure method (Fig. 2.3).

The proposed framework provides a unique set of tools to holistically understand the key organizational patterns that emerge in human settlements, as all six strategies are closely interlinked. Shifting to the next stage requires a new combination of three components with three dimensions. Each new combination adds skills for operating the components differently and generating a new kind of synergetic effect. It means that the governance of a settlement stage-by-stage gains in complexity and evolves from the preceding strategy to an organizational model with more possibilities. Furthermore, the government of a human settlement is learning to use three basic components as organizational tools from two perspectives: time and space. The possible combinations of components and dimensions represent three pairs of strategies covering organizational actions in space and time. The extensive growth, specialization, and collaboration strategies are space-focused organizational models, while the intensification, diversification, and innovation strategies are time-focused organizational models.

The first pair of strategies (extensive growth and intensification) seeks to increase the number of inhabitants. Both strategies focus primarily on internal processes of settlement establishment and development, aiming to increase the settlement's attractiveness to inhabitants. The extensive

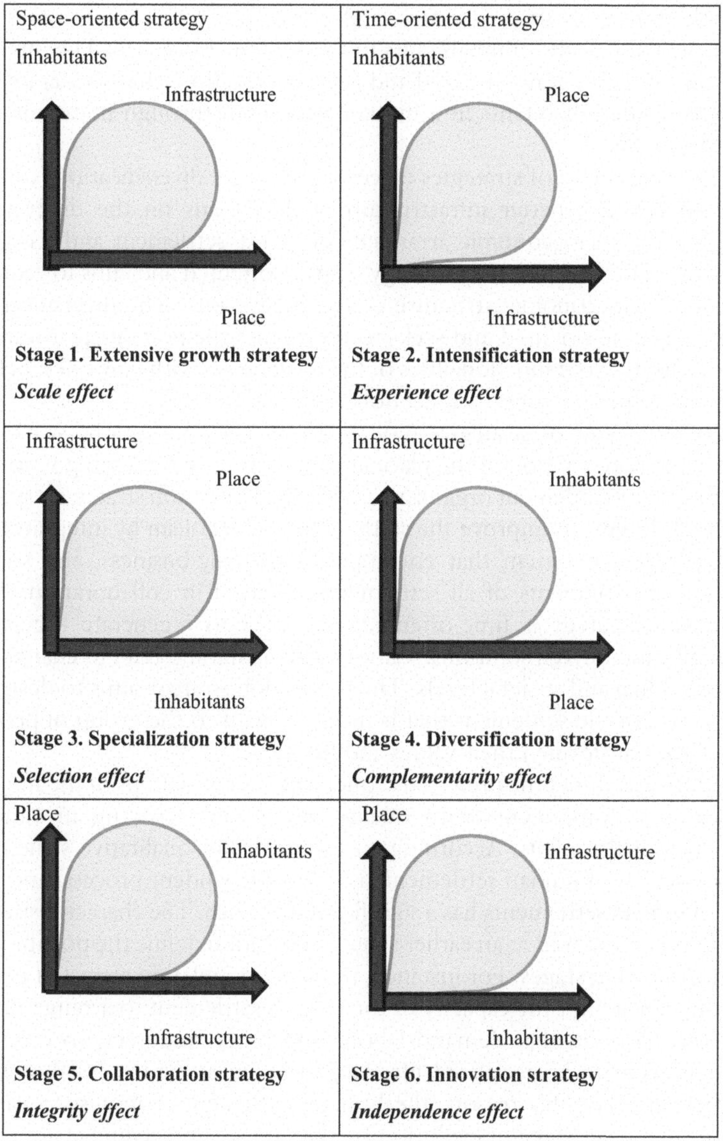

Fig. 2.3 The evolutionary path of a human settlement through different combinations of components and quality dimensions. (Source: Author's figure)

growth strategy is space-oriented and strives to provide more room to meet the daily needs of inhabitants in the settlement's place. The intensification strategy is time-oriented and focuses on actions that accelerate the growth of the inhabitants in a human settlement through infrastructure improvements.

The second pair of strategies (specialization and diversification) can be used to create a better infrastructure with a focus on the differences between the socioeconomic arrangement of the settlement and its environment. The specialization strategy is space-oriented and aims to reorganize the socioeconomic structure of the inhabitants. The diversification strategy is time-oriented and seeks to regenerate the place by providing a combination of old functionalities of the settlements with new ones, better adapted to the changing socioeconomic environment.

The third pair of strategies (collaboration and innovation) strives to ensure the regeneration of the place and adapt it to the changing vision of a high-quality settlement organization. The collaboration strategy is space-oriented. It aims to improve the settlement's metabolism by integrating it into a larger ecosystem that encompasses natural, business, and sociopolitical environments of all settlements involved in collaboration. The innovation strategy is time-oriented and seeks to regenerate the place through value-driven solutions. Values are dynamic and tend to change on the individual and societal levels. The innovation strategy aims to design a new vision of the settlement that is more relevant to the group of people who have transformed their values and lifestyle.

Figure 2.3 shows the preferred sequence of combinations of the human settlement's components with quality dimensions resulting in various organizational toolkits. According to the theory of qualitative structure, the evolution of human settlements is a path-dependent process, and the past of human settlements has a significant influence. The characteristics of a settlement achieved at an earlier stage of evolution define the possibilities in the following stages. For instance, the small population attracted in the first stage will limit the capacity of the human settlement to arrange infrastructure facilities that demand labour and other resources, to create a community with a specialized lifestyle, to be an attractive collaboration partner, etc. For this reason, the human settlement cannot successfully jump to a higher stage of evolution by skipping the preceding stage(s). It is essential to follow the sequence of changes described, as the six stages of the evolution cycle are designed in such a way that the transition to each subsequent stage of evolution means moving from simpler to more complex and professional strategic thinking.

Settlement governance practice, however, contains many examples of ignoring stage-by-stage evolution. Initiatives to implement a strategy that requires higher self-organization quality are failing due to a lack of knowledge and skills to generate the simpler synergetic effects that should be learned to create in earlier stages of settlement evolution. Understanding how the quality of a settlement governance evolves stage by stage and why the combination of three components (inhabitants, place, and infrastructure) and three dimensions of the quality structure (organizational construction, functioning, and communication with the external environment) should follow the sequence described above is the essential success factor for evolution.

Of course, the speed at which a human settlement evolves can vary greatly. However, the main task is to follow the sequence of changes in the combination of settlement components. The evolution of a settlement, defined as its quality shift to a more complex state, can be achieved only by following the sequence described in the framework.

The concepts of extensive growth, intensification, specialization, and diversification strategies are well-known in the social sciences literature, particularly within various fields of business management. However, governance theories and models do not examine them as interconnected or based on the same structural components. The proposed spatio-temporal framework of closely connected strategies offers new insights, facilitating the purposeful formation of spatial and temporal structures and functions within human settlements.

Strategic Goals and Characteristics of the Six Stages that Compose One Evolutionary Cycle

The evolutionary framework of human settlement organization, based on the Qualitative Structure approach introduced in the Section "How Human Settlements Evolve: a Framework of Six General Strategies", comprises a set of six strategies that form one evolutionary cycle of any human settlement. According to the linear time concept, each evolutionary cycle begins with the innovation strategy. However, a more straightforward way to explain how the quality of human settlement improves step by step is to start with the simplest organizational model—the extensive growth strategy.

The sequence of changes in possible combinations of three basic components (place, inhabitants, and infrastructure) with three dimensions of qualitative structure (organizational construction, functioning, and communication with the external environment) is based on the logic of increasing complexity. The term 'increasing complexity' refers to the ability of human settlements to manage their three interconnected basic components through a more diversified collection of relationships among them. Each new combination of relationships between basic components and dimensions of qualitative structure adds skills for managing the settlement from a new perspective and generating a new kind of synergetic effect.

Stage 1: The Extensive Growth Strategy

The development of each physically established start-up human settlement begins with an extensive growth strategy. The care of a newly established settlement is focused on its size. The strategy uses the simplest organizational model, where the size is the primary indicator of a settlement's quality. The quality of human settlements is measured in terms of the size of the assimilated area and the number of inhabitants.

The extensive growth strategy is space-oriented. The component 'place' represents the active force in human settlement growth, as the inhabitants' absorbing capability is directly dependent on the characteristics of the place (Fig. 2.4). Not all areas are suitable for human habitat. The place occupied for a new settlement should ensure the well-being of its inhabitants. At a minimum, a place should meet the basic physiological needs of humans. It must provide the inhabitants with a sustainable food

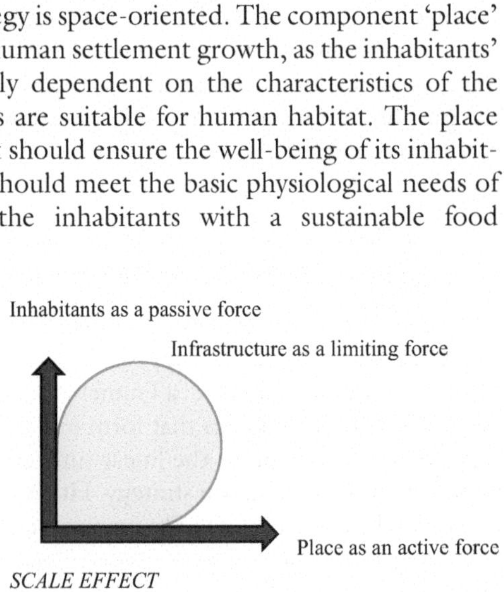

Fig. 2.4 Qualitative structure of the extensive growth strategy. (Source: Author's figure)

availability, tolerable climatic conditions, and shelter that offers protection from unfavourable situations.

The extensive growth strategy has two goals:

1. Ensure the viability of a newly established settlement,
2. Generate a positive scale effect.

The first step in the conscious evolution of a start-up human settlement is to ensure the viability of a newly established settlement. According to a holistic approach, this objective can be reformulated as a strategic task to maintain the settlement's wholeness.

Theories of critical mass, activation energy, and tipping point serve as crucial concepts for understanding how to implement this task through the extensive growth of the population in the settlement. Previously, the mentioned theories were used only to explain physical and chemical processes. Currently, they are applied in various fields, including biological and social sciences, and provide invaluable insights into the general rules that govern the quality changes of any whole entity.

In the case of human settlements, the specific requirement to maintain wholeness is dealing with the 'critical mass' of inhabitants. Like any movement or venture, a human settlement as a whole entity must reach a critical mass of inhabitants to sustain itself and succeed. The extensive growth strategy is expected to help achieve this. Of course, a settlement may exist with a single inhabitant for a while, but such settlements are the exception. People live in communities, as living in a community is essential for the continuation of the human lineage and long-term survival. How few people could be in the human settlement? The minimum population a settlement needs to maintain its viability depends on many factors, but it always exists. Each village defines its own size. Moreover, the size of the critical mass can change over time.

The second task of the extensive growth strategy is to generate a positive *scale* effect. Critical mass theory suggests that exponential growth or accelerated change will occur once a certain size is reached. When the settlement reaches a critical mass of inhabitants, a scale effect emerges and grows.

The scale effect influences the scaling of several desirable settlement characteristics, particularly those related to social outcomes (Bettencourt et al., 2020). For this reason, large human settlements have an advantage over small ones.

Many aspects of the extensive growth strategy investigate urban scaling theory. According to urban scaling researchers, population size plays a critical role in the development of a settlement because various characteristics of human settlements change systematically with city size. As indicated by studies, city-level characteristics, for example, wealth, crime, pollution, consumption patterns, and energy expenditure, scale with variations in city size (Bettencourt, 2013).

Many settlements can continue to scale for a long time. However, extensive growth always has a limit. This means that all settlements have a limited capacity to absorb migrants and/or the natural growth of inhabitants. What are the reasons?

First, population growth can limit the characteristics of a place. Physical or socio-political landscapes can seriously obstruct the development of a settlement and the accommodation of ongoing population growth. However, empirical research shows that place characteristics are not the only barrier to settlement growth. Each settlement has its capacity for growth, which depends on the ratio between a place's size and population. The massive and uncontrolled growth of the population in the settlement area can lead to a decline in its quality (Hoch, 1976; Cramer et al., 2004; Haase et al., 2013). Where a large number of people live in a relatively small area, the scale effect does not increase linearly but follows an inverse U-shaped curve. When the population of a settled place reaches a certain level, a negative synergetic scale effect occurs.

The limiting force in the settlement's extensive growth strategy qualitative structure is the component 'infrastructure', which refers to the basic physical facilities (residential, industrial, and commercial buildings; roads; power supplies; etc.) and social organizational infrastructure needed to operate a settlement. The significant growth of the settlement's population can lead to the failure of its overtaxed infrastructure. If infrastructure facilities that provide the inhabitants' basic needs, such as water, sanitation, and physical and virtual communication facilities, fail or malfunction, the consequences can be severe. Households and businesses may be disrupted, and health risks and environmental impacts may arise.

The growing negative effects suggest that the extensive growth strategy is no longer relevant for improving the quality of a human settlement, as the limiting component—infrastructure—creates a threshold for further development of the settlement. Under these conditions, a human settlement has only one alternative for future evolution—adopting a new organizational strategy. The most effective way to improve the quality of a settlement is to adopt a new governance model—the strategy of intensification. The shift to this strategy makes perfect logical sense for a human settlement seeking a new evolutionary step: the organizational activities move from extending a place for living to improving infrastructure, as this component is a primary obstacle that limits the growth of inhabitants in the settlement.

Stage 2. The Intensification Strategy

The intensification strategy is time-oriented and seeks to accelerate the growth of inhabitants by enhancing the living conditions offered by a settlement place (Fig. 2.5). The active force for improving the settlement's quality is the component 'infrastructure', and the strategy is implemented by building and renovating physical and social infrastructure facilities. Settlement infrastructure is generally performed by engineering systems (including political and social engineering) that aim to improve residents' quality of life. The place represents a limiting force in the second stage of evolution, and the possibility of infrastructure development depends on the characteristics of the place; for example, desirable infrastructure facilities cannot be arranged technically due to the specific physical characteristics of the place's landscape.

The analysis of the impact of infrastructure on the well-being of inhabitants lies at the heart of this strategy. The quality of human settlement should be analysed to identify which infrastructure facilities accelerate or slow down the growth of its attractiveness as a place to live. Learning from the best practices is also important, as the best solutions in the neighbourhoods may be a source of inspiration to increase settlement attractiveness by improving residents' quality of life through infrastructure facilities.

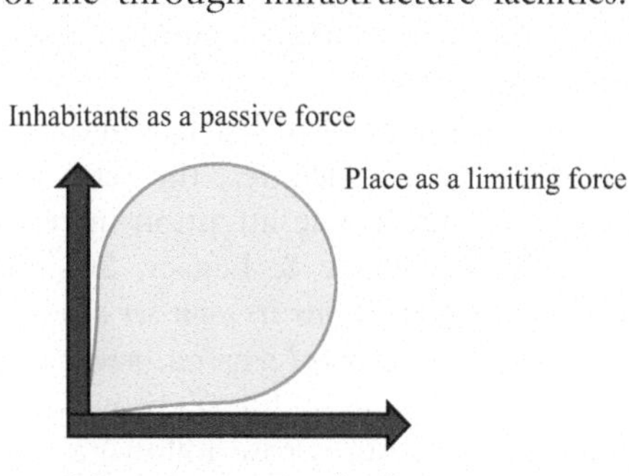

Fig. 2.5 Qualitative structure of the intensification strategy. (Source: Author's figure)

Applying global urban management practices to infrastructure development has become particularly popular in the twenty-first century, in the era of globalization and information technology.

The inhabitants' judgements of the basic infrastructure facilities necessary for the settlement are changing. Historical analysis through the lens of post-industrial theory reveals that the most significant changes in infrastructure arrangements occurred in tandem with the turn to a new paradigm of the economic system organization. With each shift to a new economic system, the areas of human life that require infrastructure facilities have undergone radical transformation. For example, the Agricultural Revolution marked a significant transition in human *civilization*, from small, nomadic bands of hunter-gatherers to larger, settled agricultural communities. It was a period of radical change during which humans began cultivating plants, breeding animals for food, and forming permanent settlements. The permanent settlements were designed and built in a step-by-step process, incorporating affordable residential and agricultural infrastructure facilities. As a result, the traditional set of infrastructure facilities in an agrarian activities-oriented settlement was significantly different from that of a settlement of hunter-gatherers. With the Industrial Revolution, technology has become a significant catalyst for transforming urban infrastructure, and technological innovations have fundamentally altered the perception of high-quality human settlement infrastructure.

In the twenty-first century, scientific advancements offer numerous solutions for enhancing physical urban infrastructure. However, implementers of the intensification strategy must keep in mind that the development of infrastructure facilities is not only a positive process; sometimes, it can generate a negative impact on the quality of the settlement. For example, dense road infrastructure can cause environmental pollution and result in severe traffic congestion, leading to increased travel times and economic costs.

Due to the need to balance underdevelopment and overdevelopment of infrastructure facilities, the term 'critical infrastructure' has recently received considerable attention in research and urban policy (Cantelmi et al., 2021; Steele & Legacy, 2017; Zebrowski & Sage, 2017). *Each human settlement has its own set of critical infrastructures, which are also referred to as essential services, whose interruption or failure would have a severe impact on daily life* (Zebrowski & Sage, 2017). The significance of these infrastructures rose following concern over the exposure of infrastructure to terrorist attacks, disruption through disasters, rising awareness of the interdependent nature of infrastructure in modern urban systems, and changes in the ownership of and responsibility for infrastructure assets (Steele et al., 2017).

If the population of a settlement is oriented towards various economic activities and lifestyles, infrastructure development can trigger social and environmental conflicts. Big infrastructure projects induce various impacts on stakeholders, which can lead to strong opposition to the project. For example, the conflict can be driven by disagreements over the purpose and effects of public investments, the use of land or other natural resources for building infrastructure objects, their location, and the construction process. When significant variations in the needs of inhabitants for infrastructure facilities become evident, the settlement governance faces many challenges. Such a situation provides an incentive to reorganize the settlement's population structure into a more homogenous one from the perspective of their basic needs in infrastructure. Doing this intentionally means entering the next stage of human settlement evolution, which can be referred to as a specialization strategy.

Stage 3. The Specialization Strategy

The large diversity of inhabitants causes variations in their needs for infrastructure facilities and can create problems with the development of physical and social infrastructure, as each specific group of inhabitants requires a differentiated approach to planning and funding their infrastructure needs. The needs depend on the characteristics of the inhabitants, including their livelihood, wealth, role in hierarchical structures, age, and other factors. Moreover, the needs of one inhabitant influence the needs of others. As noted by Star (1999, p. 380), 'Experiences of infrastructure are highly contingent, where one person's infrastructure is another person's difficulty'. The active force of the specialization strategy is the component 'inhabitants', and the strategy directs governments of human settlements to make critical decisions about the composition of the inhabitants' structure. Reducing the diversity of inhabitants allows for reducing the diversity of their infrastructure needs (Fig. 2.6).

Settlement specialization sometimes arises naturally due to external factors that enable inhabitants to develop new economic activities, which become the primary source of their livelihood. For example, due to the growth of long-distance trade in the agrarian era, many agrarian settlements have evolved into commercial cities, profiting from the passing

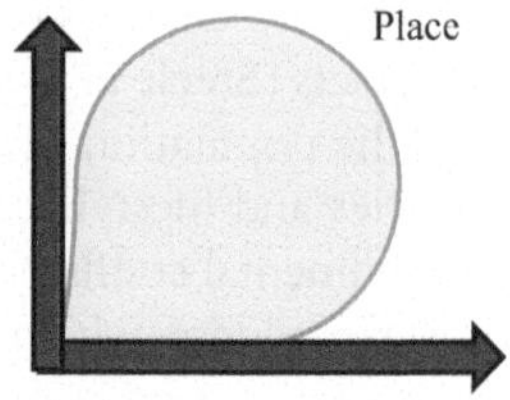

Fig. 2.6 Qualitative structure of the specialization strategy. (Source: Author's figure)

trade routes by providing merchants with a place to rest, eat, and exchange goods. However, the structure of inhabitants can also be changed intentionally. It can occur through the decisions of hierarchically organized social institutions, such as political authorities, religious organizations, guilds, classes, and kinship groups, which operate across the settlement system. For example, the military settlement may be established when the government decides to allocate a particular area for troop accommodation and military exercises.

Settlement specialization is usually related to the inhabitants' particular livelihood. It primarily refers to the differentiation of inhabitants according to their economic activities that require specific infrastructure facilities, such as mining, large-scale fishing, or leisure services. Some settlements are focused on the differentiation of inhabitants according to their spiritual and religious beliefs or cultural values. There are numerous examples of religious groups establishing monasteries as separate settlements, as religion and urbanity have continually shaped each other (URBREL, 2019). Religious settlements can also be established during periods of religious strife between different faiths. In every heterogeneous society, religious difference serves as a source of potential conflict (Brahm, 2005). Due to significant differences in cultural values, religious beliefs, and practices among groups, isolated settlements or urban zones can be established where people belonging to the same group reside and develop specific infrastructure.

The growth of specialized villages, towns, and cities reflects the region's local culture and social development. Living in a specialized settlement means residents share similar economic and social values or religious beliefs and practices. They also want to enjoy infrastructure facilities tailored to their specific lifestyle. It implies that specialized settlements aim to have infrastructure facilities that are typically not available in ordinary settlements.

The success of the specialization strategy derives from the clearly defined specificity of shared infrastructure, whether for defence, trade, collaboration in specific economic activities, religious practices, or entertainment. For example, capital cities are centres of political power and governance. They house government institutions, have military constructions designed for the defence of territories in warfare, and are used to establish rule in a region during peacetime. A well-defined focus within the realm of the local people's dominant competencies enables the more effective use of local resources. A human settlement with well-developed specific infrastructure becomes famous in the region. It gains a competitive advantage over other human settlements as an attractive place to live or visit.

In small settlements, the highest level of specialization may be the most effective solution for a long time, and a human settlement has no incentive to seek a more complex strategy. However, the limiting force in the settlement's specialization strategy—the component 'place'—is constantly influenced by external factors. This means that the relevance of the settlement's place characteristics to its specialization is dynamic and can change over time. For example, characteristics such as accessibility and connectedness of a place are essential for a settlement that specializes in tourism. However, they can be significantly altered by the development of transportation technologies, political and business solutions, and other factors. If the changes take an undesirable direction, the settlement loses its attractiveness as a tourist destination. When radical changes occur in a settlement's place characteristics due to external impacts, a high-level specialization can start to generate a negative effect on settlement quality.

As factors outside the settlement influence the characteristics of a place, its government typically has limited power to influence external factors. In this case, the leaders of a human settlement should seek a new strategy. This means that a specialized settlement must start managing the risk of degradation. The best way to avoid reducing the settlement's quality is to shift to the next evolution stage, which helps to reorganize the settlement by regenerating the component 'place'.

Stage 4. The Diversification Strategy

The diversification strategy is time-oriented and seeks to reorganize the spatial and social arrangement of the settlement's place according to the radical changes in the environment. Human settlements are not isolated or cut off from outside influences, and many of their problems are challenges imposed by external factors. For example, in a scenario of industrial decline and growing unemployment, the risk to company towns is progressive economic marginalization, demographic collapse, and an overall decrease in place quality (Lazzeroni, 2020). Changes in business, political, or natural environments transform lifestyle. Together, social characteristics and the needs of inhabitants for place organization and infrastructure facilities are changing. The diversification strategy can help mitigate the risk of a settlement's sustainability, especially for those that are strongly specialized.

The component 'place' is an organizational construction of the diversification strategy (Fig. 2.7). Like any living organism, each place has native attributes encoded in its individual deoxyribonucleic acid (DNA). Just as the DNA of any living organism changes with time and responds to variations in the environment, the local DNA of a place continuously responds to external factors. Advancing a settlement towards a viable future requires an understanding of this local DNA, such as carefully assessing the unique individual traits of a place (Schurig & Turan, 2022). The place should be reorganized to prepare for the future in accordance with the philosophy of sustainable human development, which aims to create an environment where future generations can thrive and develop. The diversification strategy should be implemented with an orientation towards the interests of key groups of inhabitants, considering their changing needs and potential livelihoods, over *an extended period*. The strategy building should consider new opportunities and challenges and offer solutions to the

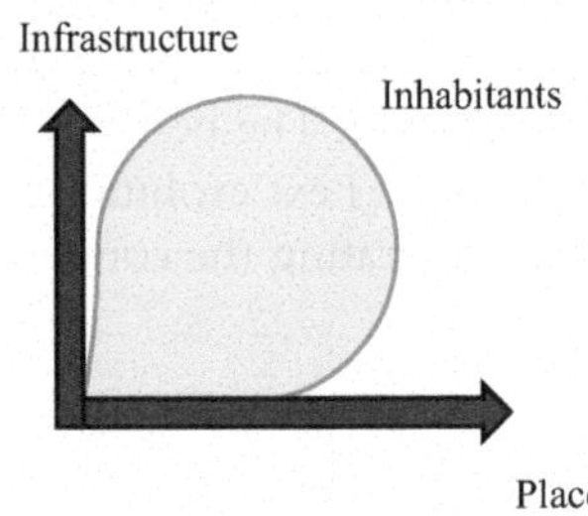

Fig. 2.7 Qualitative structure of the diversification strategy. (Source: Author's figure)

settlement inhabitants on how to regenerate their living place according to the requirements of the time.

The concept of complementarity lies at the heart of the diversification strategy. A diversification strategy should help generate a complementarity effect between the old characteristics of the place and new ones (in this stage of settlement evolution, the place covers all local resources, including human, natural, and man-made). In any solution for place regeneration, attention should be geared towards the best combination for the chosen time perspective. The size of the complementarity effect depends on two factors: (1) the ability to foresee trends of socioeconomic transformations, and (2) creativity in employing tangible and intangible local resources for adaptation to transformations. Both factors are especially crucial for the success of the diversification strategy in periods of radical socioeconomic transformations in the external environment.

Searching for the best combination of old settlement functions with new opportunities that are relevant to inhabitants' competencies and needs is a continuous process. The strategy is time-oriented, and strategic solutions should be revised periodically to identify new opportunities to enhance the complementarity effect or mitigate emerging risks to the settlement's sustainability.

The limiting force in the diversification strategy is the component 'inhabitants'. Resistance to change is a natural human response driven by such factors as fear of the unknown, comfort with the status quo, and concerns about the impact of change (Smollan, 2011; Jost, 2015; Khaw et al., 2023). In the context of the failed success of the settlement's specialization, the resistance of inhabitants to changes can manifest as scepticism about the effectiveness of diversification. The unwillingness of local people to adapt to new circumstances or ways of doing things can be a serious obstacle to regenerating the settlement.

There are many ways to revitalize a settlement and make it an attractive place to live, taking into account changing circumstances. For this reason, most human settlements tend to procrastinate the transition into the next stage of evolution. However, when economic or social conditions are not favourable and appear to be at risk of further decline, a greater number of people will probably migrate to a place with a better outlook for living. When migration and other negative forms of resistance by inhabitants to the offered ways of the place transformation get out of control, it is time to seek entirely new strategic solutions. Difficulties in financing and managing public services because of an increasing dynamism in factors influencing living place decisions motivate human settlements to initiate collaborative activities with other settlements.

Stage 5. The Collaboration Strategy

The collaboration strategy aims to rearrange the settlement's infrastructure, which is the active force in this organizational model (Fig. 2.8). However, infrastructure should be improved from a different perspective than implementing the intensification strategy in the second stage of human settlement evolution. Both strategies have the same component in the role of active force: infrastructure. However, in Stage 5, the focus of infrastructure development shifts to the settlement's metabolism, rather than providing specific facilities. Similar to the metabolic processes within a living organism, settlement metabolism refers to the flow of energy, information, and materials within a human settlement. Infrastructure provides the channels through which they flow. Analysing settlement metabolism through the flows of energy, water, air, food, raw materials, information, and other resources helps find constraints that slow down processes and make a place unattractive for inhabitants.

The collaboration strategy should be based on a management philosophy that emphasizes focusing on the most critical constraint in a system (the Theory of Constraints refers to this as a bottleneck) and implementing solutions to alleviate it. These bottlenecks can occur due to various factors, such as limited resources, inefficient processes, or capacity constraints. However, the main factor is the lack of coordination between infrastructure development in the settlement and the neighbourhoods' infrastructure. This requires a broader perspective and a vision for infrastructure development on a much larger scale—regional, national, continental, or even global. Understanding and addressing bottlenecks caused

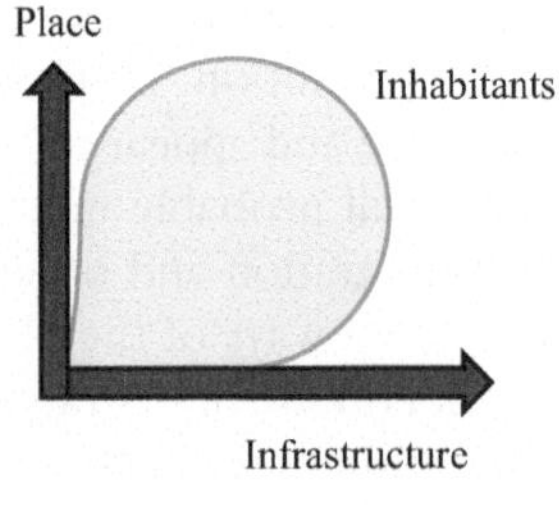

Fig. 2.8 Qualitative structure of the collaboration strategy. (Source: Author's figure)

by a bigger system is crucial for mature settlements to implement the collaboration strategy successfully. Orientation to the needs and potential of a larger system enables the creation of more value collectively than a human settlement could achieve by building infrastructure individually. This means that strategic actions should focus on collaboration to achieve shared goals.

Collaborative initiatives should enable settlements to pool resources and reduce duplication of public services, generating an integration effect. A broad spectrum of possible strategic collaborations exists between human settlements. They can undertake a range of projects that improve the flow of local products and resources, including building and running roads, bridges, and transport hubs such as ports or railway stations. Many settlements have developed the ability to share various infrastructure facilities, including irrigation systems, waste recycling facilities, educational centres, emergency services (police, fire, and ambulance), correctional facilities, courts, law enforcement services, and other public services.

Collaboration projects should modify the places involved in collaboration in a way that enables the inhabitants of all participating settlements to organize their lives more effectively. For example, an improved road between two settlements can reduce travel time, connect workers to new jobs, children to schools in another location, and bring consumers and producers closer to local markets, all while increasing the comfort of travellers, among other benefits.

The collaboration strategy can also help reduce the gaps between the desired and acquired capacities to apply the four previous strategies, as changes in economic, natural, and social environments necessitate ongoing adjustments in strategic decisions. Human settlements should periodically evaluate their quality to identify strategies with either too low or too high capacity. If a human settlement cannot maintain the desired limits of capacities, it is essential to start collaboration with other settlements. Through joint efforts, the members of a collaborative entity can break the constraints to maintain the desired capacity by transforming the component that plays the role of the limiting force. For instance, at the end of the twentieth century, access to education, medical, and social services in rural settings was identified as crucial in preventing people from leaving rural regions (Muijs, 2015; Iurchenko & Iurchenko, 2022). However, maintaining basic infrastructure facilities, such as a medical unit, a school, and a kindergarten, in a depopulated village becomes too expensive. Suppose a settlement cannot provide its inhabitants with some of the basic public services mentioned above. In this case, it becomes a place of residence that cannot maintain a minimum population, which is critical for the vitality of the traditional rural settlement. Collaboration projects with a neighbouring big city and/or other small settlements can be a solution. They enhance the capacities of the extensive growth strategy to maintain the vitality of the settlement by pooling resources for the transformation of the limiting force—infrastructure. For example, projects where schools collaborate to share human and material resources can ensure the schools' survival and help to contain population exodus (Muijs, 2015).

The similar collaborative solutions are also applicable to the other three strategies. The capacity of the intensification strategy depends on the characteristics of the limiting force—place. Collaboration fosters the sharing of experiences on how to increase the effectiveness of infrastructure solutions and offers learning opportunities for all participating settlements. The application of best practices accelerates the intensification of metabolic processes in the settlements.

Collaboration can help increase the capacity of the specialization strategy through the coordination of infrastructure-sharing projects, where each settlement focuses on developing different physical and/or social infrastructure facilities necessary for the inhabitants. For example, collaboration between specialized educational centres located in different settlements supports lifelong learning and broadens the locally available curriculum (Evans & Savage, 2015). Joint projects can also help increase the capacity of the diversification strategy if the infrastructure facilities of partnering settlements complement each other. For example, the increasing importance of tourism in the local, regional, and national economy requires active cooperation between settlements. The most effective way to develop a settlement into a tourism destination is through strategic collaboration with other settlements by developing themed routes as tourist attractions (Mandić et al., 2018; Pedrosa et al., 2022; Vada et al., 2023).

The role of collaboration between human settlements is growing in the current economic climate, characterized by limited resources, increasing demands on services, and complex community expectations. Almost any problem today is too complex to be addressed individually or by organizations working alone in their silos. Synergy-oriented approaches are necessary at every stage of infrastructure facility development, including planning, financing, construction, and maintenance.

The collaboration strategy should be based on the principles of mutuality and reciprocity. All settlements involved in a specific partnership should benefit from the collaborative activities. However, the role of the inhabitants as a limiting force on the capacity of a collaboration strategy can be significant due to a lack of willingness and/or knowledge of how they can act to create mutual benefit.

The biggest challenge to the collaboration strategy is transforming competitive relationships between settlements. A key problem relates to the territorial dimension of infrastructure policy. The goal is to undergo isolated development, but because infrastructure decisions are directly influenced by political will, the government structures of settlements often prioritize the interests of one settlement over creating the common good (Crosby & Bryson, 2005; Prager, 2010). The success in collaboration depends on synergy-oriented thinking, which suggests that partnering settlements should achieve more together than they would by working independently, by integrating their knowledge, resources, approaches, and operational cultures.

Another systemic challenge deals with a lack of strategic thinking. Local development and public governance studies note that public and non-profit administrators often stumble into collaboration without a strategic orientation (Norris-Tirrell & Clay, 2010; O'Donnell, 2012). The debate about infrastructure should begin with values and goals, not investments or technical solutions. The technical expertise of engineers and scientists cannot circumvent the political nature of allocating scarce investment resources. Technical experts can answer the question of what can be built, but not the question of what should be built. The knowledge of development experts is needed for providing insights into what is feasible and the trade-offs of different investment alternatives.

The collaboration strategy, however, is not a panacea in a highly integrated and dynamic environment. Growing numbers of various collaboration networks are constantly evolving the business and social ecosystems. Networks provide various platforms designed to enhance settlement quality according to different visions of an ideal settlement. Lack of a common vision creates confusion in understanding infrastructure development goals and chaos in their coordination. Finally, some collaborative projects or platforms start to generate a negative integrity effect. Instead of reducing uncertainty, collaboration without a shared view introduces additional dynamism to human settlements by creating new connections and breaking down old ones.

The development of new technologies, new types of resources, changes in consumption practices, and numerous other factors influence the attractiveness of living places. When the collaboration strategy is insufficient to reorganize living conditions within the framework of the old lifestyle paradigm, some people take the initiative to create a new living place. The organizational culture acquired during the implementation of the collaboration strategy guides the efforts of founders to create a new vision of an ideal human settlement through the revision of all three basic components: inhabitants, place, and infrastructure.

Stage 6. The Innovation Strategy

The way people live and organize themselves in communities is constantly evolving, and settlements should also be reorganized in response to these changes. The previously introduced five strategies aim to enhance the quality of a settlement through continuous improvements in the organization of human settlement components designed according to the traditional socio-economic paradigm. The innovation strategy seeks to improve the quality of a settlement by radically changing (making different) what exists.

The organizational construction in the sixth stage is the component 'inhabitants' (Fig. 2.9). This means that a group of people who want to live in a differently organized settlement should emerge. If people cannot find a settlement that is attractive to them, they attempt to pursue an innovation strategy. Acting as a group of people with common aspirations for living conditions that are more relevant to their lifestyle, a group initiates a pilot project to envision their vision of a more qualitative living place. This strategy should help them generate an effect of independence from traditional lifestyle, cultural values, and social norms. If the founders of a newly organized settlement succeeded with a pilot project, it could be regarded as a prototype for designing and building countercultural,

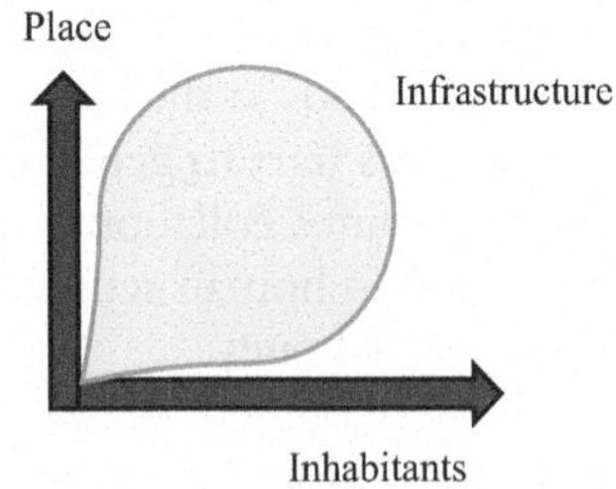

Fig. 2.9 Qualitative structure of the innovation strategy. (Source: Author's figure)

alternative places for alternative inhabitants. By serving as practical examples and research platforms, innovative settlement prototypes play a crucial role in advancing the development of the overall human settlement system.

Despite the common general orientation, groups can offer very different visions of innovative settlement organization based on their worldview, needs, and knowledge. Which one will become popular in the future depends on the general trajectory of humanity's evolution in the region and globally. World history has documented a diverse array of utopian settlements, including survivalist camps, communes, ecovillages, religious communities, and mystical retreats (Van Bueren & Tarlow, 2006). However, only a few have been used as a prototype and have become dominant in the region or worldwide. They have begun a new socio-economic evolutionary cycle of the global human settlement system.

According to linear time logic, the evolutionary cycle starts with an innovation strategy based on a new economic paradigm. The other five strategies of the qualitative structure framework can be referred to as paradigm-developing strategies (Fig. 2.10).

However, explaining the evolutionary logic as the stage-by-stage growth of settlement quality is easier when starting with the simplest organizational model—the extensive growth strategy. Therefore, Fig. 2.3 presents the framework of six strategies in the sequence of combinations between a human settlement's components and quality dimensions most appropriate for learning purposes.

Each human settlement has the opportunity to evolve by applying all six strategies stage by stage; however, this is only an opportunity, not a guarantee that it will occur. Many human settlements established according to the dominating settlement model halt their evolution at the first or second stage of their evolutionary path. The reasons can vary, but a lack of a holistic approach and understanding of the settlement's qualitative structure is one of the biggest obstacles to continuing along the evolutionary path.

Evolutionary knowledge is fundamental during periods of economic paradigm shifts. Currently, as we transition from the industrial to the post-industrial economic paradigm, society needs guidelines on how to reorganize the industrial human settlement system in accordance with the rules of the service economy. Understanding the evolutionary path of human settlements through the known socio-economic historical eras provides a 'big picture' and encourages future-minded thinking.

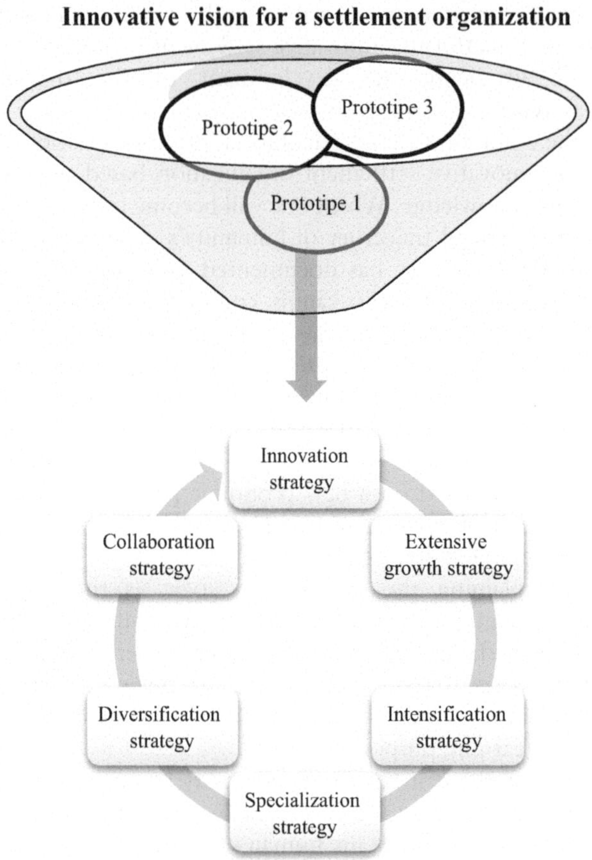

Fig. 2.10 The evolutionary cycle of a human settlement model. (Source: Author's figure)

Bibliography

Bai, X., McPhearson, T., Cleugh, H., Nagendra, H., Tong, X., Zhu, T., & Zhu, Y. G. (2017). Linking urbanization and the environment: Conceptual and empirical advances. *Annual Review of Environment and Resources, 42*(1), 215–240. https://doi.org/10.1146/annurev-environ-102016-061128

Bartlett, C. A., & Ghoshal, S. (1998). *Managing across borders*. Harvard Business School Press.

Bartuska, T. J. (2007). Understanding environment(s): Built and natural. In McClure, W. R., & Bartuska, T. J. (Eds.), The built environment: A collaborative inquiry into design and planning (pp. 33–43). John Wiley & Sons.
Bettencourt, L. M. (2013). The origins of scaling in cities. *Science, 340*(6139), 1438–1441.
Bettencourt, L. M., Yang, V. C., Lobo, J., Kempes, C. P., Rybski, D., & Hamilton, M. J. (2020). The interpretation of urban scaling analysis in time. *Journal of the Royal Society Interface, 17*(163), 20190846.
Borsdorf, A., & Stadel, C. (2015). Rural and urban settlements. In *The Andes* (Springer Geography). Springer. https://doi.org/10.1007/978-3-319-03530-7_6
Boulangeat, I., et al. (2022). From human-nature dualism towards more integration in socio-ecosystems studies. In I. Misiune, D. Depellegrin, & L. Egarter Vigl (Eds.), *Human-nature interactions.* Springer. https://doi.org/10.1007/978-3-031-01980-7_4
Brahm, E. (2005). Religion and conflict. In G. Burgess & H. Burgess (Eds.), *Beyond intractability.* Conflict Information Consortium, University of Colorado. http://www.beyondintractability.org/essay/religion-and-conflict
Brown, D. L., & Cromartie, J. B. (2017). The nature of rurality in postindustrial society. In *New forms of urbanization* (pp. 269–283). Routledge.
Cantelmi, R., Di Gravio, G., & Patriarca, R. (2021). Reviewing qualitative research approaches in the context of critical infrastructure resilience. *Environment Systems and Decisions, 41*(3), 341–376.
Choudhry, K. Z., Coles, R., Qureshi, S., Ashford, R., Khan, S., & Mir, R. R. (2015). A review of methodologies used in studies investigating human behaviour as determinant of outcome for exposure to 'naturalistic and urban environments'. *Urban Forestry & Urban Greening, 14*(3), 527–537.
Cimatti, F. (2016). Beyond the human non-human dichotomy: The philosophical problem of human Animality. *Humanimalia, 7*(2), 35–55. https://doi.org/10.52537/humanimalia.9665
Cramer, V., Torgersen, S., & Kringlen, E. (2004). Quality of life in a city: The effect of population density. *Social Indicators Research, 69*, 103–116.
Crosby, B. C., & Bryson, J. M. (2005). A leadership framework for cross-sector collaboration. *Public Management Review, 7*(2), 177–201.
Cyriac, S., & Firoz C, M. (2022). Dichotomous classification and implications in spatial planning: A case of the rural-urban continuum settlements of Kerala, India. *Land Use Policy, 114*, 105992. https://doi.org/10.1016/j.landusepol.2022.105992
Dabson, B. (2019). Regional solutions for rural and urban challenges. *State and Local Government Review, 51*(4), 283–291.
de Roo, G., & Miller, D. (2017). *Integrating city planning and environmental improvement: Practicable strategies for sustainable urban development.* Routledge.

Delgado-Viñas, C., & Gómez-Moreno, M. L. (2022). The interaction between urban and rural areas: An updated paradigmatic, methodological and bibliographic review. *Land, 11*(8), 1298.

Doernberg, A., & Weith, T. (2021). Urban-rural interrelations—A challenge for sustainable land management. In T. Weith, T. Barkmann, N. Gaasch, S. Rogga, C. Strauß, & J. Zscheischler (Eds.), *Sustainable land management in a European Context. Human-environment interactions, vol 8*. Springer. https://doi.org/10.1007/978-3-030-50841-8_6

Doxiadis, C. A. (1968). *Ekistics: An introduction to the science of human settlement*. Oxford University Press.

Doxiadis, C. A. (1970). Ekistics, the science of human settlements: Ekistics starts with the premise that human settlements are susceptible of systematic investigation. *Science, 170*(3956), 393–404.

Dunlap, R. E., & Catton, W. R., Jr. (1983). What environmental sociologists have in common (whether concerned with "built" or "natural" environments). *Sociological Inquiry, 53*(2–3), 113–135.

Dymitrow, M., & Stenseke, M. (2016). Rural-urban blurring and the subjectivity within. *Rural Landscapes: Society, Environment, History, 3*(1), 4–4.

Evans, W., & Savage, J. (2015). *Developing a local curriculum: Using your locality to inspire teaching and learning*. Routledge.

Fang, C. (2022). On integrated urban and rural development. *Journal of Geographical Sciences, 32*(8), 1411–1426.

Galbraith, J. R. (1994). *Competing with flexible lateral organizations*. Addison-Wesley.

Haase, D., Kabisch, N., & Haase, A. (2013). Endless urban growth? On the mismatch of population, household and urban land area growth and its effects on the urban debate. *PLoS One, 8*(6), e66531.

Hawkins, R. (2006). Introduction: Beyond nature/culture dualism: Let's try co-evolution instead of "control". *Ethics and the Environment, 11*(2), 1–11. http://www.jstor.org/stable/40339121

Herlin, I. S. (2004). New challenges in the field of spatial planning: Landscapes. *Landscape Research, 29*(4), 399–411.

Hoch, I. (1976). City size effects, trends, and policies: The consequences as a city grows in population and recent patterns of US urban growth are examined. *Science, 193*(4256), 856–863.

Hugo, G. (2017). *New forms of urbanization: Beyond the urban-rural dichotomy*. Routledge.

Iurchenko, S., & Iurchenko, O. (2022). Social infrastructure as a factor of sustainable development of the territory. The Journal of VN Karazin Kharkiv National University. Series: International Relations. Economics. *Country Studies. Tourism*, (15), 139–145.

Jost, J. T. (2015). Resistance to change: A social psychological perspective. *Social Research: An International Quarterly, 82*(3), 607–636.

Kalinauskas, I. N. (1991). *Najedine s mirom*. Oktiabrj.
Kalinauskas, I. N., & Reinin, G. P. (1995). Method of qualitative structures (MQS). *Moscow Aviation Institute Information Bulletin, 4*.
Karmanov, D., & Hamel, R. (2008). Assessing the restorative potential of contemporary urban environment (s): Beyond the nature versus urban dichotomy. *Landscape and Urban Planning, 86*(2), 115–125.
Karvonen, A., Cvetkovic, V., Herman, P., et al. (2021). The 'new urban science': Towards the interdisciplinary and transdisciplinary pursuit of sustainable transformations. *Urban Transformations, 3*, 9. https://doi.org/10.1186/s42854-021-00028-y
Keith, M., O'Clery, N., Parnell, S., & Revi, A. (2020). The future of the future city? The new urban sciences and a PEAK urban interdisciplinary disposition. *Cities, 105*, 102820. https://doi.org/10.1016/j.cities.2020.102820
Khaw, K. W., Alnoor, A., Al-Abrrow, H., Tiberius, V., Ganesan, Y., & Atshan, N. A. (2023). Reactions towards organizational change: A systematic literature review. *Current Psychology, 42*(22), 19137–19160.
Knight, K. (1976). Matrix organization: A review. *Journal of Management Studies, 13*(2), 111–130.
Lazzeroni, M. (2020). Industrial decline and resilience in small towns: Evidence from three European case studies. *Tijdschrift voor Economische en Sociale Geografie, 111*(2), 182–195.
Li, L., Ma, S., Zheng, Y., & Xiao, X. (2022). Integrated regional development: Comparison of urban agglomeration policies in China. *Land Use Policy, 114*, 105939.
Li, X., Yu, L., & Chen, X. (2023). New insights into urbanization based on global mapping and analysis of human settlements in the rural–urban continuum. *Land, 12*(8), 1607. https://doi.org/10.3390/land12081607
Liu, J., Zheng, B., & Tang, H. (2023). The science of rural human settlements: A comprehensive overview. *Frontiers in Environmental Science, 11*, 1274281.
Lobanova, L. (2003). Human resources transformation: Framework of problem. *Tiltai, 1*(22), 23–38.
Mandić, A., Mrnjavac, Ž., & Kordić, L. (2018). Tourism infrastructure, recreational facilities and tourism development. *Tourism and Hospitality Management, 24*(1), 41–62.
Marconcini, M., Esch, T., Bachofer, F., & Metz-Marconcini, A. (2019). Digital earth in Europe. In *Manual of digital earth* (pp. 647–681). Springer Singapore.
Melnikienė, R., & Vidickienė, D. (2019). Evaluation of the Lithuanian agricultural policy based on the analysis of qualitative structure. *Public Policy and Administration, 18*(1), 52–67.

Motta, P., Jaime, C., & Escobar, F. S. (2022). Transformation of urban–rural relationships in the context of global challenges. *The International Journal of Social Quality, 12*(2), 25–50. https://doi.org/10.3167/IJSQ.2022.120203
Muijs, D. (2015). Collaboration and networking among rural schools: Can it work and when? Evidence from England. *Peabody Journal of Education, 90*(2), 294–305.
Næss, P. (2015). Critical realism, urban planning and urban research. *European Planning Studies, 23*(6), 1228–1244.
Pateman, T. (2011). Rural and urban areas: Comparing lives using rural/urban classifications. *Regional Trends, 43*, 11–86.
Pedrosa, A., Martins, F., & Breda, Z. (2022). Tourism routes: A scoping review. *European Journal of Tourism Research, 32*, 3216–3216.
Prager, K. (2010). Local and regional partnerships in natural resource management: the challenge of bridging institutional levels. *Environmental Management, 46*(5), 711–724.
Savini, F., Ferreira, A., & von Schönfeld, K., Eds. (2022). Post-growth planning: Cities beyond the market economy. Routledge.
Scharper, S. B., & Leman-Stefanovic, I. (Eds.). (2012). The natural city: Re-envisioning the built environment. University of Toronto Press.
Schurig, S., & Turan, K. (2022). The concept of a 'regenerative city': How to turn cities into regenerative systems. *Journal of Urban Regeneration & Renewal, 15*(2), 161–175.
Scott, A., Carter, C., Reed, M., Larkham, P., Adams, D., Morton, N., Waters, R., Collier, D., Crean, C., Curzon, R., Forster, R., Gibbs, P., Grayson, N., Hardman, M., Hearle, A., Jarvis, D., Kennet, M., Leach, K., Middleton, M., … Coles, R. (2013). Disintegrated development at the rural–urban fringe: Re-connecting spatial planning theory and practice. *Progress in Planning, 83*, 1–52. https://doi.org/10.1016/j.progress.2012.09.001
Seto K. C., Dhakal, S., Bigio, A., Blanco, H., Delgado, G. C., Dewar, D., Huang, L., Inaba, A., Kansal, A., Lwasa, S, McMahon, J. E., Müller, D. B., Murakami, J., Nagendra, H., & Ramaswami, A. (2014). Human settlements, infrastructure and spatial planning. In O. Edenhofer, R. Pichs-Madruga, Y. Sokona, E. Farahani, S. Kadner, K. Seyboth, A. Adler, I. Baum, S. Brunner, P. Eickemeier, B. Kriemann, J. Savolainen, S. Schlömer, C. von Stechow, T. Zwickel, & J. C. Minx (Eds.), Climate change 2014: Mitigation of climate change. Contribution of Working Group III to the Fifth Assessment Report of the Intergovernmental Panel on Climate Change. Cambridge University Press.
Shaw, B. J., van Vliet, J., & Verburg, P. H. (2020). The Peri-urbanization of Europe: A systematic review of a multifaceted process. *Landscape and Urban Planning, 196*, 103733.

Shmakov, B.V. & Egorov I. V. (2007). Managerial processes modelling of distribute firm product flows (system approach), : Publishing House of SUSU.
Smollan, R. K. (2011). The multi-dimensional nature of resistance to change. *Journal of Management & Organization, 17*(6), 828–849.
Star, S. L. (1999). The ethnography of infrastructure. *American Behavioral Scientist, 43*(3), 377–391.
Steele, W., & Legacy, C. (2017). Critical urban infrastructure. *Urban Policy and Research, 35*(1), 1–6.
Steele, W., Hussey, K., & Dovers, S. (2017). What's critical about critical infrastructure? *Urban Policy and Research, 35*(1), 74–86.
Sy, T., Beach, L., & D'Annunzio, L. S. (2005). Challenges and strategies of matrix organizations. *Human Resource Planning, 28*(1), 39–48.
Tandoh-Offin, P. (2010). The evolving rural and urban interdependence: Opportunities and challenges for community economic development. *Journal of Geography and Regional Planning, 3*(12), 339–345.
Taylor, P., Derudder, B., Saey, P., & Witlox, F. (2006). *Cities in globalization: Practices, policies and theories.* Routledge.
URBREL. (2019). Religion and urbanity: A brief introduction. Religion and urbanity: Reciprocal formations. Retrieved June 24, 2025, from https://doi.org/10.58079/v3at.
Vada, S., Dupre, K., & Zhang, Y. (2023). Route tourism: A narrative literature review. *Current Issues in Tourism, 26*(6), 879–889.
Van Bueren, T. M., & Tarlow, S. A. (2006). The interpretive potential of utopian settlements. *Historical Archaeology, 40*(1), 1–5.
Van Vliet, J., Birch-Thomsen, T., Gallardo, M., Hemerijckx, L. M., Hersperger, A. M., Li, M., et al. (2020). Bridging the rural-urban dichotomy in land use science. *Journal of Land Use Science, 15*(5), 585–591.
Vidickienė, D. (2013). *Evolution of the manufacturer's strategic thinking based on the qualitative structure method.* Working paper No. 13-1, Naujos ekonomikos institutas.
Vidickienė, D. (2023a). Theory of qualitative structure as a conceptual framework for understanding Servitization. In *Rural transformation through Servitization: A qualitative structure approach* (pp. 15–44). Springer International Publishing. https://doi.org/10.1007/978-3-031-47186-5_2
Vidickienė, D. (2023b). Framework of product-driven business model transformation based on the theory of qualitative structure. In *Rural transformation through Servitization: A qualitative structure approach* (pp. 171–198). Springer International Publishing.
Vidickienė, D. (2023c). Territorial Servitization as a challenge to reorganizing the rural development of the industrial era. In *Rural transformation through*

Servitization: A qualitative structure approach (pp. 201–217). Springer International Publishing.

Vidickienė, D. (2023d). Framework of networking strategies based on the qualitative structure approach. In *Rural transformation through Servitization: A qualitative structure approach* (pp. 345–361). Springer International Publishing.

Vidickienė, D., & Melnikienė, R. (2014). *Evolution of rural policy.* Lietuvos agrarinės ekonomikos institutas.

Vidickienė, D., Gedminaitė-Raudonė, Ž., & Simonaitytė, V. (2019). Servitization of farming: Business model "product plus service" in Lithuania [Ūkininkavimo servitizacija: verslo modelio "produktų gamyba plius paslaugų teikimas" apraiškos Lietuvoje]. Lithuanian Institute of Agrarian Economics. ISBN: 978-9955-481-71-3 (In Lithuanian).

Vidickienė, D., Gedminaitė-Raudonė, Z., Melnikienė, R., Simonaitytė, V., & Lankauskienė, R. (2021). The role of multi-sided collaborative networks and their platforms in the process of servitization of the economy of rural regions. Lithuanian Centre for Social Sciences. ISBN 987-609-96239-1-7 (In Lithuanian).

Vidickiene, D., Gedminaite-Raudone, Z., Simonaityte, V., & Lankauskiene, R. (2023). The role of social movements in transformative tourism development: Lessons learnt from a case study in Lithuania. *European spatial research and policy, 30*(1), 79–101. https://doi.org/10.18778/1231-1952.30.1.04

Vidickienė, D., Lankauskienė, R., Melnikienė, R., Gedminaitė-Raudonė, Ž., & Simonaitytė, V. (2024). *Rural transformation through Servitization.* Springer Books.

Wandl, D. A., Nadin, V., Zonneveld, W., & Rooij, R. (2014). Beyond urban–rural classifications: Characterising and mapping territories-in-between across Europe. *Landscape and Urban Planning, 130*, 50–63.

Westlund, H. (2018). Urban-rural relations in the post-urban world. In T. Haas, H. Westlund (Eds.) *In the post-urban world: Innovative transformations in Global City regions*, (pp. 70–81). Routledge.

Yang, Y., Bao, W., Wang, Y., & Liu, Y. (2021). Measurement of urban-rural integration level and its spatial differentiation in China in the new century. *Habitat International, 117*, 102420.

Yuzhe, W. U., Hualou, L. O. N. G., Pengjun, Z. H. A. O., & Hui, E. C. M. (2022). Land use policy in urban-rural integrated development. *Land Use Policy, 115*, 106041.

Zebrowski, C., & Sage, D. (2017). Resilience and critical infrastructure: Origins, theories, and critiques. In *The Palgrave handbook of security, risk and intelligence* (pp. 117–135).

CHAPTER 3

Impact of Livelihoods on the Organization of the Human Settlements System

Dalia Vidickienė

Big Cycles in the Evolution of the Global System of Human Settlements

A vision of a high-quality human settlement organization develops over time. It depends on the people who choose *to live* there and their reaction to changes in natural, economic, and social environments.

However, from time to time, evolution calls for groundbreaking ideas that alter how human society is organized and functions. Radical transformations in the socio-economic system demand re-evaluating the previous understanding of high-quality human settlement characteristics. This suggests that an innovation strategy is necessary to implement essential changes oriented towards a fundamentally new vision for human settlement organization. The objective of an innovation strategy is to initiate the next cycle of the evolution process by establishing a new vision that replaces the prevailing perceptions of what constitutes a qualitative life place organization.

The need to revise traditional settlement models and develop new ones is driven by significant cognitive, behavioural, and cultural changes, commonly referred to as paradigm innovations. Paradigm innovation concerns

D. Vidickienė et al., *Human Settlement in the Service Economy Era*, Palgrave Advances in Bioeconomy: Economics and Policies, https://doi.org/10.1007/978-3-032-19390-2_3

the transformation of the underlying assumptions, beliefs, values, and mental models that guide human actions and decisions. Since human settlement is a highly complex system, paradigm innovations can cover many aspects of human life. According to current traditions in scientific research, paradigm innovations related to human settlement evolution are defined within the framework of disciplines such as architecture, geography, transportation engineering, urban planning, and rural development. In such a case, the redesigned vision of the ideal human settlement considers the need for radical changes in only one component of the settlement's qualitative structure. For example, the internal combustion engine in the late nineteenth century brought the large-scale mechanization of transportation modes, especially road transport (Rodrigue, 2024). The diffusion of cars, buses, and trucks followed it. The technological paradigm shifts in transportation led to a radical reorganization of the settlement's infrastructure, as a new kind of transport necessitated the restructuring of urban roads, the construction of new transportation gateways, and the establishment of public transport hubs, among other changes. Technological paradigm innovations in infrastructure are essential steps in the history of human settlement; however, they do not encompass our research object—the global human settlements system. Understanding the big picture of human settlement evolution requires a more comprehensive examination of changes at a higher level of abstraction.

At the current period, the highest level of abstraction in examining human settlements is achieved by defining radical changes in the frameworks of several dimensions of sustainable human development. Usually, economic, social, and ecological dimensions are discussed. Efforts to improve the quality of human settlements within social, economic, and environmental frameworks have led to the development of numerous more sustainable ways of living worldwide. However, the holistic approach requires one more step—the integration of social, economic, and ecological aspects of human life. Understanding their synergistic interactions is critical to the governance and development of human settlements in the post-industrial era.

The most comprehensive generalization to describe the social, economic, and environmental aspects of settlement evolution in an integrated manner is related to livelihoods, allowing people to construct a living and satisfy their daily needs and long-term objectives. Livelihoods encompass all possible assets, abilities, and activities that enable humans to survive and achieve self-realization. Over the last few decades, the urban and rural development literature has increased attention to livelihoods and their role (Beall & Kanji, 1999; Owusu, 2007; De Haan, 2012; Scoones, 2013; Singh & Muhuri, 2024). However, applying livelihood thinking in the context of global human settlement evolution is still rare. The main obstacles are the following:

1. Narrow understanding of the term 'livelihood'.
2. Focus on an individual's livelihood.
3. Lack of long-term perspective in examining livelihood system transformations.

Obstacle 1. Academic literature often employs a narrow understanding of livelihood, focusing solely on its materialistic meaning. This narrow approach is primarily driven by the practice of promoting sustainable livelihoods through the eradication and alleviation of poverty (Murray, 2001). As satisfaction of basic physiological human needs is a prerequisite for human survival, in sustainable development frameworks, a livelihood typically comprises the capabilities, assets, and activities necessary for subsistence. This narrow understanding became a key framework for academic research and policy circles when the concept of sustainable livelihoods was introduced by the Brundtland Commission on Environment and Development at the United Nations Conference on Environment and Development in 1992. The orientation towards survival values, linked to economic and physical security and stability, is a logical political decision, as, according to the findings of distinguished political scientists Ronald Inglehart and Christian Welzel, survival values prevailed in the industrial era (Inglehart & Welzel, 2005). However, the livelihood approach should emphasize the relevance of the broader context in which people's capabilities, assets, and activities are embedded. Maslow (1954) proposed that humans possess two sets of needs arranged in a hierarchy: physiological needs at the bottom and the more creative and intellectually oriented 'self-actualization' needs at the top. Most current definitions of livelihood include only the physiological (survival) needs and the economic activities that serve as tools for people to provide for their subsistence. They cover the biological requirements for human survival, such as air, food, drink, shelter, clothing, warmth, sex, and sleep. However, many people move up the hierarchical pyramid to fulfil other needs. High living standards in developed countries enable the basic physiological needs to be met, allowing more people to focus on self-expression and self-actualization. The data analysis of the 7th Wave (2017–2022) in the World Value Survey indicates that people tend to move their focus from survival values to self-expression values (World Value Survey, 2022). This means that a broad definition of livelihood should include the higher needs of human beings by describing livelihood as part of a person's or community's identity. Central to the rising 'well-living' paradigm in twenty-first-century society are such qualities as harmonious coexistence, aspirational foresight and purposefulness, solidarity, autonomy, authenticity, and integrity, thereby promoting an integrated approach to living in balance with oneself, others, and the natural world (Hosseini, 2023).

The broad concept of livelihoods, which comprises the capabilities, assets, and activities required to satisfy all human needs according to their values and a shared 'well-living' vision, is crucial for reimagining quality of life in the face of current global socio-ecological challenges and understanding the logic of the big cycles in the evolution of human settlements.

Obstacle 2. Current scientific research and global political initiatives are primarily focused on enhancing the livelihoods of individual persons or households. Examination of an individual's livelihood provides information about possible sources of subsistence and how people with various backgrounds adapt and respond to multiple forms of crisis (Scoones, 2009); however, it has little impact on our understanding of the human settlements' evolution trajectory, as human settlements are developed according to the collective needs of inhabitants. Human needs profoundly shape cultural and social structures. Essential factors include customs, social and gender norms, limited access to resources due to property rights, local knowledge of natural or man-made environments, and other relevant considerations. The large government, economic, and political systems also significantly influence the livelihoods of individuals. Consequently, scientific inquiry into the evolution of human settlements should focus on a collective understanding of livelihoods and their changes. However, it still dominates the opinion that macro features of livelihoods in a settlement, country, or region should be relegated to the status of 'context' that does not need to be researched on its own in close relation to people's livelihoods. The initiatives to link local livelihood issues closely to broader economic and political features and their changes have remained at the margins. Only the traditional approach survives to characterize rural livelihoods as based on agricultural activities in contrast to urban ones that are focused on manufacturing. Such a situation is a serious obstacle to understanding the general laws of human settlement evolution.

Obstacle 3. Current livelihood research is limiting itself to the production of studies presenting almost endless variations of local livelihoods (De Haan, 2012). However, changes in economic activities within a settlement have a negligible impact on the evolution of the overall human settlement system if they are well-known in neighbouring settlements. The communities specializing in particular economic activity have already perfected their settlements' organizational model and have designed a prototype relevant to the specific lifestyle. For the research into changing livelihoods to be illuminating and helpful in understanding the big cycles in the evolution of human settlements, it is essential to examine the transformation of the collective livelihood system from a long-term perspective. This approach involves a broader understanding of cause and effect over an extended period, incorporating historical context, and considers how current actions might influence the future.

Removing all three mentioned obstacles is crucial for understanding the evolutionary path of the global system of human settlements, as insights from historical analysis suggest that a shift in the collective livelihood paradigm, prevalent in a large region or globally, and innovation in the settlement model are closely related.

The process of evolution of the globally predominant human settlement model can involve several cycles. Over time, as a society shifts towards innovative economic and social activities, the demand for an innovative settlement model emerges. The mass shift to a new livelihood and lifestyle necessitates adapting the design and organization of the prevailing human settlement model to new circumstances. This involves creating an innovative vision of human settlement and managing its design, building, and organization according to a new economic paradigm based on a radically new type of livelihood. For example, the livelihood of the hunter-gatherer community, which predominated in the pre-agrarian era, is very different from the livelihood of farmers, which predominated in the agrarian era, or from the livelihood of the fabric worker households that predominated in the industrial era. Each of the three mentioned eras elaborated its own vision of what characteristics are necessary for high-quality human settlement. Hunter-gatherers preferred to live in mobile camps, whereas agriculturists preferred a settled lifestyle in villages. The society oriented to manufacturing developed the prototype of the city centred around industry.

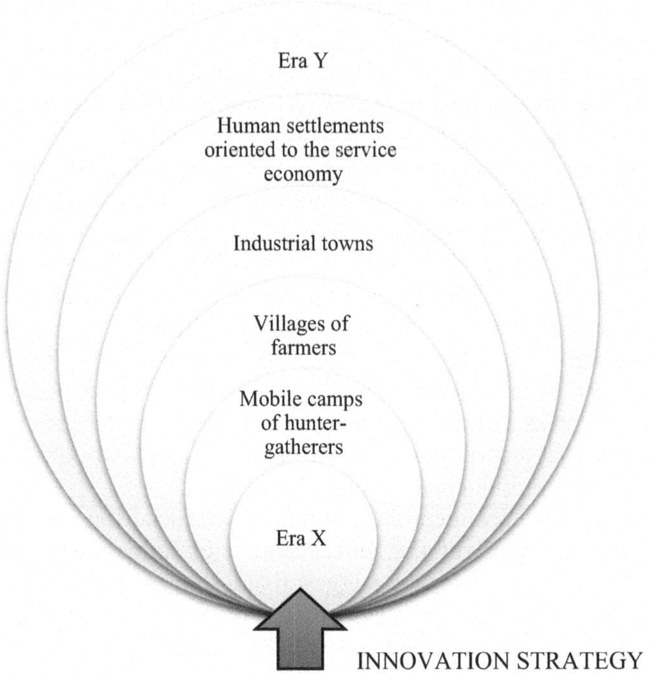

Fig. 3.1 The spiral trajectory of the globally predominant human settlement model evolution. (Source: Author's figure)

The evolution follows a spiral trajectory, which can be imagined as a helix curve (Fig. 3.1). Each new cycle is more complex compared to previous ones, as a new human settlement model incorporates all the best characteristics of its predecessors.

The inquiry into mass livelihood change provides the 'big picture' of how an innovation strategy based on a new livelihood paradigm influences the evolution of human settlements from a global long-term perspective. Exploring the shift from the dominant paradigm of livelihood activities is the best way to gain insight into how this shift shapes a new big cycle in the socio-economic evolution of human settlement. This understanding is vital at the moment, as numerous signs indicate that the life cycle of the global industrial economic system has entered its decline phase. Innovative service-driven business models are gradually replacing traditional product-driven business models, and the service economy has become the dominant force. The servitization concept-based economic system enables the emergence of a new type of livelihood, leading to new lifestyles. The activities of social movements like Transition Towns, intentional communities, and ecovillage movements demonstrate that humanity needs a new vision for high-quality human settlements that are relevant to the lifestyles of people involved in a service-driven livelihood system. For identifying key characteristics of human settlements oriented to the service economy, knowledge of the impact of the dominant livelihood on the formation of previous settlement models is necessary. As the visions of high-quality human settlements developed in agrarian and industrial eras are most visible and can be supported by academic research, the following two subchapters examine how the shift from the dominant livelihood paradigm influenced the traditional settlement model. They describe (1) the new characteristics of three basic settlement components at the stage of innovation strategy, and (2) the essential challenges to the following five paradigm-developing strategies of human settlement management in the agrarian and industrial eras. The analysis is based on the evolutionary framework designed by Qualitative Structure Theory introduced in the Chap. 2.

The Shift from the Pre-Agrarian to the Agrarian Settlement Model

Hunter-gatherer communities moved from place to place to find food, and settlements were places for sleeping and resting. The community had to change their living place as they used up local food resources or followed the seasons. Seasonal settlements have been developed in the form of winter villages, summer base camps, and specific-purpose campsites structured around the seasonal gathering of food and other resources.

The agrarian era saw people switch from nomadic hunter-gatherer lifestyles to farming as a primary livelihood activity. Most historians agree that, from approximately 11,000 BCE, people gradually transitioned from a hunter-gatherer lifestyle to one that involved cultivating crops and raising animals for food (Montgomery, 2012; Carey, 2023). The shift to agriculture is believed to have occurred independently in several parts of the world, including northern China, Central America, and the Fertile Crescent, a region in the Middle East that cradled some of the earliest civilizations (Childe, 1949; Hillel, 1991). The speed of transition to food production varied considerably among regions (Smith, 2001a, 2001b; Diamond, 2002), as the emerging agricultural lifestyle had to compete with the established hunter-gatherer lifestyle. However, by 5000 BCE, agriculture was practised in every major continent except Australia (Bulliet et al., 2008). By approximately 6000 BCE, most of the farm animals familiar to us today had been domesticated (Hillel, 1991).

Naturally, changes have not always gone in one direction. If, in expanding their settled areas, farmers reach areas unsuitable for agricultural activity, they can survive by returning to the lifestyle of hunters and gatherers (Diamond & Bellwood, 2003). As undoubted examples of reversion, anthropologists and archaeologists often provide the derivation of Polynesian hunter-gatherers on the Chatham Islands and New Zealand's South Island from ancestral Polynesian farmers (Anderson, 2003; Bellwood, 1987; Kirch, 2017), and of Punan hunter-gatherers in Borneo rainforests from other Austronesian farmers (King, 1993; Bellwood, 2007).

The transition from hunter-gatherer subsistence to agro-pastoralism had a profound impact on the evolution of the human settlement system. As the development of agriculture transformed the way humans lived, communities of agriculturally oriented people designed a different vision of a good place to live than hunter-gatherer communities.

Vision of Agrarian Human Settlement According to the Innovation Strategy

When traditional hunter-gatherer livelihoods were swept aside in favour of a reliable food supply, early agri-pastoralist societies began to evolve their understanding of high-quality settlement characteristics. To reconcile their domestic life with farming, people had to use strategic thinking and focus on creating a radically innovative settlement pattern. History testifies that agriculture-oriented livelihoods and lifestyles affected all three components of the qualitative structure of human settlements—inhabitants, place, and infrastructure. Each component of the qualitative structure of the agrarian human settlement was designed in accordance with the new way of life. The characteristics of agrarian settlement components at the stage of *innovation strategy* can be briefly described in the following way:

Component A: Inhabitants as Agriculturists
Communities that have learned to raise crops and keep domestic livestock have become less dependent on hunting, fishing, and gathering wild plants. Most people were looking for a future in crop or livestock farming and identified themselves as farmers. Some community members may often carry out other functions necessary for the community or take on roles such as priest, teacher, craftsman, soldier, hunter, fisherman, etc. However, their activities are also coordinated with agricultural activities and seasons. The strategic task for the community of agriculturists was to find a place that was not only suitable for living but also for farming.

Component B: Place Suitable for Farming
The places chosen for human habitation in the agrarian era generally differed from those where hunter-gatherer camps were typically established. The primary criterion for selecting a location for a settlement of agriculturists was the availability of land suitable for crops or pasture. Some crops require specific conditions; for example, rice can only be grown in seasonally inundated habitats, such as lake and marsh margins. For this reason, early agricultural communities developed settlements along rivers, where agriculture thrived due to fertile land and access to water (Jeunesse, 1997; Bakels, 2009). The place chosen for human habitation should also ensure long-term food security for the community.

Component C: Infrastructure Oriented to Agricultural Activities
Key infrastructure facilities in the settlement of farmers are connected to agricultural activities. Early agrarian communities were oriented to installing gardens, orchards, and pastures. Later, buildings for the secure storage of the harvest and other infrastructure to support farming operations were developed. The transition from the hunter-gatherer lifestyle to food production encouraged people to settle near their permanent gardens, orchards, and pastures, rather than migrating to follow seasonal shifts in wild food supplies. [Some hunter-gatherer communities in very productive environments were also sedentary (Bowles & Choi, 2013; Dow & Reed, 2015), but most were not.] Although the transition from wild harvesting was gradual, the communities oriented towards agricultural activities eventually preferred a more sedentary lifestyle, which opened up new opportunities for more comfortable housing.

The initial model of a settlement, adapted to the lifestyle of agrarian livelihood-oriented communities, has evolved. History testifies that the following stages of the evolutionary path of agrarian settlement, which was established according to the innovative socio-economic paradigm, can be viewed as the implementation of the following five paradigm-developing strategies described as an evolutionary framework in the Chap. 2, Section "Strategic Goals and Characteristics of the Six Stages that Compose One Evolutionary Cycle":

1. Extensive growth strategy
2. Intensification strategy
3. Specialization strategy
4. Diversification strategy
5. Collaboration strategy

Each strategy is a tool to enhance the quality of agrarian settlement by modifying its basic components: place, infrastructure, and inhabitants. Implementing each strategy stage by stage according to the mentioned sequence makes a settlement more complex and increases its quality. The next sub-chapters will shortly describe challenges for each stage of the evolutionary cycle of the agrarian human settlement. The evolutionary path explains how the agrarian human settlement system evolved or can evolve (many of the agrarian villages stopped the evolution at the second stage).

Challenges to the Extensive Growth Strategy in the Agrarian Era

The primary task for a community that has decided to shift from gathering and hunting to an agricultural activities-oriented livelihood is to find a suitable location to establish a permanent settlement, as not all areas are suitable for agricultural development. The characteristics of the place are critical at this stage, as the component 'place' is used as an organizational construction in the extensive growth strategy. The place chosen for a new settlement should be relevant to provide the community with a sustainable food supply through farming activities. It had to prove to the inhabitants that farming makes life more predictable and less dependent on chance. This feature of the place is crucial for maintaining the vitality of a newly established agrarian settlement.

A key challenge in newly established agrarian community governance has been balancing the population with the amount of food produced. As the active force of the extensive growth strategy is a component 'place', the agrarian community attempted to expand its habitat in line with population growth. A growing community required more new lands to be opened to cultivation. If the area for cultivating food crops was limited, people tried to reclaim land from forests. Studies have shown that deforestation has been a great symbol of the expansion of human settlement during the agrarian era (Duffy, 2008). Lacking land suitable for farming, agrarian communities also drained swamps and converted them into farmland or pastures belonging to the village. Even tanks, ponds, reservoirs, streams, and creeks were reclaimed to be turned into farms. Adopting farming as a primary livelihood activity transformed the small and mobile groups of hunter-gatherers into non-nomadic communities that reside in the farmland areas. To tend their fields, people had to stop wandering and begin to settle in one place. They moved into permanent settlements established in one location where a community remained for an extended period.

In many regions, crop cultivation and animal domestication allowed surplus food production, making such places attractive to live. The surplus food provided by agriculture, along with its planned supply, made it possible to sustain larger populations (Diamond, 2002), leading to more populated settlements than would have been possible with a hunter-gatherer lifestyle.

Challenges to the Intensification Strategy in the Agrarian Era

The component 'infrastructure' represents the active force of the intensification strategy, and the characteristics of the settlement's infrastructure are essential in the second stage of its evolution. When agriculture became the mainstay of livelihood for most inhabitants, it brought further challenges to the quality of a settlement. The actions taken to implement the intensification strategy during the agrarian era have focused on the development of agricultural facilities and housing.

As permanent settlements can provide more than a survival shelter with a campfire, the development of non-portable architecture has progressed rapidly. Antique housing architectural solutions were designed to adapt as much as possible to climatic conditions, and building technologies were oriented to local construction materials (Guedes, 2016). Agrarian human settlement layouts typically included residential structures, storage facilities, and communal spaces for social and ritual activities (Singh et al., 2024). Village structures were often centred around a carved-stone central grain or food storage facility, which was also used to practise social and religious rituals. As animal domestication became prominent, some societies began to structure shelters for their livestock, adapting them to the local climate and specific needs. Seeking to protect their inhabitants against external threats, ancient agrarian villages also constructed defensive infrastructure facilities, such as walls or moats, in response to the threat of natural disasters and/or attacks from neighbouring communities.

The building of shelters for people, domesticated animals, and food storage was complemented by agricultural infrastructure facilities, which helped farmers cope with the inherent unpredictability of climatic parameters, including seasonal variations, droughts, floods, and limited agricultural land. Water management was crucial for ancient agrarian societies, particularly in locations that relied on river flooding. Canals, dams, reservoirs, and water-lifting devices ensured efficient water use, helping sustain agriculture even in dry seasons (Sadhale, 2006; Singh et al., 2024). Some societies radically modified their natural environment through the use of irrigation systems for specialized food-crop cultivation (Duffy, 2008). Varied landscapes also led to the development of terraced farming, particularly in hilly areas. Terraces were constructed with stone walls to create productive lands that minimized erosion and conserved water. For example, some of the best archaeological evidence of early farmers' lives in the Andes Mountains shows that South America's region became a centre of agriculture because people developed terraces in the mountains. Terracing freed communities from farming only in fertile lowland river areas by developing flat areas on steep slopes (Sandor & Eash, 1995). A wide variety of improved and complicated field implements were employed around the world during the agrarian era. All agricultural infrastructure facilities became an inseparable part of agrarian settlements.

Agricultural livelihood-oriented communities need infrastructure not only for agrarian field improvement. Storage infrastructure, including grain silos, warehouses, and cold storage, was essential to the agricultural communities. Demand for equipment to process raw agrarian products has also grown. For example, a wind or water-powered mill was a desirable infrastructure facility in a village.

The success in developing agricultural infrastructure increased productivity, leading to a surplus of food production. It made some villages more prosperous, and people considered them particularly desirable places to live. Surplus food production also contributed to rapid population growth, driven by increased birth rates and declining death rates. The intensive population growth was a sign that the implementation of the intensification strategy was going successfully in the settlement. However, only economically strong communities in populous settlements can afford technologically innovative and/or resource-intensive infrastructure facilities. In less successful communities, disagreements began to emerge among community members about which direction to prioritize in developing village infrastructure.

Most villages solved the problem through hierarchical decision-making systems, as a primary driver of disagreements from the perspective of sedentary agricultural communities living in densely populated settlements was social differentiation. Whereas hunter-gatherer societies generally viewed resources as belonging to everyone, agriculture led to a system of ownership over land, food, and currency that was not equitably distributed among the people (Price, 1995; Montgomery, 2012). A basis for social differentiation was the lack of agricultural land. As differences in inhabitants' access to land and other resources were transferred along kinship lines (Jeunesse, 1997; Mulder et al., 2009; Shennan, 2011; Bentley et al., 2012), social inequalities have grown in every generation. Gradually, food surpluses enabled the development of social elites who were not otherwise engaged in agriculture but dominated their communities by monopolizing decision-making on village infrastructure.

Most of the agrarian settlements stopped their evolution at the second stage. The intensification strategy remains the primary approach for enhancing the quality of agrarian livelihood-oriented settlements, as it offers numerous new solutions to strengthen and develop agrarian infrastructure and improve living conditions for farmers. However, too high and rapid agricultural productivity gains can generate negative effects. The limiting force in the intensification strategy is the component 'place'. Due to intensified agricultural activities, the land's ability to support specific forms of agricultural production can decrease. Some communities have lost viable land due to inappropriate agricultural practices, overgrazing, soil erosion, and other factors. The lack of productive land for farming led to increased property ownership. In the long run, social differentiations among inhabitants became visible, and disagreements arose not only over the need to develop the settlement's infrastructure but also over the capacity of each community member to contribute to this process (Müller, 2022).

As early civilizations began to take shape, political and religious leaders rose to rule them, creating classes of 'haves' and 'have-nots' (Hillel, 1991).

Some peasants were entirely landless, while others had small plots of land or garden space, sometimes insufficient to support their families. They were forced to seek an alternative means of subsistence. A growing number of landless or near-landless inhabitants in agrarian villages became the basis for the formation of specialized settlements.

Challenges to the Specialization Strategy in the Agrarian Era

As the component 'inhabitants' represents the active force in the specialization strategy, the primary task is to concentrate inhabitants with similar needs for infrastructure facilities in a settlement. In the context of agrarian settlement evolution, the grouping of inhabitants with similar needs primarily occurred due to growing social stratification within an agrarian community, based on their success in managing agricultural activities and social life. As the trade in food products outside the settlement was poor, agrarian communities lacked the opportunity to specialize in growing monoculture crops used for food. To ensure a steady supply of food for various diets of inhabitants, villages avoided adopting a specialization strategy based on their food production activities. Only the specialization in crops for which food usage is secondary, such as flax, hemp, or cotton, is testified by historical research (Fuks et al., 2025).

Intensified agriculture, however, has provided the basis for the specialization of community members in non-agrarian activities that are important for the community's well-being. The storable food surpluses resulting from agriculture, as well as the transition from nomadism and a hunting-gathering economy, gave people time for non-agrarian activities, such as tool-making, weaving, spiritual practices, training in the art of fighting, and inventing. Success in agriculture can feed some community members who are fully involved in other jobs, such as soldiers, priests, teachers, and craftsmen.

As non-agricultural activities require a completely different infrastructure, the needs of non-farmers for specific infrastructure were a driver in starting to manage the settlement according to the qualitative structure of the specialization strategy. World history indicates that most specialized settlements in the agrarian era were established to serve the interests of three groups focused on non-agrarian activities: soldiers, priests, and craftsmen. Gradually, three main types of specialized settlements emerged with special infrastructure needs: defensive, religious, and commercial. Defensive settlements emerged as fortified locations built on hills or elevated areas to offer advantages for protection against attacks. Over time, they evolved from simpler refuges into more complicated structures, featuring increasingly elaborate ramparts, gateways, and other defensive infrastructure. Another large group of specialized settlements was religious settlements, particularly monasteries. They served as focal points for spiritual practice, attracting individuals seeking a life of contemplation and service. Depending on the religious doctrine, local culture, and social development of the place, they developed original infrastructure facilities.

The evolution of the agrarian settlements was most influenced by the emergence of settlements where skilled craftsmen concentrated. The storable food surpluses resulting from agricultural activities could feed full-time craftspeople, leading to the development of various non-agricultural economic activities, including pottery, textiles, metalwork, jewellery making, and stone carving. The growing demand for handicrafts encouraged the establishment of workshops where individual crafts were practised. For some people, crafting became a primary source of income, prompting a shift away from farming. The flourishing of various crafts in the agrarian settlement encouraged the growth and strengthening of the community of craftsmen. The concentration of craftsmen in the settlement provided a basis for a shift from a traditional focus on developing agricultural infrastructure to infrastructure more relevant to the craftsmen's needs. The formation of the specialized settlement has led to a redesign of the village layout, tailored to the lifestyle of craftsmen, enabling inhabitants to build specialized buildings and other infrastructure facilities for crafting. Gradually, some agrarian settlements were rearranged into areas where people lived and worked close to their workshops. They became prototypes for preindustrial cities characterized by a high concentration of people in a relatively small area (Sjoberg, 1955; Davis, 2011).

As the number of landless people in the region grew, the trend intensified to establish specialized villages with reinforced strategic infrastructure designed by military, spiritual, and crafting-oriented communities. However, if the governments of a specialized settlement do not have the political and social power to provide the army or monks with food, clothing, and other life-sustaining resources from external sources, the daily subsistence of the core population becomes a significant challenge. The problem of self-subsistence has also been encountered by craftsmen, especially in remote regions, as the transition from a subsistence to a commercial economy was a slow process in agrarian societies. The communities of craftsmen can survive only by combining crafting with agrarian activities or when a settlement becomes a marketing centre that provides goods and services to the surrounding locality (Casson & Lee, 2011). As the limiting force in the specialization strategy is the component 'place', such settlements needed to urgently shift to the next step in the evolution of a specialized settlement—the diversification strategy.

Challenges to the Diversification Strategy in the Agrarian Era

In the agrarian era, diversification of economic activities was mainly necessary for the subsistence of specialized communities. The economy of agrarian settlements was organized to be self-sufficient, producing all the food and other resources needed to support daily life. If the community wanted to engage in other activities, it had to find ways to supply the necessary resources to meet both the daily and specific needs of its members.

The active force in the diversification strategy is the component 'place'. The religious and defensive settlements most quickly felt the need to apply the diversification strategy to provide a regular food supply for their inhabitants. For example, monasteries engaged in agriculture, crafts, and trade, creating economic opportunities that drew in laypeople for work and to buy their goods. Monasteries could also offer protection and security to the surrounding population, especially in times of conflict, thereby acting as a catalyst for settlement and community growth around their walls.

A growing share of the population that was not directly involved in farming led to the rapid development of exchange relationships. On the one hand, craftsmen needed to sell their products. On the other hand, a settlement based on a craft economy depended on food and raw materials obtained from outside for its existence; for this reason, it became a marketing centre (Sjoberg, 1955). Gradually, such villages were transformed into densely populated market towns based on a craft economy and hosting regular food and craft markets. The growth of exchange relationships led to the emergence of new types of livelihoods. A broad range of retailers congregated in market towns; some were professional traders who occupied a local shopfront such as a bakery or alehouse, while others were casual traders who set up a stall or carried their wares around in baskets on market days (Davis, 2011). In some villages, the diversification of economic activities has enabled a radical transformation of the place, designing prototypes of the pre-industrial city based on the craft economy.

From a social perspective, the pre-industrial city is viewed as having a rigid system of stratification (Burke, 1975). The power was concentrated in the hands of ruling families or occupational groups (especially guilds), who were themselves associated with long-established areas ('quarters') of the city. Its craft economy saw trades clustered in specific quarters, but there was no functional differentiation in land use, with an intermingling of houses, shops, workshops, and markets. A pre-industrial city maintained close links with the countryside, notably through ties of landownership and by serving as a marketplace (Gold, 2009).

Diversified activities encouraged the development of a mixed infrastructure of the settlement. The layout of settlements varied, but most of them combined physical infrastructure for crafting and trading with fortifications (walls, towers, moats) and religious infrastructure facilities, such as temples, churches, mosques, and monasteries. Some of the cities that successfully implemented the diversification strategy flourished as administrative, cultural, and trading centres.

The expansion of trade and the increasing ambitions of farmers and elites to have innovative or large-scale infrastructure facilities for agrifood production, warfare, commerce, traveling, and education encouraged a shift to the next stage of evolution, a collaboration between settlements.

Challenges to the Collaboration Strategy in the Agrarian Era

The collaboration strategy aims to rearrange the settlement's infrastructure, which is the active force in this organizational model. The rearrangements should alter the characteristics of the component 'place' with a positive impact on all settlements involved in collaborative actions.

The agrarian villages collaborated to develop infrastructure primarily through shared labour and resources for agricultural needs and defence. This collaboration was crucial for tasks like clearing land, building irrigation systems, and constructing fortifications. For many agrarian villages, collaborative efforts to develop infrastructure still mainly focus on organizing mutual agricultural facilities, such as large-scale irrigation systems, and coordinating actions to maintain their functioning. Contemporary research has conducted a deep examination of incentives for cooperation on dams on shared rivers, highlighting that without cooperative management, negative impacts can occur as new dams affect downstream ecosystems and water infrastructure (e.g., Hensengerth et al., 2012; Arjoon et al., 2016; Gonzalez et al., 2021; Harou, 2021).

At the end of the agrarian era, a strong new incentive for the collaboration of settlements emerged. A growing surplus of food production in farms and diversification of economic activities through crafting led agrarian settlements to exchange their products with outside groups. As the organization of an uninterrupted food supply was vital for towns whose populations were concentrated in non-agricultural activities, a collaboration strategy was necessary to develop the exchange of products.

The biggest challenge to the collaboration strategy during the agrarian era was the creation of infrastructure that facilitated the movement of food and other products between settlements. The primary obstacle to maintaining and developing exchange relationships was the poor state of the roads. Aiming to utilize the regional potential of trade in agricultural products and crafted commodities more effectively, settlements focused on developing mobility infrastructure. For example, two or more settlements cooperated in building bridges, roads, or transport hubs, such as river or sea ports.

Collaboration was also used to create and improve infrastructure facilities that help increase mobility and communication between people residing in different settlements. For example, improved roads enabled the development of various so-called coach travel systems of horse travel. Teams of horses pulled stage coaches and mail coaches, stopping to change tired horses with fresh ones. In parallel to their primary function of carrying passengers, goods, and information, coach travel systems had a significant influence on the economic development of several towns and villages. Each station established an inn as accommodation and food were required by travellers, and stabling was necessary for the teams of horses. For long-distance travel, a network of coaching inns should be organized in settlements along the stages and mail routes.

One of the famous historical examples of a global collaboration project in the agrarian era, which can serve as an illustration of how connections between settlements change characteristics of the component 'place', is the Great Silk Road (Kuzmina, 2008; Andrea, 2014; Franklin, 2024). Today, we define it as a network of caravan routes crossing the ancient and middle Eurasian continent from the Mediterranean Sea to China via land and sea. The development of the network has been going on for nearly two thousand years. The collaboration energized settlements along the trade routes. Cities grew up along the Silk Roads as essential hubs of trade, fostering economic prosperity (Elisseeff, 2000; Ni et al., 2017). From Xi'an in China to Bukhara in Uzbekistan, from Jeddah in Saudi Arabia to Venice in Italy, cities supplied the ports and markets that punctuated the trade routes and gave them momentum. They developed as commercial cities and profited from the passing trade. Cities also provided an opportunity for travellers to rest; here, merchants, pilgrims, missionaries, soldiers, diplomats, and others came to a stop after travelling for weeks on end across inhospitable deserts and dangerous oceans. The Silk Road was not just about the collaboration for the development of trade by products and services, but also an example of a platform for cultural exchange. Merchants not only brought goods from their own regions but also introduced new products and technologies to foreign markets. The exchange of ideas, beliefs, and customs helped many Silk Road cities attract scholars, teachers, theologians, and philosophers, and, over time, became great centres for intellectual and cultural exchange, forming the building blocks of the development of civilizations throughout history (Hansen, 2012; Samoylovskiy & Samoylovskiy, 2024).

The international collaboration fundamentally transformed the primary vision developed at the beginning of the agrarian era, of what constitutes high-quality human settlements. It encouraged the development of crafting and exchange relationships, transforming lifestyles and prompting people to seek innovative solutions for organizing settlements that are more relevant to inhabitants oriented towards livelihoods based on income from their non-agrarian activities.

The Shift from the Agrarian to the Industrial Settlement Model

The first Industrial Revolution marked a major turning point in history, comparable only to humanity's adoption of agriculture in terms of material advancement. It shifted societies from an agrarian and craft economy to an industrial economy, where products were no longer made solely by hand but by machines. In the agrarian era, most production occurred in small workshops that employed a few skilled people using hand tools and craft methods (Chandler, 1977). With the Industrial Revolution, workshops evolved into integrated factories using power-driven machinery attended by large numbers of lower-skilled workers who performed increasingly specialized tasks (Wilson, 2000). Technical innovations in production and capital accumulation led to a new organization of work known as the factory system, which entailed increased division of labour among members of the working collective for specialization of functions (Fothergill et al., 1986; Geraghty, 2002).

Industrialization, as the process of applying mechanical, chemical, and electrical sciences to reorganize production with inanimate energy sources, ushered the world into a new era. From the perspective of human settlement organization, many transformations also occurred. In the agrarian era, full-time craftsmen primarily lived in small towns and cities, where they often operated workshops attached to their homes. The factory system was a new way of manufacturing in which goods were made at the factory instead of at home. Large-scale production and innovations in transportation technology enabled a separation of home from work. Earlier forms of work and ways of life began to disappear.

Vision of Industrial Human Settlement According to the Innovation Strategy

Industrialism ultimately required the formation of new human settlements, organized to meet the needs of large-scale manufacturing. People involved in manufacturing have a different vision of a good living place from that preferred by farming livelihood-oriented communities. New livelihoods affected all three components of the qualitative structure of human settlements—inhabitants, place, and infrastructure. Each component of the qualitative structure of the industrial human settlement was designed in accordance with the newly dominant livelihood. The characteristics of three industrial settlement components at the stage of innovation strategy can be briefly described in the following way:

Component A: Inhabitants as Employees

Industrialization led to the formation of a specific social group known as the working class. It consists primarily of people employed in unskilled or semi-skilled manual or industrial work. The working class is traditionally defined as individuals who must sell their labour power to earn a living. The most important livelihood asset is primarily their own labour, followed by other household assets (physical, financial, social, and natural). The working class sells its labour-power in discrete amounts of time (paid by the hour) or output piecework in return for a wage. The way of life for the working classes is dictated by the factory clock, with people taking their identity from their place in the workforce (Gold, 2009). In a work situation, the working class comprises those who are in an entirely subordinate role, such that this is a key feature of their labour contract.

In contrast to social life in rural settlements, which is based on collectivist cultures, the representatives of the working class do not tie individual identity closely to group membership. Growing competition for employment and in the workplace for better wages has fostered a trend of individualism in all spheres of social life, including changes in family structure. The compact, nuclear family became more common, replacing the extended family as the primary social unit in agrarian societies (Sassler, 2010).

Due to a tendency towards individualism, inhabitants' opinions on how a settlement should be organized are often quite different. Moreover, the objectives of workers and firms in industrial town development usually do not align with collective welfare (Combes & Gobillon, 2015). The lack of a coordinated vision is one of the primary obstacles to creating a high-quality settlement.

Component B: Place as a Hub for Employment

The most important requirement of the working class for a good living place in the industrial era was the availability of a job with a salary sufficient for subsistence. Consequently, a settlement should serve not only as a residential area but also as the primary hub for employment.

The key criteria in choosing a place for a new industrial settlement were the needs of the manufacturing plant, not the quality of life of the local population. The plant location had to be chosen to achieve the best operating costs and effectiveness (Perreur, 1998). The primary factors in choosing the site are the following (Weber, 1909):

- Availability of raw materials
- Nearness to the potential markets
- Availability of labour
- Transport communication facilities
- Availability of power, fuel, and water
- Finance and research facilities.
- Government policies

The working class focuses more on the availability of a secure workplace than on the settlement's location and physical features, such as relief, vegetation, and climate. Moving from one settlement to another did not represent a significant challenge for workers. The main criterion when choosing a place to live is the possibility of finding a job.

Component C: Infrastructure Oriented to Industrial Activities
The infrastructure of industrial settlement consists of two groups of facilities. The first group serves the interests of businesses that provide employment opportunities for inhabitants. A must-have component of an industrial city's infrastructure is at least one industrial plant that provides jobs for the city's inhabitants. However, the presence of one or several plants in the settlement as the key infrastructure facility is insufficient. The business models of manufacturing enterprises encompass a broader range of industrial activities than just production operations. The full range of activities that industrial businesses do to bring a product from its conception to its end use includes supplying raw materials and intermediate goods, storing, marketing, and moving goods to the customer or end user. Consequently, the industrial settlement must be equipped with essential infrastructure facilities to support all economic activities that create a large employment base, including modern energy and water supply systems, as well as transport infrastructure that encompasses roads, railways, seaports, airports, and other transport hubs.

The second group of industrial settlement infrastructure facilities should be organized according to the basic demands of the dominant group of inhabitants, the working class. At the beginning of the industrial era, the workers' requirements for a residential area and the town's layout were minimal. The satisfaction of the primary needs of the working class, such as housing and access to healthcare services, depended on individual efforts and was planned in line with wage-based incomes. A settlement can also provide a more comfortable standard of living through the development of public infrastructure essential for personal mobility, household management, social interaction, and leisure activities, but this depends on economic prosperity and the goodwill of local businesses and regional authorities.

The primary vision of an ideal industrial settlement, which realized the described characteristics of all three components, has been realized by establishing so-called company towns centred on a large production factory, such as a lumber or steel mill or an automobile plant. Establishing a company town was a pragmatic decision to ensure the company had a sufficient workforce, especially in remote locations such as railway construction sites, timber camps, turpentine camps, or coal mines, where a shortage of workers was common. The factory employed most inhabitants of the company town, and only a small part of them worked in one of the smaller businesses. To make a town an attractive place to live, a company offered unparalleled convenience as everything people need is within reach. From work to shopping, dining, and recreational activities, inhabitants can find all the amenities just a short distance away, saving their valuable time and reducing commuting stress. The company may also donate a church building to a local congregation, operate parks, host cultural events, and so on.

When world-scale industrialization proceeded, a largely rural society became a largely urban one. Cities grew because industrial factories required large workforces, and workers and their families needed places to live near their jobs. In the twentieth century, the urban lifestyle was adopted by the vast majority of the world's population. The United Kingdom is a valuable example of how rapidly the Industrial Revolution transformed the organization of the human settlement system. In 1801, approximately one-fifth of the population of the United Kingdom resided in towns and cities with 10,000 or more inhabitants. By 1851, two-fifths were so urbanized, and, if smaller towns of 5000 or more are included, as they were in the census of that year, more than half the population could be counted as urbanized. The world's first industrial society had become its first truly urban society as well. By 1901, the census recorded three-quarters of the population as urban (two-thirds in cities of 10,000 or more and half in cities of 20,000 or more) (Encyclopædia Britannica, 2025).

The initial model of an industrial settlement evolved through implementation of the five industrial paradigm-developing strategies described as an evolutionary framework in Chap. 2.

Challenges to the Extensive Growth Strategy in the Industrial Era

The labour force that made industrialization possible consisted of millions of newly arrived migrants from rural areas (Khan, 2024). To maintain the vitality of a newly established company town, most companies offered wages that were better than those received by agricultural workers. This has encouraged rural people to migrate to industrial towns in search of work. Most of them became not only factory workers but also permanent inhabitants of an industrial settlement. In this case, family members of the new worker arrived together. As a result, many company towns evolve into regular cities as they grow, attracting other business enterprises. Industrial plants have also begun to set up in market towns that were established during the agrarian era, as larger populations in small areas meant that the factories could draw on a big pool of workers. When a technological boom led to the expansion of the manufacturing sector, manufacturing plants required new workers, and the population of cities started to expand.

The growth of industrial cities was primarily driven by their ability to provide employment opportunities. Most cities grew in an uncontrolled and cumulative manner following the cost-and-profit calculations of entrepreneurs (Fothergill et al., 1986). The key challenge to the extensive growth strategy was to balance employment opportunities with the available workforce. However, uncontrolled migration to urban areas is rarely addressed in policy-making (Niva et al., 2019), and many cities have failed to keep this balance.

The lack of capability to manage city growth was especially evident after the Second World War, when the massive industrialization of the agricultural sector gave new impetus to urban expansion. The mechanization of agrarian work deprived many rural people of their traditional livelihoods, causing a powerful new wave of rural-to-urban migration. Most people considered the city a better place to live than the countryside, as it offered more income-generating opportunities for its inhabitants.

Uncontrolled population growth in cities generates many negative effects. Rapid urban population growth, resulting from rural-to-urban migration and natural increase, has led to frequent expansion of slums and the formation of other types of informal settlements (Okyere & Kita, 2015; Alene, 2022) that can be referred to as a manifestation of weak urban planning and land governance. Poorly planned urbanization also leads to health problems, pollution, congestion, higher crime rates, increased levels of inequality, and social exclusion (Beall et al., 2010; Kuddus et al., 2020).

Most of these negative effects were due to a failure to match the city's population growth with its infrastructure. This taught the local authorities that a strategy focused on infrastructure improvements is necessary to transform a rapidly expanding town into a well-functioning system, as the uncontrolled flow of people burdens the available infrastructure and worsens living standards.

Challenges to the Intensification Strategy in the Industrial Era

The component 'infrastructure' represents the active force of the intensification strategy, and the characteristics of the settlement's infrastructure are essential in the second stage of industrial town development. The role of infrastructure in urban development is to provide a conducive environment for the local economy to grow, thereby increasing the standard of living for urban inhabitants. At the early stages of industrialization, the intensification strategy was vital in cities with rapidly developing manufacturing sectors, as the overall growth of manufacturing created competition between cities for workers. The increasing availability of jobs in newly established or developed factories is not the only criterion for choosing a particular city as a place to live. Urban population growth can be hindered by inadequate infrastructure. Consequently, the winners in the competition for the necessary workforce were the cities with affordable housing, basic public services, and shopping areas.

At the beginning of the industrial era in the eighteenth–nineteenth century and after the mass industrialization of the agrarian sector in the second half of the twentieth century, a shortage of residential premises in working cities was a key challenge (Deane, 1979; Davis, 2019). The conditions varied, but the housing of the working classes in many cities was overcrowded, with excessive rents, and many accommodations were extremely unsanitary and unhealthy. The support of charitable organizations for poor families was insufficient, and governments began experimenting with social housing building programmes. Several approaches have evolved to meet the growing demand for affordable housing through the efforts of city governments. Some cities involved model dwelling companies that were able to offer a solution to the 'housing problem' by profitably providing decent working-class accommodation (Morris, 2001). Despite their success, other growing cities faced the persistent problem of privately rented slums. Public housing provision remains a crucial tool for local authorities to match housing to the needs of low-income workers.

People living in industrial towns and cities also need to have access to a decent level of social infrastructure. A whole range of physical and institutional infrastructures is crucial for cities to operate as social spaces in the industrial era (Klinenberg, 2018; Latham & Layton, 2019). Among vital public services for people are well-known functions such as social care, schools, sanitation, and health care services. A list of basic public services in each city strongly depends on the economic and political situation in the region, local cultural traditions and values (Michaud et al., 2009; Batley & Mcloughlin, 2015).

Another important challenge to the intensification strategy in industrial cities is the creation of public infrastructure facilities that support businesses, serving as a solid source of income for inhabitants. As manufacturing plays a central role in the economy, at the beginning of the industrial era, the responsibilities of city authorities were to develop public urban infrastructure, which covers main facilities and services required by local enterprises to support industrial operations, including transportation, energy, water, wastewater, solid waste, and information and communication technologies. Pre-industrial commercial cities, with narrow streets and tightly packed old buildings, have faced a significant challenge in developing urban infrastructure to meet the requirements of large industrial enterprises.

The intensification strategy is time-oriented; consequently, towns and cities depend on continuous infrastructure improvements to support economic prosperity and a good quality of life. It should consider not only the risk of infrastructure failure due to the age of the facility but also the changing character of the infrastructure needs, which are influenced by many factors. For example, the capacity of urban roads and transport hubs such as railway stations, riverports, or seaports can become insufficient to serve all the city's industries due to the emergence of new enterprises in the city. Revolutionary technological innovations also require essential improvement and reorganization of urban infrastructure. For example, the Electrification Revolution in the late nineteenth century radically transformed cities. The electric lamp gave people complete control over lighting inside their homes and workplaces. Cities used electricity for street lighting and trams. As pointed out by Stott (1992), electricity was the last of a sequence of 'urban amenities' that altered city life with indoor plumbing, running water, central heating, and gas in the nineteenth century. New challenges to city infrastructure improvement come with each radical invention offered by the Industrial Revolution.

The limiting force of the intensification strategy is the component 'place'. Some characteristics of the settlement's place, such as a lack of local raw materials or government policies, may become a decisive obstacle to industrial development in the city. At the end of the twentieth century, the role of a place as a barrier to a city's manufacturing sector development became more visible due to environmental regulations, causing factories to relocate from cities. The opportunities to continue manufacturing in a city area mainly depend on the price of real estate and environmental regulations (Beatley, 2012; Tang & Dou, 2021; Crevoisier et al., 2025).

During the industrial era, improvements to town or city infrastructure were heavily dependent on investments. As an industrial settlement's infrastructure consists of many systems that are not technically linked, there is constant competition to decide which system will receive more public funding. Decision-making is particularly challenging in big cities due to the diverse needs of manufacturing enterprises in energy and water supply, the capacity of the urban road transport network, and transportation hubs. Investments in infrastructure suitable for industrial enterprises have a positive and multifaceted impact on the well-being of the inhabitants and make a city a more desirable living place.

Understanding the lack of investment to meet the needs of all stakeholders in the industrial city necessitates a shift to the next evolutionary stage—specialization—that can deliver the proper infrastructure for a town. City specialization is a powerful tool for attracting and securing investors, which helps elevate a place's economic prosperity and increase its attractiveness to inhabitants as a hub of employment.

Challenges to the Specialization Strategy in the Industrial Era

In the industrial era, city specialization refers to a city's development focused on a dominant industry that defines its economic structure. Some authors refer to this development model as 'One town, one main industry' (Liu, 2016). The concentration of a particular industry in the city leads to the development of specialized infrastructure tailored to that industry.

Urban specialization can have many positive effects, especially for small towns. The effects of urban specialization in the industrial era can be seen from three perspectives: (1) benefits for industrial companies located in a town; (2) benefits for inhabitants of a town; (3) the quality of a town as a whole. All are important for the comparative advantage of cities, as it is jointly governed by the comparative advantage of firms, individuals, and their locational choices (Davis & Dingel, 2020).

The effects of urban specialization are most commonly studied through the prism of benefits to industrial companies. Empirical studies testify that many advantages are accrued to companies when they locate near others in the same industry. First, they can access shared infrastructure, allowing them to achieve greater economies of scale and increase production efficiency. Second, the companies have access to a large pool of labour. The concentration of workers familiar with specific operations in the town ensures that when demand grows, the factories can find the necessary labour in a short time (Jayet, 1983; Storper, 2010). Moreover, urban specialization is highly desirable for manufacturing firms because it attracts skilled workers, and the comparative advantage of individuals increases the comparative advantage of a firm (Moretti, 2004).

The second perspective concerns how attractive a specialized industrial town is to its inhabitants. Inhabitants who are employees also benefit from a better match between worker skills and employer needs (De Blasio & Di Addario, 2005). Understanding the dynamics of this matching process is essential for city governments seeking to improve the efficiency of labour markets and promote economic prosperity. Specialized job opportunities lead to natural sorting of urban inhabitants, as labour market specialization influences their locational choices.

The most important perspective in city management is the third one, which suggests an integrative approach. As the specialization strategy is a space-oriented management model, most solutions focus on urban productivity associated with agglomeration and emphasize the opportunity to regulate the development of urban agglomerations as a specialized labour market. Empirical research testifies that a city becomes more productive when its growth is generated by the aggregated decisions of many firms and households to migrate towards it (Bertaud, 2014). Recent studies also indicate a reciprocal relationship between the agglomeration of skilled workers and a city's prosperity. On the one hand, the agglomeration of skilled workers influences technological growth (Ikari et al., 2022); on the other hand, a highly skilled workforce is the engine of urban development (Moretti, 2004; Liang & Lu, 2019).

Cities that rely heavily on a single industry may enjoy significant economic and social prosperity during boom times. However, focusing too much on one branch of economic activity makes them vulnerable to economic downturns or shifts in global demand. A classic example is Detroit, which thrived as a hub for the auto industry but suffered severe economic decline when the industry faced challenges (Fitzgerald, 2022).

The limiting force in the specialization strategy is the component 'place', and its characteristics mainly depend on exogenous events or forces. Risks of specialization in the industrial era mainly depended on the place characteristics, which were key factors in starting manufacturing businesses, such as government policies, nearness to the markets and raw materials. When radical changes occur in a settlement's place characteristics due to external impacts, high-level specialization can generate a negative effect on settlement quality. Negative effects boost out-of-town migration, resulting in shrinkage in some parts of a city or an entire urban area.

At the end of the industrial era, globalization and deindustrialization of the world economy caused severe disruptions, drastically altering the manufacturing business and economic landscape. This led to the movement of manufacturing enterprises from one region or city to another in search of lower costs, better infrastructure, or more favourable regulatory environments. Many old industrial towns were experiencing economic decline due to the partial or total relocation of manufacturing activities to new locations. This phenomenon has left behind a large number of abandoned sites and buildings. Especially vulnerable are one-company towns. If the primary company experiences hardship or fails outright, it will transform the industrial town into a residential one. Without a source of employment, the town loses population as people leave to find work elsewhere. Communities in shrinking towns also experience declines in property value, poverty, and higher crime rates (Gu et al., 2019; Han, 2014; Wiechmann & Pallagst, 2012).

Faced with the challenge of failed city specialization, governments can improve the quality of a settlement through a diversification strategy, which is the next stage in the evolutionary path. This strategy helps to adapt industrial and business spaces built in the past to the new demands and trends of modern industries and advanced service activities.

Challenges to the Diversification Strategy in the Industrial Era

The diversification strategy is time-oriented, and strategic actions for reorganizing the component 'place' should align with the general situation in the regional socioeconomic system. During the industrial era, this strategy was primarily employed to mitigate the risks associated with overspecialization. The task was to reorganize a city into a place that offers a diversified portfolio of jobs, thereby creating the city's infrastructure necessary for its economic and social sustainability.

At the early stages of the industrial era, most attention was given to the effects of diversifying economic activities in the manufacturing sector. Many large cities have a diversified manufacturing sector, which was integrated into the urban area due to the uncontrolled and unplanned growth of the settlement. However, some of them have consciously applied the diversification strategy, as economic research has found that when a city hosts a range of industries, it is less dependent on industry-specific downturns. This is because diversification of economic activities offers flexibility and adaptability to changing economic conditions (Duranton & Puga, 2000). Empirical studies have shown that cities with more diverse economies tend to exhibit long-term resilience compared to those that rely heavily on a single specialized sector (Jacobs, 1969; Glaeser et al., 1992).

Since the Industrial Revolution, cities and industry have grown together (Taft, 2018). Towns and metropolitan regions have evolved around factories, and cities were referred to as places of production (Hatuka & Ben-Joseph, 2022). After Second World War, however, cities that depended on manufacturing for their lifeblood increasingly diversified their economies. Many cities, especially large ones, have successfully maintained sustainability by shifting from sectoral diversification within manufacturing to developing financial, legal, insurance, and other business services. A greater variety of business services for headquarters and sector-specific intermediaries within a city emerged. As a result of the development of the finance and business services industry, the infrastructure of many cities was changed—instead of manufacturing plants, buildings of banks and offices emerged.

Later, strategic planning of industrial cities applied a more complex approach in reorganizing their component 'place' by combining the development of services for businesses with services for inhabitants. The growth of high-profit corporate service firms in the city led to the emergence of a high-income professional class. The growing well-being of the population has pushed cities to diversify their economies through retail and leisure sectors. Many cities have taken strategic actions to revitalize their urban areas by creating luxury consumption spaces (Sassen, 2009).

The development of public spaces with commercial, recreational, and leisure infrastructure facilities has been adapted to the changed structure of employment in industrial cities, favouring the service sector. Seeking sustainable development, the industrial cities were transformed into mixed-use zones where housing, manufacturing, social public services, leisure, and amenities are interwoven in a way that most comfortably supports modern life. This has been particularly useful in cities where deindustrialization processes have been prominent due to the transition towards sustainable manufacturing, which represents a pivotal change in how businesses approach production, blending environmental care with economic viability and social good. The transition towards sustainable manufacturing in developed countries prompted steel manufacturers, automakers, and other industrial behemoths that were once mainstays of city life to leave urban cores and relocate production to the suburbs or less developed foreign countries (Taft, 2018). It created a lack of jobs and has left many urban manufacturing facilities abandoned and unused.

Some industrial cities successfully revitalize empty urban factories and abandoned urban areas, such as car parks, shopping areas, or railway stations, into city infrastructure facilities with new functions. For example, in New York, the economic crisis of the 70s led to the shutdown of many factories and warehouses in sectors like SoHo. These abandoned facilities were soon transformed into low-rent residential buildings, often for artists and craftspeople who needed large spaces for their work. Revitalization of many of the world's defunct manufacturing facilities and city zones has already occurred in numerous global cities. Many cities have taken bold steps to revitalize their urban areas, turning them into inspiring models of transformation. For some cities, however, the mass departure of factories proved to be very challenging. It remains crucial to consider what to do with outdated city zones and unused infrastructure facilities, as well as how to diversify the city's economy.

In an evolving society, the new needs of inhabitants and entrepreneurs require constant improvements in the design and functional organization of the component 'place'. However, local initiatives to diversify the city's functions often fail to keep pace with globalization processes. In such cases, the quality of a city can be improved by implementing a collaboration strategy.

Challenges to the Collaboration Strategy in the Industrial Era

The collaboration strategy encourages a shift from focusing on the improvement of city infrastructure to a larger system of settlements. It aims to rearrange the settlement's infrastructure, which is the active force in this organizational model. The rearrangements should positively change the characteristics of the component 'place' and benefit all settlements involved in collaborative actions.

In the industrial era, the biggest challenge to a collaboration strategy was creating infrastructure that facilitated a better flow of the workforce. Most often, the strategy was used to increase cooperation between the core city and its surrounding rural municipalities. As rural people have limited access to jobs in their village, the strategy can be employed to support active commuting through interventions aimed at improving the convenience of public transport and constructing new roads, transport terminals, and safe bicycle routes. Good transport links can widen people's job-search area and help them find employment. It can also reduce commuting times and the cost of living. Inhabitants of small settlements also need better access to education, healthcare, and social services. Collaboration on commuting infrastructure can make a positive difference by facilitating journeys of rural inhabitants to urban social infrastructure centres such as schools, kindergartens, and medical facilities. Rural-urban collaboration to improve commuting opportunities in the metropolitan area also generates positive effects on the economic development of cities. First, an expanded labour market is becoming available for industrial and service companies based in the cities. Second, urban firms involved in providing social and business services to city inhabitants can expand their activities into the wider metropolitan area.

Collaboration could find solutions to many other issues in the settlement system development, such as housing, which recognizes the need to ensure the protection of the environment when it comes to building planning. Collaboration between the city and its neighbouring rural communities is also used to boost opportunities for local entrepreneurship. Examples range from projects related to tourism and the development of innovative local food systems to those using urban–rural cooperation to produce renewable energy and reach self-sufficiency.

Successful collaboration projects create long-lasting links between all the settlements involved and encourage the formation of city-regions that can be referred to as areas where daily journeys for work, shopping, and leisure frequently cross administrative boundaries. Emerging city-regions have been reshaping traditional spatial patterns of cities and their hinterlands (Pain, 2012; Healey, 2013). They are seen as contemporary engines of the national economy; thus, all over the world, governments attempt to increase problem-solving capacities in city-regions by institutional reform and a shift of functions (Zimmermann & Feiertag, 2022).

Strengthening connections between the settlements is essential for building resilient infrastructure at the end of the industrial era, but collaboration ideas are often hindered by administrative issues. In most countries, urban financial resources are based on the city's budget and tax system, which city inhabitants fund. This restricts the budget from restoring and maintaining resources in rural areas, as they come under a separate jurisdiction. Policymakers' and inhabitants' mind-sets often support the administrative obstacles to using taxpayers' money beyond city boundaries.

The collaboration strategy is used not only to solve problems in a specific geographic region. At the end of the industrial era, the evolution of the global economic system inevitably led to the collaboration of settlements on a more global level. International networks offer cities a means to address complex problems collaboratively, particularly in the absence of national action (Zeemering, 2012). Inter-city collaboration can take many forms and deliver many kinds of value. However, empirical research shows (Robb et al., 2023; LeRoux & Carr, 2010) that cities are more likely to collaborate when dealing with politically and culturally neutral infrastructure systems maintenance functions (e.g., public transit, water systems) rather than lifestyle functions (e.g., education, recreation).

Collaboration opportunities are growing as the changes associated with developments in information and communication technologies at the end of the twentieth century have increased the ability of economic actors to communicate, conduct knowledge-based transactions, and trade products over any distance virtually instantaneously. This ability is developing the familiar territorial patchwork of 'places' and constructs a new geography in which information economy 'flows' would come to dominate (Pain, 2008). New, issue-based city networks have emerged globally, and their prevalence has increased dramatically in the twenty-first century (Acuto, 2016; Bouteligier, 2013). These networks often focus on specific issues, such as climate change or urban resiliency, and facilitate the diffusion of innovative policies among cities (Lee & Painter, 2015). Since the 1970s, transport and communication/computing technologies have fostered an expansion and intensification of inter-city collaboration (Davidson et al., 2019; Lusk & Gunkel, 2018). Under conditions of contemporary globalization, an important city is no longer identifiable by its stable embeddedness in a given territorial milieu (Taylor et al., 2006). It is instead a changing connective configuration with variable actors, which can be thought of as 'nodes' of local and global networks (Dematteis, 2000).

At the beginning of the twenty-first century, it has become apparent that the collaboration strategy cannot solve all problems of the global urban system oriented to the industrial socioeconomic model. During the industrial era, cities were recognized as the key locations for advanced economic activity, but recent evidence shows economic trajectories leading to the decline and shrinkage of many global industrial cities. As recently as the 1970s, many great cities were in physical decay and losing people, firms, key roles in the national economy, and their share of national wealth (Sassen, 2009). Studies testify that the most radical economic and structural changes occurred in cities reliant on 'traditional' industries such as metallurgy, engineering, shipbuilding, textiles, and chemicals, where deindustrialization was intense (Djurkin et al., 2023). However, some cities that are oriented to post-industrial transformations have re-emerged as attractive living places. Consequently, the next step in the evolution of the human settlements system should be oriented towards paradigm innovations in the global economic system and livelihoods.

The Shift from the Industrial to a Post-Industrial Settlement Model

A post-industrial society represents the next step beyond industrial society, which fundamentally transformed agrarian human settlements. We still lack a clear understanding of how to define the key differences between industrial and post-industrial eras. Most people describe a post-industrial economy as one in which the service sector dominates instead of the manufacturing sector. However, this definition encompasses only the quantitative aspects of the global shifts in the economic system. To emphasize the essential qualitative changes, the concept of servitization must be understood.

The term 'servitization' was introduced in 1988 by Vandermerwe and Rada in the article 'Business Servitization: Adding Value by Increasing Service Volumes'. In the current state of post-industrialism development, servitization can be defined as 'the penetration of service delivery elements into all areas of the economy by the gradual shift from product-driven business model to service-driven business model' (Vidickienė, 2017, p. 474). This penetration happens similarly to the penetration of industrial technologies at the beginning of the industrialization era. However, the current transformation of society is not driven by technological innovations. The transformation of the economic system occurs due to organizational innovations, which involve the introduction of new ideas, processes, and practices.

In the business sphere, transformation is based on shifting to innovative service-driven business models (Lightfoot et al., 2013; Khanra et al., 2021; Lankauskienė, 2024; Vidickienė et al., 2024). Entrepreneurs are realizing that it is no longer enough to make products. They began to focus not only on selling products but also on providing various services wrapped around the produced products and available resources. This new business organization trend brings significant improvements in the way a business operates and is gaining popularity in both economic activities that shaped previous human settlement systems: manufacturing and farming.

Servitization plays a crucial role not only in reorganizing business models but also in shaping consumption practices. Individuals enter a world where all aspects of their lives, including housekeeping, work, leisure, and even personal development, are delivered as on-demand services. The idea of 'Life as a Service' (LaaS) has gained popularity in recent years, as technology has made it easier to deliver services in a flexible and scalable way. In a LaaS world, people would no longer have to worry about owning assets like cars, homes, or even clothes, as everything would be available for rent or use on demand. Services such as transportation, housing, food, and entertainment would be provided through subscription-based models and accessed via digital platforms.

The penetration of service delivery elements into all areas of the economy transforms the industrial livelihood system based on the division of labour. Separating a work process into several tasks, each performed by a separate person or a group of persons, is one of the basic organizing principles of the product-driven business model. In post-industrial society, the dominant occupation has become service provision. Service businesses cannot be managed using the same organizational tools as manufacturing. Services cannot be delivered, and the provision of most services requires individualized solutions. It led to the reorganization of the occupational structure, arranged according to the division of labour applied to mass production systems.

The most visible changes are at the sectoral level, as servitization signifies the emergence of a new specific way a society organizes its economy. It is a mode of production in which the boundary between the service, manufacturing, and agricultural sectors is blurring, as all human activities increasingly incorporate service-oriented components. In this context, dividing economic activities into manufacturing, agrarian, and service sectors is no longer meaningful. From the perspective of human settlement evolution, servitization plays a crucial role in the division of labour between urban and rural populations.

The development of complex supply networks also requires revising jobs established according to a linear supply chain organization in the industrial economic system. In large companies and institutions, operations, marketing, logistics, and information systems are still managed separately. However, service-related relationships are irrelevant to the division of business processes into building blocks, as established by the linear logic of the supply chain. Product supply chains focus on production processes, while service provision supply chains emphasize efficient delivery and customer experiences. As storing services for later use is usually not possible, the focus shifts to building service relationships based on collaboration with clients. The task is to ensure a good match between the client's needs and the service provider's capacities. Building service relationships fosters creative and innovative approaches that seek mutual benefits, leading to a spread of symbiotic thinking that takes into account the role of symbiosis in the functioning of life on Earth. From the perspective of human settlement evolution, the application of service-driven business models encourages the adoption of a symbiotic approach to organizing human settlements. Experience in the service business helps design settlements that apply a symbiotic thinking concerning all human and nonhuman actors. Newly established post-industrial settlements strive to establish a symbiotic relationship with the natural environment and to be managed in a way that fosters a symbiotic lifestyle in human relationships.

The disappearance of boundaries between the main building blocks of the industrial livelihood system signifies that humanity is at the forefront of a massive paradigm shift that greatly influences livelihoods and lifestyles. Together, the criteria for choosing a place to live are changing. During the industrial era, people sought housing close to their workplaces. If the job was lost and there were no other acceptable job opportunities in the town, the family had to relocate to another city. Relocation to specialized towns was also a solution to earn a better wage. A service-driven business model supports the practice of working from home or another location, rather than from an office. Many services are provided at the client's premises rather than at the permanent workplace. Consequently, there is no need to live close to the workplace. The changing nature of jobs and livelihoods in a service-driven economic system presents new opportunities for choosing a place to live and becoming an active co-creator of a post-industrial settlement model.

The following part of the book presents a series of case studies that demonstrate the variety of solutions in designing an innovative human settlement model relevant to the realities of rising post-industrial society in European countries and ways to evolve it. Case studies also present new challenges to the other five strategies in the evolutionary framework, designed according to the Theory of Qualitative Structure (see Chap. 2).

Bibliography

Acuto, M. (2016). Give cities a seat at the top table. *Nature, 537*, 611–613. https://doi.org/10.1038/537611a

Alene, E. T. (2022). Determinant factors for the expansion of informal settlement in Gondar city, Northwest Ethiopia. *Journal of Urban Management, 11*(3), 321–337. https://doi.org/10.1016/j.jum.2022.04.005

Anderson, A. (2003). *Prodigious birds: Moas and moa-hunting in New Zealand.* Cambridge University Press.

Andrea, A. J. (2014). The silk road in world history: A review essay. *Asian Review of World Histories, 2*(1), 105–127.

Arjoon, D., Tilmant, A., & Herrmann, M. (2016). Sharing water and benefits in transboundary river basins. *Hydrology and Earth System Sciences, 20*(6), 2135–2150.

Bakels, C. C. (2009). *The Western European loess belt: Agrarian history, 5300 BC–AD 1000.* Springer Science & Business Media.

Batley, R., & Mcloughlin, C. (2015). The politics of public services: A service characteristics approach. *World Development, 74*, 275–285. https://doi.org/10.1016/j.worlddev.2015.05.018

Beall, J., Guha-Khasnobis, B., & Kanbur, R. (2010). *Urbanization and development: Multidisciplinary perspectives.* Oxford University Press.

Beall, J., & Kanji, N. (1999). *Households, livelihoods and urban poverty.* University of Birmingham, International Development Department.

Beatley, T. (2012). *Green urbanism: Learning from European cities.* Island Press.

Bellwood, P. (2007). *Prehistory of the indo-Malaysian archipelago: Revised edition.* ANU Press.

Bellwood, P. S. (1987). *The Polynesians.* Thames and Hudson.

Bentley, R. A., Bickle, P., Fibiger, L., Nowell, G. M., Dale, C. W., Hedges, R. E., et al. (2012). Community differentiation and kinship among Europe's first farmers. *Proceedings of the National Academy of Sciences, 109*(24), 9326–9330.

Bertaud, A. (2014). Cities as labor markets. Marron Institute on Cities and the Urban Environment, New York University.

Bouteligier, S. (2013). Inequality in new global governance arrangements: The north– South divide in transnational municipal networks. *Innovation: The European Journal of Social Science Research, 26*, 251–267. https://doi.org/10.1080/13511610.2013.771890

Bowles, S., & Choi, J. K. (2013). Coevolution of farming and private property during the early Holocene. *Proceedings of the National Academy of Sciences, 110*(22), 8830–8835.

Bulliet, R. W., Crossley, P. K., Headrick, D. R., Johnson, L. L., & Hirsch, S. W. (2008). *The earth and its peoples: A global history, Volume I.* Houghton Mifflin.

Burke, P. (1975). Some reflections on the pre-Industrial City. *Urban History Yearbook, 2*, 13–21. http://www.jstor.org/stable/44610848
Carey, J. (2023). Unearthing the origins of agriculture. *Proceedings of the National Academy of Sciences of the United States of America, 120*(15), e2304407120. https://doi.org/10.1073/pnas.2304407120
Casson, M., & Lee, J. S. (2011). The origin and development of markets: A business history perspective. *Business History Review, 85*(1), 9–37.
Chandler, A. (1977). *The visible hand: The managerial revolution in American business*. Belknap Press.
Childe, V. (1949). The origin of Neolithic culture in northern Europe. *Antiquity, 23*, 129–135.
Combes, P. P., & Gobillon, L. (2015). The empirics of agglomeration economies. In *Handbook of regional and urban economics* (Vol. 5, pp. 247–348). Elsevier.
Crevoisier, O., Theurillat, T., Rota, M., Segessemann, A., & Merckhoffer, A. (2025). The role of real estate in the development of cities and regions: Territorial real estate and economic systems. *Progress in Economic Geography, 3*(1), 100040. https://doi.org/10.1016/j.peg.2025.100040
Davidson, K., Coenen, L., Acuto, M., & Gleeson, B. (2019). Reconfiguring urban governance in an age of rising city networks: A research agenda. *Urban Studies, 56*, 3540–3555. https://doi.org/10.1177/0042098018816010
Davis, D. R., & Dingel, J. I. (2020). The comparative advantage of cities. *Journal of International Economics, 123*, 103291. https://doi.org/10.1016/j.jinteco.2020.103291
Davis, H. (2019). *Working cities: Architecture, place and production*. Routledge.
Davis, J. (2011). *Medieval market morality: Life, law and ethics in the English marketplace, 1200–1500*. Cambridge University Press.
De Blasio, G., & Di Addario, S. (2005). Do workers benefit from industrial agglomeration? *Journal of Regional Science, 45*(4), 797–827.
De Haan, L. J. (2012). The livelihood approach: A critical exploration. *Erdkunde, 66*(4), 345–357.
Deane, P. (1979). *The first industrial revolution*. Cambridge University Press.
Dematteis, G. (2000). Spatial images of European urbanisation. In *Cities in contemporary Europe* (pp. 48–73).
Diamond, J. (2002). Evolution, consequences and future of plant and animal domestication. *Nature, 418*(6898), 700–707.
Diamond, J., & Bellwood, P. (2003). Farmers and their languages: The first expansions. *Science, 300*, 597–603.
Djurkin, D., Antić, M., & Djordjević, D. Ž. (2023). Demographic aspects of urban shrinkage in Serbia: Trajectory, variety, and drivers of shrinking cities. *Sustainability, 15*(22), 15961. https://doi.org/10.3390/su152215961

Dow, G. K., & Reed, C. G. (2015). The origins of sedentism: Climate, population, and technology. *Journal of Economic Behavior & Organization, 119*, 56–71. https://doi.org/10.1016/j.jebo.2015.07.007

Duffy, P. (2008). Historical geographies, rural. *International encyclopedia of Human Geography*, 136–145. https://doi.org/10.1016/B978-008044910-4.00392-8

Duranton, G., & Puga, D. (2000). Diversity and specialisation in cities: Why, where and when does it matter? *Urban Studies, 37*(3), 533–555.

Elisseeff, V. (Ed.). (2000). *The silk roads: Highways of culture and commerce.* Berghahn Books.

Encyclopædia Britannica. (2025). Impact of the Industrial Revolution Google Encyclopædia Britannica, 21 August 2025, https://www.britannica.com/topic/urbanization/Impact-of-the-Industrial-Revolution

Fitzgerald, C. (2022). Detroit's decline: How the automobile capital of America fell into poverty. https://www.abandonedspaces.com/towns/detroit-michigan-decline.html.

Fothergill, S., Gudgin, G., Kitson, M., & Monk, S. (1986). The De-industrialisation of the City. In *The geography of de-industrialisation* (pp. 214–237). Macmillan Education UK.

Franklin, K. (2024). Archaeology of the silk road: Challenges of scale and storytelling. *Journal of Archaeological Research, 32*(2), 263–308.

Fuks, D., Schmidt, F., García-Collado, M. I., Besseiche, M., Payne, N., Bosi, G., Bouchaud, C., Castiglioni, E., Dabrowski, V., Frumin, S., Fuller, D. Q., Hovsepyan, R., Muthukumaran, S., Peña-Chocarro, L., Jordá, G. P., Ros, J., Rottoli, M., Ryan, P., Spengler, R., et al. (2025). Orphan crops of archaeology-based crop history research. *Plants, People, Planet, 7*(3), 562–589. https://doi.org/10.1002/ppp3.10468

Geraghty, T. M. (2002). *Technology, organization, and complementarity: The factory system in the British industrial revolution.* Northwestern University.

Glaeser, E. L., Kallal, H. D., Scheinkman, J. A., & Shleifer, A. (1992). Growth in cities. *Journal of Political Economy, 100*(6), 1126–1152.

Gold, J. (2009). City, modern. In *International encyclopedia of human geography (Second Edition)* (pp. 247–253). https://doi.org/10.1016/B978-0-08-102295-5.10884-4

Gonzalez, J. M., Matrosov, E. S., Obuobie, E., Mul, M., Pettinotti, L., Gebrechorkos, S. H., ... & Harou, J. J. (2021). Quantifying cooperation benefits for new dams in transboundary water systems without formal operating rules. *Frontiers in Environmental Science, 9*, 596612

Gu, D., Newman, G., Kim, H., Park, Y., & Lee, J. (2019). Neighborhood decline and mixed land uses: Mitigating housing abandonment in shrinking cities. *Land Use Policy, 83*, 505. https://doi.org/10.1016/j.landusepol.2019.02.033

Guedes, P. (Ed.). (2016). *Encyclopedia of Architecture and Technological Change*. Springer.
Han, H. S. (2014). The impact of abandoned properties on nearby property values. *Housing Policy Debate, 24*(2), 311–334.
Hansen, V. (2012). *The silk road*. Oxford University Press.
Harou, J. J. (2021). Quantifying cooperation benefits for new dams in transboundary water systems without formal operating rules. *Frontiers in Environmental Science, 9*, 596612.
Hatuka, T., & Ben-Joseph, E. (2022). *New industrial urbanism: Designing places for production*. Routledge.
Healey, P. (2013). City regions and place development. In *The futures of the city region* (pp. 43–55). Routledge.
Hensengerth, O., Dombrowsky, I., & Scheumann, W. (2012). *Benefit-sharing in dam projects on shared rivers* (no. 6/2012). Discussion Paper.
Hillel, D. (1991). *Out of the earth: Civilization and the life of the soil*. University of California Press.
Hosseini, S. H. (2023). The well-living paradigm: Reimagining quality of life in our turbulent world. *Discover Global Society, 1*(1), 19.
Ikari, H., Kono, T., & Zhou, Y. (2022). Industrial specialization patterns across cities, agglomeration of skilled labour and technological growth. *Spatial Economic Analysis, 17*(3), 311–331. https://doi.org/10.1080/17421772.2021.2014944
Impact of the Industrial Revolution. (2025, August 21). 'Google' Encyclopædia Britannica. https://www.britannica.com/topic/urbanization/Impact-of-the-Industrial-Revolution
Inglehart, R., & Welzel, C. (2005). *Modernization, cultural change and democracy: The human development sequence*. Cambridge University Press.
Jacobs, J. (1969). *The economy of. Cities*. Penguin Books.
Jayet, H. (1983). Chômer plus souvent en région urbaine, plus longtemps en région rurale. *économie et Statistique, 153*(1), 47–57.
Jeunesse, C. (1997). Pratiques Funéraires au Néolithique Ancien: Sépultures et Nécropoles Danubiennes 5500–4900 av. J. C., Éditions Errance.
Khan, F. (2024). Impact of industrial revolution on urbanization patterns in 19th-century Europe. *European Journal of Historical Research, 3*(3), 49–60. https://doi.org/10.47672/ejhr.2465
Khanra, S., Dhir, A., Parida, V., & Kohtamäki, M. (2021). Servitization research: A review and bibliometric analysis of past achievements and future promises. *Journal of Business Research, 131*, 151–166.
King, V. T. (1993). *The peoples of Borneo*. Blackwell.
Kirch, P. V. (2017). *On the road of the winds: An archaeological history of the Pacific Islands before European contact*. University of California Press.

Klinenberg, E. (2018). *Palaces for the people: How social infrastructure can help fight inequality, polarization, and the decline of civic life*. Penguin.

Kuddus, M. A., Tynan, E., & McBryde, E. (2020). Urbanization: A problem for the rich and the poor? *Public Health Reviews, 41*(1), 1.

Kuzmina, E. E. (2008). *The prehistory of the silk road*. University of Pennsylvania Press.

Lankauskienė, R. (2024). State of the art in Servitization research. In *Rural Transformation through Servitization: A Qualitative Structure Approach* (pp. 47–67).

Latham, A., & Layton, J. (2019). Social infrastructure and the public life of cities: Studying urban sociality and public spaces. *Geography Compass, 13*(7), e12444. https://doi.org/10.1111/gec3.12444

Lee, T., & Painter, M. (2015). Comprehensive local climate policy: The role of urban governance. *Urban Climate, 14*, 566–577. https://doi.org/10.1016/j.uclim.2015.09.003

LeRoux, K., & Carr, J. B. (2010). Prospects for centralizing services in an urban county: Evidence from eight self-organized networks of local public services. *Journal of Urban Affairs, 32*(4), 449–470.

Liang, W., & Lu, M. (2019). Growth led by human capital in big cities: Exploring complementarities and spatial agglomeration of the workforce with various skills. *China Economic Review, 57*, 101113.

Lightfoot, H., Baines, T., & Smart, P. (2013). The servitization of manufacturing: A systematic literature review of interdependent trends. *International Journal of Operations & Production Management, 33*(11/12), 1408–1434.

Liu, M. (2016). The strategic thinking on promoting the specialized towns' new-style urbanization construction in Guangdong Province. *Journal of Service Science and Management, 9*(06), 501.

Lusk, K., & Gunkel, N. (2018). *Cities joining ranks—Policy networks on the rise*. Boston University. https://open.bu.edu/server/api/core/bitstreams/73ed206e-9b7b-4585-8fea-6a2fa3149f2a/content.

Maslow, A. H. (1954). The instinctoid nature of basic needs. *Journal of Personality, 22*(3), 326–347.

Michaud, K. E. H., Carlisle, J. E., & Smith, E. R. A. N. (2009). The relationship between cultural values and political ideology, and the role of political knowledge. *Political Psychology, 30*(1), 27–42. http://www.jstor.org/stable/20447183

Montgomery, D. R. (2012). *Dirt: The erosion of civilizations, with a new preface*. University of California Press.

Moretti, E. (2004). Human capital externalities in cities, Ch. 51. In V. Henderson & J.-F. Thisse (Eds.), *Handbook of regional and urban economics, vol. 4* (pp. 2254–2291). North-Holland: Elsevier.

Morris, S. (2001). Market solutions for social problems: Working-class housing in nineteenth-century London. *Economic History Review, 54*, 525–545.
Mulder, M. B., Bowles, S., Hertz, T., Bell, A., Beise, J., Clark, G., et al. (2009). Intergenerational wealth transmission and the dynamics of inequality in small-scale societies. *Science, 326*(5953), 682–688.
Müller, M. (Ed.). (2022). The Routledge handbook of medieval rural life. Routledge. https://doi.org/10.4324/9781003194866.
Murray, C. (2001). Livelihoods research: Some conceptual and methodological issues. Chronic Poverty Research Centre Working Paper, (5).
Ni, P., Kamiya, M., & Ding, R. (2017). Cities network along the silk road. In *The global urban competitiveness report* (pp. 15–29).
Niva, V., Taka, M., & Varis, O. (2019). Rural-urban migration and the growth of informal settlements: A socio-ecological system conceptualization with insights through a "water lens". *Sustainability, 11*(12), 3487. https://doi.org/10.3390/su11123487
Okyere, A. S., & Kita, M. (2015). Rethinking urban informality and informal settlements growth in urban Africa: A literature discussion. *Journal of Sustainable Development in Africa, 17*(2), 101–124.
Owusu, F. (2007). Conceptualizing livelihood strategies in African cities: Planning and development implications of multiple livelihood strategies. *Journal of Planning Education and Research, 26*(4), 450–465.
Pain, K. (2008). City regions and economic development. In C. Johnson, R. Hu, & S. Abedin (Eds.), *Connecting cities: City-regions. Connecting cities* (pp. 20–47). Metropolis.
Pain, K. (2012). Spatial transformations of cities: Global city-region? Mega-city region. In *International handbook of globalization and world cities* (pp. 83–93).
Perreur, J. (1998). Industrial location theory in German thought–Launhardt and Weber. *Recherches Économiques de Louvain/Louvain Economic Review, 64*(1), 75–96.
Price, T. D. (1995). Social inequality at the foundations of agriculture. In T. D. Price & G. Feinman (Eds.), *Foundations of social inequality* (pp. 155–188). Platinum Press.
Robb, K. A., LaPointe, M., Hemsing, K., Anderson, G., & Anderson, J. (2023). Inter-city collaboration: Why and how cities work, learn and advocate together. *Global Policy, 14*(5), 663–675. https://doi.org/10.1111/1758-5899.13292
Rodrigue, J. P. (2024). Concept 3: The emergence of mechanized transportation systems. The Geography of Transport Systems, 20.
Sadhale, N. (2006). Water harvesting and conservation in ancient agricultural texts. *Asian Agri-History, 10*(2), 105–120.
Samoylovskiy, A. L., & Samoylovskiy, A. L. (2024). The great silk road and its impact on cultural exchange and economic development in ancient civilizations. *Наука. Общество. Оборона, 12*(3 (40)), 27–27.

Sandor, J. A., & Eash, N. S. (1995). Ancient agricultural soils in the Andes of southern Peru. *Soil Science Society of America Journal, 59*(1), 170–179.
Sassen, S. (2009). Cities in today's global age. *SAIS Review of International Affairs, 29*(1), 3–34.
Sassler, S. (2010). Partnering across the life course: Sex, relationships, and mate selection. *Journal of Marriage and Family, 72*(3), 557–575.
Scoones, I. (2009). The politics of global assessments: The case of the international assessment of agricultural knowledge, science and Technology for Development (IAASTD). *The Journal of Peasant Studies, 36*(3), 547–571.
Scoones, I. (2013). Livelihoods perspectives and rural development. In *Critical perspectives in rural development studies* (pp. 159–184). Routledge.
Shennan, S. (2011). Property and wealth inequality as cultural niche construction. *Philosophical Transactions of the Royal Society B: Biological Sciences, 366*(1566), 918–926.
Singh, A., Negi, A., & Thakur, R. (2024). Ancient agricultural practices: Lessons from the past for sustainable farming today. *Nature Science, 1*(4), 18–21. https://www.researchgate.net/publication/385533116_Ancient-Agricultural-Practices
Singh, I., & Muhuri, S. (2024). Assessment of livelihood sustainability during urban development-induced rural displacement and resettlement (UDIRDR): A literature review. *Canadian Journal of Development Studies/Revue canadienne d'études du développement, 45*(1), 136–160.
Sjoberg, G. (1955). The preindustrial city. *American Journal of Sociology, 60*(5), 438–445.
Smith, B. D. (2001a). Low-level food production. *Journal of Archaeological Research, 9*(1), 1–43.
Smith, B. D. (2001b). Documenting plant domestication: The consilience of biological and archaeological approaches. *Proceedings of the National Academy of Sciences, 98*(4), 1324–1326.
Storper, M. (2010). Why does a City grow? Specialization, human capital, or institutions? *Urban Studies, 47*(10), 2027–2050. https://doi.org/10.1177/0042098009359957
Stott, R. (1992). Urban electrification [review of the Electric City: Energy and the growth of the Chicago area, 1880–1930, by H. L. Platt]. *Reviews in American History, 20*(2), 211–215. https://doi.org/10.2307/2703103
Taft, C. (2018, June 25). Deindustrialization and the Postindustrial City, 1950–present. Oxford Research Encyclopedia of American History. Retrieved May 2, 2025, from https://oxfordre.com/americanhistory/view/10.1093/acrefore/9780199329175.001.0001/acrefore-9780199329175-e-574
Tang, C., & Dou, J. (2021). The impact of heterogeneous environmental regulations on location choices of pollution-intensive firms in China. *Frontiers in Environmental Science, 9*, 799449.

Taylor, P., Derudder, B., Saey, P., & Witlox, F. (2006). *Cities in globalization: Practices, policies and theories*. Routledge.

Vandermerwe, S., & Rada, J. (1988). Servitization of business: Adding value by adding services. *European Management Journal, 6*(4), 314–324.

Vidickienė, D. (2017). Economic regulation directions regarding the essential shift in the structure of the economy. *Public Policy and Administration, 16*(3), 468–481.

Vidickienė, D., Lankauskienė, R., Melnikienė, R., Gedminaitė-Raudonė, Ž., & Simonaitytė, V. (2024). *Rural transformation through Servitization*. Springer Books.

Weber, A. (1909). Uber den standort der industrien, Tubingen. Traduction anglaise*: Theory of the location of industries*. University Press.

Wiechmann, T., & Pallagst, K. M. (2012). Urban shrinkage in Germany and the USA: A comparison of transformation patterns and local strategies. *International Journal of Urban and Regional Research, 36*(2), 261–280.

Wilson, J. M. (2000). History of manufacturing management. In P. M. Swamidass (Ed.), *Encyclopedia of production and manufacturing management*. Springer. https://doi.org/10.1007/1-4020-0612-8_406

World Value Survey. (2022). Retrieved May 5, 2025, from https://www.worldvaluessurvey.org/WVSDocumentationWV7.jsp

Zeemering, E. S. (2012). The problem of democratic anchorage for interlocal agreements. *The American Review of Public Administration, 42*, 87–103. https://doi.org/10.1177/0275074010397532

Zimmermann, K., & Feiertag, P. (2022). *Governance and city regions: Policy and planning in Europe*. Taylor & Francis.

CHAPTER 4

Extensive Growth Strategy: Challenges to Establishing and Growing Human Settlements Beyond the Urban–Rural, Work–Leisure, and Human–Nature Divide

Vitalija Simonaitytė and Živilė Gedminaitė-Raudonė

The past several decades has witnessed the emergence of human settlements that challenge conventional territorial and social boundaries. These include ecological communities, intentional settlements, and ecovillages that are designed not only as places of residence but as spaces for holistic living. Central to their development is a vision that dissolves the rigid dichotomies between urban and rural, work and leisure, and human and nature. These settlements attempt to reimagine human habitation as a more integrated, responsive, and regenerative way of life, responding to deepening concerns about environmental degradation, alienation in urban environments, and the unsustainability of life patterns developed during the industrial era.

At the heart of the new vision of post-industrial settlement is a radical redefining of three components of any settlement: place, infrastructure, and inhabitants. The concept of 'partnering with place' is a foundational principle of these alternative settlements (Masterson et al., 2019; Steffen et al., 2015; Adger et al., 2011). Rather than imposing a design logic from above, these communities choose and organize their living place in response to local ecological, cultural, and historical specificities. This

D. Vidickienė et al., *Human Settlement in the Service Economy Era*, Palgrave Advances in Bioeconomy: Economics and Policies, https://doi.org/10.1007/978-3-032-19390-2_4

approach emphasizes relationality—the inhabitants are seeking to live with the landscape, rather than against it; they develop place-based knowledge systems and governance frameworks; and they incorporate nature as both boundary and participant in the settlement's unfolding design. In many cases, this means reconfiguring long-standing assumptions about the separation of human needs from environmental limits and moving towards what could be termed a *symbiotic human ecology*.

The transition to a new lifestyle requires a comprehensive rethinking of infrastructure, both physical and social. Traditional infrastructure serves to delineate roles, functions, and spaces—work occurs in offices, rest in homes, and leisure in parks. In contrast, the settlements analysed here blur these boundaries. Gardens serve as places of both sustenance and recreation. Shared spaces merge co-working with communal gatherings. Homes are often places of enterprise, healing, and education. This multifunctionality challenges the institutional separation of public and private life and calls for new forms of governance and design that can accommodate fluidity, ambiguity, and emergence (Basiouny, 2024; Springer & Kaza, 2024).

Furthermore, these settlements often evolve through bottom-up or hybrid governance models, frequently drawing on cooperative, sociocratic, or even permacultural principles. Community building is based on decision-making processes embedded in the everyday life of the community, involving inhabitants in deliberation and responsibility-sharing (Sociocracy For All, n.d.). These emergent governance practices attempt to mirror the ecological ethos of the settlements themselves: non-linear, adaptive, and participatory. Yet such approaches face critical challenges, including the high demands they place on participants' time and skills, the difficulty of sustaining engagement over time, and the tendency for informal hierarchies to persist despite horizontal aspirations (May, 2022; Baird et al., 2019; Leach et al., 1997).

From a socio-spatial perspective, these developments complicate prevailing planning categories. They are often not fully urban, yet far from being traditionally rural. They incorporate forms of productivity (agriculture, small-scale manufacturing, digital work) but resist standard models of economic zoning. Similarly, they host both temporary and long-term residents, blurring the line between habitation and mobility. These dynamics render such settlements difficult to classify or support through conventional policy and planning mechanisms. The settlements discussed in this chapter offer a prism through which to examine these tensions. Although emerging from different national and cultural contexts, they all exemplify how ecological visions of living can be implemented through relational design approaches. The case studies generate in-depth, multi-faceted explorations of three different types of Human Settlements Designed Beyond the Urban–Rural, Work–Leisure, and Human–Nature Divide. The research also examines how ecovillage leaders are seeking to maintain the vitality of the settlement by growing the number of inhabitants, and what challenges to the extensive growth strategy arose. Each case study demonstrates how localized and often family-initiated efforts have been scaled into viable and evolving communities. Yet the path is neither straightforward nor uniform. The diversity of these initiatives speaks to both the adaptability and fragility of this emerging settlement model.

Ultimately, this chapter positions the ecovillages not merely as lifestyle experiments or architectural curiosities, but as living laboratories of socio-ecological transformation according to the rules of post-industrial society. As a decline in manufacturing jobs and a rise in professional service-oriented occupations continue to unsettle existing paradigms of development, these alternative settlements provide valuable insights into how we might reconceive the very structure of human habitation. They invite us to ask: What does it mean to grow a residential community not just in numbers, but in depth? How might we design infrastructures that foster interdependence rather than separation? And what role can place-based innovation play in shaping futures that are more liveable, just, and ecologically attuned?

The following subchapters on three cases: Understenshöjden, Amatciems, and Kardokai reflect an innovative symbiotic approach to eco-settlement development, wherein human habitation is reimagined as a co-evolutionary process with nature rather than a dominating force over it. These settlements exemplify how new forms of human–nature relations can be crafted avoiding the socio-ecological disconnection developed during the industrial era. Establishers and eco-entrepreneurs in each case play a pivotal role in translating ecological ethics into spatial, technological, and communal practices that facilitate mutual flourishing. Rather than treating nature as a backdrop or resource, these initiatives foster integrated systems of living and blurring the boundaries between dwelling and landscape, culture and ecology. Ultimately, these examples underscore a broader cultural transition towards relational living, where eco-settlements serve as laboratories for developing the prototypes of villages more relevant to a post-industrial lifestyle.

Understenshöjden, a pioneering eco-settlement located on the urban fringe of Stockholm, offers a compelling example of how ecological values and middle-class aspirations were integrated into suburban housing development during the rise of environmentally conscious planning in the late twentieth century. This neighbourhood, largely initiated and shaped by a group of engaged citizens in collaboration with sympathetic architects and developers, reflects a deliberate attempt to reconfigure conventional suburban living by embedding ecological principles directly into the built environment. Rather than rejecting modern comforts, Understenshöjden (n.d.) reimagines them through a symbiotic life lens—emphasizing collective values, shared infrastructure, passive solar design, energy efficiency, and natural building materials. Its formation expands the spatial boundaries of the Stockholm city, thus exemplifying the potential of hybrid settlement models that transcend traditional dichotomies of urban versus rural and private versus communal. Importantly, Understenshöjden was not a grassroots initiative born in isolation but emerged through negotiations among local actors, including municipal authorities, planning professionals, and future residents, thereby demonstrating how institutional frameworks can be leveraged to foster ecological transitions in housing. Yet, while it realized many of its ecological goals, the settlement also highlights enduring tensions between environmental idealism and socio-economic realities—particularly in its demographic composition, which tends to reflect a relatively homogenous, educated, and resource-rich middle class. In this way, Understenshöjden exemplifies both the promise and limitations of early eco-settlement models: it is a real-world laboratory for environmentally attuned residential design, yet its scalability and accessibility remain open questions in broader efforts to mainstream ecologically sound living beyond niche enclaves.

Amatciems, located in the Gauja National Park region of Latvia, represents the eco-settlement that reconfigures the traditional spatial and functional dichotomies between urban and rural, work and leisure. Initiated in the 1980s and developed in early 2000s by local entrepreneur, this eco-settlement was envisioned as a high-end residential community that blends the aesthetics of rural idyll with the conveniences of contemporary life. What sets Amatciems apart is its integration of advanced infrastructure—fiber-optic internet, modern heating systems, and sustainable water and waste management—within a carefully preserved natural environment, featuring lakes, forests, and open landscapes as essential elements of the residential experience. The development explicitly caters to urban professionals and expatriates seeking an alternative to city life without compromising connectivity or comfort, thereby creating a hybrid space where remote work, leisure, and nature coexist seamlessly. This blurring of boundaries between professional life and restorative living aligns with broader post-urban trends in which digitalization enables mobile lifestyles and flexible forms of work. In Amatciems, homes are not isolated rural retreats but functional nodes within global networks, allowing residents to participate in international business or creative industries while enjoying the serenity of natural surroundings. The settlement also reframes the notion of luxury by intertwining exclusivity with ecological consciousness—regulations prohibit fences, non-natural landscaping, and intrusive architectural styles, thereby preserving visual and environmental continuity. However, despite its innovative integration of work–leisure–nature synergies, Amatciems raises questions of inclusivity and replicability. Its model, heavily reliant on private capital and oriented towards a select demographic, demonstrates the potential of privately initiated eco-developments but also highlights the socio-economic limitations of such ventures in addressing broader systemic transitions. Nonetheless, Amatciems contributes a vital perspective to the discourse on new human settlements by illustrating how intentional design can foster symbiotic relationships between technological modernity and natural immersion, all within a ruralized yet globally connected framework.

Kardokai, an eco-settlement nestled in the rural landscape of Lithuania, presents a compelling case of how grassroots initiatives can reconfigure human-environment relations through a deeply embedded ecological worldview. Initiated by a single family and gradually expanding through like-minded settlers, Kardokai (n.d.) draws inspiration from the '*kin's domain*' concept popularized by the *Anastasia* movement—a vision in which each family stewards a parcel of land not simply as property, but as an integral part of their extended being. This vision enacts a radical rethinking of human dwelling: rather than positioning nature as a resource or backdrop, Kardokai settlers cultivate symbiotic relationships with the land, animals, and nature elements, thereby dissolving the ontological divide between human and nature. In Kardokai, forest, gardens, and wild meadows are not managed landscapes but co-actors in the creation of a meaningful life. Architecture follows organic design principles, food systems are regenerative and diversified, and daily rhythms are attuned to seasonal changes and ecological feedback. Here, the human body and mind are situated within, rather than apart from, the ecosystem—blurring the modern dichotomies of nature and culture, wild and domesticated, subject and environment. This deeply relational mode of inhabiting space not only supports biodiversity and low-impact living but also fosters a spiritual ecology in which emotional well-being, ecological stewardship, and communal identity are inextricably linked. Moreover, the community's hybrid livelihood strategies—combining subsistence gardening, artisanal crafts, environmental education, and remote work—demonstrate how Kardokai dissolves boundaries between economic utility and ecological responsibility. Although the pace of infrastructure development remains incremental, and legal ambiguities pose periodic challenges, Kardokai stands as a living prototype for post-urban settlement patterns that transcend extractive human–nature hierarchies. By reimagining settlement not as dominion over land but as co-creation with place, Kardokai articulates a future in which human flourishing is contingent upon, rather than opposed to, the vitality of the more-than-human world.

Eco-Settlement at the Urban Fringe: Understenshöjden, Sweden

Foundations of a Vision: Citizen-Led Beginnings at Understenshöjden

Understenshöjden ecovillage, located in the Björkhagen, just outside the city centre of Stockholm, Sweden, emerged in the late 1980s as part of a growing movement towards sustainable urban development. The initiative began in 1989, when a group of like-minded individuals formed an association called EBBA (Ekologiskt Byggande i Björkhagen—Ecological Building in Björkhagen). This founding group was composed of people deeply concerned about environmental degradation, resource consumption, the ecological footprint of traditional housing, and the social isolation and alienation often found in conventional urban developments. The founders envisioned a housing community that would prioritize ecological responsibility, social cooperation, and democratic self-governance. Their goal was not just to build houses, but to create a new way of life—one that integrated ecological design with strong eco-community bonds. The EBBA group took a proactive, grassroots approach—driven by the belief that citizens themselves should lead the creation of sustainable living environments. Their vision extended beyond environmental sustainability to include social cohesion, participatory governance, partnering with place and a deep connection with nature (Tellus Think Tank, 2015).

They reached out to public authorities, architects, and developers to seek partnerships and support, ultimately forming collaborations with HSB (n.d.), Sweden's biggest federation of cooperative housing, and SMÅA-hus, a construction firm open to ecological experimentation. Through collective effort, shared decision-making, and years of advocacy and planning, this citizen-led initiative laid the foundation for what would become one of Sweden's first and most well-known urban ecovillages.

Securing land from the Stockholm municipality was a pivotal moment in the project's history, as it demonstrated growing institutional support for sustainable living models in urban areas. Throughout the early 1990s, the planning phase was characterized by extensive participatory design workshops, where future residents were involved in decisions regarding layout, materials, and energy systems. This co-creation process ensured that the resulting homes were not only environmentally friendly but also met the needs and values of those who would inhabit them. In 1995, after several years of careful planning and construction, the project was completed with 44 housing units arranged in a compact, pedestrian-oriented layout that encouraged interaction and minimized environmental impact.

What made Understenshöjden particularly innovative for its time was its commitment to ecological principles embedded in every aspect of its design. Homes were built using natural and locally sourced materials. The settlement incorporated solar panels, pellet-based heating systems, and composting, along with well-developed systems for rainwater management and waste separation. But beyond technology and design, the settlement also fostered a vibrant communal life. Residents formed working groups for maintenance, gardening, and organizing activities—ensuring a sense of shared ownership and responsibility. Over the years, Understenshöjden has become a reference point in Sweden and beyond for ecovillage development within an urban context, combining the benefits of proximity to a major city with the ecological and social integrity of village life, that is, connecting rural and urban aspect of living.

Design Phase: Ideal Settlement Vision of Understenshöjden

The founding members of Understenshöjden had a clear and ambitious vision for the ideal settlement—one that harmonized ecological sustainability, eco-community life, and human-scale urbanism. The desirable characteristics of the inhabitants were that they would be environmentally conscious, cooperative, and actively involved in the development and ongoing life of the community. Social responsibility and democratic participation were as important as technical solutions. The place itself was imagined as a village within the city—small enough to foster strong interpersonal relationships, yet integrated into the urban fabric of Stockholm to allow for accessibility to services, work, and education.

In terms of living infrastructure, the settlement was to be built from natural and non-toxic materials, minimize ecological impact, and incorporate energy-efficient systems, such as solar panels, pellet heating, and insulation optimized for the Nordic climate. Housing units were envisioned as compact, warm, and light-filled. The outdoor environment would encourage biodiversity, play, communal gardening, and shared social spaces. Walkability, green spaces, and a sense of aesthetic harmony with the natural surroundings were core to the vision.

Design Concept of Understenshöjden

Understenshöjden was not designed according to a rigid external urban development programme or a single exemplar model, but it was inspired by broader ecological architecture and cohousing principles that had gained traction in Scandinavia and Europe during the 1980s and early 1990s. While there was not a single blueprint, the project drew from permaculture thinking, passive solar housing, and Scandinavian co-housing developments that emphasized private living units alongside shared spaces and responsibilities.

The design process also reflected an understanding of regional planning priorities in Stockholm at the time, which included interest in compact city development and urban infill that respected surrounding green spaces—Understenshöjden borders the Nacka nature reserve. Thus, the settlement bridged grassroots initiative with emerging public policies that supported ecological experimentation.

Organization of the Participatory Design Process

The design process was participatory from the outset. The EBBA association, comprised of future residents, led the conceptual phase and collaborated closely with architects, urban planners, and construction partners. Regular workshops and meetings were held, in which members could influence decisions on layout, building materials, energy systems, and shared amenities. This co-creative model ensured a deep sense of ownership and alignment between the residents' values and the built environment.

Future inhabitants were encouraged to envision not just the physical layout, but also the social dynamics of the village—how shared responsibilities would be managed, how common spaces would function, and how environmental goals could be embedded into daily life. This horizontal planning structure was key to creating an eco-community that not only looked sustainable but operated sustainably in practice. The result was a settlement that truly reflected its founders' aspirations, built through consensus and shared learning over several years.

Building Beyond Intent: Strategic Governance and Design in Understenshöjden's Formation

The success of Understenshöjden Ecovillage can be attributed to a series of well-considered strategic actions that integrated ecological innovation with community empowerment and participatory governance. From its inception, the project was grounded in a clearly articulated vision shared by a collective of environmentally conscious citizens. By establishing the association EBBA (*Ekologiskt Byggande i Björkhagen*), these individuals not only formalized their intent but also created a democratic platform through which decisions could be deliberated and enacted. This early move towards bottom-up governance was essential in fostering a strong sense of ownership, cohesion, and long-term commitment among future residents.

Crucially, the group understood the importance of cross-sector collaboration. Rather than pursuing the project in isolation, they strategically partnered with institutional actors such as HSB, a prominent cooperative housing organization, and SMÅA-hus, a construction firm receptive to sustainable experimentation. These alliances were pivotal in bridging grassroots activism with professional expertise, ensuring that the community's ecological ideals could be translated into technically and legally feasible housing solutions. Furthermore, the group's capacity to align its aims with broader municipal sustainability goals played a significant role in acquiring a valuable land parcel in Björkhagen. The municipality's support not only legitimized the project but also demonstrated how civic initiative and public policy can be mutually reinforcing in sustainable urban development.

Another defining strategy was the application of participatory and inclusive design processes. Future inhabitants were actively involved in all phases of planning and construction, contributing to the layout, architectural materials, energy systems, and shared spaces. This co-creative approach ensured a high level of responsiveness to user needs while simultaneously embedding democratic culture into the physical and social fabric of the community. It also served to minimize post-construction conflict and fostered the collective capacity to manage shared responsibilities over time.

The design of the built environment was itself a strategic achievement. Ecological integrity was not treated as an add-on but embedded holistically into living infrastructure, including the use of non-toxic, natural materials; solar energy systems; pellet heating; and sustainable water and waste systems. These technical features were complemented by the cultivation of a shared culture of maintenance, stewardship, and cooperation. Residents were organized into self-managed working groups responsible for everything from communal gardening to building upkeep, thereby ensuring that the ideals of sustainability were practised not just environmentally, but socially.

Finally, Understenshöjden's role as a publicly visible, research-friendly, and pedagogically relevant example of urban ecological living further amplified its success. By participating in public discourse, welcoming study visits, and engaging with the broader sustainability movement, the community extended its impact beyond its geographical boundaries. It has become a reference point for policy-makers, urban planners, and other grassroots initiatives, serving not only as a home for its residents but also as a living laboratory for post-industrial, post-carbon eco-community models.

In sum, Understenshöjden's success lies in its synthesis of visionary grassroots mobilization, strategic institutional engagement, integrated ecological design, and a sustained commitment to participatory, place-based living. It illustrates that ecovillages, when underpinned by coherent strategy and social innovation, can play a formative role in shaping sustainable urban futures.

Current Situations: Characteristics of Inhabitants

Understenshöjden is home to a relatively small but stable eco-community composed of 44 households, forming a close-knit neighbourhood. The demographic structure has evolved since the community's inception in the mid-1990s. Originally, most residents were young professionals and families with children who were actively engaged in ecological issues and urban sustainability. Over the years, however, a portion of the population has aged in place, and a generational shift is now evident. Some of the original founders still live in the village, but there has also been an influx of younger households and new families attracted to the ecovillage's values, aesthetics, and reputation. This intergenerational composition contributes to social stability while gradually refreshing the community's energy and perspectives.

In terms of livelihoods, residents are typically engaged in a wide range of urban professions, including education, healthcare, design, architecture, IT, and environmental consultancy. The community benefits from its location in Stockholm, which allows inhabitants to pursue professional careers while maintaining an ecologically grounded lifestyle. As such, Understenshöjden does not operate as an economic cooperative or subsistence-focused ecovillage; rather, it is a residential model of sustainable urbanism where daily life incorporates ecological practices within a conventional urban economic framework.

Regarding population growth and sustainability, the village's small size limits large-scale expansion, but its housing units remain in high demand. As such, there is a consistent turnover and interest from newcomers, which helps sustain its vitality. However, the ecovillage does not produce a 'scale effect' in the conventional economic sense due to its limited housing capacity and absence of income-generating services. Instead, its influence is felt qualitatively, as a demonstration project and reference model for sustainable urban design and community-based living. Its continued visibility in policy, academic, and architectural discourse ensures its impact beyond its physical boundaries.

Culturally, Understenshöjden is characterized by a collaborative and participatory ethos. The eco-community shares values such as ecological responsibility, mutual support, consensus-based decision-making, and inclusivity. These principles are practised through regular community meetings, shared responsibilities (e.g., maintenance groups, gardening), and social events. While residents maintain their private lives and autonomy, there is a strong underlying culture of reciprocity and interdependence. This social infrastructure, though informal, is essential to the ecovillage's resilience and long-term success. It not only enables practical cooperation but also fosters a deep sense of place attachment and collective identity.

Defining Features of Living Infrastructure in Understenshöjden

Understenshöjden's living infrastructure reflects a deliberate and thoughtful integration of ecological design, human-scale planning, and community cohesion. The settlement comprises 44 housing units, arranged in a compact, village-like configuration that encourages social interaction and minimizes ecological impact. Homes are primarily row houses and semi-detached buildings, constructed using natural, non-toxic materials, such as untreated wood, solid spruce flooring, clay plaster, and brick interiors in bathrooms and kitchens. The facades are treated with iron vitriol, which helps them blend into the forested surroundings of the nearby Nackareservatet nature reserve.

The spatial layout emphasizes pedestrian orientation: there are no internal roads for cars, which are parked at the edge of the site, ensuring that shared paths and green spaces between homes remain safe and tranquil. Small gardens, shared courtyards, play areas, and gathering spaces are interspersed throughout the site, creating a woven network of communal and semi-private spaces that promote informal encounters and strengthen neighbourly ties. The natural landscape is preserved, mature-inspired solutions are adopted and integrated into the community, with native vegetation and trees forming an ecological buffer and habitat.

In terms of property ownership, Understenshöjden operates under a housing cooperative (bostadsrättsförening) structure. Each household owns the right to occupy their home (as in a condominium model), while shared spaces and infrastructure—such as the paths, green areas, community tools, and certain systems (e.g., waste and heating)—are held in collective ownership. This model enables a balance between individual autonomy and communal responsibility, encouraging residents to take part in both private maintenance and shared duties.

The governance system is characterized by collective decision-making, grounded in consensus and participation. Residents hold regular meetings to make decisions about budget allocations, maintenance, use of shared spaces, and community initiatives. Sub-groups or working groups are voluntarily formed to manage specific tasks, such as gardening, facilities upkeep, event coordination, and new member orientation. The cooperative board, elected from among the residents, handles administrative and legal matters, while ensuring that decisions reflect the community's values and priorities.

Infrastructure development occurred in phases. The initial planning phase (1989–1993) involved vision-building, participatory design, and negotiation with public and private partners. Construction took place between 1993 and 1995, resulting in the initial housing units and essential eco-services, such as waste management systems and heating infrastructure. In subsequent years, the community continued to invest in upgrades, including the installation of solar panels, improvements to the pellet heating system, and experiments with composting and greywater recycling. These adaptations reflect the community's ongoing commitment to eco-innovation and sustainability, adjusting infrastructure as technologies and needs evolve.

In sum, Understenshöjden's living infrastructure serves as a physical embodiment of its values: ecological awareness, social connection, and participatory governance. It demonstrates how infrastructure can support—not just symbolize—sustainable and collaborative ways of life within a modern urban setting.

Place-Specific Attributes of Understenshöjden

Understenshöjden is uniquely situated on the urban–nature boundary in the Björkhagen district of southern Stockholm, adjacent to Nackareservatet, one of the city's largest and most ecologically significant nature reserves. This location imbues the settlement with distinct landscape qualities—it is surrounded by forests, rock outcroppings, native shrubs, and biodiversity corridors that enhance not only visual aesthetics but also ecological integrity. The terrain is gently sloped, offering natural drainage and views across the green surroundings. Walking and cycling trails connect the settlement to both nature and the city, offering residents immediate access to recreational green infrastructure such as hiking, skiing, and birdwatching trails—an invaluable asset in promoting mental and physical well-being.

While Understenshöjden does not occupy a site of protected cultural heritage, its character is strongly influenced by Scandinavian vernacular aesthetics and the legacy of the Swedish ecological design movement of the 1980s and 1990s. The architectural style reflects principles of simplicity, functionality, and integration with nature, with careful attention paid to materiality and climate responsiveness. As one of Sweden's earliest purpose-built urban ecovillages, Understenshöjden has itself gained heritage value within the environmental and social housing discourse, often cited as a pioneering project in sustainable urban development.

In terms of land ownership and financing, the land was originally acquired from the Stockholm municipality through collaboration with HSB, and it is now managed by the cooperative housing association. Individual households purchase occupancy rights (similar to condominium ownership), while common infrastructure and grounds are collectively owned and maintained. This financing model promotes affordability and long-term community stewardship, as profits are not extracted for private gain but reinvested in maintenance and ecological upgrades.

Understenshöjden also offers favourable conditions for remote work and work from home professional activity. Each housing unit includes flexible interior spaces that can be adapted as home offices, and residents often report having quiet, naturally lit work areas that enable productive telecommuting. The community benefits from reliable high-speed internet, essential for modern professional and educational engagement. Its proximity—just a short metro ride—to central Stockholm also enables hybrid work models and easy access to meetings, cultural events, and institutional resources. Several residents work in creative, environmental, or knowledge-intensive sectors that allow for flexible or remote arrangements.

The settlement provides a safe, healthy, and quiet living environment. Vehicular traffic is restricted to the outer perimeter, ensuring that internal paths and green spaces remain child-friendly and pedestrian-focused. Air quality is excellent due to both the natural buffering of surrounding forest and the eco-community's low-emission heating systems. Noise pollution is minimal, and the sense of security is enhanced by strong social cohesion—residents know and look out for each other, which adds an informal but effective layer of communal care. The combination of natural tranquillity, green surroundings, and low-stress social design contributes to a notably high quality of life, often cited by residents as a key reason for long-term residency.

The Regeneration of the Understenshöjden Project

For those aspiring to initiate an ecovillage or regenerative settlement, the first and most crucial step is to build a committed and values-aligned founding group. Successful communities begin with people who not only share ecological ideals, but who are also prepared to invest time in democratic processes, compromise, and mutual learning. Formalizing the group into a legal entity—such as an association or cooperative—helps provide structure and clarity. It's important to articulate a shared vision early on, addressing not only environmental goals but also expectations around governance, finances, and community culture. This foundational phase should include outreach to gather interest, skills mapping among members, and a commitment to participatory decision-making, which builds long-term resilience and trust.

The second major tip is to engage strategically with institutions and professional stakeholders from the outset. Collaborations with municipalities, housing cooperatives, ethical developers, and architects can accelerate access to land, funding opportunities, and regulatory approvals. Early discussions with local governments can also reveal how the project aligns with public sustainability goals, urban planning frameworks, or land-use priorities—opening the door to mutually beneficial partnerships. Importantly, choose design professionals who are receptive to ecological and participatory design methods. Co-design workshops between professionals and future residents are an effective way to bridge vision and feasibility, translating abstract ideals into technically sound, liveable infrastructure.

Finally, it is essential to balance ecological ambition with long-term liveability and adaptability. While passive house standards, renewable energy, and green infrastructure are critical, so too are reliable internet, well-designed indoor workspaces, and access to transportation and eco-services. Communities that thrive over time are those that plan not just for building performance, but also for evolving social needs, generational change, and economic realities. Embedding flexibility—such as shared spaces that can be repurposed, or governance models that can be periodically reviewed—helps ensure the settlement remains relevant and responsive. Ongoing education, openness to newcomers, and a culture of collaboration can help transform the initial idea into a long-lasting, living eco-community.

Amatciems: An Example of Creating a Unique Village Based on Nature-Inspired Solutions

From Retreat to Regeneration: The Origins of Amatciems Village

Initially, there was no idea about the village. In 1987, successful businessman Aivars Zvirbulis (Čiris) and his wife resided in Riga, the capital of Latvia, and were actively involved in city activities as residents. Activities were demanding and stressful, as was the lifestyle in cities. They wanted to find a nice place for holidays outside the city with a beautiful landscape surrounded by nature. They found a nice spot near the forest, but the problem was that no communications or services were available. So, Čiris slowly raised the idea of creating a settlement based on nature-inspired solutions and modern communication and services. The initiator aimed to integrate three natural elements into the living infrastructure—water, land, and forests.

The Highlight of Amatciems: the unique landscape is made up of all the basic elements of nature: flowing **land**scape, clear **water**, fresh **air**, a warm **fire** in the fireplaces, glorious sunset rays, thousands of **trees**, and ancient **stones**. (Source: www.amatciems.lv)

Čiris purchased land 38 years ago in Amata municipality covered by forests, but the implementation of the project started around the Year 2000. When he constructed his family house, relatives and friends were impressed by the idea and were willing to have a settlement nearby. The initiator of this idea has understood that if he wants to have a good living infrastructure, he needs to develop this place as a village and invite more people to join this project. This was how Amatciems village was established. Later, the internal rules of this village were created for like-minded people (e.g., no fences in the area, no loud music in the evenings and at night, etc.). The initiator of the village defines Amatciems as a village of detached houses of unified architectural quality in a picturesque location.

Amatciem village is now a home for the initiator of this idea, for his children and grandchildren, friends, and other people who have similar approaches to the living place they reside in. The initiator of this idea emphasizes that the symbiosis between the environment, developed infrastructure, and visual aesthetics creates the image of a premium-class village, demonstrating the harmony between humans and nature. Amatciems also provides a perfect and practical transition from the city to the countryside, as the village combines the rural idyll with modern technology (Amatciems, n.d.).

Founding Amatciems: A Nature-Inspired Vision by Aivars Zvirbulis

The idea of establishing a settlement came to Aivars approximately 40 years ago. He and his family lived in Riga and successfully engaged in business activities. Work was as challenging, intensive, and stressful as life in the capital city. So, Čiris and his wife wanted to find a peaceful place in nature outside the city for their holidays or more extended weekends. In 1987, they purchased the first hectares of land in the Amata municipality, located near Riga, the capital of Latvia (approximately 80 km from Riga). Some years ago, the motivation for realizing this idea even got stronger. In the early 1990s, the recession affected businesses in Europe, and a global economic downturn occurred worldwide. Aivar's business was also affected by these events. At this time, walking in the mountains and hiking (where he was treating the health problems affected by stress and felt the beneficial effects of nature), he decided in his life to create something for himself, what he likes, not following rules as in proper business and with a mind to leave something for the future. He has sold the remaining business and begun investing in new projects based on his ideas. His friends were visiting a new place, and they liked his idea, the place itself, and how it had been developed. A decade later, the developer of Amatciems village purchased land plots in the neighbouring areas, and the territory increased to 300 ha in the year 2000.

Integrating Water, Land, and Forest: Ecological Design Strategies in Amatciems

Initially, the project's initiator was willing to find a location outside the city with a beautiful landscape, surrounded by forests and lakes. He wanted to create a desirable place that satisfied his desire to live in an environment with nature-inspired solutions. There were also a few more requirements he was willing to adapt to this settlement. He wanted to have infrastructure that people used in cities as city residents. Additionally, he envisioned this place as a holiday home, with relaxation being the primary activity upon arrival, rather than maintenance tasks. For example, having cut grass in the summer, a road with no snow in the wintertime, etc. Also, you can feel safe in this natural place in the middle of nowhere. To sum up, the idea of creating a village was to realize the desire to live in a well-maintained, picturesque property surrounded by forest and water.

Later, when his first steps in the idea were realized and the property was built, he was open to inviting more inhabitants to purchase land and properties on his land. The most essential requirement for potential inhabitants is that they share similar values regarding their living place and livelihood, are willing to partner with this place, and aim to abide by its internal rules.

The creation of living infrastructure was based on the initial idea that each settlement in the village would have sufficient privacy in the area, with no regular fences, and would feature a piece of forest, water, and another natural element, in line with the principle of partnership with this place. The landscape was changed by digging ponds, creating hills, and replanting trees. Nevertheless, the biological rhythms of nature were observed when performing any of these activities. The main roads were paved with asphalt, lined with lights, and left space for walks along natural forest paths.

The internal rules were developed based on the experience of similar villages in other countries and the initiator's vision. Internal rules have been established to define the organization of the village's living infrastructure, the behaviour of its inhabitants towards nature, non-human habitats, and other inhabitants of Amatciems. For example, the plots by individual houses cannot have fences to allow free movement of wildlife (for deer, foxes, birds, and other animals). During the evening and nighttime, loud noises are not allowed. Dogs are treated as friends of people and cannot be chained. Internal rules for village inhabitants with similar values were not considered restrictive; instead, they promoted harmony and calmness in the village.

The settlement was designed according to an original concept created by Aivars Zvirbulis, the initiator of this idea. Previous experiences in his life greatly helped him in creating a vision and a roadmap for implementing it. Aivars was very experienced in orienteering sports and arts, among other things. In orienteering sports, he gained knowledge about various landscapes, flora, and fauna, and also created maps for orientation activities. In the arts, he had a perfect sense of space and shape.

So, activities in the past helped him draw his idea of the settlement on paper, then put it on a map, plan activities for implementation, and create a roadmap for implementation. The initiator created this place as he imagined it in this dream and painted it on the map. He trusted in himself and his ideas.

The examples that Čiris saw in the World also had an impact. For example, in rural villages in Sweden, there are very narrow roads, which gave him confidence that we can drive slowly and respectfully towards our fellow road users and that we should not exaggerate the width of the road. After a trip through Sweden, the width of the roads was replanned, and broader, greener roadsides were achieved. A family of Latvian builders from America provided valuable advice, categorically recommending against the initial idea of building individual septic tanks for individual sewage wastewater. This was because, in the event of an accident, the water quality in the ponds would be compromised, and a local ecological disaster could occur. In Amatciems, there is a central water and sewage system.

The design process began with paperwork, involving planning for the landscape and living infrastructure on the purchased land, as there were no prior communications. Later, physical work started for the installation of the first communications and the construction of buildings. Finally, the remaining infrastructure was created according to the needs of the initiator, which became important at the time of living.

Firstly, landscape and land plots were planned for approximately 100 settlements in the area. Secondly, landscape formation work was organized, including digging the land, creating hills, forming ponds, and planting trees. The biological rhythms of nature were observed when performing any of these activities. Secondly, communication installations have started: electricity, water, and sewage systems. Step-by-step, a living infrastructure was created as planned in the vision. The main roads were paved with asphalt, and lighting was provided along the route for safe walking in the darkness. An optical cable was installed to ensure remote work capabilities. Non-human habitats were also considered to allow them to move freely in the area and avoid any fences in the village.

During the design stage, the developer also sought a suitable solution and model for service provision in the area. As he tried to have a good living infrastructure similar to the existing one in the cities, on the one hand, and also to ensure security in this remote area, on the other hand, he concluded that more inhabitants are needed to provide services and sustain the settlement's vitality. In the design stage, economic assessment has helped to identify that 100–200 houses are required if you want to provide services in the area.

From Founding to Flourishing: Strategic Dimensions of a Village

Aivars Zvirbulis applied an original and intuitive approach to the creation of Amatciems village, guided by personal vision, sensitivity to the natural landscape, and evolving community needs. This place was created not as an ordinary business model but as an attractive place for himself, his family, friends, and later, for like-minded people. He did not employ many specific advertisements or communication strategies to attract more residents. Čiris developed this village step by step by observing nature and the needs of himself and the inhabitants.

Living in Symbiosis: The Rhythm of Life in Amatciems

In the first years, mainly three types of inhabitants purchased land and/or houses in Amatciems village: the first group was digital nomads (e.g., people working in the IT sector); the second group was families with children who could work from home, remotely (as advocates or designers); and the third group was people in the age of retirement and close to retirement. A unifying characteristic among the residents is the gradual dissolution of the traditional boundary between professional activity and leisure, reflecting a lifestyle in which work and personal life are increasingly integrated.

After the COVID-19 pandemic, starting in 2021, when people's thinking and working habits have changed, new types of inhabitants have decided to choose this place:

- The first group is young families with young children aged 30–40 years with different professions (digital nomads, designers, doctors, business people);
- The second group consists of people who can work partly in the office and partly from home (with more diversified professions compared to the early years of settlement development). Commuting is about 60 minutes to Riga, the capital of Latvia, and inhabitants have identified that this time is also good for summarizing work ideas or clearing their minds from day-to-day activities.
- The third group consists of people in their 50 s and 60 s, most of whom are pre-retirement. They are economically active but willing to slow down their everyday lives and live close to nature.

New trends among inhabitants with diverse lifestyles and livelihoods emerged in 2024. The first groups of inhabitants are young couples, approx. 25 years, with other nationalities (so-called mixed couples), usually one person with Latvian nationality and another from abroad with a different nationality. They are looking for a place with a high quality of life where they can work from home, enjoy a good climate, and partner with a place. Another type of inhabitants—people from abroad, from other EU countries, mainly from southern Europe—expressing their desire to live in picturesque landscapes, in green areas, with four seasons a year, willing to have seasonal changes and good air quality. Some countries to mention are Switzerland, Germany, France, Israel, and Portugal. New residents also highlight that Amatciems provide not only a good quality of life but also high-quality buildings at reasonable prices. There is also the option of purchasing local food to lead a healthier life.

From 35% to 40% of families live permanently, and the remaining amount have a house as a second home for weekends. Some have different types of working practices (e.g., working from abroad for one month, then living in Amatciems for one month).

Currently, there are about 100 houses in the Amatciems villages. The existing population is not sufficient to sustain the settlement's vitality. Based on the economic calculations, around 150–200 houses should generate a scale effect. Hundred houses are still too few.

Amatciems have unique testing for shared values and culture for newcomers. Before purchasing a property in Amatciems, the initiator of this idea discusses the place with potential stakeholders, emphasizing its peaceful and quiet environment, where it is possible to work creatively and relax with family and friends. They aim to assess whether there are a common understanding and acceptance of the values of this place. Usually, if people like a place and a home with no fences, they tend to be open-minded. Internal rules guarantee a harmonious lifestyle and like-minded neighbours who respect nature and peace. The internal rules of the village are intended for like-minded individuals who do not view them as restrictive, but rather as promoting quiet and peace.

Collaboration in Amatciems between inhabitants is naturally organized, based on the needs of the inhabitants. If some inhabitants share common interests, they often organize everyday activities. For example, in Amatciems, a group of gourmands like to do testing events in different houses. Another example is art lessons and painting lessons for children. Additionally, there is a room in Amatciems for co-working activities. Some events, such as New Year's Eve and summer concerts, are organized collectively. All these events come from residents' individual initiatives.

The creation of living infrastructure in Amatciems village was based on the following principles:

- *Physical infrastructure* should be similar to that in cities for the convenience of inhabitants (e.g., installation of water, heating, sewage systems in houses, paved roads, and lights along the main roads);
- *Safety of place.* As the area is in a remote rural location, the safety of residents and settlements was a key concern (e.g., ensuring safe walks for families with young children when they stay at home alone).
- *Provision of main services.* For more than half of the residents, Amatciems village is a home for holidays, with the main activity being to relax and avoid maintenance activities in the settlement upon arrival. For example, there is cut grass in the summer, a road with no snow in wintertime, etc. So, there was a need for services.
- *Possibilities to work remotely.* Most of the inhabitants wanted to take advantage of the opportunity to work from home, so there was a need for high-speed internet.

Buildings and the arrangement of homes. Each house was designed to incorporate all elements of nature, protecting the peace and health of its residents while providing a harmonious balance with the natural environment. The primary criteria for selecting the building's location were the relief, landscape, and cardinal points. The house should blend seamlessly into the landscape while offering its residents the best views of nature from within.

The house can be built using one of three types of construction—timber framed, log building, or stone building, supplementing it with a boulder, decorative timber facing, painted plaster, or glass exterior walls and allowed roof coverings—reeds, torn wood chips, clay or cement tiles, and lawn coverings. There are two options for potential inhabitants to purchase a house: they can choose a house that is already built or select an individual project and get confirmation from the initiator of this place that this project is in line with the stylistic requirements for this place (Amatciems, n.d.).

Infrastructure. Amatciems village offers a seamless and practical transition from the city to the countryside, as it combines the rural idyll with modern technology. For the convenience of the residents, Amatciems has all modern communications: part of the required capacity of green electricity is generated by a solar panel park, drinking water is obtained from a deep well, sewage is discharged outside the village to municipal treatment plants, high-speed trunk optical networks and modern technologies guarantee uncompromising internet speed (Amatciems, n.d.).

Amatciems has 24/7 technical security, which can respond quickly to calls. Thus, the village area is a safe environment for its permanent residents and those who choose Amatciems as their second home. The roads have been lit, pavements and paths have been created, and bridges have been built for villagers and visitors to stroll (Amatciems, n.d.).

In the Amatciems village, the 'Smart village' concept was also adopted by the management company. Each household can submit requests and orders, receive a response, etc. Each inhabitant can access records and statistics on the resources they consume. Smart meters enable the determination of the cause and reason behind a reading, especially when it appears too high. Smart meters alert you about temperature changes in your house (e.g., low temperatures—5°C or high temperatures above 25°C, etc.), information notifications from the building manager about planned or emergency interruptions in the supply of water, electricity, or internet, problems with communication networks, or other types of information affecting the residents. It is possible to keep the property safe and take care of it remotely (Amatciems, n.d.).

Services. The initiator of the village has established a management company to provide all the services that Amatciems village residents need, aiming to integrate modern technologies into this living environment. The first type of service is related to maintaining the houses and territory (some services are for public areas, while others are for individual needs). The second type of service is a construction company that can build a house according to your needs. The third type of service is the Customer Support Service. The management company provides round-the-clock support to residents to solve any problem or customer request as quickly as possible, operating the village infrastructure and other household issues.

Arrangement of public spaces. In Amatciems village, the entire area can be described as a public space surrounded by forest and water, featuring small hills, ponds, and no fences between houses.

> In Amatciems, the forest has not been turned into a city park, but a flowering meadow is next to a well-kept lawn. A mown lawn usually has no fireflies, but in Amatciems, hundreds of little lights glow in the grass on warm summer nights. A sonorous chorus of green frogs can be heard in the ponds.Source: www.amatciems.lv

There is one room in the Amatciems for co-working activities. There are also areas in the main building where common activities are held, such as art lessons, children's painting lessons, and summer concerts.

Property co-ownership. Inhabitants own houses and land plots. Roads are owned by the management company. Internal rules provided information on how building and other infrastructure work should be organized.

Amatciems village is located in a remote rural area with a changed landscape, as viewed by the initiator of this idea: an area with hills, ponds (natural and formed artificially), forests, and many trees. In the village, the balance between the environment, developed infrastructure, and visual aesthetics creates an image of a premium-class village, demonstrating the harmony between humans and nature.

Favourable conditions exist for performing work duties at home for digital nomads. Each household in Amatciems is connected to the internet via optical fibre cable using FTTH (Fiber to the Home) technology. This enables villagers to utilize the resources available on the public internet for both local and international traffic, with guaranteed, uncompromising download and upload speeds (Amatciems, n.d.).

Most inhabitants use private transportation, but public transportation is also available (a 10-minute walk to the train or bus station). Individual spaces at each settlement can be used for client or team meetings.

The inhabitants of Amatciems village define this place as a place for a good quality of life, with a healthy and quiet environment, fresh air, good infrastructure for travel, remote work, provision of services, and good safety.

Designing with Purpose: Recommendations for Emerging Regenerative Settlements

For people wishing to set up a similar settlement, the main advice is to follow the main idea that the person has in mind and is willing to implement.

> No matter what you do, just follow your heart and implement your ideas with passion. All difficulties can be solved.*Laura Zvirbule, daughter of Aivars Zvirbulis*

Another important aspect is hard work. One should understand that implementing this idea may require a significant amount of time, energy, and continuous effort every day. A prerequisite is also to enjoy it.

Kardokai Community: A Case Study of Nature-Based Rural Settlement and Straw-Bale Architecture in Lithuania

From Vision to Village: The Origins and Evolution of the Kardokai Community

The initial efforts to establish the Kardokai Community began in 2006. The principal initiator of the settlement, Raimundas Vaičiūnas, along with his wife, was residing in Kaunas at the time, the second-largest city in Lithuania, and actively engaged in urban life. However, following the establishment of their family, the couple underwent a re-evaluation of their living environment and lifestyle priorities. This introspection led to the recognition of a shared aspiration to relocate from the urban context to a rural setting, motivated by the desire to raise their children in symbiosis with nature. Consequently, Raimundas Vaičiūnas commenced the search for a location that would be conducive to the creation of a nature-oriented settlement aligned with these values.

Inspiration for the content of the settlement came from the series of books *Ringing Cedars of Russia* by Vladimir Megre and his heroine Anastasia (Megre, 1997). Known as 'Kin's Domain' settlement, these are a new generation of ecovillages with a focus on sustainability for future generations of families. Supporters of this idea were creating 'Anastasia clubs' in Lithuanian cities and discussing the ways of creating settlements with nature-inspired solutions.

In 2006, Raimundas acquired approximately three hectares of land, marking the initial step in the implementation of his envisioned settlement project. By 2010, his family had relocated to a newly constructed residence on the site. As the family settled into rural life and their children matured, a growing need for increased social interaction emerged. In response to these evolving social needs, the initiators recognized the potential to develop the area into a broader, village-like community.

This realization prompted a strategic shift in the project's trajectory from an individual homestead to an ecovillage. Accordingly, the initiators began actively inviting other individuals and families who shared similar ecological and communal values to participate in the initiative. This marked the beginning of the Kardokai Community's development, as new residents acquired land and constructed homes that reflected the architectural and environmental ethos of the original homestead.

As of 2025, the Kardokai Community comprises approximately 20 individual land plots, with 13 residential houses inhabited on a permanent basis. The total population of the settlement is estimated at 47 residents. Each household occupies a private land parcel ranging in size from one to three hectares, reflecting the community's foundational emphasis on spacious, nature-integrated living.

Nature, Place, and Intention: The Foundational Vision of the Kardokai Settlement

The conceptualization of establishing a rural settlement emerged approximately two decades ago, initiated by Raimundas and his spouse. At the time, both individuals resided in Kaunas and were actively engaged in the city's socio-cultural life. However, the formation of their family prompted a reassessment of their living environment. They came to the shared understanding that they wished to raise their children in a countryside setting, fostering a lifestyle in symbiosis with nature.

Motivated by this vision, they have searched for a suitable land parcel that would support their aspirations. After evaluating several potential locations, they identified promising options that aligned with their environmental and social values. In 2005, the initiator of the project acquired the initial hectares of land in the municipality of Kazlų Rūda, located approximately 36 kilometres from Kaunas, Lithuania's second-largest city. This location was particularly favourable due to its forested surroundings, distance from major transport infrastructure, and its potential to facilitate the implementation of nature-inspired solutions and the cultivation of place-based partnerships.

In subsequent years, the settlement's initiator expanded the landholdings by acquiring additional plots in the neighbouring area. He also began to engage individuals who shared similar values, inviting them to purchase land and establish their own homesteads within proximity. This organic and value-driven process led to the formation of what is now known as the Kardokai Community.

From Family Vision to Community Formation: The Kardokai Settlement Story

At the inception of the project, the initiator envisioned establishing a residential settlement in a rural environment. His primary objective was to create a living space for his family that would enable the integration of nature-based solutions and ecological principles. The selection criteria for the location prioritized environmental suitability for sustainable living over the availability of conventional infrastructural amenities.

Subsequently, as the initiator's children began to grow, the evolving needs of the family highlighted the importance of social interaction and communal life. This realization led to a shift in focus from a solely family-centred initiative to one oriented towards community-building. In response, the initiator began to actively seek like-minded individuals who shared similar values and aspirations regarding lifestyle, environmental sustainability, and collaborative living.

To support the development of a broader community, the initiator acquired additional parcels of land in adjacent areas, which he offered to prospective community members. A core prerequisite for participation in this emerging community was a shared commitment to environmentally conscious living, alignment in livelihood perspectives, and a willingness to engage collaboratively in the co-creation of the settlement. According to the initiator's vision, the Kardokai Community is intended to comprise approximately 100 inhabitants.

The creation of living infrastructure was based on the initial idea that each settlement in the village would have its own land, ranging from 1 to 3 hectares, and organize physical infrastructure according to its own views, following nature-inspired solutions. Most of the members have chosen to build straw houses with the help of other community members. In later years, when the project was developed, they decided to name their community Kardokai Community—Straw Houses Capital.

During the conceptual design phase of the settlement, inspiration was drawn from the book series *The Ringing Cedars of Russia* by Vladimir Megre, particularly through the philosophical and lifestyle ideals embodied by the character Anastasia (Megre, 1997). Central to these writings is the notion of the *Kin's Domain*—a model of sustainable settlement structured around family homesteads. This model represents a new generation of ecovillages, emphasizing long-term environmental stewardship, intergenerational continuity, and self-sufficiency.

The earliest *Kin's Domain*-inspired settlements began to emerge in the early 2000s (2001–2002) across various post-Soviet countries, including Russia, Lithuania, Latvia, and Belarus. These settlements appealed to individuals and families seeking alternatives to both urban life and the communal structures characteristic of Western ecovillages. In particular, the emphasis on individual family plots rather than collective ownership resonated with those who held critical memories of the Soviet-era forced collectivization policies, thereby making the *Kin's Domain* model more culturally and historically acceptable in post-socialist contexts.

Over time, Megre's books were translated into multiple languages, facilitating the global dissemination of the *Kin's Domain* concept (see Fig. 4.1). As a result, the model gained popularity not only throughout Europe but also across other continents, contributing to broader discussions on alternative rural development, intentional communities, and sustainable living.

Supporters of this idea from Lithuania were creating 'Anastasia clubs' in various Lithuanian cities and discussing ways to create settlements in various areas in Lithuania using nature-inspired solutions. This network of people was the perfect base for information and data collection, exchange of experiences, searching for potential inhabitants in eco-settlements with

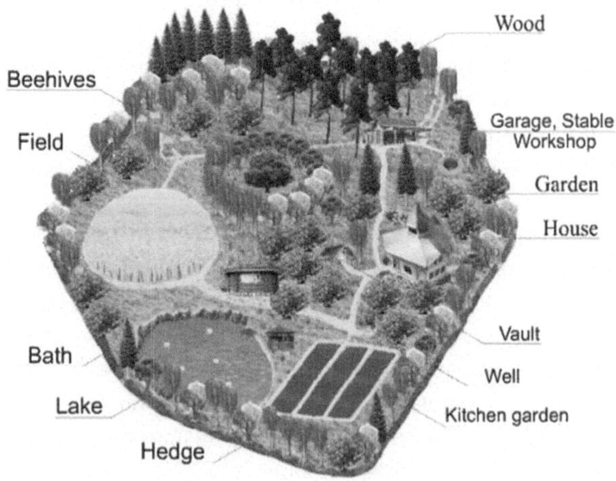

Fig. 4.1 Kin's Domain design. (Source: https://kinscommunity.com/kins-domain-history/ and Vidickiene, 2013)

similar views, and sharing experiences on building practices on nature-inspired solutions (e.g., houses from straw, from clay, etc.).

In the subsequent stages, once the initiators had acquired land and commenced the development of their respective settlements, the intensity of their previously active networks gradually diminished. This shift was largely attributable to the considerable time and financial resources required for the establishment of individual homesteads, which demanded sustained personal involvement and investment. As a result, the original collective vision underwent a process of transformation and decentralization, becoming more closely aligned with the specific needs, capacities, and aspirations of each individual settlement and its emerging community.

The design process has begun with planning the landscape and living infrastructure on a purchased parcel of land in Kardokai. The design process started in 2006, and in 2010, the family moved to this settlement. The initiator decided to build a straw house from natural materials. He was contacting other colleagues and friends to get ideas on how to build this type of house.

The creation of this place was centred on striking a balance between materiality and spirituality. Additionally, he sought to adopt a natural lifestyle in this environment, drawing inspiration from the series of books *Ringing Cedars of Russia* (Megre, 1997). Raimundas wanted to integrate nature-inspired solutions in living infrastructure and to partner with this place. Step by step, the living infrastructure was created as it was planned in the vision. This process has not stopped, as the family continually has new ideas for construction, gardening, and creating new attractions on their land plot (e.g., an outdoor seating area by the fire).

Initially, only one family had settled in Kardokai. After several years of living in the new settlement, they have begun to invite more supporters of this idea to join the project. The invitation was advertised on newly created platforms for like-minded people or at their events (e.g., on the platform www.ekogyvenvietes.lt). There was the possibility to purchase a plot of land in the nearby area. When some of the newcomers purchased land, more potential newcomers expressed their interest as well. The initiator of this idea decided to purchase land plots in a nearby area and later offer the opportunity to purchase these plots to others. In this way, the creation of the Kardokai community started.

Stages of development of Kardokai Community:

1. The design stage and first settlement: 2006–2010. Since 2008, when the building process began, many people have visited this site to observe the project's implementation.
2. The development stage: 2010–2016. During the development stage, the purchase of land and the recruitment of newcomers were the most significant activities.
3. Creation of the Kardokai Community and continuous growth, from 2016 to the present. Designing of community rules, creation of needed infrastructure (initiation of school establishment, cooperation for economic activities, etc.)

During the initial development phase, Raimundas Vaičiūnas did not implement a formal selection process for individuals interested in acquiring land within the emerging settlement. However, over time it became evident that some newcomers lacked a clear understanding of the foundational vision underpinning the project. In response to these challenges, Raimundas introduced motivational interviews as a means of evaluating prospective residents' alignment with the community's core principles.

These interviews served to assess individuals' motivations for joining the settlement, their commitment to living in close interaction with nature, their support for the implementation of nature-based infrastructural solutions, and their willingness to actively participate in the life of the community. Moreover, an additional aim of this procedure was to ensure continuity in the physical development of the site, by confirming that new members intended to establish a tangible presence and contribute to the ongoing material realization of the settlement.

The construction of most settlements in Kardokai village was characterized by a high degree of community involvement and mutual assistance. Community members regularly organized collective labour initiatives, during which participants contributed to various stages of the building process, such as the insertion of straw bales into wall structures, plastering, and other forms of manual support. These cooperative efforts were typically followed by communal gatherings involving shared meals, informal conversations, and social activities, which played a crucial role in fostering social cohesion and reinforcing a sense of belonging among residents.

In certain instances, the settlement's initiator, Raimundas Vaičiūnas, extended transitional housing support to newcomers by offering temporary accommodation until they were able to construct their own homes. This practice further reflected the community's ethos of solidarity, reciprocity, and support during the formative stages of settlement development.

Strategic Actions Without a Blueprint: The Iterative Development of the Kardokai Community

The initiator, Raimundas Vaičiūnas, guided the process primarily through personal intuition and a desire to create a living environment that resonated with his own values and lifestyle aspirations. At the time of the initial land acquisition, there were no additional vacant land parcels available in the immediate vicinity, which limited the potential for coordinated expansion.

In the subsequent stages of development, Raimundas actively sought opportunities to acquire additional land suitable for settlement. This process involved direct engagement with local residents and the dissemination of information about the community through interpersonal networks and various local gatherings. In this way, the expansion of the Kardokai Community occurred incrementally, reflecting an organic, step-by-step evolution shaped by emerging opportunities and contextual constraints.

The family employed only selective and informal communication strategies aimed at attracting like-minded individuals. These efforts were primarily channelled through word-of-mouth networks, thematic clubs, public meetings, and community events supported by advocates of the *Kin's Domain* concept. The village's development was thus driven not by top-down planning mechanisms but by a gradual alignment of ecological observation, personal needs, and shared values among prospective residents.

From Aspiration to Daily Life: The Realities of the Kardokai Settlement

The inhabitants of the Kardokai Community represent a diverse group in terms of livelihood strategies and individual lifestyles. However, they are united by shared values and aspirations related to ecological living, such as seeking proximity to nature, consuming healthy and sustainably produced food, and raising children in a natural environment. These common ideals form the normative foundation of the community, despite variations in personal and professional trajectories.

During the early development phase of the settlement, the initiator, Raimundas Vaičiūnas, actively sought to attract like-minded individuals by inquiring whether prospective residents were familiar with *The Ringing Cedars of Russia* book series by Vladimir Megre and the ideas presented by its central character, Anastasia (Megre, 1997). Initially, alignment with this philosophical framework was common among early settlers. However, over time, the requirement for ideological alignment became less pronounced. Newcomers were simply asked whether they had encountered the books, with no obligation to adhere to their vision. Nevertheless, it remained expected that prospective residents would demonstrate a commitment to ecological values, including living in harmony with nature, adopting nature-inspired infrastructure solutions, and practising environmentally conscious consumption patterns, such as permaculture-based food production.

Demographically, most residents fall within the age range of 30 to 50 years, and the majority are families with children. As of 2025, the community consists of approximately 20 land plots, with 13 houses inhabited on a permanent basis, comprising a total of around 47 individuals, of whom 22 are children. On average, each household includes three children, and each family owns between 1 and 3 hectares of land.

In terms of livelihood, many residents aim to derive income from local or home-based activities to avoid daily commuting. Some have undertaken significant professional transitions upon relocating to Kardokai. For instance, several community members have shifted from previous careers—such as information technology—to engage in the local construction sector, often collaborating as a team to offer building services. Others remain in remote work roles. A number of women are involved in childcare, while others engage in artisanal and craft production, selling their goods at community events and regional gatherings. These patterns suggest that self-realization and occupational reinvention are common outcomes of permanent settlement in Kardokai.

The original vision anticipated a community of approximately 100 inhabitants. Currently, based on the available 20 plots, the expected population may reach around 80 individuals. However, achieving the target of 100 residents is constrained by a limited availability of land in the surrounding area. According to the initiator, a community of 20 families—or approximately 100 individuals—would constitute a functionally sufficient population for maintaining vibrant social and economic activity.

While the developmental phase of the settlement was characterized by a high degree of initiative and engagement, the transition to a more mature phase has revealed certain challenges. Notably, there has been a decline in the frequency and diversity of community-led activities, and collaboration among residents is perceived as insufficient. A key structural limitation is the absence of dedicated communal infrastructure, such as shared indoor or outdoor spaces suitable for gatherings or economic initiatives. At present, meetings are held either in private residences or within the premises of the nearby Kardokai Nature School. Collective action within the community emerges organically, driven by shared interests and resident initiatives rather than formal governance structures.

During the COVID-19 pandemic, beginning in 2020, the Kardokai Nature School played a pivotal role in attracting new interest in the village. Several individuals associated with the school approached Raimundas to inquire about the possibility of relocating permanently to Kardokai. This led to the emergence of new initiatives and a renewed interest in expanding the community.

The Kardokai settlement comprises 20 individual land plots, each ranging in size from 1 to 3 hectares, of which 13 currently host residential houses. The spatial organization of the village reflects a dispersed settlement pattern, with most settlements situated at a considerable distance from one another. Residents typically access neighbouring households via public forest paths or rural roads. At present, the community lacks designated communal infrastructure; as a result, meetings and collective gatherings are held either within private residences or at the Kardokai Nature School.

In recognition of the prevalent use of straw-bale construction techniques, the community has collectively adopted the informal title *'Kardokai—Straw Houses Capital'*. This designation reflects both a material and ideological commitment to environmentally sustainable building practices. The design of each house intentionally integrates natural elements, aiming to preserve the tranquillity and health of its inhabitants while fostering a harmonious relationship with the surrounding environment.

All residential buildings and land plots within the Kardokai settlement are privately owned by community members, while roads and access routes remain public infrastructure. In 2013, the settlement's initiator, Raimundas

Vaičiūnas, established a formal organization—the Kardokai Community Association—to serve as a legal entity for communication and collaboration with public institutions and external stakeholders.

Despite the existence of a formal structure, most community governance and decision-making processes are organized informally. Decisions are typically discussed during general meetings, where activity plans and community-related issues are presented and discussed. Thematic or issue-specific discussions are delegated to temporary working groups, which form on a voluntary basis. Participation in these groups is open to all residents, and the outcomes of their deliberations are subsequently shared with the broader community for collective consideration.

Responsibility for the development of individual living infrastructure lies with each resident. The process generally begins with land acquisition, followed by a series of construction and habitation phases. Informal, non-commercial assistance, particularly during the early stages of settlement, is often extended to new residents, especially young families. This mutual aid approach facilitates initial integration and helps overcome practical challenges. Subsequent phases of infrastructure development are typically organized by individual households.

The *Kardokai Community—Straw Houses Capital* is situated in a remote rural locality within Kardokai village, surrounded by the expansive Kazlų Rūda forest massif. This forest complex, ranked as the third largest in Lithuania, spans approximately 58,700 hectares, of which 47,000 hectares are forested. It is located in the southwestern part of the country and stretches across the administrative territories of Marijampolė, Kazlų Rūda, Šakiai, and Kaunas district municipalities. Geographically, the massif lies approximately 12 kilometres west of Kaunas and to the northwest of the Kaunas–Marijampolė transport corridor.

While the region is characterized by its relative remoteness, it does have internet connectivity, albeit with limited bandwidth, which allows for the performance of certain professional duties from home. Nonetheless, the community primarily emphasizes local livelihood strategies, with a focus on service-oriented and place-based economic activities. These include construction services, artisanal and handicraft production, and employment opportunities within the nearby Kardokai Nature School, located approximately 0.5 to 1 kilometre from the settlement.

Transportation within and beyond the community is facilitated exclusively by private vehicles, as public transport infrastructure is currently unavailable. In response to this limitation, community members frequently engage in cooperative practices such as carpooling or shared errands to urban areas for essential goods and services. Furthermore, residents have adapted their private residential spaces to accommodate professional engagements, such as client consultations and team meetings.

From the perspective of its inhabitants, Kardokai is perceived not merely as a place of residence, but as a locus of high quality of life. The community is valued for its peaceful atmosphere, ecological integrity, and close relationship with the natural environment—attributes considered integral to the vision of sustainable rural living espoused by its residents.

Towards Regenerative Living: A Guide for Aspiring Community Creators

For people wishing to set up a similar settlement, the initiator of this community gives some good tips and pieces of advice:

1. Be careful in selecting the location of your place. If you want to be close to nature, it can pose some challenges with connection links. This is very important for young families.
   (a) It is important to have public transport nearby.
   (b) There is a need to have good roads in all seasons. It can be challenging with rural and forest roads during winter, spring, and other seasons. Clarify who is responsible for maintaining these roads.
2. If community and common activities are important, start by creating your place through communal building. Common spaces help bring people together and connect them.
3. Large distances are not a significant threat. Nevertheless, the existence of a larger city nearby makes your living environment and commuting easier.
4. It is essential to find a quiet spot near a forest. The initiator did not recommend choosing a location near agricultural land with intensive farming.
5. It is recommended to create rules describing living practices for newcomers. Additionally, it is essential to establish when rules can be revised and updated.

6. It is recommended to define the vision of your community at the time of establishment.
7. Spirituality should be an integral part of the community's life. It is something that brings people together. It is needed because the population needs to find a source of community and joy.

References

Adger, W. N., Barnett, J., Chapin, F. S., & Ellemor, H. (2011). This must be the place: Underrepresentation of identity and meaning in climate change decision-making. *Global Environmental Politics, 11*(2), 1–25. https://doi.org/10.1162/GLEP_a_00051

Amatciems. (n.d.). https://amatciems.lv/

Baird, J., Plummer, R., Schultz, L., Armitage, D. R., & Bodin, Ö. (2019). How does socio-institutional diversity affect collaborative governance of social–ecological systems in practice? *Environmental Management, 63*(2), 200–214. https://doi.org/10.1007/s00267-018-1123-5

Basiouny, N. (2024). *Eco-villages and Utopian communities around the world: A global overview.* ConnollyCove. https://www.connollycove.com/eco-villages-and-utopian-communities/.

HSB. (n.d.). Cooperative housing. https://www.hsb.se/in-english/

Kardokai. (n.d.). https://www.kardokai.lt/

Leach, M., Mearns, R., & Scoones, I. (1997). Challenges to community-based sustainable development: Dynamics, entitlements, institutions. *IDS Bulletin, 28*, 4–14. https://doi.org/10.1111/j.1759-5436.1997.mp28004002.x

Masterson, V. A., Enqvist, J. P., Stedman, R. C., Tengö, M., Giusti, M., Wahl, D., & Svedin, U. (2019). Sense of place in social–ecological systems: From theory to empirics. *Sustainability Science, 14*(3), 555–564. https://doi.org/10.1007/s11625-019-00695-8

May, C. K. (2022). Complex adaptive governance systems: A framework to understand institutions, organizations, and people in socio-ecological systems. *Socio-Ecological Practice Research, 4*(1), 39–54. https://doi.org/10.1007/s42532-021-00101-7

Megre, V. (1997). Ringing cedars of Russia. https://vmegre.com/books/. [3 April 2025].

Platform of ecosettlements in Lithuania. (2025). https://ekogyvenvietes.lt/. [3 April 2025].

Sociocracy For All. (n.d.). *Sociocracy in intentional community.* https://www.sociocracyforall.org/sociocracy-in-intentional-community/

Springer, J., & Kaza, N. (2024). The relational shift in urban ecology: From place and structures to processes and relations. *Ambio, 53*(1), 1–12. https://doi.org/10.1007/s13280-024-02001-y

Steffen, W., Broadgate, W., Deutsch, L., Gaffney, O., & Ludwig, C. (2015). The trajectory of the Anthropocene: The great acceleration. *The Anthropocene Review, 2*(1), 81–98. https://doi.org/10.1177/2053019614564785

Tellus Think Tank. (2015). *Understenshöjden: One of Sweden's first eco villages.* https://www.tellusthinktank.com/featuredarticle/understenshojden-one-of-swedens-first-eco-villages-no006/

Understenshojden.se. (n.d.). *About Understenshöjden.* https://understenshojden.se

Vidickiene, D. (2013). *Living in harmony: Inspiring stories from ecovillages* (D. Vidickiene, Ed.). BMK Publisher. ISBN 978-609-8080-33-9.

CHAPTER 5

Symbiotic Living: Intensification Strategies That Redefine Education, Governance, and Communal Life in Eco-Settlements

Živilė Gedminaitė-Raudonė, Vitalija Simonaitytė, and Rita Lankauskienė

The intensification strategy in eco-settlements development emerges as a crucial next step following the initial stage of extensive growth, in which the primary focus lies on the physical expansion of eco-settlements, both in terms of population and area. During this stage, eco-communities typically design and implement environmentally conscious residential models that address pressing ecological concerns, including renewable energy systems, decentralized water management, sustainable transportation solutions, and low-impact waste treatment technologies. However, as these initiatives mature, a limitation of infrastructure often becomes evident.

The biggest challenge is the absence of a robust social infrastructure capable of sustaining long-term communal life in alignment with the ecological values espoused by the settlement. Experiences from various eco-settlements have demonstrated that even when physical infrastructures succeed in nature-friendly solutions, new constraints inevitably emerge. Chief among them is the growing tension between environmental ideals and the realities of social organization. Without adequate infrastructure for education, healthcare, governance, and cultural life, the initial

D. Vidickienė et al., *Human Settlement in the Service Economy Era*, Palgrave Advances in Bioeconomy: Economics and Policies,
https://doi.org/10.1007/978-3-032-19390-2_5

ecological momentum risks stagnation. Over time, communities may find it increasingly challenging to maintain shared decision-making structures and collective coherence, especially in the face of diverging expectations or generational change.

Seeking to make life in the ecovillage more attractive for inhabitants, the intensification strategy is applied. Rather than expanding in size or physical footprint, ecovillages entering the second stage of their evolution seek to deepen the quality and coherence of internal life by investing in the creation of 'living infrastructure'. This includes not only tangible facilities—such as schools, community centres, or cooperative workspaces—but also intangible systems of knowledge-sharing, mutual care, governance, and education that reaffirm the community's founding values. The intensification strategy underscores the importance of transforming eco-settlements into hubs of innovation that can develop solutions more relevant to a new lifestyle oriented to symbiosis with nature and community.

Among the key challenges to the intensification strategy is the development of innovative educational infrastructure, particularly for children, which must intensify the ecological, communal, and developmental ethos of the community. Conventional education systems often fall short in this regard. Lithuanian public schools, for example, face mounting difficulties related to curriculum rigidity, emotional disengagement, and limited responsiveness to environmental and local socio-cultural contexts (European Commission, 2020; OECD, 2022). In response, residents of ecovillages are increasingly seeking alternative educational models that emphasize nature-based, holistic learning approaches, recognizing children as multi-dimensional beings whose development must be nurtured intellectually, emotionally, physically, and spiritually (Šiugždinienė, 2022).

As Haselsteiner (2025) argues, ecovillages serve as experimental platforms for social innovation, providing real-life testing grounds for nature-inspired holistic education, healing, co-living, and participatory governance methods. Innovative infrastructure solutions can increase resilience and empower residents to navigate complex societal and ecological challenges more effectively.

An examination of the practical concerns of ecovillage residents reveals that they are seeking integrated models of living, learning, and coexisting with nature. The best practices of the ecovillage movement underscore the importance of integrating environmental, social, and political dimensions when designing an infrastructure for post-industrial settlements. By fostering application and creation of innovative educational, governance, and care systems, ecovillages reduce dependence on external institutions and enhance self-sufficiency. This does not imply isolation, but rather the cultivation of resilient socio-ecological systems that can exchange with broader society while maintaining internal integrity. In this sense, intensification represents a strategic deepening of ecovillage life: not expanding outward, but rooting inward—into values, into community, and into place.

The practical ways to solve key challenges to the intensification strategy in the post-industrial era are illustrated with three case studies. The first case, Kardokai Nature School in Lithuania, serves as an example of a non-traditional educational infrastructure that fosters children's symbiosis with nature. The second case—sociocracy in ecovillages—exemplifies an innovative governance model in symbiosis between people that serves as social infrastructure, enabling communities to co-create development trajectories grounded in participation, shared values, and collective well-being. Third case—Resonancia Community in Spain—serves as an example of a laboratory of living infrastructure creation through alternative ways that intensifies communal life through experiential learning, and co-creating a temporal living place adapted to the needs of neo-nomads through nature inspired design.

A case study on *Kardokai Nature School* illustrates how value-based, holistic education can serve as an essential component of social infrastructure that deepens community cohesion and long-term viability. Unlike conventional educational institutions, Kardokai Nature School integrates ecological awareness, experiential learning, and emotional development into its pedagogy. This nature-embedded approach not only addresses gaps in formal education but also reinforces shared community values, making the settlement more attractive to families seeking meaningful, alternative education reflecting the current needs of society. Over time, this educational model has gained national visibility, drawing scholars from across Lithuania and transforming the school into a hub for value-aligned learning beyond its immediate locality. In addition to its primary educational function, the school provides a range of supplementary services that support the social metabolism of the community and the quality of relationships and interactions among its members. These include nature-based summer camps for children, experiential learning programmes, and thematic seminars for adults. Together, these offerings position the school as a dynamic platform for lifelong, community-integrated learning.

A case study on *sociocracy in ecovillages* introduces sociocracy and related governance systems as integral components of innovative social infrastructure—the institutional and cultural scaffolding that enables people to live and thrive together symbiotically. In the face of growing societal, ecological, and demographic challenges, communities around the world are increasingly exploring new governance and social infrastructure models that foster collaboration, inclusion, and resilience. Among these, sociocracy, holacracy, and similar organizational systems have emerged as promising frameworks for enabling collective decision-making, shared responsibility, and trust-building within intentional communities, ecovillages, and other types of emerging innovative residential clusters. In contrast to traditional top-down governance models, sociocratic systems centre on local agency and responsiveness, allowing communities to co-create their own development trajectories. They are particularly relevant in contexts seeking to attract residents to eco-settlements by offering not only physical amenities, but also an infrastructure that prioritizes participation, shared values, and well-being. As housing and regional development strategies increasingly shift from purely economic metrics towards quality-of-life indicators, new forms of social infrastructure become indispensable. The design of inclusive governance, meaningful participation, and collaborative problem-solving not only improves co-living but also enhances the attractiveness of eco-settlement as a place to live. The spread and more intensive use of these decentralized self-governance systems not only support democratic governance at the micro level but also offer blueprints for creating infrastructure that encourages more symbiotic relationships between people at larger scales. In this light, sociocracy is not merely a governance tool—it is a strategic asset in the evolution towards resilient and socially cohesive living environments.

The third case introduces the activities of *Resonancia Community*, located in southern Spain, which provides an opportunity to experience living in a non-traditional eco-settlement. Resonancia Community offers an environment for temporary living, experiences, and exploration, providing inspiration and knowledge to help you set up your life's dream. You will not find an established community of permanent residents here, but instead a flexible community of free souls, many of whom practise a neo-nomadic lifestyle. Rather than relying on a fixed blueprint, this ecovillage functions as a laboratory for creating living infrastructure that focuses on co-evolution with the place and its inhabitants. Communal spaces serve as both practical facilities and social technologies, fostering a sense of belonging and creative exchange, enabling one to experience a sense of community without conforming to pre-existing social structures.

The three case studies illustrate how an intensification strategy enhances the internal vitality of human settlements by developing living infrastructure. Together, these cases demonstrate how focusing on building innovative education and governance systems creates an experiential environment that not only supports but also intensifies the spread of a symbiotic lifestyle in society.

Kardokai Nature School: Creating an Infrastructure for Holistic Education and Human–Nature Symbiosis

Shared Values, Shared Action: The Initiation of Kardokai Nature School. The conceptual foundation for the Kardokai Nature School began to take shape between 2010 and 2013, in response to the needs of the growing Kardokai Community. The idea was closely tied to the vision of Raimundas Vaičiūnas, the founder of the Kardokai ecovillage, who actively encouraged like-minded individuals to acquire land in the vicinity and establish a community grounded in shared values. Among the newcomers were numerous families with young children, whose presence underscored the pressing need for accessible, locally based educational provision aligned with the community's ethos. The school's establishment was preceded by nearly a decade of community-led educational activities, primarily in the form of children's camps. These earlier initiatives laid the groundwork for the idea to establish a formally recognized educational institution. This initiative culminated in the official registration of the Kardokai Nature School in 2017, under the jurisdiction of the Kazlų Rūda municipality.

Rethinking Education in Lithuania: The Emergence of Kardokai Nature School as an Important Step in Improving the Infrastructure of Kardokai Ecovillage. Kardokai Nature School was created in response to the shortcomings of traditional education. The formal education system in Lithuania is currently confronting several systemic challenges that impede its effectiveness and inclusivity. Key issues include chronic underfunding, resulting in inadequate resources and infrastructure, particularly in rural areas (Luobikienė, 2018). This financial strain has contributed to a persistent shortage of qualified teachers, particularly in STEM disciplines, resulting in increased class sizes and a corresponding decline in educational quality. Compounding this issue is the aging profile of the teaching workforce: between 2009 and 2018, the number of teachers aged 25 or younger decreased by 71%, while those aged 55 or older increased by 48% (Rutkiene & Kaminskienė, 2023). This demographic imbalance presents a long-term threat to the sustainability of the teaching profession. Moreover, the national curriculum has been criticized for being outdated and overly theoretical, with limited emphasis on practical competencies required in a modern, knowledge-based economy (European Commission, 2020). These deficiencies are reflected in international assessments, where Lithuanian students have consistently underperformed relative to their European peers (OECD, 2022). Additionally, the centralized and rigid governance of the education system has hindered timely reforms and local-level innovation (Urbanovič & Patapas, 2012). Across Lithuania, formal educational institutions face mounting challenges related to curriculum rigidity, emotional disengagement, and a disconnection from local socio-cultural and environmental realities (European Commission, 2020; OECD, 2022). Conventional schools often prioritize academic outcomes over emotional intelligence, creativity, and ecological awareness, which are increasingly recognized as essential competencies in the twenty-first century. In light of these persistent challenges, there is growing recognition of the need for alternative educational models that emphasize personalized learning, community participation, and integration with the natural environment—models that can better respond to contemporary social, ecological, and developmental needs (Šiugždinienė, 2022). Against this backdrop, families who settled in Kardokai village during the early 2010s recognized the need for an alternative educational model grounded in community values and child-centred pedagogy.

In this context, the Kardokai ecovillage community recognized a dual need: first, for an educational institution situated near their residential area; and second, for a learning environment that aligns with their values and worldview—one that diverges from the principles and practices of conventional education. The founders of the ecovillage envisioned an education model that prioritizes ecological consciousness, experiential learning, and holistic human development, embedded within the rhythms of community life and natural systems. This vision catalysed the creation of the Kardokai Nature School as a cornerstone of the village's second stage of evolution, marking a shift from housing and foundational community-building efforts to the intentional construction of values-based educational infrastructure.

Planting the Seeds of Change: How Kardokai Nature School Was Conceived. The conceptual foundation for Kardokai Nature School began to emerge between 2010 and 2013. During this period, community members organized informal children's camps that prioritized exploration, connection with nature, and experiential activities, laying the groundwork for what would later become a formal educational institution.

Before the formal establishment of the Kardokai Nature School, extensive discussions took place concerning the vision of an ideal school. During this deliberative phase, two distinct perspectives surfaced within the community.

One group advocated for a comprehensive, pre-defined vision to be developed prior to initiating any practical activities. This approach emphasized the importance of outlining key elements such as pedagogical content, institutional governance, and infrastructure design before moving forward. In contrast, a second group proposed a more pragmatic path, favouring immediate action over prolonged conceptual debates. They expressed concern that extended discussions on ideal characteristics—whether related to community structure, infrastructure, or broader educational philosophy—might indefinitely delay the implementation process.

By 2017, the efforts to have innovative infrastructure culminated in the official registration of Kardokai Nature School under the jurisdiction of the Kazlų Rūda municipality. This milestone signified a shift from grassroots experimentation to an intentional, structured, and recognized model of education, shaped by years of lived experience and evolving pedagogical insight.

At its core, the school responds to a critical gap left by mainstream education: the need for *nature-based learning* that fosters curiosity, critical thinking, and meaningful engagement with the environment. From its inception, Kardokai Nature School embraced an outdoor-focused pedagogy, encouraging students to spend substantial time in natural settings regardless of weather conditions. Such immersive contact with nature supports cognitive flexibility, physical well-being, and sensory integration—elements often neglected in traditional classroom settings. Outdoor learning is not a supplementary activity but a cornerstone of the school's educational philosophy, wherein children learn through direct interaction with natural elements, seasonal rhythms, and ecological cycles.

Parallel to this nature-oriented approach is the school's commitment to *holistic education*, which seeks to develop the child as a whole person—emotionally, intellectually, socially, physically, and spiritually. The pedagogical model at Kardokai Nature School prioritizes emotional maturity, empathy, creativity, and self-confidence. These values are operationalized through hands-on learning experiences, collaborative projects, and reflective dialogue, aiming to cultivate not just academic competence but personal integrity and social responsibility. The symbolic learning journey—from the question 'Who am I?' to the affirmation 'I am Happiness'—captures the school's deep-rooted emphasis on self-awareness and well-being as educational outcomes in their own right.

> Kardokai Nature School is a safe space for children *to discover, explore, create, and grow*. Knowledge is transmitted lovingly, in a lively way, based on practice and experience. We nurture an emotionally mature, creative, self-confident, and empathetic personality.
>
> We instill a love of self, neighbor, nature, and the world through common moral values. Under the roof of the school, we bring together a sustainable, cohesive, and thriving community of teachers, children, and parents. All this so that our children can walk the path of '*From - who am I? To - I am Happiness.*'
>
> *Source: https://kardokugamtosmokykla.lt/*

Building an Educational Ecosystem in an Organic Way. The founding process of Kardokai Nature School was organic and iterative, grounded in the shared aspiration of creating an inviting and meaningful educational environment for children and the broader community. The initiators adopted a step-by-step approach, allowing the school to evolve in response to emerging needs and contextual realities.

The Kardokai Nature School was officially registered in 2017 under the jurisdiction of the Kazlų Rūda municipality. At its inception, the school enrolled 17 students and appointed a director to oversee the development process. Subsequently, the community embarked on a creative phase that included the design of learning content, the development of physical infrastructure, and the articulation of a coherent institutional vision.

From the outset, the initiators aspired to establish an alternative educational model that diverged from conventional urban schools, particularly in terms of its community dynamics, physical setting, and environmental integration. The geographical location of Kardokai village—situated in a forested area, distant from major roads—provided favourable conditions for realizing these ambitions. The setting allowed for the implementation of nature-inspired educational and infrastructural solutions, the cultivation of an environment in symbiosis with natural ecosystems, and the fostering of a strong place-based identity.

The educational model adopted by Kardokai Nature School was underpinned by a value-based framework that integrates moral development, self-awareness, ecological consciousness, and social responsibility. The school community, comprising educators, learners, and parents, collaborates to cultivate a sustainable and cohesive learning environment. This community is founded on shared ethical principles, with the goal of cultivating a profound respect for oneself, others, nature, and the broader world.

The school aspires to nurture learners who embody creativity, critical thinking, integrity, and compassion. By situating educational processes within the natural environment, the school fosters a sense of interconnectedness between human development and ecological sustainability. This integration is considered essential for shaping socially responsible and environmentally conscious individuals who can contribute to both personal and societal well-being.

Although the initial phase of the school's establishment was characterized by a sense of joy and creative enthusiasm, the process also necessitated a critical refinement of the original concept. The transition from visionary ideals to operational realities required substantial effort in defining and aligning the school's pedagogical and organizational principles.

Kardokai Nature School was conceived as a distinctive educational initiative, drawing inspiration from established pedagogical paradigms, particularly those aligned with humanistic educational philosophy. The development of the school's conceptual framework was organized as a participatory process involving diverse stakeholders, including members of the school administration, parents of enrolled students, and other members of the Kardokai Community with a vested interest in education. The co-creation of the school's foundational vision spanned approximately two to three years, during which consensus was gradually achieved.

Initially, the school's pedagogical practices emphasized the integration of natural elements into the learning process. However, over time, the community recognized that despite these efforts, the school's approach remained insufficiently differentiated from that of conventional educational institutions. This realization prompted a renewed effort to refine and deepen the school's conceptual identity, leading to a more coherent and purpose-driven educational model.

The overarching aim of Kardokai Nature School is the holistic development of individuals who are both conscious and content—learners equipped not only with cognitive competencies but also with emotional intelligence and social responsibility. The school places a strong emphasis on fostering cooperation, co-creation, and a vibrant sense of community. It envisions itself as a dynamic learning community grounded in core values such as mutual respect, awareness, responsibility, generosity, compassion, joy, and intellectual curiosity.

Functioning as a collaborative ecosystem, the school promotes reciprocal learning among students, educators, and parents. Knowledge transmission is characterized by experiential, interactive methods that emphasize moral development and encourage reflective, ethically grounded thinking. Through this approach, Kardokai Nature School seeks to cultivate individuals capable of contributing meaningfully to both their immediate communities and the broader social and ecological systems in which they are embedded.

Educators who transitioned to teaching at Kardokai Nature School after prior experience in conventional educational institutions have reported a markedly different professional and emotional experience. Notably, they observed the absence of long-term occupational fatigue commonly associated with traditional school environments. The pedagogical rhythm at Kardokai Nature School is perceived as more balanced and less constrained by the pressures of rigid schedules or institutional routines, thereby reducing stress and the sense of constant urgency.

Parents, children, and teachers are members of the school community. The interpersonal climate within the school community is characterized by supportive and collegial relationships. Teachers, students, and parents collectively contribute to a school culture that fosters mutual respect, emotional safety, and a strong sense of belonging. This communal atmosphere is frequently described by members as resembling that of an extended family, emphasizing cohesion, empathy, and shared responsibility in the educational process.

Specific challenges arose during the design and construction of the school's physical infrastructure. At its inception, Kardokai Nature School consisted of a single building that accommodated both pre-school and primary-level children, as the initial enrolment consisted of only 17 pupils. From the outset, the school adopted an outdoor-based educational model, wherein both instructional and recreational activities were conducted predominantly in natural settings. Regardless of weather conditions, children were consistently encouraged to engage in play, exploration, and learning in outdoor environments. This approach fostered a dynamic and multisensory learning experience, offering conditions that stimulated holistic cognitive, emotional, and physical development in ways that differ markedly from those found in conventional classroom settings.

After the first year of operation, the need for differentiated spaces became apparent, resulting in the separation of pre-school and primary school facilities. Simultaneously, the administration recognized the practical limitations of maintaining exclusively outdoor classes throughout the year, particularly during colder seasons. This prompted the search for an alternative solution that would ensure continuity of learning activities in indoor environments when necessary.

In its second year, the school secured a rental agreement for a residential property situated near the Kardokai community, which included approximately 2–3 hectares of land. The contract, signed in 2018, provided the spatial foundation for further growth. As student enrolment increased annually, the school faced a shortage of infrastructure. In response, the administration initiated a development project in 2019 to construct modular, subject-specific learning spaces—referred to as 'mobile classrooms'. This infrastructure expansion was supported by the Kazlų Rūda Local Action Group (LAG), reflecting an important example of community-based educational development through rural partnership frameworks.

A decision-making board supports the governance of the school, although final authority resides with the three founding members. Parental involvement is actively encouraged, with parents participating in discussions and contributing to some aspects of the decision-making process, thereby reinforcing the school's emphasis on community engagement and participatory governance.

After several years of development through the collaborative efforts of all stakeholders, the mission of Kardokai Nature School is articulated through three interrelated pillars that reflect its holistic and value-oriented educational philosophy:

1. *Community.* The school functions as an inclusive and nurturing environment, fostering a strong sense of belonging, emotional security, and shared responsibility among all stakeholders, including students, parents, and educators. The aim is to support the comprehensive development of each individual while cultivating cohesive social ties and community resilience.
2. *Nature.* Environmental education constitutes a core element of the curriculum. Students engage in systematic observation and interac-

tion with the natural world, thereby internalizing a sense of ecological interconnectedness. The curriculum emphasizes the cultivation of environmental stewardship, curiosity, and ecological literacy throughout the academic year, reinforcing the principle that learners are integral components of the broader ecosystem.

3. *Human Development.* The pedagogical approach centres on the experiential cultivation of intellectual, emotional, physical, and spiritual capacities. Learning is guided by a commitment to respect, empathy, and care for both the individual and the environment. Educators play a facilitative role, supporting each child's innate curiosity and tailoring learning experiences to their developmental needs, thereby encouraging self-awareness and self-actualization (Kardokai Nature School, 2025).

Through the integration of these three pillars, Kardokai Nature School presents a model of holistic education that emphasizes community engagement, ecological consciousness, and personal development. Its pedagogical framework is grounded in lived experience, moral and ethical education, and nature-based learning, with the overarching goal of nurturing empathetic, confident, and environmentally responsible individuals.

Shifting to the Specialization Strategy. From the time the school was established in 2017, with 17 scholars in total, it has grown to have 130 scholars and 40 teachers (including remote and physical scholars) by 2025. The school population is still growing. Additionally, the school administration is willing to have approximately 100 scholars attend classes in person. Now, 60 scholars are physically attending this school. There are up to seven scholars in each class. The school is a primary school and will seek secondary school status.

Kardokai Nature School has gradually evolved into a multifaceted educational ecosystem that combines holistic pedagogy with a diverse range of service offerings. Four types of services are provided at the school:

1. *Kindergarten Programme.* The kindergarten at Kardokai Nature School is one of the first in Lithuania to apply a holistic approach to early childhood education. Set within a natural and community-integrated environment, this programme places significant emphasis on outdoor experiential learning. Young children engage in activities that support cognitive, emotional, and social development

through contact with nature, practical tasks, and community interaction.

2. *Primary and Secondary Schooling (Grades 1–12).* Kardokai Nature School offers a comprehensive general education curriculum spanning grades 1 through 12, delivered through both contact-based and family education formats. Learning is situated in a natural environment and driven by an experiential and value-oriented pedagogy. The curriculum is intentionally designed to address the intellectual, emotional, physical, and spiritual aspects of the learner, supported by the school's emphasis on moral values, environmental stewardship, and social responsibility. Students are treated as unique individuals with distinct needs and talents. The school promotes autonomy, creativity, and critical thinking by enabling learners to explore their interests and engage in real-world problem-solving projects. Educators play the role of mentors rather than traditional authority figures, fostering learning relationships based on trust, empathy, and mutual respect. The schooling experience aims to produce responsible, reflective individuals who understand their roles within the natural world and broader society.
3. *Children's Camps.* The seasonal camps organized by Kardokai Nature School offer children immersive experiences that combine recreation, personal development, and environmental education. These camps are structured around outdoor activities such as hiking, adventure games, teamwork exercises, and creative workshops, aiming to reconnect children with nature and support the development of non-cognitive skills. These short-term but intensive programmes contribute to the long-term goals of the school by reinforcing values such as cooperation, responsibility, ecological consciousness, and community engagement.
4. *Experiential Education Programmes for Children and Adults.* Kardokai Nature School also offers a variety of *experiential education modules*, which take place both within the school's premises and in the surrounding forests. These programmes are designed for both children (aged 6–12) and adults, aiming to deepen participants' connections with nature through sensory engagement, practical skills, and guided reflection. These sessions integrate curriculum-based content with nature immersion, fostering teamwork, self-confidence, environmental awareness, and creativity. All educational experiences, whether aimed at children or adults, seek to reinvigo-

rate the human capacity for curiosity, empathy, and self-knowledge. They are also designed to facilitate informal learning within the community and strengthen bonds among participants.

Parents with their children are free to choose one of the options—to participate in the educational process physically or to opt for service-education within the family. Parents with children from nearby locations typically choose to attend school in person. Other families from all over Lithuania choose to educate their children at home by utilizing the services of Kardokai Nature School. Families choose this type of learning for their children for various reasons, including large distances, the child's character or manner, negative experiences in previous schools (such as bullying), and fatigue. Typically, this type of learning yields better results.

The school also organizes seminar series and experiential days. In addition to the school community, external people are invited to participate in the workshops. The aim is to enhance teaching quality, support newcomers, and foster communication and cooperation.

In response to the COVID-19 pandemic, the school pioneered a distance learning programme that enabled families across Lithuania to engage with Kardokai's educational model. Over one hundred families from across Lithuania expressed interest in this service, enabling the school to operate as a national-level educational provider. The distance learning services finally transformed the school into a nationally recognized institution, offering both remote and in-person learning that aligns with ecological and humanistic principles.

The efforts of the school community have shifted the evolution of Kardokai ecovillage towards a specialization strategy. Through the expansion and diversification of transformative educational services, the school has consolidated its role not only as an educational institution for children but also as a centre for lifelong and community-based learning. The gradual development of the pedagogical, social, and spatial character of the school has created an infrastructure that enables it to become a leading provider of innovative services in Lithuania.

The Kardokai Nature School is situated on approximately 2–3 hectares of land in a rural setting, surrounded by forest. This natural environment provides a foundational context for the school's educational philosophy, which emphasizes ecological integration and experiential learning. The campus comprises a variety of purpose-built structures, including an administrative building, five to seven subject-specific modular classrooms—often referred to as 'mobile classrooms'—a large communal building for collective gatherings and events, and a separate facility dedicated to pre-school education. The spatial organization of these structures reflects a decentralized layout, with most buildings located at a distance from one another to maintain an open, nature-integrated environment.

Ample outdoor spaces are interspersed throughout the campus, offering diverse opportunities for children to engage in play, exploration, and learning in natural settings. These open-air environments serve as extensions of the classroom, supporting the school's commitment to nature-based, holistic education. The school grounds are secured through a long-term rental agreement, established in 2018 for a 20-year term, ensuring stability for continued development and use.

The school's geographical context offers conditions conducive to both in-person and remote educational activities. Although high-speed internet connectivity is limited, basic internet access is available, enabling the implementation of distance learning when necessary.

To address the accessibility needs of students residing in other cities or towns, the school provides organized transportation services. School buses operate on predefined routes, collecting students from designated locations in the morning and returning them to the exact locations after school hours.

Members of the Kardokai Nature School community characterize the offered infrastructure facilities as highly favourable for educational and developmental purposes. It is valued for its high quality of life, healthy and peaceful surroundings, and close relationship with the natural environment.

Sociocracy as Innovative Social Infrastructure for Symbiotic Co-living in Eco-Settlements

Residents of newly established ecovillages often face a shortage of effective tools and frameworks to guide community-building processes. Without clear structures for communication, decision-making, and conflict resolution, everyday collaboration can become strained or inefficient. This lack of supportive social infrastructure can hinder the development of shared identity, trust, and long-term cohesion within eco-settlements.

Even though sociocracy is not a silver bullet, in the context of ecovillages development, it might present a promising solution to one of the most persistent challenges: balancing participatory inclusivity with operational efficiency. Many intentional communities adopt egalitarian structures and consensus decision-making to reflect their values of mutual respect and equality. However, consensus, while being idealistic, can lead to decision paralysis, especially when communities grow or when members lack facilitation training (Christian, 2003). Sociocracy mitigates this problem by replacing unanimity with consent-based decision-making, where proposals move forward unless someone has a reasoned and paramount objection. This ensures that the process remains inclusive without sacrificing momentum. The time saved in meetings, combined with a continued emphasis on listening and iteration, makes sociocracy particularly suitable for ecovillages that need to balance relational harmony with timely action and seek symbiotic relationships within them (Buck & Villines, 2007).

Another key problem sociocracy addresses is the fragmentation of responsibilities and ambiguity in governance roles, which often undermine accountability in informal or overly horizontal communities. Ecovillages frequently struggle with underdefined authority structures that lead to burnout, miscommunication, or power imbalances masked by an appearance of equality. Sociocracy introduces clearly defined roles, domain-based circles, and structured processes for electing individuals to operational tasks. These mechanisms provide the clarity necessary for distributed leadership, while maintaining checks through role reviews and feedback loops (Sociocracy For All, n.d.). According to Romme (1995), such structuring allows organizations to preserve equivalence in voice while building functional specialization, which enhances coordination and organizational learning. This structural coherence is essential for ecovillages aiming to scale or engage with external partners and governance systems.

Finally, sociocracy supports the development of a resilient social infrastructure, which is often the Achilles' heel of otherwise successful ecovillage initiatives. While physical infrastructure (e.g., energy, housing, food systems) may be ecological and self-sustaining, many communities face internal conflict, emotional exhaustion, or informal hierarchies that remain unacknowledged. Sociocracy might be a tool for transparent communication, a cadence for meetings, and institutional memory through linked circles and documented policy. It creates opportunities for members to engage in their capacity while ensuring that voices are heard through delegation and representation. In doing so, it fosters a culture of shared governance, adaptive feedback, and constructive dissent—qualities that not only solve internal problems but enable the community to evolve without losing coherence (Romme, 1995; Biørn-Hansen & Håkansson, 2018). As such, sociocracy addresses the often overlooked but critical dimension of social ecology: how people govern themselves and co-create meaning over time.

However, even ecovillages without intentionally applying sociocracy establish somewhat similar practices on symbiotic approaches and engage communities in co-living and co-creation activities. Keuruu ecovillage in Finland employs 'Heart circle' as a community strengthening tool, where once a week the ecovillage residents gather together to express their emotions and feelings. The basic idea of the 'Heart Circle' is listening to others in an authentic way, cultivating a respectful attitude towards everybody, talking about ones feelings and full confidentiality (Palojärvi, 2013).

The ZEGG Forum is another example of structured group ritual developed in the ZEGG (Center for Experimental Cultural Design) ecovillage (Germany) to foster transparency, emotional honesty, and trust within communities. Designed to support deep communication, the Forum creates a safe space where individuals can express their inner experiences—including thoughts, feelings, and motivations—in front of others. Participants gather in a circle, and one person—the presenter—steps into the centre to share authentically, using both verbal and non-verbal expression. Their aim is not performance but self-revelation, guided by the principle that 'there is nothing bad or wrong inside me'. Facilitated by trained assistants, the ritual includes feedback rounds ('mirrors'), where others reflect what they observed in the presenter. These reflections are not evaluations but offerings that support self-awareness and group cohesion. The forum is practised regularly in small groups (15–35 members), and its continuity fosters long-term trust, emotional resilience, and collective learning (Meyer-Stoll & Ecker, 2013).

ZEGG also integrates the Forum into larger thematic events and intensive community gatherings. Alongside other tools such as Nonviolent Communication, communal meals, seasonal festivals, and shared work, the Forum serves as a cornerstone of co-creation and social innovation—helping the community navigate conflict, build mutual understanding, and sustain vibrant, cooperative living (Meyer-Stoll & Ecker, 2013).

Hessel Tabor (2024) carried explicit analysis on three Dutch ecovillages (Luna, Terra, Nova) and agreed that the level of sociocracy principles varies, and communities implement not all principles to its greatest extent. Tabor's (2024) study revealed four key challenges in how Dutch ecovillages apply sociocracy. While consent-based decision-making is generally practised, communities face persistent ambiguity around what qualifies as a valid objection, largely due to the broad and interpretive nature of their mission statements, which complicates consistent evaluation—a problem noted by Christian (2012, 2023). Emotional tensions were also common during decision-making, not necessarily due to sociocracy itself, but rather the lack of adequate training and the method's tendency to expose underlying interpersonal dynamics (Buck & Endenburg, 2012; March & Simon, 1993; Hamilton & Gioia, 2010). Furthermore, most ecovillages did not fully implement the hierarchical circle structure central to SCM, with General Circles either missing or stripped of decision-making authority, reflecting a cultural resistance to hierarchy despite its functional abstraction in sociocracy. Finally, the double link principle—vital for feedback and power balance between circles—was inconsistently or not at all applied, often due to the perception that elected representatives are burdensome or unnecessary, even though their absence undermines accountability and contradicts the communities' stated non-hierarchical ideals (Tabor, 2024). The findings suggest that adaptations to sociocracy in Dutch ecovillages are driven more by cultural norms and practical limitations than by misunderstanding of the method—offering a nuanced understanding of how governance ideals are negotiated in intentional communities (Tabor, 2024). However, this suggests that sociocracy is a useful tool when it is applied systematically, and it follows methodologies of the tool.

Sociocracy as a Management System and Form of Governance. Sociocracy is a governance system grounded in principles of equivalence, transparency, and effectiveness, designed to ensure that all members of an organization or community have a voice in decision-making. The term derives from the Latin *socius* (companion) and the Greek *kratein* (to rule), literally meaning *rule by the companions.* The intellectual origins of sociocracy trace back to Auguste Comte, the nineteenth-century French philosopher, who proposed a society governed by scientific reasoning and ethical cooperation rather than coercion or majority rule (Comte, 1851). However, the modern sociocratic method was first practically developed by Kees Boeke, a Dutch Quaker and educator, in the mid-twentieth century. Influenced by both Quaker consensus and pacifist ideals, Boeke implemented sociocratic principles in his school, *Werkplaats Kindergemeenschap*, promoting inclusive and respectful participation (Buck & Villines, 2007; Czekaj et al., 2020).

The system was later formalized and expanded by Gerard Endenburg, who adapted sociocracy for organizational management in the 1970s.

Endenburg (1998) integrated cybernetic principles and system thinking of creating what is now known as the Sociocratic Circle-Organization Method (SCM), emphasizing circular structures, double-linking, sociocratic elections, and consent-based decision-making. In this SCM model, power is distributed horizontally through semi-autonomous circles that govern specific domains, connected via roles that link each level of decision-making. Rather than seeking unanimity or majority vote, decisions are made by consent, meaning that no member has a reasoned and paramount objection. Sociocracy has since gained international recognition as a dynamic governance model that enhances both individual agency and collective intelligence, and it is increasingly applied in cooperatives, non-profits, and intentional communities, particularly ecovillages, where relational accountability and resilience are core values (Romme, 1995; Romme, 2019; Christian, 2003, 2013).

Sociocracy Defining Elements. A defining structural feature of sociocracy is its use of nested circles—semi-autonomous groups responsible for specific domains of work or governance. These circles are double-linked, meaning that each one sends both an operational leader and an elected representative to the next-higher circle, ensuring two-way communication and feedback. This architecture balances autonomy and coordination, allowing decisions to be made at the most relevant level while preserving systemic coherence. Inspired by principles from cybernetics and systems theory, this circular design enables distributed authority and adaptability in complex environments. Romme (1995) emphasizes that such structural innovations enable sociocracy to function as a 'learning organization', where coordination is achieved without rigid hierarchy (Fig. 5.1).

Another element—sociocratic elections are a cornerstone of distributed governance, ensuring that roles are filled through a transparent, participatory, and fair process that fosters both legitimacy and trust. These elections are a consent-based method for assigning individuals to roles within an organization, grounded in transparency, equality, and shared responsibility. The process begins with defining or reaffirming the role description, including its purpose, duration, and evaluation criteria. Each circle member then submits a written nomination, followed by a round where nominators explain their choices in relation to the role's needs. After hearing all arguments, members are invited to adjust their nominations, and the facilitator proposes a candidate based on the discussion. A consent round follows, where each member, including the nominee (last), is asked whether they consent. If objections arise, the circle addresses them or restarts the

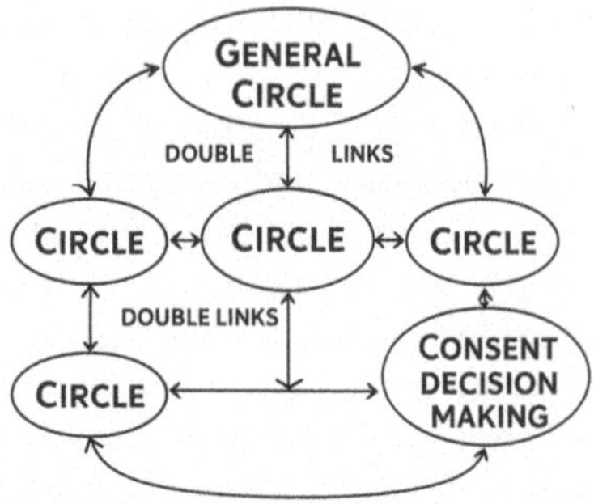

Fig. 5.1 Circular governance in sociocracy: Distributed authority through nested and linked circles. (Source: Romme, G. (1995))

process. This structured dialogue ensures that the selected person is well-suited and accepted by peers. Sociocratic elections build trust and psychological safety, promoting a sense of ownership and accountability, while also allowing for regular review and renewal through term limits and performance feedback (Buck & Villines, 2007; Sociocratisch Centrum Nederland, 2020).

At the core of sociocracy lies the principle of consent-based decision-making, which departs from traditional governance models based on majority voting. In sociocratic practice, a decision is adopted when no participant has a 'paramount and reasoned objection', rather than requiring full consensus or a majority threshold. This mechanism supports both inclusivity and efficiency, making it particularly attractive for organizations and communities that value participation without sacrificing functionality. Consent ensures that each voice is respected and integrated, thus fostering a high level of commitment to collective decisions. Buck and Villines (2007) highlight that this approach contributes to a culture of psychological safety, responsiveness, and mutual accountability, making it well-suited for intentional communities, cooperatives, and agile teams.

Consent decision-making matters in sociocracy, because, first, it allows the group to make decisions efficiently, avoiding endless deliberation; second, it preserves minority concerns without stalling the group; third, it is well-suited for adaptive, living systems like ecovillages, where psychological safety and flexibility are vital. As Romme (1995) notes, sociocracy fosters 'dynamic governance', where feedback and dialogue enhance both organizational effectiveness and individual inclusion.

Equally important are the mechanisms for transparency, role clarity, and ongoing evaluation. Sociocratic organizations define roles and responsibilities explicitly and conduct regular reviews of both policies and individual roles to adapt to changing needs. These institutional practices are not just procedural; they are cultural tools that nurture cooperation, alignment, and reflective practice. As Romme (1995) notes, sociocracy represents not only a set of techniques but a philosophy of organizing that integrates democratic values with operational effectiveness.

When compared to consensus decision-making, commonly used in activist networks and ecovillages, sociocracy provides a more structured and scalable approach to collective governance. Consensus often demands unanimity, which can lead to decision paralysis or domination by those unwilling to compromise. Sociocracy, by using consent rather than consensus, allows decisions to move forward as long as no 'reasoned objection' is raised, fostering both forward momentum and psychological safety (Buck & Villines, 2007). In addition, sociocracy embeds clear role differentiation, evaluation mechanisms, and structured meeting formats—components often missing in more informal consensus models. While both systems value inclusivity, sociocracy achieves it through systematization, making it more sustainable in larger or more complex organizational environments.

In recent years, holacracy has emerged as a contemporary alternative to both sociocracy and hierarchical governance. Like sociocracy, holacracy promotes distributed authority and circle-based decision-making. However, it is more rule-bound and prescriptive, emphasizing operational roles and tactical meetings over social cohesion and relational dynamics (Robertson, 2015). Holacracy is frequently adopted in tech companies and startups, where clarity of task execution and accountability are paramount. In contrast, sociocracy maintains a softer, more human-centred orientation, grounded in the values of community, mutual respect, and dialogue. It offers more flexibility in tailoring governance to cultural and relational contexts, especially in ecovillages or cooperatives where values alignment and shared purpose are as critical as efficiency. Therefore, while holacracy and sociocracy share systemic roots, their practical implementations reflect different priorities and social assumptions.

Sociocracy distinguishes itself from traditional hierarchical governance through its commitment to distributed authority, consent-based decision-making, and cyclical organizational structures. In contrast to conventional top-down management, where decisions flow unilaterally from executives to subordinates, sociocracy operates through semi-autonomous circles with two-way linking between levels of decision-making. This structure allows for more responsive, context-sensitive governance, reducing bottlenecks and enhancing employee or member engagement (Romme, 1995). While traditional hierarchies often rely on positional authority and compliance, sociocracy emphasizes equivalence—the idea that all voices hold weight in policy formation, regardless of formal status. This shift from control to participation makes sociocracy particularly attractive in mission-driven organizations, cooperatives, and intentional communities (Table 5.1).

When to Apply Sociocracy and Similar Innovative Infrastructures? Sociocracy is most useful to employ when an ecovillage reaches a level of complexity that renders informal or consensus-based governance ineffective or overly time-consuming. This typically occurs when a community grows beyond a handful of core members and begins to manage multiple domains of activity—such as housing, food production, education, and community outreach. At this point, the need for coordination, accountability, and efficient decision-making becomes critical. Sociocracy offers a governance model that is both systematic and human-centred, capable of handling organizational complexity while preserving community values of inclusion, autonomy, and shared power (Romme, 1995). Its circle structure and role differentiation provide clarity in how decisions are made and who is responsible for what, reducing confusion, duplication of effort, and emotional strain.

Crucially, sociocracy is not only a framework for new ecovillages but can be successfully implemented in existing communities seeking to overcome governance fatigue or organizational stagnation. In many mature ecovillages, founding members may feel overburdened by informal leadership roles, while newer members may struggle to find entry points into meaningful participation. Sociocracy can be introduced as a regenerative intervention, offering a shared vocabulary and structure for re-evaluating internal governance in a non-confrontational way. Its modular and scalable design allows communities to start small—perhaps by applying sociocratic methods within one working group or for a specific project—and then expand incrementally. This phased adoption lowers resistance to change and enables cultural adaptation, especially when facilitated with appropriate training and reflection processes (Buck & Villines, 2007).

Moreover, sociocracy proves most valuable when a community seeks to align ecological systems thinking with social systems thinking—an ambition increasingly common in ecovillage movements. Just as permaculture designs for energy and nutrient flow, sociocracy designs for information

Table 5.1 Key features of alternative and traditional governance models

Feature	*Sociocracy*	*Consensus*	*Holacracy*	*Traditional Hierarchy*
Decision-making method	Consent (no paramount objections)	Unanimous agreement	Consent for governance; roles execute tasks autonomously	Top-down; authority-based decisions
Governance structure	Nested, double-linked circles	Flat or loosely structured	Circle-based roles and domains	Rigid vertical hierarchy
Authority distribution	Decentralized, dynamic, with double-linking	Fully horizontal, collective authority	Distributed by roles, structured authority through constitution	Centralized, positional authority
Scalability	High (supports complex organizations and communities)	Limited (effective mostly in small or aligned groups)	High (designed for large, fast-moving organizations)	Very high (used in corporations, governments)
Flexibility and adaptability	Moderate–high; adaptable to social and cultural contexts	High in values, low in structure	Moderate; structured but rigid in practice	Low; changes slow and often bureaucratic
Conflict handling	Objections integrated into dialogue; evaluated for relevance	Often struggles with persistent dissent	Process-driven, structured feedback loops	Typically managed by superiors; low procedural input
Role clarity and evaluation	Clear roles; regular reviews and elections	Often informal or emergent roles	Highly specified roles and domains	Defined by job descriptions and reporting lines
Values orientation	Equality, transparency, collaboration	Equality, inclusivity, deep dialogue	Efficiency, autonomy, purpose alignment	Efficiency, control, predictability
Context suitability	Ecovillages, cooperatives, mission-aligned organizations	Small activist groups, intentional communities	Startups, tech firms, agile business environments	Corporations, government bodies, traditional institutions

Source: Prepared by authors, based on Romme, G. (1995) and Robertson, (2015)

and influence flow and symbiosis, ensuring that feedback circulates throughout the system and that decisions are made where the relevant knowledge resides. This not only enhances community resilience but also supports long-term sustainability by making governance a living, adaptive process rather than a fixed structure. As Biørn-Hansen and Håkansson (2018) notes, ecovillages that incorporate flexible, yet robust governance systems are better positioned to integrate newcomers, resolve conflicts, and maintain coherence across changing circumstances. Sociocracy thus becomes not just a governance method, but a social technology for deep adaptation, appropriate at any stage of community development.

In conclusion, sociocracy can be understood not merely as a governance tool but as a vital component of social infrastructure within ecovillages. As communities grow and evolve, informal consensus mechanisms often prove insufficient for managing complexity, particularly when interpersonal disagreements hinder progress. Sociocracy provides a structured yet flexible framework that supports inclusive participation, role clarity, and consent-based decision-making—foundational elements for sustainable collective action. In the second stage of ecovillage development, where strategic coordination becomes critical, sociocracy enables groups to move beyond idealistic agreement towards functional governance. Institutionalizing dialogue, symbiotic relationships, accountability, and feedback helps communities navigate the tensions of diversity and ensures that their social systems can support long-term ecological and cultural goals.

Valley of Sensations of the Resonancia Community: A Living Laboratory for Ecovillage Infrastructure Innovation

Nestled in the Alpujarra region of southern Spain, near the village of Yátor, the Resonancia Community was established in 2000 by German artist and craftsman Achim Burkard (2025). Inspired by his prior endeavours—such as the 'Wild Rose' Ecovillage in Germany and the 'Casa el Morisco' retreat centre in Málaga—Burkard envisioned a place where individuals could engage in creative, communal living deeply intertwined with nature. The Resonancia Community welcomes digital nomads,[1] artists, facilitators, and

[1] A digital nomad is *a person who travels freely while working remotely* using information and communications technology such as the Internet (Haider, 2023).

seekers of alternative lifestyles. The community emphasizes trust, self-responsibility, and deep interpersonal resonance, encouraging members to co-create their experiences without rigid structures or expectations (Resonancia Community, 2025).

Distinct from traditional ecovillages, Valle de Sensaciones operates without a permanent resident community, allowing for a fluid and dynamic exploration of communal living. This approach facilitates a unique environment where temporary participants co-create the community experience, fostering adaptability and continuous innovation (Sensaciones, 2025).

The settlement was designed as a camp with infrastructure adapted for short-term stays. Central to the valley's ethos is the concept of 'living infrastructure', where shelter and other facilities are constructed using natural materials like clay, wood, and stone, harmonizing with the surrounding environment. These constructions not only serve functional purposes but also act as artistic expressions, embodying the integration of ecological design and aesthetic creativity (SPACES Archives, 2025).

Over time, it has become evident that the vitality of the camp depends on the participation of individuals committed to medium- or long-term engagement, who are prepared to assume responsibilities and provide a consistent human presence. However, the camp infrastructure is not designed to support long-term residency, and the nearby village of Yátor offers no rental housing options. In response to these limitations, a privately initiated community housing project was established in the village: the 'Casa de Resonancia' Coliving. As a result, the Resonancia Community unites two legally independent but deeply connected projects: the non-profit Ecovillage Laboratory, managed by the Association 'Valle de Sensaciones' (Valley of Sensations), and the privately managed Coliving Hub, 'Casa de Resonancia'. Both offer complementary ways of engaging with conscious, community-based living in a rural Andalusian setting. Clear legal separation ensures sustainability while allowing shared vision and collaboration to thrive.

Resonancia is deeply integrated into the village of Yátor. Residents of the Resonancia Hub are encouraged to engage with local neighbours, participate in village life with respect for local cultural norms, and foster mutual appreciation and shared experiences.

This place is not defined by architecture or infrastructure alone, but by the lived intensity of temporary inhabitants who pass through and transform it in the process. The community, ever in flux, resists static models. Instead, it explores what it means to belong without possessing, to dwell without permanence, and to live in ways that remain deeply rooted in place, presence, and people.

At its core, the project helps to solve the challenges to the intensification strategy of the post-industrial era, which aims to enhance the quality of life by integrating social and physical infrastructure systems. Here, the concept of infrastructure extends beyond daily utilities—it encompasses shared spaces for expression, learning, and co-creation that offer opportunities to live in a community without conforming to pre-existing social structures.

The experience accumulated in the ecovillage offers valuable insights into the development of human settlements oriented towards a **neo-nomadic lifestyle**.

Seeds of Renewal: How the Valley of Sensations Was Imagined into Being. The initiative to establish and regenerate the Valley of Sensations Ecovillage originated from a collective of visionaries, artists, and ecological thinkers who sought to create a living laboratory where infrastructure is not merely functional but deeply interwoven with environmental consciousness, communal experimentation, and holistic well-being. This grassroots initiative did not emerge from institutional planning but from a shared desire to reimagine human settlements as spaces of intentional living, guided by alternative values such as resilience, self-sufficiency, and sensory connection to the environment.

The regeneration strategy was shaped by both the physical limits and the sensory potential of the site, where conventional engineering solutions had to adapt to the hilly terrain and natural constraints. These challenges fostered innovation: structures were built using natural materials, water and energy cycles were closed-looped, and communal systems for food, knowledge, and cultural exchange became central features of the settlement.

This initiative exemplifies a model where infrastructure development is community-driven and continuously refined through iterative practices and feedback from residents. The focus is on the symbiosis of soft (social) and hard (technical) infrastructures, ensuring the ecovillage remains adaptive to demographic and informational flows. By learning from global best practices—yet firmly rooted in the local context—the Valley of Sensations not only offers improved living standards but redefines what constitutes 'quality of life' in a post-industrial settlement. The village's approach demonstrates how grassroots settlement regeneration can serve as a model which goes beyond sustainable lifestyle and is embedded in local identity, sensory richness, and ecological balance.

From Soil to Soul: Designing a Living-Lab-Based Ecovillage. The Valley of Sensations ecovillage, as presented by Resonancia Community, represents a living laboratory where infrastructure is approached not as a physical necessity but as a means of enhancing the human experience in profound and regenerative ways. Within the intensification strategy framework, which aims to improve the quality of life by optimizing social and physical infrastructure, this settlement presents an innovative case for symbiotic lifestyle. The ecovillage offers a deliberate reimagining of how people, place, and systems interact to generate vitality, well-being, and sustainability. Conceptually, the project aligns with movements such as the Global Ecovillage Network (GEN), permaculture principles as articulated by David Holmgren (2002) and Bill Mollison (1988), and elements of bioregionalism. However, it avoids a rigid template.

The design process in Resonancia is treated as a constant inquiry rather than a fixed pre-existing structure. The ecovillage design was developed through a decentralized, iterative, and participatory process. Workshops, retreats, and immersion events served as both planning forums and testing grounds. The village engaged a wide array of contributors—from architects and permaculture designers to artists and spiritual practitioners. This ensured that the design incorporated diverse expertise and cultural perspectives.

Crucially, the infrastructure design was treated as an evolving metabolic system. This aligns closely with the intensification strategy: rather than building for maximum capacity from the outset, infrastructure was developed gradually, monitoring its effects on community metabolism, and thus solving the imperfections of a place as a limiting factor. For example, the introduction of compost toilets, solar dryers, and biogas digesters was phased in through cycles of use, feedback, and refinement. This allowed the community to measure which interventions led to greater energy flow efficiency, health improvements, or social cohesion, and adjust accordingly.

The physical limitations of the site—such as water table levels, slope gradients, and soil types—guided the specificity of required infrastructure scale and typology. Rather than trying to overcome the limits of a place through industrial solutions, the community embraced them, seeing constraints as a design opportunity to innovate low-tech, place-responsive systems. Informational resources, such as documentation from other ecovillages and networks, were used extensively to avoid reinventing the wheel.

Communication technologies also played a vital role. Online collaborative platforms allowed for asynchronous design collaboration, while documentation of practices was continuously refined and shared with the broader community and global networks. Inhabitants' perceptions and feedback were treated as vital data points for evaluating and revising the infrastructure strategy, fostering a real-time adaptive planning model.

Overall, the Valley of Sensations serves as a compelling case for the intensification strategy in alternative settlements. Its design phase illustrates how physical infrastructure, social cohesion, and environmental synergy can be jointly pursued to enhance the metabolism and attractiveness of a place, to diminish its limiting attribute. Rather than imposing a predefined urban model, the settlement evolves organically through a careful balance of vision, experimentation, and responsiveness to the constraints and gifts of its landscape. This participatory and iterative approach allows the community to remain resilient, vibrant, and deeply rooted in both place and purpose via changing infrastructure composition and design.

Designing Infrastructure to Fulfil Both Utilitarian Functions and Catalyse Transformative Social Experiences. The Valley of Sensations seeks to accelerate the metabolism of human-environment interactions while acknowledging and adapting to the place's constraints. At the core of Valley of Sensations' strategic actions are the creation of infrastructure that serves both utilitarian and transformative purposes. Far from being a backdrop to human activity, the wild, rugged terrain of the valley plays an important role in shaping the experience of living. The site itself is remote and untamed—a narrow basin cradled by steep hills, laced with springs and shaded by Mediterranean forest. The land imposes limits: there is no road access to the valley floor, no reliable utilities, and no pre-existing infrastructure. And yet, it is precisely these constraints that enable new ways of life to take form.

The village's founders explicitly conceptualize their location as a 'laboratory' for researching and constructing life-support systems that are both symbiotic and sensorially rich. This 'laboratory' includes permanent and semi-permanent shelters, experimental gardens, bio-construction workshops, and open-air social spaces. These are not traditional infrastructure elements in the conventional sense, but they fulfil the same systemic role—serving as conduits for energy, information, water, and social interaction.

The Valley of Sensations builds essential infrastructure using local materials and low-tech methods, creating climate-responsive *shelters* adapted to steep terrain and Mediterranean conditions. *Water* is managed through rain capture, greywater reuse, and composting toilets—systems that align use with place and well-being. *Energy* comes from solar and human-powered tools, fostering off-grid resilience. *Food systems* combine permaculture, biodiversity, and shared meals, weaving nourishment into daily life. *Social structures*—workshops, residencies, and collective decision-making—support adaptability and cohesion. Flexible *timeframes* and rhythms help align human presence with ecological cycles, ensuring infrastructure serves both people and land.

The Valley of Sensations exemplifies the intensification strategy through its conscious efforts to build and refine infrastructure in a symbiotic way, elevating living conditions while remaining attuned to the material and ecological characteristics of place. By integrating physical engineering with social innovation, and by aligning infrastructural development with environmental biorhythms and constraints, the ecovillage demonstrates how settlement can emerge symbiotically from grassroots experimentation and collaborative place-making.

Temporary Roots for Lasting Change: Pros and Cons of Realities of the Valley of Sensations. One of the most distinctive features of the Valley of Sensations is its approach to time-bound participation. While it attracts a constantly shifting demographic (ages 20–45, including short-term visitors and long-term collaborators), residents are required to stay at least two lunar months to allow for deeper integration. There are observed two—positive and negative—sides concerning the adaptation of such temporary residency model.

The positive aspects are nested, first, in the encouragement of deep engagement by allowing participants to immerse themselves fully without the pressure of long-term commitment. It also brings a constant renewal of ideas, energy, and cultural diversity, keeping the community dynamic and creatively charged. By avoiding permanence, it reduces the social rigidity that can develop in more static environments. Residents get to experience of modifying communal living in concentrated bursts, making each cycle purposeful and transformative.

On the other hand, the lack of long-term continuity can pose challenges for sustaining projects over time. With each new wave of residents, organizational memory must be rebuilt, often from the ground up. The infrastructure must remain highly adaptable to accommodate ever-changing needs and lifestyles. Emotional bonds, while often powerful, can be fleeting—requiring participants to cultivate emotional resilience.

This dual nature—rootedness without permanence—demands a redefinition of what it means to be a 'resident' or 'member' in contemporary communal settings. This transient population model supports a lifestyle based on communal exploration, creativity, and personal growth. Given its design, Valley of Sensations does not aim for population growth in the traditional sense. Instead, it thrives on the continuous influx of new participants, ensuring a vibrant and ever-evolving community dynamic.

The community emphasizes values such as trust, authenticity, and open communication. The ecovillage features a variety of unique, nature-integrated living spaces, that are designed to blend seamlessly with the natural environment, promoting symbiosis and aesthetic harmony. Decision-making processes are inherently participatory, with the community co-creating norms and practices during their time together. This approach ensures that the infrastructure and social systems remain adaptable and responsive to the group's evolving needs. Since its inception in 2000, the village has undergone continuous development, guided by principles of symbiosis and artistic expression. While the site itself is off-grid, the nearby Resonance Hub provides co-living and co-working facilities equipped with internet, enabling participants to maintain professional engagements during their stay at Valley of Sensations—excellent conditions for neo-nomads. Although the site itself is off-grid, the nearby Resonance Hub offers co-living and co-working facilities with internet access, allowing participants to sustain their professional activities during their stay at the Valley of Sensations—ideal conditions for neo-nomads. This proximity ensures that individuals can balance work responsibilities with immersive community experiences. The environment prioritizes health and well-being, featuring amenities like compost toilets, solar-heated showers, and spaces dedicated to relaxation and healing. The integration of natural elements into daily living supports a lifestyle that is both sustainable and enriching and allows a shift to symbiotic organization.

Creating Settlements Through Infrastructure with the Force of a Dynamic Community Ahead. Creating a settlement in the spirit of the Valley of Sensations is less about building physical infrastructure and more about cultivating a dynamic symbiotic way of life. It's an evolving process of social, ecological, and cultural development—shaped not by fixed plans, but by lived experience. For those envisioning similar projects, key insights emerge from this neo-nomadic approach.

Founders are best served by incrementalism: allowing the place to grow organically through cycles of use, reflection, and adaptation. Rather than aiming for a complete design from the start, early stages should prioritize essential functions—shelter, food, sanitation—while remaining open to evolving complexity. Valley of Sensations exemplifies this through its iterative growth, where each layer of development emerges in response to the limits of the place and the unlimited desires of those inhabiting it.

A vital element here is community culture. Rather than a static population, a fluid mix of short- and long-term participants fosters creative energy and resilience. With clear values and shared rituals, even temporary residents can contribute to a deeply engaged social fabric. This rotating dynamic avoids stagnation and sustains a vibrant, evolving commons.

Flexibility is essential. Spaces should accommodate both autonomy and togetherness, with a focus on collective rituals, gatherings, and shared labour. These are not just functional spaces with adaptive infrastructure, but also numerous symbiotic social channels through which meaning, culture, and belonging are shared.

Crucially, the specificity of neo-nomadic projects benefits from maintaining links to broader networks. Hybrid models—combining remote immersion with digital connectivity—enable participants to sustain symbiotic livelihoods while staying rooted in regenerative practice.

Above all, the settlement must be viewed as a living laboratory. With a mind-set of experimentation and co-evolution, every system or process becomes a site of learning. Success lies not in permanence, but in the project's ability to remain responsive, value-driven, and embedded in its legal, ecological, and cultural context.

References

Biørn-Hansen, A., & Håkansson, M. (2018). Building momentum: Scaling up change in community organizations. In *CHI '18: Proceedings of the 2018 CHI conference on Human Factors in Computing Systems* (Paper No. 410, pp. 1–13). Association for Computing Machinery. https://doi.org/10.1145/3173574.3173984.

Buck, J., & Villines, S. (2007). *We the people: Consenting to a deeper democracy.* Sociocracy.info Press.

Buck, J. A., & Endenburg, G. (2012). The creative forces of self-organization [Technical report]. Sociocratic Center.

Burkard, A. (2025). Philosophy of Valle de Sensaciones. Resonancia Community. Retrieved June 7, 2025, from https://resonancia.community/en/philosophy-valle-sensaciones

Christian, D. (2003). *Creating a life together: Practical tools to grow ecovillages and intentional communities.* New Society Publishers.

Christian, D. L. (2012). Busting the myth that consensus-with-unanimity is good for communities: Part I. *Communities, 155*, 42–49.

Christian, D. L. (2013). Transparency, equivalence, and effectiveness: How sociocracy can help communities: Part I. *Communities, 160*, 59–63.

Christian, D. L. (2023, May 5). Using sociocracy successfully in communities [conference presentation]. *Sociocracy in intentional communities conference 2023.* Sociocracy For All.

Comte, A. (1851). *Système de politique positive.* Carilian-Goeury.

Czekaj, J., Walczak, M., & Ziębicki, B. (2020). Towards the sociocratic organization model. *Organization Review, 10*(969), 13–19. https://doi.org/10.33141/po.2020.10.02

Endenburg, G. (1998). *Sociocracy: The organization of decision-making: "No objection" as the principle of sociocracy.* Eburon Academic Publishers.

European Commission. (2020). *Education and training monitor 2020: Lithuania.* Publications Office of the European Union.

Global Ecovillage Network. (2025). *Global Ecovillage Network.* Retrieved June 9, 2025, from https://ecovillage.org

Haider, S. (2023, February 16). How to become a digital nomad. Harvard Business Review. Retrieved June 7, 2025, from https://hbr.org/2023/02/how-to-become-a-digital-nomad

Hamilton, A. L., & Gioia, D. A. (2010). Organizational identity and strategic decision making. In P. C. Nutt & D. C. Wilson (Eds.), *Handbook of decision making* (pp. 139–164). Wiley.

Haselsteiner, E. (2025). Ecovillages and transition towns—What can we learn from them for a regenerative future? In C. Cobreros, E. Giorgi, & T. Cattaneo (Eds.), *Regenerative design: Cities and nature* (pp. xxx–xxx). Springer. https://doi.org/10.1007/978-3-031-76890-3_12

Holmgren, D. (2002). *Permaculture: Principles and pathways beyond sustainability*. Holmgren Design Services.

Kardokai Nature School. (2025). About us. https://kardokugamtosmokykla.lt/ (Accessed April 11, 2025).

Luobikienė, I. (2018). Evaluation of the prospects of educational availability in Lithuanian districts in the context of the social development of the country's territories. Society. Integration. Education. *Proceedings of the International Scientific Conference, 2*, 320–331. https://doi.org/10.17770/sie2018vol1.3111

March, J. G., & Simon, H. A. (1993). Organizations (2nd ed.). Wiley.

Meyer-Stoll, I., & Ecker, A. (2013). ZEGG forum: A ritualized form of communication for larger groups, Germany. In D. Vidickienė (Ed.), *Living in harmony: Inspiring stories from ecovillages* (pp. 56–58). BMK leidykla.

Mollison, B. (1988). *Permaculture: A designer's manual*. Tagari Publications.

OECD. (2022). *PISA 2022 results (volume I & II): Country notes—Lithuania*. OECD Publishing. https://www.oecd.org/pisa/

Palojärvi, A. (2013). Heart-circle as a community-strengthening tool in Keuruu ecovillage, Finland. In D. Vidickienė (Ed.), *Living in harmony: Inspiring stories from ecovillages* (pp. 55–56). BMK leidykla.

Resonancia Community. (2025). *Ecovillage laboratory*. Retrieved June 7, 2025, from https://resonancia.community/en/ecovillage-laboratory

Robertson, B. J. (2015). *Holacracy: The new management system for a rapidly changing world*. Henry Holt and Company.

Romme, A. G. L. (2019). Climbing up and down the hierarchy of accountability: Implications for organization design. *Journal of Organization Design, 8*(1), 20. https://doi.org/10.1186/s41469-019-0060-y

Romme, G. (1995). The sociocratic model of organizing. *Strategic Change, 4*(4), 209–215. https://doi.org/10.1002/jsc.4240040404

Rutkienė, A., & Kaminskienė, L. (2023). Teacher Education in Lithuania: Striving for Professionalism. In M. Kowalczuk-Walędziak, R. A. Valeeva, M. Sablić, & I. Menter (Eds.), *The Palgrave Handbook of Teacher Education in Central and Eastern Europe*. Palgrave Macmillan, Cham. https://doi.org/10.1007/978-3-031-09515-3_16

Sensaciones. (2025). Philosophy of Valle de Sensaciones. Retrieved June 7, 2025, from https://www.sensaciones.de/en/philosophy-valle-sensaciones

Šiugždinienė, J. (2022, June 1). *Experts share insights on Lithuanian education and the challenges ahead up to 2050*. Vilnius University. https://www.vu.lt/en/news-events/news

Sociocracy For All. (n.d.). *Homepage*. https://www.sociocracyforall.org/

Sociocratisch Centrum Nederland. (2020). Homepage. https://sociocratie.nl/

SPACES Archives. (2025). Achim Burkard—Valle de Sensaciones. Retrieved June 7, 2025, from https://www.spacesarchives.org/explore/search-the-online-collection/achim-burkard-valle-de-sensaciones/

Tabor, H. (2024). *How sociocracy is applied in the Dutch ecovillage: Insights from Dutch ecovillage inhabitants and sociocracy experts* (Master's thesis, University of Twente). University of Twente Student Theses. https://essay.utwente.nl/102580/

Urbanovič, J., & Patapas, A. (2012). Decentralisation reforms of education management: Theoretical and practical issues. *Public Policy and Administration, 11*(4), 659–671.

CHAPTER 6

Specialization Strategy: Different Platforms for Building a Service-Oriented Lifestyle Community

Rita Lankauskienė and *Goda Lukoseviciute*

In the industrial era, settlement specialization was mainly focused on a dominant industry that led to the development of specialized infrastructure tailored to that industry. As the service economy encourages humanity's transition into more symbiotic living, the evolution of human settlements necessitates a re-evaluation of traditional community structures. Central to this transformation is the *specialization strategy*, wherein communities are designed around specific service-oriented lifestyles that go beyond ecological and social sustainability. This chapter examines how ecovillages implement the specialization strategy for the creation of intentional communities to cultivate shared cultural identities rooted in *Ecocracy (Symbiocracy)* principles, which emphasize the integration of physical, social, and spiritual dimensions in communal living.

In contrast to the specialization strategy during the industrial era, the specialization of post-industrial settlements is not focused on economic activities. A service-oriented lifestyle inspires people to take a broader view of homogeneous group characteristics, emphasizing shared interests and values. Grouping by interests and values creates communities that may be based on various collaborative platforms. Most groups collaborate to create new value through transformative services for inhabitants and outside

D. Vidickienė et al., *Human Settlement in the Service Economy Era*, Palgrave Advances in Bioeconomy: Economics and Policies,
https://doi.org/10.1007/978-3-032-19390-2_6

the settlement. Transformative services are those that create lasting positive change in the well-being of individuals, communities, and ecosystems, going beyond simple satisfaction to improve life quality, happiness, financial well-being, and overall life satisfaction for those with specific needs, like refugees or people with special needs. Providing transformative services usually does not require expensive grey infrastructure facilities. The most important thing is to create intangible infrastructure in the settlement.

The first step is to create the community's culture, shifting from traditional hierarchical governance and communication methods. For example, adopting Ecocracy refers to emerging governance models that recognize the intrinsic value of all life forms and prioritize ecological equilibrium over human-centred development, which also corresponds to sociocracy. Ecocracy emphasizes governance systems that integrate human well-being with ecological integrity, recognizing that sustainable societies must operate within planetary boundaries and co-evolve with natural systems (Naess, 1989; Folke et al., 2016). Symbiocracy extends this principle by framing governance as the cultivation of mutually beneficial relationships between humans and their socio-ecological environment, where community resilience emerges through cooperation, reciprocity, and interdependence (Margulis & Sagan, 2002; Capra & Luisi, 2014). *Sociocracy*, as a method of decision-making and organizational design, operationalizes these values at the human-social level through consent-based governance, distributed authority, and feedback loops, thereby enabling communities to embody symbiotic and ecocratic principles in practice (Endenburg, 1988; Buck & Villines, 2007) (for more details, also see the Case 'Sociocracy as Innovative Social Infrastructure for Symbiotic Co-Living in Eco-Settlements'). These approaches represent a fundamental shift from anthropocentric to post-anthropocentric paradigms, challenging long-standing assumptions of human dominance over nature (Washington et al., 2017; Albrecht, 2020). As humanity confronts the limitations of industrial modernity, Ecocracy advocates for societies structured as interdependent components within complex ecological systems (Braidotti, 2013).

Under Ecocratic principles, communities do not merely reside in ecosystems—they co-evolve with them. Such a framework necessitates the redefinition of cultural transmission systems, particularly enculturation and socialization. Enculturation, traditionally focused on embedding dominant social norms within individuals, is reoriented to prioritize *ecological literacy, empathy towards non-human life*, and *relational accountability* (Motevalli et al., 2022). Socialization, similarly, shifts from instilling competitive individualism to fostering values of cooperation, mutual respect, and environmental stewardship (Kopnina et al., 2018). This cultural shift aligns with the principles of posthumanism, which rejects the centrality of the human subject and embraces an ethics of entanglement with all life forms (Haraway, 2016). Ecocracy thus implies a relational ontology where governance is symbiotic, not hierarchical, and where power is exercised through care, regeneration, and responsibility. Communities that embed these principles actively contribute to the emergence of a 'Symbiocene' era—an ecological epoch characterized by reciprocal flourishing between human and more-than-human worlds (Albrecht, 2019).

Enculturation, the process by which individuals internalize the cultural norms, values, and worldviews of their society, is central to the formation of ecological identities within intentional communities. When cultural practices are consciously aligned with ecological principles, enculturation becomes a tool for fostering collective environmental ethics and more sustainable behaviour (Motevalli et al., 2022). In such contexts, socialization agents—such as community education programmes, intergenerational mentorship, and participatory rituals—transmit values of ecological stewardship, interdependence, and post-anthropocentric ethics (Tilbury, 1995). These agents reinforce pro-environmental norms not only through formal education but also through lived experience and community interaction. As ecological consciousness becomes embedded in everyday practices—such as communal farming, low-impact living, and ritual connection to place—a shared cultural identity emerges, which aligns personal behaviour with broader environmental goals (Gough, 2002) and goes beyond sustainability. This process of ecological enculturation and socialization is thus foundational to the long-term viability of Ecocracy-aligned communities.

At the heart of Ecocracy lies the recognition that nature possesses intrinsic value—that is, value independent of any instrumental benefit to humans. This principle challenges dominant anthropocentric paradigms in environmental governance and aligns with ecocentric ethics, which argue for moral consideration of ecosystems, species, and abiotic entities (Washington et al., 2017). Ecocracy builds on this foundation by institutionalizing the inherent worth of the non-human world into policy, cultural norms, and community life. It promotes governance structures that prioritize ecological balance and the well-being of all life forms, not just human interests (Rolston, 1994). By embracing this ethos, Ecocracy encourages societies to transition from exploitative to reciprocal relationships with nature, fostering a worldview rooted in interconnectedness and mutual thriving. Such ethical reorientation not only supports biodiversity and ecosystem resilience but also reshapes the moral architecture of governance for the Symbiocene era.

In embracing Ecocracy, communities are compelled to establish governance systems that mirror the relational complexity and interdependence of ecological systems. This requires a reconfiguration of cultural norms and social behaviours—shifting from human-centred dominance to mutual responsibility and care for all life forms. By embedding ecological ethics into institutional practices and everyday interactions, such communities foster a more just, resilient, and sustainable coexistence with the natural world, aligning governance with the principles of ecological justice and systemic interconnectivity.

This chapter is illustrated with three case studies. Intentional communities such as Tamera and Quinta do Coelho Azul Ecovillage in Portugal, and Rožkalni in Latvia, exemplify different collaboration platforms for the creation of community with specific interests and values, and illustrate how the specialization strategy can foster lifestyles aligned with Ecocracy principles. These communities prioritize holistic development, inclusive governance, and sustainable practices, serving as models for post-anthropocentric living where human activities harmonize with ecological systems, composing symbiotic settlements.

Tamera (www.tamera.org) specializes in *peace education and ecological restoration*, integrating spiritual, social, and environmental dimensions into daily life. The community emphasizes trust, cooperation, and nonviolent communication, creating a culture rooted in interconnectedness and mutual respect. Through its focus on healing landscapes and relationships, Tamera delivers transformative services that demonstrate how ecological balance and human coexistence can be cultivated together. Guided by the principles of Ecocracy, the settlement serves as a living model of peace-oriented and regenerative culture, aligning human activities with the resilience of natural systems.

Quinta do Coelho Azul (https://www.coelhoazul.eu/en) focuses on *permaculture education and regenerative living*, functioning as an intentional off-grid community in southern Portugal. Its mission is to disseminate ecological literacy through immersive learning, including Permaculture Design Certificate (PDC) courses, natural building workshops, and experiential sustainability programmes. By integrating communal living with regenerative agriculture, the ecovillage provides transformative services that foster cooperation, ecological stewardship, and interspecies respect. Anchored in Ecocracy principles, the community demonstrates how education, shared responsibility, and ecological ethics can co-create sustainable lifestyles in harmony with local ecosystems.

Rožkalni Camphill (camphillrozkalni.lv) specialization lies in *therapeutic community living and social inclusion*, where individuals with developmental disabilities and co-workers co-create a supportive and dignified environment. By weaving together residential life, meaningful work, and cultural activities, the settlement delivers social therapeutic services that nurture belonging, purpose, and connection to nature. This approach embodies a holistic model of transformative services, where human dignity, mutual care, and ecological responsibility are central. In doing so, Rožkalni reflects the principles of Ecocracy, fostering environments in which human well-being and ecological sustainability are deeply interconnected.

The communities under examination demonstrate inclusive governance through participatory decision-making and shared responsibilities, embodying the principles outlined in the United Nations' 11 Principles of Effective Governance for Sustainable Development (Escribano et al., 2020). Their commitment to sustainable practices, such as biodynamic farming and eco-friendly construction, further exemplifies their alignment with Ecocracy principles. Tamera, Quinta do Coelho Azul, and Rožkalni illustrate how specialization strategies in intentional communities can operationalize Ecocracy principles, offering viable models for sustainable, inclusive, and ecologically harmonious living.

As humanity enters the Symbiocene era, intentional communities are pioneering specialization strategies that align with Ecocracy principles, fostering service-oriented lifestyles rooted in ecological ethics and post-anthropocentric values. Through processes of ecological enculturation and socialization, these communities cultivate cultural identities grounded in interdependence, stewardship, and relational governance. Case studies of Tamera, Quinta do Coelho Azul, and Rožkalni demonstrate how peace education, permaculture, and therapeutic living can operationalize holistic development, inclusive decision-making, and environmental sustainability. Together, they offer scalable models for resilient and ethically grounded human settlements where culture and governance evolve in harmony with nature.

Peace Education: Tamera Healing Biotope Ecovillage, Portugal

From Vision to Biotope: The Origins of Tamera's Peace Ecology. In the municipality of Odemira, in the southwest Alentejo area of Portugal, a small group of Portuguese people established Tamera Healing Biotope Ecovillage in 1995. The foundation of Tamera is a self-sufficient, sustainable, and replicable communitarian model for harmonious relationships and cooperation between people, animals, and the environment, backed by an inclusive and participatory system of government. Over 250 people, including children, co-workers, and students, live and study together in the 154-hectare Tamera Eco Village, an interconnected post-patriarchal society free from violence and conflict. In addition, Tamera serves as a networking and collaboration hub and 'free lab', where employees and researchers may exchange knowledge and work together to find answers. In this community, shared living, ecological restoration, fostering trust, and establishing robust social structures are the cornerstones of daily existence. By creating what they refer to as a 'Healing Biotope'—a place for rebirth, community, and experimentation—Tamera hopes to be a real-life illustration of what a future based on ecological harmony, peace, and self-determination can look like.

The bulk of the Tamera community's permanent population are non-Portuguese, and none of them are native to the area. The majority of the community's members speak German, with the remainder hailing from nations including Spain, Israel, Italy, the United Kingdom, France, the United States, Chile, and Greece. Approximately 60% of the population is female, and the typical inhabitant is 35 years old. The fact that 30 of the community's residents are less than 18 shows that no one under that age is excluded. The Tamera people spoke German as their first language for a long time, but as the community grew, English increasingly replaced it. From its inception, Tamera was designed not as a conventional village but as a highly specialized model for peace-building and ecological regeneration. Its specialization lies in offering transformative eco-services: healing of landscapes, relationships, and cultural systems.

Seeding Peace: The Founders' Path to a Healing Civilization. Tamera began in 1978 when Dieter Duhm together with Sabine Lichtenfels, Charly Rainer Ehrenpreis, Sarah Vollmer, and a small group of collaborators founded their first communal experiment in southern Germany. The pioneers had a common vision to give up on their professions and use their expertise and accumulated knowledge together to create an interdisciplinary research centre to develop solutions to ecological innovations, bionics, architecture, food security, and alternative technologies instead. In order to successfully create solutions to specific world problems, the idea of establishing a research centre inside a community framework necessitates taking into account the fundamental questions about human relationships that lie beneath all problems, preventing 'real solutions' like competition, greed, and jealousy. Their foundational thesis is centred around global peace, which cannot be achieved through political reform alone—it must be practised in place, through new models of living. In the Black Forest of Germany, they started a three-year communal experiment in 1983 with 50 people. They then used the findings of this study to build a functional community in subsequent initiatives across Europe until they eventually founded Tamera in 1995. Early on, the group recognized that no technical solution would be lasting without a strong, trust-based social foundation. Tamera was envisioned as a 'Healing Biotope'—a prototype for a post-capitalist, peaceful civilization. This foundation laid the groundwork for Tamera's specialization as a systemic experiment as a prototype settlement offering unique transformative eco-services to the world.

Designing a Healing Biotope: An Environment of Trust and Ecology. Building on the specialization strategy—which frames the settlement as a provider of regenerative, peace-oriented services—Tamera's design is rooted in Dieter Duhm's Healing Biotope theory. These design choices express Tamera's core specialization: offering a living demonstration of how infrastructure, social healing, and ecological balance can be integrated into a model capable of addressing global crises at the local scale.

Tamera's design did not follow a standard urban planning framework but was instead guided by the conceptual framework of the Healing Biotope, developed by Dieter Duhm. It draws on systems theory to conceptualize settlements as living organisms composed of interrelated social, ecological, and energetic subsystems (Duhm, 2015). Influenced by deep ecology, the model rejects the anthropocentric view of nature, emphasizing instead the fundamental interconnectedness and intrinsic value of all life forms (Naess, 1989; Esteves, 2017). Dieter Duhm incorporates elements of Reichian psychology, particularly Wilhelm Reich's theories of somatic energy (orgone) and emotional 'armouring', as a basis for healing trauma and fostering emotional transparency within communities (Reich, 1974; Esteves, 2017). The social component of the model promotes radical nonviolence, asserting that sustainable peace must include transformed human relationships—especially around trust, sexuality, and power (Duhm, 2005).

Moreover, the theory integrates alternative epistemologies, such as Rupert Sheldrake's concept of morphic resonance—the idea that biological and social systems inherit collective memory—and Viktor Schauberger's harmonics, which frame water and energy as living entities following natural implosive flows rather than mechanical exploitation (Sheldrake, 2011; Coats, 2001; Esteves, 2017). These concepts underpin Tamera's ecological and technological strategies, including the design of its Water Retention Landscape and solar-biogas test fields, which aim to harmonize with, rather than dominate, natural systems. While these epistemologies are often critiqued by mainstream science (Strick, 2015; Cordon, 2012), they serve as the philosophical foundation for Tamera's design of integrative sustainability.

In designing Tamera as a Healing Biotope, the vision extended beyond physical infrastructure—it required shaping a human ecology aligned with its foundational values. The ideal inhabitants are not passive recipients of a pre-built system but active co-creators of the social, ecological, and spiritual fabric of the settlement. These individuals are expected to cultivate emotional transparency, engaging in deep interpersonal work through practices such as the Forum, which fosters trust and vulnerability. They are also ecologically literate, either skilled in or open to learning regenerative practices such as permaculture, water retention, and decentralized energy. Spiritually, the community values those who are open to ritual, meditation, and sacred activism, integrating inner transformation with outer change. Additionally, residents are expected to embrace non-monogamous relationship patterns where trust and transparency are essential, as well as sexual ethics based on freedom and responsibility. Economically, they tend to reject consumerist logic in favour of gift economies, mutual aid, and post-materialist living, contributing labour and care to the commons. Lastly, ideal residents are committed to long-term place-based engagement, willing to participate in ongoing co-creation rather than temporary retreat.

The place itself is treated as an active partner in the healing process. The ideal landscape for a Healing Biotope is not pristine wilderness but degraded land with the potential for *regeneration*, offering a context where ecological repair and human healing can occur simultaneously. By implementing a water retention landscape, the site regains hydrological autonomy, reversing desertification and restoring the natural water cycle. Reforestation, agroecology, and biodiversity corridors are developed to restore habitat complexity and soil vitality, turning a once-barren region into a vibrant biotope. The land is also considered energetically alive, and infrastructure is designed to harmonize with natural flows, drawing from Schauberger's ideas of implosive energy. Culturally and spiritually, the site is rooted in the Alentejo bioregion, but it functions as a global prototype, offering a model that resonates far beyond its immediate territory. The physical environment is carefully curated to be quiet, safe, and contemplative, enabling inner work, ritual practice, and collective coherence. Central to this is the sacralization of space—where the land is not just used but revered through the creation of ceremonial zones, such as the Stone Circle and Temple of the Earth.

The living infrastructure at Tamera reflects the community's integrated approach to ecology, community, and spirit. Buildings are constructed from natural, low-impact materials such as straw, clay, and timber, and follow bioclimatic and passive solar principles to minimize energy use. Housing is designed on a human scale, clustered in a way that balances communal rhythm with personal privacy. A strong emphasis is placed on *shared facilities*, including communal kitchens, gardens, co-working spaces, educational venues, and spiritual centres, all of which reinforce interaction, mutual responsibility, and the rhythm of collective life. The infrastructure is highly decentralized, including off-grid energy systems, composting toilets, greywater reuse, and food production integrated into the landscape. Technological tools, such as internet access and digital infrastructure, are present but managed mindfully, enabling global connection without overwhelming the embodied, place-based nature of community life. *Sacredness* is embedded in the built environment—not as an add-on, but as a structural principle guiding spatial design and daily use.

The design process of Tamera was organized as a co-evolutionary, vision-led, and participatory process, guided by the principles of the Healing Biotope theory and rooted in both spiritual intuition and ecological observation. Spatial planning of the village was based on experiential knowledge, dialogue with nature, and constant feedback from both the environment and the social body of the community. *Vision-led* master planning anchored in the concept of a Healing Biotope, which influenced not only spatial decisions but also the spiritual, social, and ecological intentions behind every intervention. Collaborative input from experts in regenerative systems: for example, the Water Retention Landscape was co-designed with Sepp Holzer, while energy systems were developed with innovators in decentralized solar-biogas technologies. These technical elements were integrated with permaculture, sacred geometry, and systems thinking.

Social design processes were simultaneously developed, including the architecture of trust. These social tools were essential to organizing infrastructure in a way that supported collective responsibility and non-hierarchical governance. Non-linear development in phases: initial efforts focused on basic housing and food production, followed by strategic implementation of water systems, energy autonomy projects, educational centres (like the Global Campus), and sacred spaces. Each phase was informed by what the community had learned through practice and reflection. Ritual and spiritual anchoring played an important role. Decisions—particularly those involving land and community relationships—were often made in conjunction with rituals, vision quests, or meditative practices aimed at aligning the settlement with 'the matrix of life', as Duhm describes it.

Strategies for a Regenerative Future: Water, Trust, and Global Learning. Tamera's strategic actions are expressions of its specialization as a provider of transformative eco-services. These actions are intentionally aligned with the goal of producing ecological, social, technological, and spiritual values beyond conventional development paradigms.

Tamera ecovillage implemented the following strategies for sustainable village development as a morphogenetic field and a cultural template that can influence global patterns by existing, evolving, and being visible:

- *Ecological Regeneration: Water as the Foundation of Healing.* Action. The strategy is intimately connected with the emergence of a regional food autonomy network, leading to the design and implementation of a Water Retention Landscape (2007–2009) to reverse desertification and achieve hydrological autonomy. To achieve the strategic plans a partnership with Sepp Holzer (Austrian permaculture expert) was established, which led to implementation of small-scale earthworks such as retention lakes, swales, and terraces. Today Tamera is a water-autonomous ecovillage, dramatically increasing biodiversity and soil fertility.
- *Energy and Technological Innovation.* Action. The strategy is connected with the need for energy production autonomy, where the development of decentralized, renewable energy systems including

solar, wind, and biogas under the projects of 'SolarVillage' and 'Biospheric Test Field' was implemented. The strategy integrates off-grid energy autonomy with ecological technologies as living demonstrations of post-carbon systems leading Tamera to a partial energy self-sufficient village.

- *Social and Relational Transformation.* The strategy is centred around the creation and institutionalization of the so-called Forum, which facilitates group process for emotional transparency, community healing, and conflict resolution. The strategic aim is to build a culture of trust through daily emotional work, honest communication, and structured group process. Through such strategic approach, a high group cohesion, reduced internal conflict, and a replicable social technology for other communities have been achieved.
- *Education and Global Outreach.* The strategy is linked with the need to have an independent and non-traditional live classroom at the village to train activists, scholars, and intentional community founders. This approach has led to the creation of the Global Campus, Terra Nova School, and Escola da Esperança, a school for kids and young people. Today thousands of trainees worldwide are visiting the village and sharing the knowledge with global partner projects (e.g., in Colombia, Kenya, Palestine).
- *Spiritual-Cultural Anchoring.* The strategy is centred around the need to have a spiritual centre at the village through rituals, sacred activism, and the creation of spiritual infrastructure (e.g., Stone Circle, Temple of the Earth). The objective is to reconnect humans with nature and the divine through ceremony, meditation, and collective intention. Through this strategy an integration of inner and outer transformation as well as cultural depth and resilience is achieved.
- *Economic Experimentation and Internal Commons.* The strategy is centred around the need to pilot a gift economy model based on shared labour, non-monetary exchange, and collective funding (solidarity funds). The aim is to decommodify life within the community while supporting the global solidarity economy. The applied strategy helped to increase internal resilience and a practical alternative to capitalist resource flows.
- *Network Building and Movement Support.* The strategy targets participation in the Global Ecovillage Network (GEN), International Peace Workers Network, and alliances with grassroots movements. It

aims to position Tamera as part of a broader ecosystem of regenerative, peace-building projects. Today Tamera has amplified impact beyond the site and collaborative knowledge exchange.

Through these interconnected strategies, Tamera operationalizes its specialization model—offering not only local solutions, but a transferable framework for communities seeking systemic healing.

Realizing the Vision: People, Place, and Everyday Infrastructure. Tamera's population and the way of life reflect its role as a specialized settlement. Inhabitants are not only residents—they are co-producers of the eco-social services the village aims to deliver.

Tamera is home to approximately 170 permanent residents, including adults, children, elders, and rotating groups of students, interns, and guests. The *community* includes individuals with diverse backgrounds in ecology, education, arts, healing, activism, construction, and information technology, reflecting a multifunctional livelihood structure centred on collective labour, self-sufficiency, and global peace work. While the population remains relatively stable, growth is intentionally limited, driven by value alignment rather than expansionist aims. In terms of age, the population is predominantly middle-aged adults (30s–50s), with a smaller proportion of youth and elders, raising long-term questions about generational continuity and youth retention.

Culturally, Tamera is a collaborative, values-driven community built around the principles of truth, trust, and love. Inhabitants engage in emotional transparency practices, where group dialogue is used to build psychological safety and resolve interpersonal tensions. Daily life is shaped by a non-hierarchical ethos, shared responsibilities, and a strong commitment to nonviolence, ecological stewardship, and spiritual inquiry. Many residents practise free love or polyamory, embedded in a framework of conscious relational ethics and communication. While the community operates in Portugal, the majority of residents are German speaking, which has been noted as a cultural barrier to deeper local integration. Nevertheless, Tamera's social fabric is held together by shared rituals, educational programmes, cooperative work rhythms, and a collective vision of building a regenerative culture. The current population is sufficient to maintain the settlement's vitality, although further efforts may be needed to diversify demographics and ensure long-term intergenerational resilience.

The living infrastructure of Tamera is designed not for general habitation but to support a high-functioning ecosystem of care, education, experimentation, and ecological restoration—core to its specialization as a Healing Biotope. The *infrastructure* has evolved over multiple phases since its founding in 1995, following an organic, need-responsive, and ecologically conscious development model. The initial phase focused on basic housing, communal facilities, and food cultivation infrastructure. Later phases included the construction of specialized buildings for education (Global Campus), spiritual practice (Temple of the Earth), technological experimentation (Solar Test Field, Biospheric Test Field), and guest accommodation. Residential areas are arranged in clustered housing units, designed for communal living while allowing for personal privacy. Homes are primarily built using natural and low-impact materials (e.g., adobe, wood, straw bale) and follow bioclimatic principles to ensure energy efficiency. Public spaces—such as communal kitchens, dining areas, meditation halls, gathering circles, and permaculture gardens—are interwoven with residential zones to foster daily interaction and social integration.

Land and core infrastructure are held collectively through a legal structure involving several interconnected entities, including Ilos Lda. (land trust), the GRACE Foundation (educational body), and the AMH (Association for the Healing Biotopes). This structure reinforces collective ownership and long-term stewardship rather than individual property rights. Decision-making follows a decentralized, non-hierarchical model based on a critical process of direct, public communication among community members, in which self-expression, including verbal and emotional elements, as well as care work, has a central role. The design and governance of infrastructure reflect Tamera's values of shared responsibility, ecological integrity, and spiritual purpose, with each phase of development serving both practical needs and symbolic functions within the larger vision of a Healing Biotope.

Tamera's place-based strategy is a critical dimension of its specialization. The biophysical and spiritual qualities of the landscape are central to its role as a provider of transformative eco-services. With regard to *place characteristics*, Tamera is situated in a rural landscape historically marked by semi-arid conditions, soil degradation, and seasonal water scarcity. Through the implementation of a large-scale Water Retention Landscape, the community has restored ecological vitality to the area, creating a lush, biodiverse, and agriculturally productive environment. The terrain now includes man-made lakes, terraced gardens, native tree plantings, and microclimates that support both food sovereignty and ecological research.

The land holds symbolic and cultural value, as it has been transformed from degraded pasture into a model of regenerative design—an embodiment of the Healing Biotope vision. While not officially classified as a heritage site, Tamera assigns spiritual and ecological significance to the land, often referring to it as a living being and integrating ritual and ceremony into its care.

The land is owned collectively through Ilos Lda., a legal trust, and managed by associated non-profit and educational entities, allowing the community to avoid private ownership models and maintain long-term stewardship. In terms of infrastructure for working and living, Tamera is relatively well-equipped for remote and home-based work. It provides reliable internet access, enabling residents to participate in online meetings, remote collaboration, and educational outreach. While the rural location limits public transport, car-sharing systems and local ride arrangements are used within the community. The overall environment is quiet, safe, and health-promoting, with minimal noise pollution, abundant natural beauty, clean air, and spaces for reflection and healing. These conditions support both individual well-being and professional productivity, particularly for those involved in research, writing, education, digital media, or spiritual facilitation. The landscape and built environment together foster a deep sense of place, purpose, and belonging—critical to Tamera's long-term viability as a transformative settlement.

Lessons from a Healing Biotope: Blueprints for Systemic Transformation. A number of significant factors should be taken into account when attempting to develop a transformative settlement based on the Tamera Healing Biotope model. These factors go beyond basic sustainability and touch upon deep ecological, social, and cultural systems.

First, it is essential to establish strong ecological foundations. Beginning with a regenerative land-use strategy—not merely conservation should be considered. The strategy should ensure water autonomy through landscape hydrology techniques such as water retention basins, swales, and soil restoration. This is foundational to long-term resilience, especially in arid or degraded environments. In addition, biodiversity restoration and closed-loop systems (water, food, energy) should be core design principles from the outset.

Secondly, avoid treating ecological regeneration and community building as separate tasks. It is crucial to develop a place-based culture where emotional healing, social trust, and ecological care are inseparable. With regard to design spaces such as gardens, kitchens, forums, and sacred spaces, they should serve both ecological and relational functions. Recognize that peace work must include emotional processing, conflict resolution, and shared values, not just activism or green infrastructure.

Tamera's example following project should integrate systems thinking, spiritual ecology, deep psychology, and post-capitalist economics. Replicators should articulate their own guiding vision or philosophical framework early, which can serve as a compass for difficult decisions and long-term coherence. Trust should be built through structured group processes such as the Forum, shared rituals, deep communication training, and a willingness to face conflict directly. It is important to avoid replicating only the visible infrastructure; instead, invest in invisible architecture—social agreements, decision-making frameworks, conflict mediation systems, and spiritual practice.

Moreover, following Tamera's lead by placing land in foundation or trust-based structures, one should avoid speculation and private commodification. This ensures long-term access, equity, and ecological accountability, and opens possibilities for intergenerational continuity. As Tamera began with less than 20 people and minimal infrastructure, it is important to not overplan on large teams. Instead, prototype, reflect, and adjust. The idea is to allow the land and the community to co-evolve and let the design evolve in time, aligning with the rhythm of nature and the community's capacity.

Finally, one should create educational platforms that can both finance the project and spread its values. Schools, workshops, residencies, and open-source publications are essential for outreach and sustainability. Education should serve both the inner transformation of participants and the outer replication of regenerative systems.

To replicate a settlement with a specialization strategy like Tamera's, one must go beyond conventional sustainability and design for the provision of systemic, regenerative services—ecological, emotional, social, and spiritual.

Education in Agriculture and Communal Living: Quinta do Coelho Azul Ecovillage and Self-Sustainable Permaculture Project (Portugal)

From Abandoned Fields to Living Ecovillage: The Birth of Quinta do Coelho Azul. In the region of Algarve, near Faro, a Belgian couple established an ecovillage Quinta do Coelho Azul (the 'Farm of the Blue

Rabbit') based on the principle of permaculture (Mollison et al., 1991). The fundamental idea of permaculture is that by using biological resources, holistic design that is modelled after natural ecosystems, humans may lessen or even replace energy- and pollution-intensive industrial technologies, particularly in agriculture. The initiative to establish the ecovillage began in 2014 when a couple acquired and renovated an old farmhouse in Quelfes, east of Olhão, and began transforming two hectares of citrus, almond, and olive groves into a permaculture food forest. This was the beginning of the process of creating a self-sufficient, regenerative community that was integrated with the local ecology.

The origins of the *Quinta do Coelho Azul* trace back to the late 1990s, when a wave of counter-urban migration began to shape the rural landscapes of southern Portugal. Located in the foothills of the Serra do Caldeirão, the land had historically been used for subsistence farming, featuring olive trees, cork oaks, and dryland orchards. However, by the 1980s, the property had been largely abandoned, as younger generations migrated to cities or abroad, and traditional agriculture declined due to economic centralization and EU market shifts. In the early 2000s, the land was rediscovered by a group of international environmentalists, educators, and eco-entrepreneurs who were drawn to the Algarve for its Mediterranean climate, low land prices, and relatively loose rural zoning policies. The group began with camping and provisional structures while restoring ancient stone terraces, dry-stone walls, and water retention systems—many of which dated back to the Moorish era. Within time, a self-sustaining, community-oriented permaculture farm and ecovillage, with a vision of ecological restoration, shared living infrastructure, and educational outreach was developed. Following a cooperative land purchase involving private funds and international crowdfunding, the settlement's site spans approximately 14 hectares and has since grown to house a rotating population of 20–30 long-term residents, alongside volunteers, seasonal workers, and permaculture students.

Living the Change: Founders Who Planted Seeds of Symbiosis. The project was created and started by a Belgian couple in their early 40s who had both quit their jobs as landscape designers and environmental consultants. Disillusioned by the gap between ecological rhetoric and practice in urban Europe, they started looking for a place where they could actually 'live the change' rather than just support it. The couple purchased the site in 2010 in Algarve after an extended exploratory journey through southern Europe. Their founding vision was strongly informed by permaculture ethics and design principles, particularly the idea of symbiosis—where human activity could integrate harmoniously with ecological processes to co-create abundance. Rather than impose a masterplan, they adopted a 'listening to the land' approach, observing seasonal flows, soil patterns, water lines, and native plant behaviour over the course of the first full year. The founders were also inspired by intentional community models in France, Spain, and Australia. Their goal was to avoid the pitfalls of both eco-isolation and rigid collectivism. Instead, they envisioned a modular, semi-autonomous living system: one where residents could co-create shared value but also retain individual agency. They developed an early set of community guidelines rooted in nonviolent communication, consensus decision-making, and shared labour exchange systems—tools that remain foundational today.

The early phase of the project attracted like-minded individuals through word-of-mouth, permaculture networks, and online platforms such as WWOOF, Workaway, and GEN Europe. In 2012, the founders formalized the project under a Portuguese non-profit cooperative structure, allowing for co-ownership models and eligibility for EU rural development grants. As the community expanded and diversified, the founders shifted from central leadership to facilitation roles. They continue to live on-site, offering guidance, mentoring, and historical continuity, while newer generations of residents take on project coordination, teaching, and innovation. Their foundational intent remains clear: to build a place where humans and ecosystems thrive together, not through control or domination, but through mutual adaptation and respect.

Designing with the Land: A Permaculture Blueprint for Community. The founders envisioned the ecovillage as a living system—a place where ecological health, social well-being, and experiential learning would co-evolve. The ideal was a self-sufficient, bioregionally grounded eco-community capable of producing food, conserving water, generating livelihoods, and cultivating civic agency. Key characteristics included:

- Inhabitants living lightly on the land, in modest, energy-efficient structures with a culture of shared responsibilities and mutual care.
- Landscape resilience, achieved through agroecological mosaics: food forests, keyline-inspired cultivation, hedgerows, orchards, and windbreaks integrated with water-harvesting infrastructure (swales, ponds, contour paths).

- Regenerative infrastructure, including composting toilets, greywater systems, renewable energy (solar), and natural building techniques using clay, straw, and recycled materials.
- Communal spaces designed for education, hosting, cultural exchange, and group governance—functioning as both civic infrastructure and symbolic heart of the settlement.
- Integration with the wider bioregion, where the farm's activities would contribute to local food systems, restoration networks, and regional drought resilience.

The design was rooted in permaculture ethics and principles (care for earth, care for people, fair share) as articulated by Mollison and Holmgren (1978). Influences also came from Findhorn Ecovillage in Scotland, a model for integrating spiritual practice, sustainability, and cooperative governance (Copeland et al., 2023); Tamera ecovillage in Portugal, a pioneering intentional community experimenting with healing biotopes, water retention landscapes, and sociocratic decision-making (Esteves, 2017); Transition Towns and Ecovillage Design Education (EDE) frameworks, especially the Gaia Education curriculum, which structured early pedagogical offerings; Membership in Ecosystem Restoration Communities (ERC), which provided a framework for embedding the site within a global constellation of restoration camps, with shared protocols for learning design, impact tracking, and volunteer engagement.

The development of Quinta do Coelho Azul was iterative, combining vision-led planning with adaptive management. Key elements included:

- Participatory design charrettes involving residents, staff, permaculture consultants, and local artisans. Early phases mapped hydrology, prevailing winds, sun paths, and soil characteristics to inform site zoning.
- Prototyping through action: rather than blueprinting everything up front, many features (e.g., greywater systems, communal kitchens, volunteer housing) were trialled, used, and then refined.
- Agroforestry pilots tested different guild combinations of Mediterranean trees, shrubs, and groundcovers, adapting species choice to observed microclimates and water behaviour.
- Community infrastructure (meeting spaces, kitchens, eco-lodges) was built incrementally, with attention to both aesthetic coherence and functionality. Materials were sourced locally whenever possible.

- Feedback loops: reflection circles, weekly reviews, and seasonal evaluations allowed residents, interns, and guests to give input on what worked, what didn't, and how practices should evolve.
- Design literacy was cultivated among participants, with workshops in permaculture design, landscape reading, and group facilitation ensuring that everyone could contribute meaningfully to shaping the space.

Overall, the design process mirrored the principles of ecological succession: start simple, build soil (social and literal), diversify, and adapt to feedback from the system. The founders imagined a self-sufficient eco-community that could integrate food production, water stewardship, social cohesion, and visitor education. Desirable characteristics included inhabitants living lightly on the land with shared infrastructure; a thriving landscape combining food forests, gardens, and water-harvesting features, low-impact buildings, and communal spaces for learning, hosting, and governance.

The physical layout of the ecovillage:

- Zone 0/1 (heart): communal kitchen, dining area, educational spaces, and administration buildings.
- Zone 2/3: market gardens, animal systems, orchards, and agroforestry belts, managed with rotation and polyculture principles.
- Zone 4/5: wild areas, experimental restoration paddocks, and natural habitats for biodiversity enhancement.

Housing was clustered to reduce footprint, encourage social interaction, and facilitate shared services (laundry, tool storage, internet hubs). The design drew heavily on permaculture principles (Mollison & Holmgren, 1978) and was informed by exemplar projects such as Findhorn (Scotland) and Tamera (Portugal). More recently, its membership in the Ecosystem Restoration Communities (ERC) network linked it to a global methodology of restoration camps. The process combined participatory workshops with professional design input. Successive phases included mapping hydrology, soils, and access; trialling agroforestry; creating communal living facilities; and embedding educational programmes. Feedback loops with residents, volunteers, and visiting trainers shaped successive iterations of land use and governance.

Strategies of Regeneration: Soil, Soul, and Social Architecture. Quinta Vale da Lama's strategic development was guided by systemic regeneration—restoring land, empowering people, and designing governance and finance mechanisms that could support resilience and long-term continuity.

The site underwent a regenerative land-use transformation. Keyline design principles were implemented to manage water flow and prevent erosion. The land, once degraded pasture, was transitioned into a diverse agroforestry mosaic that integrated Mediterranean tree crops such as carob, olive, and fig, alongside annual gardens and fodder hedgerows. Soil regeneration practices were deployed through composting, cover cropping, rotational grazing, and mulching to rebuild fertility and improve water retention. In terms of integrated water management, swales, ponds, and terraces were designed and constructed to slow, spread, and sink rainwater. Greywater systems were installed, and low-tech water-reuse loops were piloted in kitchen and accommodation areas. The project also actively advocated for basin-level collaboration with local authorities and networks to improve regional drought resilience.

The educational ecosystem was strategically developed in parallel. Associação Novas Descobertas was established to focus on youth and family learning. Seasonal programmes were launched, including Permaculture Design Courses (PDC), Ecosystem Restoration Camps, and long-term internships. To address adult learning needs related to climate adaptation and desertification, the Mud Valley Institute was co-created as a focused educational initiative.

Social architecture and governance were foundational elements. Horizontal decision-making tools such as sociocracy, rotating facilitation, and a culture of feedback were embedded into daily life. Residents and interns were regularly trained in group dynamics, role-sharing, and restorative conflict resolution. Agreements were created for asset sharing, land stewardship, and cohabitation to ensure long-term cohesion. Economic diversification was a deliberate strategy to manage financial risk. A blended revenue model was developed, combining farm produce sales, course fees, and conscious tourism via the seasonal operation of Casa Vale da Lama eco-resort, grants, and value-added product enterprises. Residents and alumni were encouraged to develop entrepreneurial initiatives, such as herbal goods, fermentation labs, and repair services.

Strategically, the community focused on building strong networks and advocacy channels. By joining the Ecosystem Restoration Communities

(ERC) platform, the project attracted volunteers, shared curricula, and documented impacts. Active partnerships were built with local schools, universities, and municipal agencies to promote bioregional education. Members also contributed to broader discussions around water justice, regenerative tourism, and rural revitalization.

Infrastructure development was phased carefully. Multi-use buildings and scalable utilities—such as solar power systems, composting toilets, and mobile classrooms—were prioritized to maximize flexibility and reduce upfront costs. Development followed a sequence that began with gardens, moved to housing, and later added hospitality infrastructure. Funding came from a combination of EU funds, local grants, and alignment with regional climate resilience programmes. These actions—ecological, educational, social, economic, and political—were coordinated not through top-down control, but through shared values and a commitment to learning-in-action.

A Living Laboratory: Regenerative Living in Practice. The ecovillage today stands as a living experiment in regenerative living—a place where agroecology, community dynamics, and educational missions intertwine. It is a grounded attempt to model sustainable human-nature relations under real-world constraints. The resident population is modest, numbering a few dozen core individuals, complemented by a fluid ecosystem of interns, seasonal volunteers, visiting educators, and eco-tourists. The core community includes long-term residents between 30 and 50 years of age who take on key roles in land management, programme delivery, governance, and mentorship. Younger cohorts join through Erasmus+, WWOOF, or other structured learning programmes, creating intergenerational and intercultural exchanges. Many residents cooperate farming duties with teaching, research, remote work, or artisanal production. Some operate as part of the farm's organizational ecosystem, while others are independent entrepreneurs aligned with the community's values. Remote work is viable due to stable internet access, allowing members to contribute to international networks or consultancies while rooted in place-based living.

The community emphasizes values over numbers: rather than pursuing population growth, it seeks a functional scale—where human presence does not exceed the land's carrying capacity and where social cohesion remains manageable. The broader network of alumni, programme participants, and collaborators forms a distributed community that reinforces the project's vitality without demanding co-location. Shared values are central: regeneration of ecosystems, participatory governance, cooperative living, and hands-on education. These are not abstract ideals but daily practices embedded in work rhythms, decision-making rituals, and the care of place and people.

The physical infrastructure is humble, modular, and deliberately low-impact. It includes communal spaces built from natural materials for gatherings, workshops, and meals; volunteer and intern housing in yurts, domes, or cabins; a renovated farmhouse functioning as an eco-tourism lodge and training centre; compost toilets, solar showers, greywater systems, and tool-sharing areas. Structures are intentionally clustered to foster social interaction and reduce ecological footprint. The arrangement supports spontaneous encounters—through shared meals, joint workdays, or fire circles—while maintaining enough privacy for rest and reflection.

Governance is structured around weekly assemblies, sociocratic facilitation, and rotating roles, ensuring that decision-making is distributed and adaptive. Conflict is addressed through restorative dialogue, and feedback loops are embedded into both infrastructure design and social agreements. Infrastructure evolved organically: initial phases prioritized essential farm buildings and volunteer shelters; later phases added educational spaces and upgraded tourism facilities. Financial constraints and seasonal rhythms shaped the pacing, with a consistent commitment to reinvesting in community-serving structures rather than private accumulation.

The site itself—43 hectares of coastal Algarve land—is both a constraint and an inspiration. The terrain features rolling hills, arid summers, and seasonal torrents. Traditional Mediterranean orchards (carob, fig, olive) echo past land uses, forming a cultural and agroecological backbone. The farm sits within a vulnerable bioregion marked by rural depopulation, water scarcity, and increasing tourism pressure. Rather than retreating from these dynamics, the ecovillage engages them proactively—using its visibility and partnerships to model alternatives. Land tenure is based on private ownership by a founding family, yet the governance and use of the land are shared through long-term agreements with the resident association and education non-profits. This hybrid model allows for legal clarity while supporting commons-based stewardship.

Financing has combined ethical private investment, EU grants, programme revenue, and income from eco-tourism. The project's mixed economy is key to its resilience: no single stream dominates, and surpluses are directed into infrastructure, land care, and educational access. Despite its rurality, the site is accessible and offers adequate digital infrastructure for hybrid livelihoods. This enables residents to participate in European learning platforms, online research, and remote collaborations—blending place-based and networked modes of living. Ecologically, the site has seen dramatic improvements: reforestation, increased soil organic matter, restored water retention, and biodiversity recovery. Wildlife corridors have returned, and previously eroded fields now support layered agroforestry systems.

More than just a functional settlement, the ecovillage operates as a living symbiosis—a mutually beneficial coexistence between soil and soul, ecology and economy, permanence and adaptation. It is not static; the system is continually shaped by feedback from the land, the climate, and the community. Cultural rhythms such as shared meals, solstice rituals, farm markets, and storytelling nights nurture not only resilience but joy. Children are home-schooled or co-schooled in partnership with local institutions, using the land itself as a learning laboratory. Elders share not just knowledge, but perspectives on long-term thinking. Conflicts arise but are held within a framework of dialogue and repair. The community doesn't claim to be finished—it claims to be alive. Its greatest achievement is not the infrastructure or the yields, but the ongoing commitment to co-evolution: with the land, with each other, and with the challenges of our time.

However, the ecovillage is not static and evolves through cycles of experimentation, success, and failure. There are challenges—burnout, land-use regulations, climate shocks, interpersonal tensions. But the project's core strength lies in its resilience mindset: mistakes are composted into learning, structures are adapted, social tools are upgraded.

Composting Experience into Wisdom: Lessons for Future Ecovillages. In order to start a regenerative settlement one of the first and most important steps is to start with observation, not intervention. It is important to understand the land: its water flows, soil health, native species, and climate patterns. Likewise, understanding the cultural landscape—who lives nearby, what histories are held in the soil, what forms of knowledge already exist—is also an additional step. Regeneration must begin with context, not concept. The design process should be participatory from the beginning, even if the initial team is small. Bring in not just experts, but also those who will live, work, and learn on the land. Co-create the vision through dialogue, mapping exercises, and shared meals. Aim for slow but deep alignment around values—ecological care, cooperation, resilience, and justice. These will serve as anchors when difficult decisions arise, as they inevitably will.

When it comes to land and legal structure, flexibility and foresight are key (Wenger, 1998). Whether through co-ownership, lease agreements, or stewarding models, ensure that governance is transparent, equitable, and adaptable over time. Sociocratic or consent-based systems can help avoid burnout and power struggles later. It is crucial to start small and build in phases, aligned with both ecological capacity and human bandwidth. Focus on foundational systems first: water, soil, shelter, and food. One must prioritize infrastructure that is multi-use, low-impact, and capable of evolving. Further, it is important to avoid over-investing in aesthetics or technology too early. A single well-designed compost toilet or water swale can do more than a solar panel array if it's embedded in a functioning system.

Economic diversity is another pillar (Wright, 2019). One must avoid dependency on a single income stream such as grants or tourism and combine regenerative agriculture, education, remote work, product development, and seasonal hospitality to create a resilient web of livelihoods. Encouragement of residents to develop small enterprises that align with the project's ethics—whether herbal production, fermentation, eco-construction, or online facilitation—is also a key. Designing such a project as a place of learning—formally and informally—attracts new energy, builds partnerships, and distributes responsibility. It is important to host workshops, internships, or camps that allow people to contribute labour while learning skills.

One should create time for group reflection, celebration, and rest, and build in practices like shared meals, weekly circles, storytelling nights, or work parties. These small rituals hold the community through change and stress. Lastly, regenerative settlements can't be islands—they must engage with surrounding communities, schools, governments, and ecosystems. It is essential to contribute to local food systems, watershed councils, or cultural events. Regeneration is not only about healing land—it's about restoring relational infrastructure between people and place, between humans and nonhumans, between present and future (Lockyer & Veteto, 2013).

Therapeutic Community Living and Social Inclusion: Rožkalni Camphill, Latvia

Planting the Seeds of Belonging: the Settlement's History Evolves. Rožkalni Camphill was established in 1999 by a Latvian couple Vilnis and Inga Neimaņi, in Latvia, near Valmiera city, 100 km north from Riga—capital city of Latvia. The basic principle of the Camphill movement is to include people with disabilities in society, thus also learning to build harmonious relationships themselves: working together, caring for each other, loving and forgiving, celebrating holidays, etc. Working and living in harmony with the needs of the community and in close connection with nature contributes to the mental health and personal development of each participant.

After intensive training and experience in Camphill communities in Norway, they returned to their homeland to establish the first (and currently the only) Camphill village in Latvia. With the assistance of friends and volunteers, they transformed a simple rural house in the village of 'Rožkalni' in Rencēni parish into a dynamic community for individuals with special needs. In its early stages, the community provided home and familial support to young people from orphanages.

Later on, the newly acquired friends from the Camphill movement in Norway travelled to Rožkalni to help build the second residential house—'Zenta Mauriņa house', which was one of the early straw houses in Latvia. On May 27, 2023, a spark from a chimney struck the roof of this residential building, resulting in significant damage to the substantial structure. Fortunately, none of the villagers and co-workers were injured in the fire calamity. However, 13 individuals lost everything they owned (Šatrovska, 2023). Public support for Rožkalni was publicly initiated through a donation to the house's restoration in order to guarantee the village's ongoing narrative (Matisone, 2023).

Visionaries of Inclusion: The Founders and Their Mission. The initiative to establish Rožkalni Camphill was led by Vilnis and Inga Neimaņi, a Latvian family of two adults and two children. Before establishing the settlement, the Neimaņi family participated in Camphill communities in Norway, where they received training and gained experience in *anthroposophy*. The integration of spiritual and practical aspects of life, particularly in education and social development, is the primary focus of this philosophical approach, which was developed by Rudolf Steiner (Steiner, 2013). Considering the gathered knowledge and experience in anthroposophy, Vilnis and Inga started cherishing a vision to create a supportive environment where individuals with developmental disabilities could live and work together, fostering a sense of community and belonging. Thus, the dedication of the founders to establishing and developing Rožkalni Camphill demonstrates a strong commitment to social responsibility, community building, and the integration of individuals with special needs into society.

Through the prism of a symbiotic settlement, the above-outlined characteristics connect the attributes of organizers' lifestyle with creativity, willingness to collaborate, and focus on relationships ahead to the service-driven business model, with particular dedication—services to individuals with special needs, i.e., specialization.

Designing for Dignity: Building a Targeted Community Around Shared Lives. The specialization strategy encourages tailoring infrastructure to meet the specific needs of particular groups of inhabitants who share similar lifestyles. In this approach, the primary driving force is the component of 'inhabitants', and the strategy guides the governors of human settlements to make deliberate decisions regarding the composition of the population. By reducing diversity among inhabitants, it becomes possible to design and implement infrastructure more effectively, aligning it closely with the shared needs and expectations of the community. Rožkalni is a purposefully developed therapeutic settlement rooted in the Camphill movement, where individuals with developmental disabilities engage in meaningful work, participate in community life, and experience a sense of belonging. As a specialized social innovation strategy, Rožkalni addresses the complex needs of its inhabitants not through traditional institutional care, but by creating a self-sustaining, inclusive, and nature-integrated community (Polis, 2015).

From the outset, Rožkalni was conceived as more than just a residential facility—it is a transformative settlement structured around collective life, shared goals, and mutual support, where inhabitants co-create a meaningful and dignified existence. This intentional community structure is based on the understanding that individuals with special needs flourish best within supportive social ecosystems, rather than isolated care systems.

The organizational foundation of Rožkalni is a community of residents, co-workers, and volunteers united by shared values and a clear social mission. This post human-centred governance model emphasizes cooperative decision-making, rejecting traditional hierarchies in favour of participatory and inclusive approaches. The model is not static: it is strategically oriented towards continuous adaptation, with the aim of enhancing the social infrastructure needed to meet the evolving needs of its members.

Key to Rožkalni's strategy is the cultivation of a socially and emotionally supportive environment. Through the integration of living, working, and cultural spaces, the community fosters relationships based on empathy, understanding, and mutual respect. This forms the backbone of transformative service delivery—where healing and growth emerge from shared daily life.

The organizational foundation of Rožkalni is a community of residents, co-workers, and volunteers united by shared values and a clear social mission. This *posthuman-centred governance model* emphasizes cooperative decision-making, rejecting traditional hierarchies in favour of *participatory and inclusive approaches*. The model is not static: it is strategically oriented towards continuous adaptation, with the aim of enhancing the *social infrastructure* needed to meet the evolving needs of its members.

Key to Rožkalni's strategy is the *cultivation of a socially and emotionally supportive environment*. Through the integration of living, working, and cultural spaces, the community fosters relationships based on empathy, understanding, and mutual respect. This forms the backbone of transformative service delivery—where healing and growth emerge from shared daily life.

The Rožkalni settlement is built upon the foundational principles of the Camphill movement, launched in Scotland in 1939 by Dr Karl König. Based on Rudolf Steiner's anthroposophical philosophy, Camphill *promotes the symbiosis between humans and nature* and views each individual as inherently valuable, regardless of ability. The Rožkalni strategy interprets and applies these principles by:

- Creating inclusive living environments, where individuals with and without disabilities share responsibilities and life experiences.
- Engaging all residents in meaningful and therapeutic work, such as agriculture, crafts, and workshop activities.
- Promoting spiritual and cultural development through festivals, art, and music.
- Fostering ecological responsibility through sustainable living and biodynamic farming.

These principles support a settlement model that does not merely provide care, but instead enables personal development and social contribution, thereby addressing the existential needs of post-industrial society.

The *spatial design* of Rožkalni reflects both *philosophical ideals* and *practical functionality*. Architectural solutions are guided by principles of human scale, ecological construction, and spatial interconnectedness. Residential homes are designed for small-group co-housing, balancing privacy with communal engagement. Shared spaces such as the cultural centre, dining hall, and workshops serve as hubs of interaction, creativity, and celebration.

Rožkalni's economic infrastructure is similarly strategic. Specialized workshops—such as dairy processing, herbal tea production, and paper-making—offer not only employment but also meaningful daily structure. Agricultural activity follows biodynamic principles, integrating natural rhythms and environmental care into food production and land stewardship. Importantly, the first straw house built in Latvia, located in Rožkalni, symbolizes the community's commitment to ecological building practices and local heritage. Construction materials and techniques reflect Latvian traditions while embracing modern sustainability standards.

Rožkalni's governance and ownership model strengthens its transformative impact. The community operates on a co-ownership basis, promoting shared responsibility and long-term commitment. A social enterprise structure ensures financial sustainability through the sale of organic products and crafts, while also creating real employment opportunities for residents. Rožkalni is embedded within local and international networks, including Waldorf educational institutions and other Camphill communities across Europe. These connections ensure knowledge exchange, economic support, and social innovation diffusion beyond the settlement's borders.

Rožkalni Camphill represents a new kind of rural development—one that redefines service provision through community, sustainability, and social inclusion. It offers an alternative vision to post-industrial societal challenges, emphasizing healing relationships with both people and the natural world. In this way, Rožkalni is not merely a place to live. It is a transformative settlement, a social ecosystem where architecture, work, and everyday life are co-designed to support human dignity, mutual care, and environmental harmony. It stands as a compelling model of how intentional settlements can serve as laboratories of meaningful and inclusive futures.

Strategic Growth through Service and Soil. Rožkalni Camphill's strategic approach is rooted in the idea of the community as a transformative agent. The experience of Camphill communities in countries such as the United Kingdom and Norway demonstrates that these settlements frequently extend support to young individuals emerging from institutional care systems, including orphans. In contrast, the case of Rožkalni reflects a more deliberate and narrowly defined specialization strategy: the community made a strategic decision—to purposefully organize around the needs of people with developmental disabilities, establishing a coherent social and infrastructural model aligned with this specific inhabitant group. The core specialization lies not in any singular activity, but in the integrated development of a sustainable, inclusive, and symbiotic environment. This is realized through interconnected strategic actions that align with the needs of its residents and the philosophy of symbiosis with nature—a hallmark of the Camphill movement.

Rožkalni has attained certified organic farming status through the use of biodynamic methods over its 30-hectare estate. These practices not only uphold environmental ethics but also generate work opportunities that match the abilities of the residents, referred to as villagers. They engage in horticulture, composting, and the production of dairy products. These meaningful tasks cultivate a sense of purpose and strengthen ties to the land, reinforcing the therapeutic essence of the community. Thus the community reached the integration of biodynamic agriculture and work, which is essential for creating a favourable infrastructure to live and work.

In addition to farming, Rožkalni offers structured workshops in papermaking, tea preparation, felting, and weaving. These activities ensure that all community members have a role, regardless of physical or intellectual ability, thus upholding the settlement's core values of inclusion and service. The winter months especially highlight these indoor workshops, integrating residents into year-round productivity and social participation (Krasta, 2023). Thus, crafts and social workshops contribute to the creation of a symbiotic settlement.

Next to that, from its origin as a single farmhouse in 1999, Rožkalni has evolved into a well-integrated village. The community now includes two residential houses, a cultural centre, workshops, and farming infrastructure. Its architectural layout promotes daily interaction and shared living. The recent rebuilding of 'Zenta Mauriņa House'—destroyed by fire and replaced with 'Lilijas House' in 2023—demonstrates a resilient and responsive strategy aligned with community needs and shared values. Thus, the settlement built a community-centric infrastructure.

Finally, Rožkalni's involvement in initiatives like the European Commission's 'Pats savam saimes galdam' project shows a dedication to sustainable development through external collaboration. These partnerships support not only agricultural growth but also knowledge-sharing events that enhance the residents' engagement with broader society, ensuring the collaborative development. Through these strategic actions, Rožkalni Camphill demonstrates a holistic approach to community living by incorporating services for social inclusion via sustainable agriculture and continuous symbiotic development of the settlement to improve the well-being of its members throughout all actions in the livelihood.

Living the Vision: People, Place, and Everyday Infrastructure. Rožkalni's organizational model centres on the concept of people as the core of the settlement's infrastructure. Here, infrastructure is not merely physical—it is social and emotional. The environment is curated to promote empathy, safety, and opportunities for self-expression and inclusion. The Rožkalni Camphill currently functions as a social therapeutic village for individuals with developmental disabilities. Residents live side by side with volunteers, social workers, and families in a structure of mutual care. At present, Rožkalni Camphill provides housing for ten individuals with intellectual developmental disabilities (Youth.Europa.Eu, 2025). The community's activities are intended to create an environment that offers its residents opportunities to develop skills and engage in meaningful activities. Villagers adhere to biodynamic farming principles and engage in a variety of agricultural activities, such as horticulture and farming. Additionally, they are involved in the production of dairy products, including sour cream, curd, and fresh cheese. Workshops that emphasize woodworking, felting, weaving, and the preparation of tea and spices are implemented during the winter months. These initiatives not only meet the community's requirements to sustain, but also contribute to local markets by selling home-made products.

The community has maintained a consistent population over the years in terms of population dynamics. The small scale of the community presents challenges in attaining significant economies of scale, even though the current population supports the community's operations. Nevertheless, the community's sustainability is facilitated by the integration of volunteers and the sale of products, which help mitigate these challenges. In the broader context, Latvia has experienced a population decline, with an approximate 11,000-person decrease in 2024 (Official Statistics of Latvia, 2025). This trend is especially evident in rural areas, which could potentially affect communities such as Rožkalni Camphill by restricting the local pool of potential residents and personnel.

Although the current population in Rožkalni Camphill is adequate to support daily operations, the restricted size presents obstacles to long-term development and scalability, particularly in the context of regional demographic trends.

Through co-living, open decision-making, and shared ownership, Rožkalni Camphill is a prime example of a *collaborative community*. It promotes social integration, sustainable lifestyles, and reciprocal care and is based on anthroposophical principles. Cultural events, teamwork, and a dedication to helping people with disabilities foster a united atmosphere of dignity, meaning, and purpose.

Living Infrastructure. Rožkalni Camphill underwent substantial living infrastructure development to facilitate its mission of offering a therapeutic environment for individuals with developmental disabilities. Several stages might be distinguished in infrastructure development at Rožkalni:

- *Initial Establishment* (1999): Founders Vilnis and Inga Neimaņi transformed a simple rural house into a community residence, laying the foundation for 'Rožkalni'.
- *Expansion* with 'Zenta Mauriņa House': Assistance from the Norwegian Camphill community facilitated the construction of this second residential building, notable for being one of Latvia's first straw houses.
- *Development of Workshops and Cultural Centre*: The community itself established various workshops and a cultural centre to promote skill development and social engagement among residents.
- *Reconstruction* (2023): Following a fire that damaged 'Zenta Mauriņa House', the community, with support from donors and volunteers, constructed 'Lilijas House', inaugurated on September 30, 2023.

In current times, relevant characteristics to the living spaces are defined in terms of structure and layout, property co-ownership, and collective decision-making. Considering the structure and layout, the village is composed of two residential houses, a cultural centre, stables, and workshops. The arrangement of these structures is designed to promote a communal ambiance, with shared spaces that encourage interaction among residents. The property co-ownership type of Rožkalni Camphill is a charitable foundation that collectively owns the land and structures. The Camphill philosophy of collective stewardship and shared responsibility is exemplified by this communal ownership model. Although the available sources do not provide specific governance structures, Camphill communities generally implement collective decision-making processes that involve residents, staff, and volunteers to guarantee inclusive management, as well as fostering a sense of responsibility and belonging among inhabitants.

Situated near Valmiera in Latvia, Rožkalni Camphill holds specific *place characteristics*. Rožkalni spans 30 hectares of fertile land used for organic farming. The landscape offers a serene and natural environment conducive to the community's therapeutic goals. The community has achieved organic farming status, utilizing biological preparations and minerals prepared on-site. The infrastructure supports work duties at home, with provisions for transportation and internet connectivity to facilitate communication and collaboration.

Being Latvia's first and only Camphill settlement, Rožkalni has great heritage importance. The community, which was founded by Vilnis and Inga Neimaņi following their training in Norway, reflects the Camphill movement's tenet of integrating people with developmental impairments into a nurturing setting. The 'Zenta Mauriņa House', one of Latvia's first straw houses, was a noteworthy architectural element that represented creative and environmentally friendly building techniques.

The Camphill Rožkalni Charitable Foundation is the joint owner of the buildings and land. Contributions from families, local government agencies, and social security—which pay for necessities—are among the funding sources. Donations from foundations, organizations, and people provide additional funding for therapies, cultural events, and infrastructure development.

The community's participation in numerous workshops and the sale of goods are guaranteed by functional infrastructure, which also supports these activities. For both residents and staff, the common areas are crucial for internal meetings and teamwork.

The peaceful rural environment of Rožkalni is beneficial to the health of its residents. A dedication to environmental sustainability and wellness is shown in the focus on biodynamic farming and the use of natural materials in architecture, which supports the green focus of the settlement. The activities and organization of the community foster a secure and encouraging environment for people with developmental disabilities. In conclusion, 'Rožkalni' is a prime example of the seamless blending of landscape, heritage, and community-oriented infrastructure, creating an atmosphere that is conducive to the success of people with developmental disabilities.

Lessons from Rožkalni: Growing Specialized Symbiotic Settlements. Several important aspects should be taken into consideration when aiming to replicate a similar initiative to the Rožkalni Camphill.

Comprehensive Training. Immersion in the ideologies and real-world operations of comparable models is essential before establishing a community. As Vilnis and Inga Neimaņi did, training in well-established Camphill communities, like those in Norway, provides exposure to (a) social therapy and the ideas of anthroposophy, (b) practices for community-based care, and (c) living and working conditions that are inclusive. By ensuring that founders absorb not only tasks but also the culture of these settlements, embodied learning makes it possible for genuine replication and adaptability. Thus, gaining experience in established Camphill communities or similar settings is necessary to understand the operational dynamics and philosophies.

Community Engagement. Relationships based on reciprocity, trust, and involvement form the social fabric, which is a must for a successful symbiotic settlement. Early and continuous cooperation with local inhabitants, municipalities in the region, NGOs, civic society actors, and volunteers (including foreign volunteers) creates credibility and resiliency. Rožkalni is a prime example of this, thanks to its vast network of volunteers, contributors, and supporters who helped with post-crisis reconstruction. Thus the involvement of local communities and volunteers vitally serves to build a support network and foster inclusivity.

Sustainable Practices. Instead of being an afterthought, sustainability ought to be a fundamental design element. To illustrate this, Rožkalni uses (a) organic and biodynamic farming systems (30 hectares of land); (b) natural building supplies (straw houses, e.g.); (c) resource circularity (e.g., composting, dairy processing). These methods improve community health and local food systems while reducing their negative effects on the environment. Thus implementing organic farming and eco-friendly building techniques helps in promoting sustainability and ensuring self-sufficiency.

Diverse Work Opportunities. Rožkalni Camphill practice proves that settlements must develop a range of jobs tailored to different skill levels in order to guarantee social inclusion and economic vitality. Among the examples are (a) dairy processing and farming; (b) handicrafts and paper-making; (c) making herbal tea; and (d) working with wood. Through product sales, these activities promote residents' sense of self-worth, offer meaningful participation, and support long-term financial viability. Thus various developed workshops and enterprises work to provide meaningful work and at the same time generate income.

Resilience Planning. Resilience needs to be planned for in advance, as seen by Rožkalni's response to the 2023 fire. Important elements consist of (a) plans for evacuation and emergency management procedures, (b) sufficient building insurance, (c) various sources of support, (d) mechanisms of community solidarity (donations, volunteer work). This guarantees that shocks act as stimulants for regeneration rather than endangering continuity.

Collaborative Decision-Making. Shared governance, a fundamental Camphill idea, promotes social cohesion, empowerment, and shared responsibility. Mechanisms could consist of (a) frequent gatherings of the community; (b) inclusive decision-making procedures for residents, employees, and families; (c) rotation of roles in administrative tasks. These methods foster a democratic culture that is in line with the community's common values and long-term developmental objectives.

Altogether, the above-highlighted pointers provide a comprehensive and integrated strategy for creating a symbiotic living model with specialization. The specialization strategy began with a broader desire to live differently—often led by a group seeking to create a distinct way of life, separate from mainstream norms. Rather than adapting to existing systems, they establish a new one. This is the foundation of Rožkalni Camphill: a self-created community shaped by values of inclusion, care, and ecological living. Initially inspired by a holistic vision, Rožkalni's founders gradually made a strategic decision to specialize—focusing specifically on integrating individuals with developmental disabilities into all aspects of daily life. This narrowing of purpose created a coherent, supportive environment where infrastructure, governance, and relationships are aligned around shared goals. In this sense, specialization was not a limitation, but a refinement. It enabled Rožkalni to develop a strong identity and infrastructure rooted in human dignity and mutual care. The selective nature of this strategy—choosing who to live with and how—allowed the community to function as a whole, rather than a set of services. Thus, Rožkalni shows how specialization can be a courageous act of shaping a meaningful life, together, where being 'apart' becomes a source of strength, not separation.

References

Albrecht, G. A. (2019). Earth emotions: New words for a new world. In *Earth Emotions*. Cornell University Press.

Albrecht, G. A. (2020). Negating solastalgia: An emotional revolution from the Anthropocene to the Symbiocene. *American Imago, 77*(1), 9–30.

Braidotti, R. (2013). Posthuman humanities. *European Educational Research Journal, 12*(1), 1–19.

Buck, J., & Villines, S. (2007). *We the people: Consenting to a deeper democracy*. Sociocracy.info Press.

Capra, F., & Luisi, P. L. (2014). *The systems view of life: A unifying vision*. Cambridge University Press.

Coats, C. (2001). *Living energies: An exposition of concepts related to the theories of Viktor Schauberger*. Gateway Books.

Copeland, C., MacKerron, G., & Foxon, T. J. (2023). Futures for Findhorn: Exploring challenges for achieving net zero in an ecological intentional community. *Futures, 149*, 103155.

Cordon, L. A. (2012). *Freud's world: An encyclopedia of his life and times*. Greenwood.

Duhm, D. (2005). *The sacred matrix: From the matrix of violence to the matrix of life*. Verlag Meiga.

Duhm, D. (2015). *Terra Nova: Global revolution and the healing of love*. Verlag Meiga.

Endenburg, G. (1988). *Sociocracy: The organization of decision-making*. Delft University Press.

Escribano, P., Lubbers, M. J., & Molina, J. L. (2020). A typology of ecological intentional communities: Environmental sustainability through subsistence and material reproduction. *Journal of Cleaner Production, 266*, 121803.

Esteves, A. M. (2017). Radical environmentalism and "Commoning": Synergies between ecosystem regeneration and social governance at Tamera ecovillage, Portugal. *Antipode, 49*(2), 357–376.

Folke, C., Biggs, R., Norström, A. V., Reyers, B., & Rockström, J. (2016). Social-ecological resilience and biosphere-based sustainability science. *Ecology and Society, 21*(3), 41. https://doi.org/10.5751/ES-08748-210341

Gough, S. (2002). Whose gap? Whose mind? Plural rationalities and disappearing academics. *Environmental Education Research, 8*(3), 273–282.

Haraway, D. J. (2016). Staying with the trouble: Making kin in the Chthulucene. In *Staying with the Trouble*. Duke University Press.

Kopnina, H., Washington, H., Gray, J., & Taylor, B. (2018). The 'future of conservation' debate: Defending ecocentrism and the nature needs half movement. *Biological Conservation, 217*, 140–148.

Krasta, E. (2023). Programme for the enterprising and self-employment - "Home for your own family table" [in Latvian "Pats savam saimes galdam"].https://epale.ec.europa.eu/lv/content/programma-uznemigajiem un-rosigajiem-pats-savam-saimes-galdam.

Lockyer, J., & Veteto, J. R. (2013). *Environmental anthropology engaging Ecotopia: Bioregionalism, permaculture, and ecovillages.* Berghahn Books.

Margulis, L., & Sagan, D. (2002). *Acquiring genomes: A theory of the origins of species.* Basic Books.

Matisone, G. (2023). Cleaning up to help rebuild the burnt down house in Camphill Rožkalni for people with special needs [in Latvian]. https://www.lsm.lv/raksts/zinas/latvija/20.06.2023-talko-lai-palidzetu-atjaunot-nodeguso-maju-camphill-rozkalni-ciemata-cilvekiem-ar-ipasam-vajadzibam.a513467/

Mollison, B., & Holmgren, D. (1978). *Perma-culture one. A perennial agriculture for human settlements.* University of Tasmania.

Mollison, B. C., Slay, R. M., Girard, J. L., & Girard, J. L. (1991). *Introduction to permaculture.* Tagari Publications.

Motevalli, S., Saffari, N., Michael, M. T. A., & Abadi, F. H. (2022). Enculturation, education and sustainable development: Understanding the impact of culture and education on climate change. *International Education Studies, 15*(4), 31–41.

Naess, A. (1989). *Ecology, Community and Lifestyle.* Cambridge University Press.

Official Statistics of Latvia. (2025). Population of Latvia declined by 11 thousand in 2023. https://stat.gov.lv/en/statistics-themes/population/population/press-releases/20902-number-population-latvia-2023?utm_source

Polis, A. (2015). Ekociemati Latvijā - Rožkalni. April 3, 2015, Journal "Vides Vēstis". https://videsvestis.lv/ekociemati-latvija/

Reich, W. (1974). *The discovery of the Orgone.* Vision.

Rolston, H. (1994). *Conserving natural value.* Columbia University Press.

Rožkalni Camphill. (2025). Official website. Available at: camphillrozkalni.lv

Šatrovska, A. (2023). Camphill foundation Rožkalni asks for support for the renovation of the family house in Rožkalni. https://www.valmierasnovads.lv/camphill-nodibinajums-rozkalni-ludz-atbalstu-saimes-majas-atjaunosanai-rozkalnos/?utm_source=chatgpt.com

Sheldrake, R. (2011). *The presence of the past: Morphic resonance and the habits of nature.* Icon Books.

Steiner, R. (2013). *Anthroposophical leading thoughts: Anthroposophy as a path of knowledge-the Michael mystery.* Rudolf Steiner Press.

Strick, J. E. (2015). *Wilhelm Reich, Biologist.* Harvard University Press.

Tamera. (n.d.). *Healing Biotopes Plan—A strategy for global peace*. https://www.tamera.org/healing-biotopes-plan/

Tamera. (n.d.). *Holistic Education—Political, spiritual, social, sexual & ecological*. https://www.tamera.org/holistic-education/

Tilbury, D. (1995). Environmental education for sustainability: Defining the new focus of environmental education in the 1990s. *Environmental Education Research, 1*(2), 195–212.

Washington, H., Taylor, B., Kopnina, H., Cryer, P., & Piccolo, J. J. (2017). Why ecocentrism is the key pathway to sustainability. *The Ecological Citizen, 1*(1), 35–41.

Wenger, E. (1998). *Communities of practice: Learning, meaning, and identity*. Cambridge University Press.

Wright, C. (2019). *The EcoVillage at Ithaca: Pioneering a sustainable culture*. New Society Publishers.

Youth.Europa.Eu. (2025). Camphill Nodibinajums "Rozkalni". https://youth.europa.eu/volunteering/organisation/63163_lv

CHAPTER 7

Diversification Strategy: Reorganization of the Place According to Post-Anthropocentric and Post-urban Thinking

Vitalija Simonaitytė, Rita Lankauskienė, and Paweł Chmieliński

It is easier to create a settlement adapted to a post-industrial lifestyle in an area of empty land. As demonstrated by case studies in Chaps. 4, 5, and 6, this allows for the creation of a community of inhabitants who share the same lifestyle and the building of new infrastructure. Starting from an uninhabited or sparsely used territory creates fewer conflicts of interest and allows the direct projection of new values into spatial forms and infrastructures. In this way, post-industrial values can be inscribed from the very beginning into the morphology of the settlement. This dynamic has been noted in urban studies as the 'tabula rasa effect', where the absence of legacy systems enables experimentation with alternative models of social and ecological living (Lefebvre, 1996; Harvey, 2012).

However, the transition to a new socio-economic paradigm does not mean that existing cities and villages cannot be transformed. The targeted efforts of a new generation of social movements show that this is a feasible task. The experience of Transition Towns and Ecovillage movements

D. Vidickienė et al., *Human Settlement in the Service Economy Era*, Palgrave Advances in Bioeconomy: Economics and Policies, https://doi.org/10.1007/978-3-032-19390-2_7

demonstrates that the efforts to reorganize the place take two key trajectories, oriented to post-anthropocentric and post-urban thinking. These movements have shown that urban and rural regeneration processes can be guided not only by ecological concerns but also by new cultural paradigms in which the human being is no longer the sole measure of all design decisions. As Westlund and Haas (2018) emphasize, the post-urban world challenges established planning categories and invited hybrid solutions that bridge the conventional urban and rural divide. Similarly, Haraway (2016) calls for 'making kin' with non-human species, suggesting that the reconstruction of place must include multispecies justice and ecological companionship.

The first steps in reorganizing cities with a focus on natural environment issues were taken during the industrial era by integrating nature into the city's fabric. The integration of nature improves the aesthetic and environmental quality of cities, making them healthier and more pleasant places to live. This development was historically evident in the emergence of garden cities and park systems, which sought to bring balance to the alienated industrial metropolis (Conn, 2024). However, the post-industrial values and lifestyle require more attention to the relationships between humans and the environment. As Gutierrez-Velez et al. (2022) argue, infrastructure systems must be reimagined to go beyond the 'urban' and the 'rural' if we are to enable sustainable relations between humans, non-humans, and their environments. Latour (2018) reinforces this by suggesting that modern societies must 'land' again, recognizing the Earth as a political actor that reshapes our modes of inhabitation.

Gradually, solutions oriented to urban renewal by creating green spaces and using more green technologies for infrastructure development are evolving into a more complex approach. This approach encourages a transition from a concept of urban naturation to a post-anthropocentric approach to human settlement. The application of post-anthropocentric design is a radical shift from the human-centred design of modern industrial cities. This approach promotes an ecologically conscious and equitable design practice by recognizing the intrinsic value and interconnectedness of all living and non-living entities. From the perspective of regenerative design, this means that architecture, infrastructure, and landscapes must evolve as living systems, echoing principles of circularity and reciprocity (Mang & Reed, 2012). Post-anthropocentric planning seeks to move beyond harmful human-centric practices by fostering symbiotic relationships between humans and nature through methods like biomimicry, regenerative urban planning, and circular systems that support long-term sustainability and planetary health.

At the end of the industrial era, urban decay, urban shrinkage, and even ghost cities have become recurring phenomena across the urbanized world, with areas in the biggest cities decaying or even abandoned altogether. The same processes are testified in remote rural areas, where outmigration and economic decline have created empty landscapes. Such phenomena are not only material but also symbolic, representing the exhaustion of the modernist paradigm of endless urban expansion. As Brunori (2006) observed, wealthy rural areas as well as shrinking cities are entering post-rural and post-urban processes, characterized by hybrid networks and new symbolic capital.

Thinking in the terms of the industrial era, the regeneration of urban and rural human settlements is seen as two different processes. However, the emerging post-industrial reality shows that the human settlement regeneration strategy is most productive when it is oriented to the urban–rural continuum. Entering the service economy era blurs the line between agrarian villages and industrial towns and cities. Consequently, human settlement regeneration strategies take an orientation to characteristics of the post-urban and post-rural world. As Westlund (2014) has argued, we may indeed be 'entering a post-urban world' where the analytical distinction between city and countryside loses its explanatory power. Brenner (2016) similarly argues for a 'planetary urbanization' perspective, in which all spaces, whether forests, farms, or metropolises, are implicated in global urban processes.

The key challenge is the creation of human settlements with characteristics where the meaning of concepts 'rurality' and 'urbanity' disappears. Growing servitization and deindustrialization processes are essential factors encouraging the revision of the traditional city design, adapted to the needs of the working class. Progressive communities and policymakers are seeking innovative solutions to enhance the quality of life and promote community well-being, focusing on livelihoods and lifestyles that align with a servitized economy. An important role is played by the development of transformative services that emphasize a holistic approach to health, education, and ecological well-being. As Westlund and Borseková (2025) suggest in their post-urban hypothesis, the new settlement paradigm is defined less by density or land-use patterns than by networks of services, ecological integration, and cultural imaginaries. This orientation is reinforced by concepts such as 'commoning the city' (Stavrides, 2016), where collective use and stewardship of space become central to the social infrastructure of the post-urban world.

In this context, the diversification strategy emerges as a crucial pathway: instead of uniform urban renewal projects or purely rural development programmes, it promotes adaptive, plural, and resilient reorganization. Diversification here refers not only to economic functions but also to cultural, ecological, and infrastructural dimensions of human settlements. In practical terms, it means creating settlements that are simultaneously resilient to global economic shifts, responsive to ecological imperatives, and open to multiple forms of life—human and non-human alike. As Escobar (2018) stresses, design in the pluriverse is about enabling many worlds to coexist, each grounded in relational ontologies and local practices, rather than enforcing one hegemonic model of urban modernity.

The chapter therefore presents three case studies on initiatives to develop human settlements, whose regeneration vision extends beyond the 'urban' and the 'rural' and is oriented to human/non-human symbiosis:

1. Druskininkai, Lithuania: Revitalization of the resort.
2. Smiltynė: Integrating health services, ecology, and cultural heritage.
3. Local Action Group (LAG) 'Green Neighbourhood': Unlocking the potential of the local community to create a better living.

Grounded in the Druskininkai case, the diversification strategy proposed here understands 'reorganization of place' as the purposeful build-out of living infrastructure for new kinds of services—wellness, regenerative health, low-carbon mobility, nature-based recreation, and digital work, conceived within the Symbiocene ethos of human–more-than-human co-flourishing. In a forested municipality whose mineral springs and spa heritage long prefigured health-oriented land uses, the shift after the 1990s' crisis towards an integrated portfolio of services illustrates how post-anthropocentric design can be operationalized as infrastructure rather than as rhetoric (Raymond et al., 2017; European Commission, 2019, 2020). The municipality's investments in pedestrian and bicycle corridors, a fully electric transit fleet, and EV charging stations align mobility with planetary health while coupling tourism diversification to everyday resident well-being (Banister, 2008; European Commission, 2021). At governance level, multiscale coordination—EU funds, national climate agendas, municipal planning, and LAG-led participation—has translated biophilic intent into durable assets and capabilities, enabling adaptive stewardship of forests, rivers, and mineral resources as co-design partners rather than mere amenities (Haraway, 2016; Latour, 2018). Read through a post-urban lens, Druskininkai's green transition dissolves inherited urban–rural binaries by embedding service networks and ecological functions across the settlement fabric, exemplifying Westlund's and Borseková's hypothesis that future place-making is structured less by density than by service ecologies and cultural imaginaries (Westlund, 2014; Westlund, 2017; Westlund & Borseková, 2025). Crucially, diversification here is not only economic; it is ontological: medical-wellness services interlink with ecosystem care (nature-based solutions, circular resource flows), social services (inclusive public space, participatory governance), and digital services (remote work readiness), assembling what Albrecht names the Symbiocene—'the age of living together' as a practical planning horizon (Albrecht, 2019; Mang & Reed, 2012). In this register, Druskininkai functions as a demonstrator of Symbiocene infrastructure: a place where regenerative health systems, climate-neutral mobility, and commons-based governance co-produce resilience, attractivity, and multispecies habitability along the urban–rural continuum (Bai et al., 2010; Bulkeley & Betsill, 2013).

The transformation of Smiltynė illustrates how diversification strategies can reconfigure a settlement's identity by layering new social functions onto inherited cultural and ecological infrastructures. Originally a military and resort site, Smiltynė entered decline in the Soviet era, yet its regeneration since the late twentieth century demonstrates the adaptive reuse of place-based assets. The repurposing of Nerija Fort as the Lithuanian Sea Museum and Dolphinarium created cultural and educational anchors (GPSmyCity, 2025; Baltic Seaside, 2025), while the establishment of the Dolphin-Assisted Therapy Centre in 2015 introduced a specialized health service for neurodiverse populations in partnership with universities and healthcare institutions (Kreivinienė, 2019; Lithuanian Sea Museum, 2025a). In diversification terms, Smiltynė exemplifies the principle of complementarity: heritage buildings, marine expertise, and ecological landscapes are recombined with innovative therapeutic and educational functions, generating a multifunctional identity that strengthens resilience and inclusivity (Escobar, 2018; Westlund & Borseková, 2025). Rather than restoring a mono-functional resort, the settlement evolved into a hybrid node where health, ecology, and culture intersect, providing transformative services within a UNESCO-protected landscape (UNESCO,

2025). This trajectory shows how diversification not only prevents stagnation but also curates continuity, ensuring that post-industrial settlements remain adaptive, socially relevant, and ecologically accountable.

The third case—the Local Action Group 'Green Neighbourhood'—demonstrates how peri-urban settlements can be reorganized within post-anthropocentric and post-urban paradigms. Situated in Poland's Mazowieckie region, the municipalities of Brwinów, Milanówek, and Podkowa Leśna—historically shaped by the garden city ideal—represent a socio-spatial laboratory where human and non-human agencies co-constitute new modes of living. Pressured by demographic ageing, suburbanization from nearby Warsaw, and ecological vulnerabilities, the LAG mobilizes a diversification strategy rooted in the LEADER approach and community-led governance. Through participatory consultations, intergenerational engagement, and grassroots innovation, the LAG advances a symbiotic development model where ecological assets, cultural heritage, and social infrastructures are treated not as passive backdrops but as co-design partners in territorial regeneration. Initiatives focused on environmental education, Smart Village concepts, and inclusive service infrastructures illustrate how peri-urban landscapes can dissolve rigid urban–rural dichotomies by embedding multispecies justice, ecological reciprocity, and digital-era services into everyday life. In this sense, 'Green Neighbourhood' exemplifies a transition beyond anthropocentric planning logics and modernist urban growth models, towards hybrid socio-ecological systems that enact the pluriversal ethos of post-urbanity. The case highlights how diversification of place functions, when anchored in community agency, can operationalize post-industrial imaginaries into living infrastructures.

Revitalization of the Druskininkai (Lithuania) Resort

Settlement's history. The municipality of Druskininkai is located in southern Lithuania. The territory shares borders with three rural municipalities in the north, as well as Poland and Belarus. Druskininkai city, two rural elderships, and Druskininkai municipality are its three administrative units. The name of the city comes from the Lithuanian word 'druska', which means salt. Local sources are rich in minerals and their healing effects have been known for centuries. Druskininkai was named a health resort town since 1794 and now it is balneological, mud, and climatic resort.

In the Druskininkai region, forests cover up to 80% of the land. The custom of gathering forest items, such as berries and mushrooms, has been practised by the locals since ancient times and serves as an extra source of revenue. This area has poor land that is unsuitable for farming and therefore just a fifth of the land fund is made up of agricultural land. The population of Druskininkai region is rather small—in 2021 Druskininkai municipality had about 19,000 residents, almost 3000 fewer than in 2011 and the population density of 42 people per km^2, which was almost the same as the national average of 42.8 people per km^2 (Lithuanian Data Agency).

However, despite relatively small size and being remote municipality, Druskininkai can be regarded as a leading example of a green settlement within the Lithuanian and broader Baltic context, owing to its sustained commitment to environmental sustainability, low-carbon mobility, and nature-integrated urban development. And even green city notion (Short, 2015) has gained popularity in recent years and is seen as a competitive advantage for cities in terms of attracting residents, tourists, and businesses; the greening of a city involves not only already described measures such as creating green spaces, promoting sustainable urbanism, and addressing environmental issues like air pollution, but much broader solutions such as creating living infrastructure, proposing nature-inspired solutions, ensuring the partnering with nature, offering transformative services and many more.

The municipality has implemented a range of policies and projects aligned with sustainable urban planning principles, including the construction of extensive pedestrian and bicycle infrastructure, the transition to a fully electric public transport fleet, and the promotion of electric vehicle (EV) use through the establishment of charging stations. Furthermore, Druskininkai's integration of natural assets, such as mineral springs, forests, and river systems into the urban fabric reflects a strategic alignment with biophilic and health-oriented design principles and nature-inspired solutions. The town's inclusion in national and European green networks, such as the Lithuanian Green Municipalities initiative, further reinforces its role as a model of ecological governance and innovation. These achievements position Druskininkai as not only a spa and wellness destination (Lithuanian Tourism Department, 2022), but also as a forward-thinking municipality committed to sustainable and regenerative development seeking the symbiosis with nature.

The initiation of settlement regeneration. As a resort municipality, Druskininkai settlement for many years emphasizes sustainability, good air quality, low pollution, and accessible green spaces as important elements of urban and rural development and promotion. Druskininkai region has been preserved by local people and local government where the green settlement is shaped by two factors: nature, as the region is surrounded by forests, clean air, mineral water, and mud, and for the last two decades of active human actions preserving green spaces, ensuring eco-friendly transportation, sustainable tourism and wellness services, waste management and recycling, and extensive participation in European Union (EU) green programmes related to sustainable urban development, environmental protection, and renewable energy.

However, Druskininkai is an example of the Winston Churchill's saying, 'Never let a good crisis go to waste', as in 1990s and early 2000s Druskininkai experienced the most severe economic hardship marked by exceptionally high unemployment rates. In 2000, the unemployment rate reached approximately 29%, and in 2001 it climbed to 29.9%, making it one of the highest in Lithuania at the time (URBACT, 2023; Skindarienė, 2006). These figures reflected the municipality's struggle to recover from the post-Soviet transition and the decline of state-supported industries, particularly in the health and tourism sectors. The health resorts, like the rest of the city's infrastructure, were run down, and there had been no investment in the resort for several decades. By 2005, however, the unemployment rate had significantly decreased to 10%, indicating early signs of local economic revitalization and targeted employment initiatives.

This was the period when main currently running businesses were started in the region and the region shaped its previous face from old-fashioned sanatorium-based resort to the one more focused on a variety of diversified services, starting from family activities (aqua park, skiing, bicycle infrastructure) to a more sophisticated ones, such as rehabilitation services and even a healing spa, medical spa—a hybrid facility that combines the relaxing environment of a traditional day spa with advanced medical treatments typically found in a doctor's office and bridging the gap between beauty procedures and medical care. This introduced the whole new medical tourism aspect to the resort and attracted even more diversified spectrum of tourism.

The regeneration of Druskininkai as a green and diversified settlement was initiated through a combination of local municipal leadership, national policy alignment, and EU support mechanisms. While the town's origins as a health resort date back to the nineteenth century, its transformation into a green city is rooted in post-1990 urban redevelopment efforts following Lithuania's independence. The municipal government of Druskininkai played a central role in this transition, actively pursuing sustainable development goals and leveraging EU structural funds for environmental infrastructure, public transport modernization, and green tourism (Druskininkai Municipality, 2022). The official framing of Druskininkai as a *green city* began to solidify in the early 2010s and later, particularly through its alignment with national strategic documents such as the Lithuanian National Climate Change Management Agenda (2021–2030) and the National Transport Development Programme (2014–2022). These initiatives emphasized low-emission transport, urban green space development, and integration of nature-based solutions, i.e., policies that were actively implemented at the municipal level. Additionally, Druskininkai's participation in EU-funded programmes such as URBACT and INTERREG further catalysed its environmental regeneration. These programmes encouraged participatory governance and sustainability-oriented innovation, enabling Druskininkai to rebrand itself not only as a health and wellness destination, but also as a model of regional green transformation. Thus, while the settlement's green identity evolved incrementally, it gained formal traction and visibility over the past decade through a convergence of local initiative and multilevel policy frameworks (see European Commission, 2019, 2020).

Design phase of the settlement: ideal Druskininkai settlement vision. An ideal vision for the Druskininkai settlement integrates environmental sustainability, community engagement, and a harmonious human–nature relationship. In this vision, inhabitants are envisioned as active stewards who exhibit ecological responsibility, civic participation, and adaptability. The ideal inhabitant of Druskininkai—a region known for its ecological regeneration efforts and health-oriented living infrastructure—embodies a lifestyle that is environmentally conscious, socially engaged, and future-oriented. Rooted in the municipality's unique landscape of mineral springs, forests, and therapeutic heritage, residents are expected to actively maintain a low ecological footprint through sustainable practices such as walking and cycling, energy conservation, and ecological stewardship (Druskininkai Rural LAG Strategy, 2023).

Beyond personal lifestyle choices, civic engagement plays a vital role: ideal inhabitants are those who participate in co-creating local solutions, contribute to participatory planning, and engage in collaborative initiatives that align with the municipality's green strategy. These individuals recognize themselves as part of a broader socio-ecological system and embrace the responsibilities of shared governance and collective care (Druskininkai Rural LAG Strategy, 2023). Furthermore, adaptability is key—they are willing to experiment with green technologies, support municipal innovations such as electric mobility and zero-waste initiatives, and adjust their behaviour in response to climate-related challenges. Finally, given Druskininkai's dual identity as a local community and international wellness destination, the ideal resident cultivates a balance between place-based identity and intercultural openness—welcoming visitors, contributing to a culture of hospitality, and nurturing the local commons for shared benefit. Such characteristics are essential to sustaining Druskininkai not only as a green settlement, but as a living model of human–nature harmony.

The ideal living infrastructure in Druskininkai balances modern amenities with traditional elements, integrating advanced green technologies—like renewable energy systems and digital monitoring for environmental quality—with heritage conservation. Public spaces, civic centres, and transportation networks are designed to prioritize pedestrian and bicycle mobility, reducing reliance on fossil-fuel-based transport. Community infrastructure that supports local entrepreneurship, cultural events, and educational programmes further reinforces social cohesion. In summary, the ideal vision of Druskininkai is a resilient, healthy, and inclusive settlement where the inhabitants' sustainable practices, communal engagement, and respect for local natural and cultural heritage drive continuous eco-innovation in partnering with the place, which also reflects the most recent trends in the rest of the world (see e.g., Raymond et al., 2017; Bulkeley & Betsill, 2013; Bai et al., 2010).

Design framework: urban (regional) development programme. The redevelopment of Druskininkai as a green settlement has been shaped by an integrated approach that draws on both traditional village concepts and contemporary urban development programmes. The town's regeneration strategy incorporates elements reminiscent of rural village models highlighting community cohesion, local identity, and environmental integration while also adopting innovative urban planning and sustainable mobility concepts. For example, Druskininkai's urban design process was aligned with the objectives of Lithuania's National Transport Development Programme (2014–2022) and the Climate Change Management Agenda (2021–2030), ensuring that infrastructural projects like pedestrian zones, cycle paths, and electric public transport are embedded within a broader climate policy framework.

In addition, the redevelopment leveraged frameworks associated with EU initiatives such as URBACT, which advocate for cohesive regional development through cross-sectoral strategies. This exemplar model emphasizes not only the physical redesign of urban spaces but also the revitalization of social, cultural, and economic practices. The integration of these strategies has allowed Druskininkai to preserve its heritage as a health and wellness destination while transitioning towards a more sustainable and resilient environment. With a dual focus on bottom-up innovation, highlighted by grassroots ecovillage and community-led projects, and top-down governmental support, the settlement's redesign bridges traditional values with modern green urbanism. This hybrid framework illustrates how a community can simultaneously honour its historical context and harness contemporary sustainable practices to foster long-term regenerative development (European Commission, 2019).

Organization of the design process. The design process for Druskininkai transformation into a green settlement was characterized by a multifaceted, participatory framework combining top-down policy support with bottom-up community engagement. Initially, municipal authorities collaborated with national agencies and EU programmes to secure strategic guidance and funding. Instruments such as the Lithuanian National Transport Development Programme and URBACT projects provided policy frameworks and financial resources essential for infrastructural innovations like electrified public transport and extensive non-motorized pathways. This top-down impetus was complemented by local initiatives that involved diverse stakeholders: residents, local businesses, environmental NGOs, and academic institutions, to ensure the process reflected the community's cultural identity and ecological aspirations.

Public consultations and participatory workshops were organized to gather insights and priorities directly from the inhabitants. This inclusive mechanism not only helped tailor design interventions to the specificities of the local environment but also fostered community ownership and strengthened social bonds. These participatory efforts were supported by digital planning tools and feedback loops that allowed for continuous monitoring and evaluation of the redevelopment progress. Furthermore, public–private partnerships were instrumental in bridging technical expertise with innovation, facilitating projects ranging from green infrastructure development to the installation of electric vehicle charging stations. By integrating expert-driven strategic planning with grassroots mobilization, the design process in Druskininkai set a precedent for resilient and adaptive urban planning, establishing a replicable model for holistic regeneration, enabling eco-communities, eco-services, eco-innovations, nature-inspired solutions, and overall, the partnering with the place.

Strategic actions for further development. In recent years, Druskininkai municipality has undertaken a comprehensive and forward-looking strategy to position itself as a model of green urban development in Lithuania. Central to this transformation has been a concerted focus on sustainable urban and rural mobility and infrastructure, reflecting a broader commitment to environmental resilience and climate-conscious place-based planning. The municipality has prioritized the development of an integrated pedestrian and bicycle network to encourage low-impact, active transportation and reduce car dependency. Simultaneously, efforts to modernize public transport through the electrification of municipal transit systems signify a decisive move towards reducing greenhouse gas emissions and improving urban air quality. Complementing these initiatives, the establishment and expansion of electric vehicle infrastructure, including the installation of public charging stations, has reinforced the municipality's support for sustainable private mobility. Collectively, these measures demonstrate a coordinated, multisectoral approach to building a greener, healthier, and more liveable urban environment, aligning with both national climate objectives and EU sustainability frameworks.

Sustainable urban mobility and infrastructure in Druskininkai. Druskininkai has emerged as a leading example of sustainable urban transformation in Lithuania, particularly through its investment in green mobility and environmentally conscious infrastructure. The municipality's approach is grounded in its Sustainable Urban Mobility Plan, complemented by national and EU-level strategies for climate-neutral development.

Pedestrian and bicycle infrastructure. As part of its ongoing urban greening initiatives, Druskininkai has prioritized the development of infrastructure that encourages non-motorized transport. The municipality constructed extensive pedestrian and bicycle pathways, including a green corridor along the Ratnyčėlė stream, a natural landscape asset integrated into the town's mobility design. This intervention enhances connectivity and reduces car dependency while contributing to the town's health and wellness profile. Additionally, the municipality installed 146 new bicycle parking spaces to improve accessibility and facilitate modal shifts among residents and visitors (EU Tourism Platform, 2024).

Electrification of public transport. In a significant step towards decarbonization, Druskininkai has fully transitioned to an electric public transport fleet. The replacement of fossil fuel–powered buses with electric alternatives was achieved through a public–private partnership model, positioning the town among the first in Lithuania to reach full electrification of municipal transit. This development aligns with the priorities of Lithuania's National Transport Development Programme 2014–2022, which seeks to modernize transport systems and reduce sectoral emissions (Regional Action Plan, 2020). The electric fleet reduces greenhouse gas emissions and noise pollution, aligning urban mobility with public health and environmental goals.

Electric vehicle infrastructure. To further support low-carbon mobility, Druskininkai has established a network of ten public electric vehicle charging stations. These installations facilitate the transition to cleaner individual transportation by making EV use more practical for both residents and tourists. The infrastructure supports Lithuania's Climate Change Management Agenda 2021–2030, which promotes the decarbonization of transport through the adoption of renewable energy technologies and electrified mobility (Ministry of Environment of the Republic of Lithuania, 2021a). This initiative reflects the municipality's proactive role in building the foundational infrastructure for a sustainable transport future.

For example, in 2022 the Ministry of Environment carried the Lithuanian Municipal Environmental Ranking, to strengthen the competitiveness and leadership of municipalities in the field of environmental protection and to promote the implementation of the provisions of the Government Programme of the Republic of Lithuania and the objectives of the Green Deal. The ranking assesses not only the environmental performance of municipalities, but also the promotion of environmental awareness in municipalities, and in 2022 Druskininkai Municipality ranked the second place out of 60 municipalities in Lithuania (Lithuanian Municipal Environmental Rating, 2022).

Collectively, these developments reflect a strategic integration of environmental, technological, and health considerations into local planning. Druskininkai's coordinated investments in active mobility, public transit electrification, and EV infrastructure exemplify a comprehensive approach to sustainable urban development that resonates with both local identity and broader European sustainability goals.

Current real situation. According to the 2021 Population and Housing Census, Druskininkai Municipality had about 19,000 residents—nearly 3000 fewer than in 2011 (Lithuanian State Data Agency, 2021). Census data from 2011 and 2021 show a clear demographic shift: populations in small settlements (201–1000 residents) declined, while those in larger ones (1001–2999 residents) grew significantly. Villages and towns with 201–1000 residents experienced a 47% population decrease, whereas the smallest settlements—those with fewer than 200 residents—witnessed a relatively marginal decline of 4.7% (Statistics Lithuania, 2021; Druskininkai Rural LAG Strategy, 2023).

The demographic structure of Druskininkai municipality also indicates an ageing population. The median age rose from 46 years in 2014 to 49 years in 2022, exceeding the national median of 44 years in the same year, and suggesting a growing proportion of elderly residents (Lithuanian Data Agency, 2022). Furthermore, the municipality continues to experience negative natural population change: between 2014 and 2022, the number of deaths exceeded births by approximately 1400 individuals.

While net migration in Druskininkai remained negative from 2001 onwards, a turning point occurred in 2018, with positive migration trends emerging from 2020 onwards. This reversal is attributed to several interrelated factors, including sustained investments in high-quality public infrastructure and services, an increasingly attractive living environment, and the expansion of remote work opportunities following the COVID-19 pandemic, which enabled greater residential mobility across Lithuania (Lithuanian Data Agency, 2022).

Druskininkai region enables collaborative community, expressing shared values and culture. For example, Local Development Strategy for Druskininkai Rural area (2023–2027), Druskininkai Strategic Plan (2021), i.e., Druskininkai Rural LAG Strategy prioritizes the development of the rural area of Druskininkai harmoniously, ensuring the availability of services that are important to residents and tourists will lead to a higher quality of life, increased attractiveness, and social inclusion. Local residents proposed that priority be given to increasing access to social services and healthcare, and to developing tourism infrastructure and services. This can be done by collaborating with the growing NGO sector and strong local communities, and by drawing on the success of EU funding. Indeed, these measures relate to the objectives of the most important higher-level strategic documents for the region: (1) Druskininkai Municipality Strategic Development Plan 2021–2029; (2) EU Funds Investment Programme 2021–2027; (3) Strategic Plan for Lithuanian Agriculture and Rural Development 2023–2027; and (4) National Progress Plan 2021–2030 (Druskininkai Rural LAG Strategy). And second, it is foreseen in the Druskininkai Rural LAG Strategy that people will be actively involved in local communities and develop social and community businesses and therefore the region's tourism potential—cultural heritage sites, amateur art, national heritage and crafts, traditional events, beautiful landscapes—will be employed better.

The living infrastructure of Druskininkai municipality reflects a well-balanced integration of architectural tradition, contemporary urban planning, and community-oriented spatial development. Residential buildings in the municipality range from low-density private housing to mid-rise apartment blocks, with recent construction adhering to energy-efficiency standards aligned with national and EU sustainability goals (Ministry of Environment of the Republic of Lithuania, 2021b). The spatial arrangement of homes and public spaces is characterized by functional zoning and accessibility, with residential areas closely linked to green corridors, public parks, and recreational spaces—features that promote physical activity and social interaction. A distinct feature of Druskininkai layout is the preservation of natural topography and integration of forested areas into residential zones, enhancing both ecological value and aesthetic quality (Druskininkai Municipality, 2022). Public spaces are designed to be inclusive and multifunctional, accommodating community events, cultural activities, and informal gatherings. Property ownership in Druskininkai is predominantly individual, but many apartment buildings operate under cooperative or homeowners' associations that manage shared infrastructure and participate in collective decision-making. These governance structures are supported by legal frameworks that enable co-financing of renovations, energy retrofitting, and public space improvements (National Land Service, 2020).

The development of living infrastructure in Druskininkai has progressed in phases. Initial efforts during the post-Soviet transition focused on privatization and basic service provision, while the early 2000s marked a shift towards modernization, aesthetic renewal, and the expansion of public amenities. The current phase, since the 2010s, emphasizes green regeneration, digitalization, and participatory urban governance, in line with the municipality's strategic development plans and broader European green transition objectives (European Commission, 2019).

Place characteristics. Druskininkai municipality is distinguished by its unique natural landscape, cultural heritage, and infrastructure conducive to modern, flexible living. Land ownership in the municipality is a mix of private and municipal property, with infrastructure and urban development projects often financed through a combination of EU structural funds, national programmes, and public–private partnerships.

The municipality provides favourable conditions for remote work, an increasingly relevant feature in the post-pandemic context. Residents benefit from high-speed internet connectivity, supported by national digital infrastructure initiatives (Communications Regulatory Authority of Lithuania, 2023), and from a quiet, healthy environment—attributes frequently mentioned as essential to work–life balance and productivity. Many homes and public facilities are equipped with spaces that allow for participation in virtual client meetings or team collaboration, while accessibility via regional roads and inter-city transport options ensures continued connectivity. The overall atmosphere in Druskininkai—defined by low pollution levels, minimal noise, and the presence of therapeutic natural elements—enhances the municipality's appeal as both a place to live and work, particularly for individuals seeking a sustainable, wellness-oriented lifestyle.

The regeneration of the project. Establishing a green settlement or regeneration project akin to Druskininkai requires a holistic vision that balances environmental restoration, economic sustainability, nature-inspired solutions, and community well-being. The first and most critical step is the development of a place-based strategy grounded in local natural assets, cultural identity, and socio-economic conditions. Druskininkai's transformation and revitalization into a green settlement was anchored in its historic identity as a health resort town, enabling a natural alignment between ecological infrastructure and wellness tourism. Planners and stakeholders should begin by conducting an integrated environmental and cultural landscape assessment to identify core ecological features such as rivers, forests, or mineral resources that can serve as the foundation for regenerative development and nature-based solutions (Raymond et al., 2017; European Commission, 2020).

The second imperative is the formulation of a strategic urban mobility and infrastructure plan that prioritizes low-emission transportation, accessibility, and connectivity. Druskininkai's success in pedestrianization, bicycle infrastructure development, and full public transport electrification exemplifies a systems-thinking approach to sustainable mobility. Replicating such a model requires coordination across multiple sectors, including transport, energy, and urban design. Municipalities should aim to implement policies that phase out high-emission vehicles, invest in electric mobility, and support alternative modes of transport (Banister, 2008; European Commission, 2021). This shift must be accompanied by public communication strategies that build trust and participation, fostering behavioural changes aligned with ecological goals (OECD, 2025).

Thirdly, stakeholders must adopt a governance framework that enables both top-down leadership and bottom-up participation. Druskininkai's regeneration was supported by national policies, such as Lithuania's Climate Change Management Agenda, and EU programmes like URBACT, but it was also grounded in local initiative and public–private partnerships. Cities aspiring to replicate this model should pursue multilevel governance, engaging national ministries, municipal departments, civil society organizations, and private investors. Mechanisms such as participatory budgeting, local climate councils, and citizen co-design workshops can help ensure that regeneration efforts reflect community values and generate broad-based ownership of green transitions (Smeds & Acuto, 2018; Bulkeley & Betsill, 2013).

Finally, a successful green settlement must establish mechanisms for long-term monitoring, adaptation, and learning. Ecological regeneration is not a fixed goal but an ongoing process that must respond to climate uncertainties, economic fluctuations, and social dynamics. Building resilience requires embedding adaptive capacity into urban systems through performance indicators, digital monitoring tools, and policy feedback loops (Folke et al., 2005; Bai et al., 2010). Settlements should also link their projects to international networks, such as the Global Ecovillage Network or the Covenant of Mayors, to benefit from knowledge exchange, benchmarking, and external funding (GEN Europe, 2023; Covenant of Mayors, 2022). By cultivating a culture of innovation, transparency, and iterative planning, green regeneration projects can remain responsive and effective over time, evolving towards ecological and social resilience in a rapidly changing world.

Smiltynė as a Model of Settlement Diversification: Integrating Health Services and Cultural Heritage

Smiltynė—embedded in time, oriented to the future. The history of Smiltynė, a small settlement at the northern tip of the Curonian Spit in Lithuania, is a compelling story of functional and spatial reorganization of the place. Originally established for military and logistical purposes in the twentieth century, the place has undergone significant transformations—from a military outpost to a seasonal resort town, and more recently, to a multifunctional centre for cultural, ecological, and therapeutic services. Smiltynė's transformation demonstrates how the identity of a place is not fixed but rather constructed and reconstructed through successive layers of use and meaning, shaped by changing societal needs, resource dynamics, and external pressures over time.

As part of the Curonian Spit—a UNESCO World Heritage Site renowned for its exceptional coastal landscape and ecological fragility—Smiltynė's early development was closely tied to its geographic and strategic location. Documented as early as 1429, it began as a travel post between Memel (Klaipėda) and Königsberg (Kaliningrad), offering services such as inns and ferries for merchants and travellers crossing the Curonian Lagoon. By the sixteenth century, it had developed stable logistical functions, including a tavern and post station. However, the construction of the Nerija Fort in the nineteenth century marked the formal beginning of its military role, incorporating defence structures into the area's overall layout (Smiltynė, 2025).

With the decline of military threats and the fort's diminishing strategic relevance, Smiltynė's function began to shift. The surrounding area transitioned from a militarized zone to a place increasingly oriented towards recreation and leisure. This change was formalized at the turn of the twentieth century with the construction of the Kurhaus hotel in 1901 and the town's emergence as a coastal resort for Klaipėda's affluent classes. Its calm forests and seashore attracted visitors seeking rest and rejuvenation, leading to new infrastructure centred on wellness and seasonal tourism. These developments marked the beginning of Smiltynė's specialization in hospitality and therapeutic recreation.

However, the Second World War and the subsequent Soviet occupation disrupted this trajectory. The town's elite character faded, the fort was damaged, and the resort-based economy declined. In the post-war decades, Smiltynė experienced demographic shrinkage and a loss of functional relevance—risks common in narrowly specialized settlements. Yet this decline also created space for a new stage in its evolution. In 1979, the Nerija Fort was repurposed as the Lithuanian Sea Museum, signalling a cultural and educational reorientation (GPSmyCity, 2025). The museum later expanded to include a dolphinarium in 1994, promoting marine conservation and drawing broader public interest (Baltic Seaside, 2025).

A pivotal development occurred in 2015 with the launch of the Dolphin-Assisted Therapy Centre, offering specialized services for individuals with autism, cerebral palsy, and other neurodevelopmental disorders (Lithuanian Sea Museum, 2025a). This marked a further diversification of Smiltynė's functional profile, aligning with contemporary health and social service needs. The initiative, backed by institutions like Klaipėda University and Vilnius University, exemplifies how existing infrastructure and natural resources can be repurposed to generate new forms of social value.

Smiltynė's evolution trajectory from a specialized mono-functional settlement to a diversified services provision–oriented coastal hub illustrates how 'place' can be reorganized—both spatially and institutionally to meet changing demands. The town now balances multiple roles: a tourist destination, a cultural site, a marine education centre, and a therapeutic facility. Each function serves different user groups: from casual visitors and marine enthusiasts to children with disabilities and their families, demonstrating a deepening of place-based inclusivity (Kreivinienė & Perttula, 2012).

Importantly, this transformation did not erase the town's historical identity but instead layered new functions onto old foundations. The regeneration strategy was neither abrupt nor externally imposed. Rather, it activated latent capacities rooted in Smiltynė's geography, history, and infrastructure. This incremental, place-sensitive approach to diversification shows how small settlements can avoid stagnation by internalizing adaptability as both a strategic orientation and a lived reality.

The integration of environmental stewardship into Smiltynė's development also reflects an innovative approach. Its transformation embodies a post-industrial logic where ecological sensitivity, cultural heritage, and public health are not competing values but interdependent goals. In theoretical terms, Smiltynė exemplifies how localities can mobilize tangible (infrastructure, landscapes) and intangible (identity, memory, expertise) assets to foster resilience and sustainable development.

Ultimately, Smiltynė's case offers a nuanced perspective on place-making and transformation. From a defensive node to a healing space, its changing functions have continually responded to evolving demands—military, economic, social, and ecological. This history of adaptive reorganization positions Smiltynė not only as a preserved heritage site but as a forward-looking settlement capable of navigating the complexities of twenty-first-century development.

Anchoring the future: the visionaries behind Smiltynė's renewal. The regeneration of Smiltynė as a diversified coastal settlement was not the result of a singular, top-down planning directive but rather a multi-actor initiative grounded in interdisciplinary collaboration and long-term social vision. Central to this process was the Lithuanian Sea Museum (2025b), an institution already embedded in the cultural and scientific fabric of the region. Recognizing the need to rejuvenate both the physical and social landscape of Smiltynė, the museum's leadership, in cooperation with academic and healthcare institutions, initiated a project that would bring therapeutic innovation to the fore of the settlement's identity.

The catalyst for regeneration was the introduction of dolphin-assisted therapy, developed as a formal programme within the Dolphinarium section of the museum. Officially launched in 2015, this programme emerged from prior informal engagements and experimental therapeutic sessions dating back to the early 2000s. The museum partnered closely with Klaipėda University, Vilnius University, and the public institution 'Vaiko raida' (*eng. Child Development*), pooling expertise in marine biology, psychology, special education, and public health. This intersectoral partnership was essential not only in shaping the therapeutic programme but also in aligning it with broader goals of sustainable development and beyond human-centred regeneration.

The initiative reflects what the theoretical literature on diversification describes as a regenerative strategy initiated through institutional foresight and grounded in an understanding of 'place' as a malleable but enduring resource system. Rather than allowing Smiltynė's historical decline to deepen, stakeholders recognized the value of its landscape, marine culture, and legacy infrastructure as assets that could be reoriented towards new livelihoods and social functions. In this way, the regeneration process was not simply reactive but proactively structured to accommodate future societal transformations, as emphasized in diversification theory.

Importantly, the initiative was not purely economic in orientation. Instead, it fused health, ecology, education, and community cohesion in a way that illustrates a complementary logic, where new services enhance and reinterpret older place-based functions. By embedding health services within an ecologically sensitive and culturally meaningful site, the initiators laid the groundwork for Smiltynė's revival not as a tourist enclave, but as a multifunctional, human development-oriented settlement—a hallmark goal of diversification strategy.

Designing a healing shoreline: the vision and process behind Smiltynė's regeneration. The regeneration of Smiltynė was not born of a single fixed vision, but rather from a recognition of the need to adapt to shifting social, economic, and ecological conditions. The design phase of its transformation reflects a time-oriented, diversification-driven strategy: one that rethinks existing assets, anticipates future needs, and carefully blends the old with the new. It was a design not of disruption, but of continuity through evolution, where each decision aimed to generate a complementarity effect between inherited characteristics and emerging societal functions.

At the heart of this process was the aspiration to cultivate a place that could offer healing services—not just for local inhabitants, but for a broader network of visitors, professionals, and families seeking respite, therapy, and connection. Smiltynė's future was imagined not as a return to its early-twentieth-century role as an elite seaside resort, but as a diversified, multifunctional settlement rooted in the principles of sustainable human development. This vision acknowledged the limitations of relying on single-function settlement types—be they tourism, industry, or conservation—and instead embraced layered complexity as a source of resilience.

The **ideal vision for the reorganized settlement** was shaped around three interwoven components: inhabitants, infrastructure, and place. The aim was not to encourage large-scale migration or permanent settlement, but to cultivate a flexible and adaptive human presence. The envisioned social fabric included health professionals, researchers, caregivers, families undergoing therapy, eco-tourists, and seasonal volunteers. Rather than seeking homogeneity, the design aimed for functional complementarity—diverse user groups whose activities would reinforce one another within a coherent spatial and institutional framework. The *infrastructure*, accordingly, was not designed as a monolithic project, but as a platform for dynamic services. The dolphin-assisted therapy centre became the symbolic and functional core of this approach. Facilities were created to support therapeutic sessions, but also to accommodate education, scientific research, and nature-based public programming. Small-scale, eco-sensitive design guided the development of paths, observation areas, and patient spaces. These elements were not only aesthetically and environmentally appropriate—they were also deliberately future-proof, designed to serve multiple overlapping purposes and respond flexibly to demographic or functional shifts over time. The *'place'* itself—the unique setting of Smiltynė on the Curonian Spit—was recognized as more than terrain. It was seen as an organizational construct, rich in cultural heritage, ecological value, and symbolic meaning. The design process treated place not as a passive backdrop but as an active resource to be regenerated through thoughtful use. In this way, the diversification strategy moved beyond conventional land-use planning, emphasizing instead landscape activation as a therapeutic, educational, and identity-building asset. The goal was not just to preserve nature, but to cohabit with it in ways that would reinforce Smiltynė's evolving role as a service-oriented, reflective settlement.

Importantly, the design phase did not emerge from a singular vision imposed from above. It was collaboratively produced through a network of institutional actors: the Lithuanian Sea Museum, Vilnius University, Klaipėda University, and public health organizations such as 'Vaiko raida'. These institutions brought not only technical expertise but diverse perspectives on what the future of Smiltynė could become. Their participation ensured that the design process was both strategically informed and socially accountable.

Smiltynė was not designed according to a fixed village concept or model (e.g., Causeway Coast and Glens Borough Council, 2025). Instead, it evolved in line with principles found in sustainable regeneration theory and international trends in therapeutic urbanism and place-based innovation. While not formally embedded in an EU regeneration framework, the project was fully aligned with goals in public health diversification, ecological protection, and soft mobility. It exemplified the kind of localized, service-based development called for in both national and regional policy circles.

The organizational logic behind the design was gradual and iterative. No single blueprint dictated the entire transformation. Instead, a phased and reflexive approach allowed for ongoing adjustment based on experiential feedback and shifting conditions. The design team did not aim to solve every problem in advance, but to create an open-ended infrastructure—one capable of learning, adapting, and accommodating future uses not yet foreseen.

Through this method, Smiltynė became a canvas for diversified activity: a place where health services are nested within ecological systems, where heritage meets innovation, and where the boundaries between therapy, learning, and tourism begin to dissolve. It is a model of complementary layering, where each element reinforces the next, and where infrastructure supports not only function but meaning.

In this way, the design phase of Smiltynė illustrates the essence of the diversification strategy: an adaptive, time-sensitive reorganization of space that seeks to regenerate place according to both local resources and changing human needs. It is not a case of designing anew, but of designing forward, where each step enriches the future without abandoning the past.

From decline to adaptive reuse: the rationale for diversification. Smiltynė's post-war history mirrors the trajectory of many monofunctional settlements that experienced decline following socio-political transformations. Once a luxury resort favoured by the upper classes of neighbouring city Klaipėda, Smiltynė lost its economic vibrancy and social relevance in the Soviet period. Its small population, seasonal use, and geographic insularity left it vulnerable to demographic stagnation and spatial underutilization. In such a context, continuing along a single line of specialization—be it high-end tourism or conservation alone—would risk exacerbating marginalization.

Time-oriented strategy through infrastructure adaptation. The success of a diversification strategy relies on the ability to anticipate societal changes and revise existing solutions accordingly. Smiltynė's regeneration exemplifies this principle. Rather than clinging to outdated models of mass tourism or seasonal recreation, stakeholders invested in a future where health, education, and nature-based services are central to human well-being, with a hint to what goes beyond the human-centred approach—Symbiocene. Smiltynė's infrastructure has been adapted in phases to support this shift. Initial steps included spatial reconfiguration for improved access, ecological zoning to protect sensitive areas, and the development of specialized therapeutic spaces. These interventions demonstrate a gradual, time-oriented approach, allowing the settlement to remain agile while extending its relevance.

Complementarity as a Strategic Principle. At the heart of this diversification strategy is the concept of complementarity—the creative interplay between inherited assets and newly created infrastructure facilities. Smiltynė's historical build infrastructure (port access, coastal buildings) and its natural assets (Curonian Spit's landscape, marine biodiversity) have been repurposed to support the development of innovative therapeutic and educational services. These new facilities do not displace the old but build upon them, creating a layered identity.

The dolphin therapy centre, established under the Lithuanian Sea Museum, plays an essential role seeking the complementarity effect. It draws on local marine expertise and environmental knowledge while introducing a highly specialized form of service that meets contemporary needs—particularly those related to neurodiverse populations and mental health. This strategic layering of functions increases the resilience of the settlement and ensures that existing infrastructure gains new meaning in the context of human and nature symbiosis-oriented development. It aligns with the development of service economy, wherein the settlement becomes a place for delivering adaptable services rather than static products or amenities. Infrastructure here is no longer just a physical setting—it is an enabling environment, capable of hosting therapeutic interventions, scientific research, inclusive recreation, and community learning. Inhabitants and visitors, including patients, caregivers, researchers, volunteers, and short-term visitors, engage in a dynamic service. These actors are not isolated but interdependent, and their needs continuously reshape how space is used and managed. As such, Smiltynė is transitioning from a place of passive occupation offering working places to a site of active co-creation, guided by temporal flexibility and social responsiveness.

The transformation of Smiltynė through the development of dolphin-assisted therapy services represents a compelling case of settlement diversification. Rather than restoring the area's former identity as a leisure enclave or pursuing rigid specialization, the regeneration of Smiltynė has been strategically directed towards diversification, understood here as a dynamic, future-oriented effort to reorganize the spatial, social, and functional structure of the place. Dolphin therapy is thus not merely a new economic activity; it is a social innovation that introduces a complementary function into the existing settlement, bridging tourism, healthcare, education, and environmental awareness.

The incorporation of therapeutic services also required cross-sector collaboration, particularly between cultural institutions, academia, health services, and local governance. These partnerships enabled not only the funding and design of unique infrastructure facilities, but also their alignment with national strategies on public health and sustainable regional development.

Overcoming Resistance and Managing Change. As in all diversification processes, Smiltynė faced constraints, particularly related to inhabitant inertia and institutional conservatism. The remoteness of the settlement, its small residential base, and the ecological sensitivity of its environment meant that significant transformation could only occur through careful negotiation and trust-building.

Some resistance emerged regarding the ethical implications of dolphin therapy, the appropriateness of development within a UNESCO-protected zone, and the challenge of attracting professionals to a semi-remote area. These concerns were addressed through transparent communication, ongoing evaluation, and ethical compliance aligned with international standards. The participation of research institutions also provided a framework for reflexivity and continuous learning—key mechanisms for resolving resistance and increasing strategic legitimacy.

Smiltynė's current trajectory is not a final state but part of a longer evolutionary arc. The integration of dolphin therapy into settlement's identity has brought new visibility and purpose, but this too will need to evolve. To maintain vitality, the settlement must remain open to new complementarities—perhaps expanding into broader wellness services, intergenerational educational programmes, or international rehabilitation networks.

What Smiltynė demonstrates is that diversification is not about multiplying functions indiscriminately. It is about curating continuity through thoughtful layering—matching old place characteristics with new societal needs and functions, using local resources creatively, and staying oriented towards the needs of future generations.

Living in the transition—Smiltynė's present reality in a diversified settlement. Smiltynė today stands as a settlement in active transition, embodying a careful response to the challenges and potentials of diversification. Its physical form, social composition, and infrastructure all bear the imprint of intentional transformation—guided by a long-term vision of place regeneration oriented to the needs of post-industrial society. It is not a settlement that has been reinvented overnight, but one that is being quietly recalibrated through time, partnerships, and purpose.

What defines the reality of Smiltynė most vividly is the character of its inhabitants, not in terms of numbers, but in the shared intentionality that binds them. While the permanent population remains small and insufficient to generate economies of scale in traditional terms, the people drawn to Smiltynė—whether long-term staff, visiting patients and their families, therapists, or marine scientists—form a community of alignment. They are connected by a common pursuit of healing, care, and reflective interaction with nature. This coherence of values offers a form of social density that substitutes for numerical volume. In this way, the settlement sustains its vitality not through scale, but through significance.

Rather than a fixed residential population, Smiltynė accommodates a fluid, functional community shaped by cycles of use. Health professionals, university researchers, therapy recipients, museum visitors, and environmental volunteers all pass through or remain temporarily, each contributing to the evolving identity and functionality of the place. While this structure does not offer the continuity of a traditional village, it brings the dynamism necessary for a diversified settlement to remain adaptive and relevant. At its core, Smiltynė is animated by a collaborative spirit, with its institutions and inhabitants cultivating a sense of care that extends across social and spatial boundaries.

This sensibility is mirrored in the living infrastructure of the settlement. Architecture and public space are shaped to promote emotional and physical well-being. Repurposed maritime buildings, newly designed therapy facilities, and natural walkways come together to form an environment where functionality is balanced with atmosphere. The built form favours simplicity and integration with the surrounding landscape, encouraging gentle use and sensory openness. Homes, therapeutic buildings, and public areas are organized to foster interaction without intrusion, making space for both solitude and connection.

Property ownership in Smiltynė reflects the ethos of shared responsibility. Much of the land and key infrastructure are managed by public or non-profit entities, such as the Lithuanian Sea Museum. This model ensures that infrastructure is developed with the public good in mind, rather than speculative gain. The governance of space is thus aligned with the community's broader mission, reinforcing the logic of stewardship and long-term adaptability.

The characteristics of the place in which Smiltynė sits continue to play an active role in shaping its present reality in the framework of the environmental and cultural matrix. The Curonian Spit's dramatic dunes, pine forests, and coastal air are not backdrops but essential elements of the therapeutic offering. Here, the natural world is an extension of the clinic and the classroom. The therapeutic experience is inseparable from the setting in which it unfolds. This intimate link between ecology and service transforms landscape into living infrastructure.

Moreover, the cultural legacy of the site—its historical role as a port, a retreat, and a point of maritime heritage—adds a further layer of meaning. The Sea Museum and Dolphinarium operate not just as institutions, but as anchors of identity, preserving memory while extending the settlement's function into new realms. Infrastructural upgrades have been handled with sensitivity to this heritage, ensuring that new development does not displace history, but builds upon it.

Despite these strengths, Smiltynė's reality is not without tension. Its small size limits the availability of skilled labour and constrains the organic growth of a stable resident base. The therapy services, while unique, are resource-intensive and require sustained legitimacy, scientific support, and ethical clarity. The protected status of the region imposes necessary, though complex, constraints on expansion, necessitating a constant negotiation between nature preservation and progress.

Nevertheless, these constraints are not weaknesses but part of a dynamic equilibrium. They compel the community to remain creative, cautious, and collaborative—hallmarks of a successful diversification strategy. Smiltynė's model of development, shaped by incremental adaptation and deep place sensitivity, has allowed it to remain small yet impactful, modest yet meaningful.

The current state of Smiltynė affirms that diversification is not only a question of adding new functions or attracting more people. It is about cultivating synergy between what a place has been, what it now offers, and what it aspires to become. In Smiltynė, the settlement itself has become a service—not a product to consume, but a lived environment of care, restoration, and cohabitation with nature. It is a place where past and future are held in balance, and where transformation unfolds not through rupture, but through quiet continuity.

Lessons for cultivating a diversified healing settlement. The regeneration of Smiltynė offers more than a case of successful place reorganization—it presents a meaningful roadmap for how small, underutilized settlements can reposition themselves through carefully considered new functions. The lessons drawn from this experience are not procedural steps but guiding principles, shaped by deep engagement with place, people, and purpose. For those aspiring to develop similar initiatives elsewhere, several key reflections emerge.

At the heart of Smiltynė's renewal was a strong sense of intention. The vision did not begin with infrastructure or services, but with a purposeful commitment to creating a place where healing, education, and nature could be seamlessly integrated. This foundational clarity proved essential. It guided every decision that followed and provided the settlement with a future-oriented identity rooted in sustainable human development. Other settlements looking to regenerate must begin not with a checklist of needs but with a clear narrative: what kind of life is this place intends to support, and how does that vision respond to the changing needs of both current and future generations?

A second lesson lies in the principle of complementarity. Smiltynė's transformation did not require erasing its past or importing entirely foreign functions. Instead, it focused on finding synergy between its inherited assets—coastal landscapes, maritime heritage, and cultural infrastructure—and emerging societal demands, such as innovative and inclusive health services and ecological learning environments. The dolphin-assisted therapy centre did not exist in isolation; it emerged as a natural evolution of what Smiltynė already was, creatively reimagined for contemporary relevance. This approach demonstrates that successful diversification builds on place-specific strengths, using them as foundations for meaningful innovation.

The Smiltynė case also illustrates the importance of holistic thinking. The settlement's revitalization did not unfold within economic sectors defined in industrial era, such as healthcare, tourism, or education. Instead, these domains should be deliberately intertwined. The therapy centre served simultaneously as a clinical facility, a research site, a tourist attraction, and a public education platform. This integrated approach enabled a more efficient use of space and resources and allowed Smiltynė to offer services that were flexible and responsive to seasonal and demographic fluctuations.

Another often-overlooked dimension of regeneration is the cultivation of what may be called 'soft infrastructure'—the relationships, values, and knowledge systems that allow a place to function socially and culturally. While Smiltynė's physical development was modest in scale, its institutional partnerships are far-reaching. Collaborative ties with universities, hospitals, museums, and local authorities ensured not only credibility and operational capacity but also cultural alignment. These social infrastructures were essential in generating trust, managing resistance, and enabling adaptive growth. Settlements elsewhere would do well to prioritize such forms of investment from the outset.

A defining feature of Smiltynė's diversification is its treatment of the landscape not as a passive backdrop, but as an active agent of change. Nature is not aesthetic ornament here—it is health infrastructure, symbolic anchor, and environmental commitment. The proximity to dunes, pine forests, and open sea directly shapes the therapeutic efficacy of the services provided, and reinforces the broader message that well-being is inseparable from ecological sustainability. Future initiatives should therefore resist separating 'green' design from pragmatic goals; rather, they should allow environmental logic to co-shape the regeneration model.

Smiltynė's approach to development was intentionally slow and iterative, avoiding the rigidity of fixed masterplans, typical for urban development in industrial era. Each phase of infrastructure improvement was tested against real needs, and each programme evolved through feedback from practitioners and users. This adaptive approach ensured resilience and relevance, particularly in the face of changing political and environmental conditions. Communities seeking to follow this path should build flexibility into their processes—allowing for learning, recalibration, and the creative use of uncertainty.

Inevitably, all transformations encounter resistance, and Smiltynė was no exception. Questions about the ethics of dolphin therapy, concerns over conservation restrictions, and scepticism about long-term sustainability had to be addressed. The response was not defensiveness, but dialogue. Through transparent governance and evidence-based communication, the settlement managed to transform many doubts into forms of participation. This underlines the importance of emotional intelligence and ethical clarity in managing transformation, especially when communities are asked to accept unfamiliar ideas.

Finally, the Smiltynė experience reminds us that success must be measured not solely in economic metrics, but in terms of well-being, cohesion, and adaptability. It is not the volume of visitors or the size of investment that defines value here, but the quality of relationships, the integrity of space, and the meaningfulness of services. Replication, then, is not about copying facilities or programmes—it is about adopting a mindset of place-responsive diversification, where each decision supports a long-term, inclusive vision of shared flourishing.

Local Action Group 'Green Neighbourhood' in Poland: Evolving Idea of a Garden City According to the Contemporary Needs

From garden city ideals to a 'Green Neighbourhood' vision. The Local Action Group 'Green Neighbourhood' (orig. 'Zielone Sąsiedztwo', LAG ZS; hereinafter—'Green Neighbourhood') brings together representatives of public administration, social and economic partners, and residents of three municipalities in the Mazowieckie Province. The LAG comprises Podkowa Leśna and Milanówek from the Grodzisk district and Brwinów from the Pruszków district, located in the centre of the Mazowieckie region. The area of operation forms a spatially coherent whole. Functionally and administratively, it is a uniform structure of three neighbouring municipalities, which are well connected and share the same type of low-rise buildings surrounded by green areas.

Particularly noteworthy is the situation of the southern parts of the Brwinów municipality, which are administratively separated from the main area of the municipality by Milanówek and Podkowa Leśna. The inhabitants of these areas find themselves on an administrative island—however, this has not affected their quality of life in any way. This further emphasizes the functional cohesion of the entire area. In the context of the LEADER approach, social and historical ties, similar needs and goals of residents, complementary resources, and a shared identity and cultural heritage are of key importance.

Above all, however, the idea of cooperation between the towns and residents of these three localities is based on a shared vision of the area as a place to live and work close to nature, in contrast to the large Warsaw agglomeration. There is great potential for this for two reasons. Within the LSR area, each municipality has forms of nature protection, such as the Warsaw Protected Landscape Area, established by the Warsaw Province Governor in 1997 (Brwinów and Milanówek municipalities), as well as the Parów Sójek Nature Reserve, the Bolesław Hryniewiecki Nature Reserve, the Witold Tyrakowski 'Zaborów' Nature Reserve, and the Warsaw Protected Landscape Area established by the Governor of Warsaw in 1997 (Podkowa Leśna Municipality). Within the LSR area, each of the municipalities (100% of the area) has at least one form of nature protection (protected landscape area (three municipalities) and three nature reserves (one municipality)).

In addition to their environmental values, the specific character of these settlements is also determined by their origins—they were all initiated in line with the garden city idea developed by Ebenezer Howard. This concept involved the creation of new settlements combining the advantages of the city and the countryside, based on the principle of balance between man, nature, and work (Kędzierski, 2022). It was characterized by low and scattered buildings, a significant proportion of green areas (parks, gardens, squares), the pursuit of economic self-sufficiency, and the building of healthy, accessible, and active communities. Its primary goal was to create an alternative to the crowded and polluted industrial centres of the nineteenth century. Today, urbanization pressure in agglomerations means that cities developed according to this concept are highly rated in terms of quality of life and are also extremely attractive in terms of location, in this case in relation to Warsaw, to which all three cities are connected by a local railway line, allowing commuting to work in about 30 minutes.

Demographic and economic dynamics have reshaped the overall context of the settlement (Allen, 2003). Brwinów has grown rapidly with young families settling in new housing estates, while Podkowa Leśna has seen population ageing, and Milanówek reflects both tendencies. Together, the three municipalities had nearly 50,000 residents in 2020, supported by a dense network of more than 8500 micro- and small enterprises. This peri-urban dynamic, i.e., youth inflow on one side, ageing on the other, creates both development potential and vulnerability, especially in service provision and social cohesion. Here, *diversification is not only economic but social:* strategies must respond simultaneously to the needs of seniors, newcomers, and small-scale entrepreneurs, weaving them into a coherent service ecology.

The Local Action Group 'Green Neighbourhood' was officially established in 2008 as a result of a grassroots initiative by the residents of the municipalities of Brwinów and Podkowa Leśna, who decided to enter into a partnership on the basis of municipal council resolutions. In 2014, Milanówek joined the LAG structures, made possible by a change in regulations, according to which towns with up to 20,000 inhabitants could be merged. The initiative to create the Tri-City of Gardens arose from the need to unite efforts for the development of Brwinów, Milanówek, and Podkowa Leśna. These municipalities are characterized by similar spatial, social, and economic conditions. The process began with workshops on development conditions, attended by representatives of all three local governments. The aim of this agreement was to preserve cultural and natural heritage and improve the quality of life of the inhabitants of an area whose history since the beginning of the twentieth century has been shared or very similar. Local government officials recognized that by combining the potential of their municipalities, they could respond more effectively to the needs of residents and create attractive conditions for new settlers. In the face of intensifying competition between local governments, neighbourly cooperation and joint development planning are becoming particularly important. The convergence of the LAG partnership with earlier cooperation between local governments significantly facilitates the planning and implementation of the Local Development Strategy.

The establishment of the LAG fits into the broader context of the implementation of the EU's rural development policy (Shucksmith, 2000) and the LEADER approach, which is based on a bottom-up approach, tri-sectoral partnership (public, social, and economic), and innovative actions. In accordance with the RLKS Act (2015) and subsequent EU regulations, the establishment of the LAG made it possible to use funds from the European Agricultural Fund for Rural Development (EAFRD) and to implement local development strategies in the 2007–2013, 2014–2020, and currently 2023–2027.

The history of the LAG 'Green Neighbourhood' shows a process of gradual institutionalization and professionalization of structures, which contributes not only to planning (Berkes & Ross, 2013). In the first programming period (2007–2013), over a hundred local projects were implemented, including the development of entrepreneurship, tourism, environmental education, and social integration. In the next stage (2014–2020), the LAG's activities included innovative projects such as Financial Intelligence Clubs and the '3K: Creativity, Competence, Femininity' programme, which strengthened local social capital and promoted proactive attitudes (LSR, 2024, pp. 7–8). This process corresponds to the trends observed in the literature, according to which LAGs act not only as distributors of funds, but above all as animators of innovative social and economic activities (cf. Bock, 2016).

In its latest strategy (2023–2027), the LAG 'Green Neighbourhood' has formulated a vision of development in which Brwinów, Podkowa Leśna, and Milanówek are to constitute an integrated area providing residents with a high quality of life, good working and leisure conditions, as well as access to cultural goods. A key element of this story is the consistent effort to involve the local community in the decision-making process through consultations, social research, and participatory workshops. Such participatory practices are strongly supported by research on sustainable local development, which emphasizes the importance of residents' co-decision-making for the sustainability of project results (Sørensen & Torfing, 2019).

The history of the LAG 'Green Neighbourhood' is an example of the evolution of a grassroots initiative into a mature institutional structure, which, thanks to the consistent implementation of local development strategies and the use of participatory tools, has become a permanent feature of the socio-economic landscape of the Warsaw Tri-City Gardens.

It was against this backdrop that residents and local leaders initiated the creation of the LAG in 2008, later expanded to include Milanówek (2014). By formalizing cooperation under the LEADER framework, the three municipalities turned their shared cultural and ecological heritage into the foundation of a collective development strategy. Over successive EU programming periods, the LAG matured from a grassroots initiative into a professionalized institution implementing projects in entrepreneurship, tourism, environmental education, and social innovation. This institutionalization illustrates diversification as a process of layering governance, services, and infrastructures onto inherited settlement forms, transforming a peri-urban commuter zone into a more resilient, post-urban constellation.

Read through the lens of diversification strategy, the 'Green Neighbourhood' represents a continuity of place-based values transformed into a pathway for post-urban regeneration. Its garden city origins anticipated the principles of ecological balance and service-based living, while its current orientation, focusing social innovation, ecological stewardship, and participatory governance, demonstrates how peri-urban settlements can adaptively reorganize themselves in response to demographic change, metropolitan pressure, and the demands of a post-industrial society.

Local Champions as Agents of Diversification. The initiators of the LAG 'Green Neighbourhood' were local leaders representing the municipalities of Brwinów and Podkowa Leśna, who already in 2008 adopted formal resolutions on joining the partnership. The decision was made in the spirit of multisectoral cooperation—representatives of the public, economic, and social sectors, as well as residents, were involved in the process. A key factor was the awareness that the challenges associated with local development—such as limited financial resources, urbanization pressure, and the need to protect cultural heritage—require coordinated action across municipal boundaries.

The inclusion of Milanówek in 2014 expanded the partnership's base and gave it a regional character, covering the entire Warsaw Tri-City of Gardens. This process is consistent with the findings of the literature, which points to the importance of so-called local champions—individuals and institutions capable of mobilizing communities around a long-term vision (Ray, 2006, Journal of Rural Studies). The initiators of the 'Green

Neighbourhood' demonstrated organizational competence, and their actions were a catalyst for social and economic development in the region.

Placed in the context of diversification strategy, the role of these initiators goes beyond institution-building: they acted as agents of diversification by mobilizing multisectoral resources, connecting ecological and cultural heritage with new forms of service provision, and creating governance structures capable of expanding the functional profile of the settlement from commuter towns to a diversified, post-urban community.

Designing a symbiotic settlement vision. The project phase of the LAG 'Green Neighbourhood' focused on creating a vision of sustainable development for the area, with a priority on high quality of life for residents, protection of the natural environment, and development of an economy based on services and social innovation. According to the provisions of the LDS 2023–2027, the PTO area is to be a friendly place to live and conduct business that is not harmful to the environment, while ensuring access to educational, cultural, and recreational infrastructure (LDS, 2024, pp. 6–7).

The design process was organized in a participatory manner, including public consultations, surveys, workshops, and meetings with stakeholders. It implemented the LEADER principles, which correspond to the concept of local co-governance described in the literature (Esparcia, 2014). The vision of the LAG 'Green Neighbourhood' assumes the integration of social, economic, and ecological aspects in a development model referred to as symbiotic, where work, everyday life, and the natural environment intertwine to form a coherent settlement system.

The process of creating the LDS document consisted of five important stages. During each of them, the LAG 'Green Neighbourhood' used different methods, appropriate to the needs of the local community, drawing on its experience in communicating with the local community from the periods 2007–2013 and 2014–2020. The principles of friendly communication were applied at each stage. The following stages were distinguished:

- Stage I Diagnosis and SWOT analysis.
- Stage II Definition/consultation of objectives and indicators and Action Plan.
- Stage III Development/consultation of the rules for selecting operations and local criteria.

- Stage IV Development/consultation of monitoring and evaluation rules.
- Stage V Development/consultation of the communication plan.

The main purpose of these meetings was to develop the basic assumptions for the future SWOT analysis and the objectives, indicators, and action plan appropriate to the challenges identified. Information was also obtained on the preferred methods of communication with various target groups, such as young people, seniors, and people in difficult situations.

Based on previous experience, the meetings were organized in the form of workshops led by a moderator who ensured that the plan and discussion scenario were followed. The relaxed atmosphere allowed participants to express their opinions and urgent needs that could be met using available external funds. It is worth noting that residents of various municipalities took part in the discussion, so each reported need was analysed taking into account the specific characteristics of the municipality and the quality of life of residents in a particular place.

In addition, in order to make an accurate diagnosis of the area, data from other sources, such as the Central Statistical Office (GUS), databases of member municipalities, surveys, idea cards, and interviews, were also used.

Undoubtedly, one of the most common methods of engaging the local community in the life of any organization is through surveys. The surveys were distributed throughout the area covered by the LDS and were completed by residents, including young people, seniors, disadvantaged people, and representatives of identified interest groups in the LDS area. In the survey, residents also answered questions about the potential of the municipalities in which they live and the problems occurring inthe area. What distinguished this process was a solution aimed at activating young people and involving them in the consultation process, which was the preparation of a dedicated survey that was recommended to each other by young people to fill out. In the survey, young people also expressed their opinions on the desired leisure activities.

Placed in the context of diversification, this design process illustrates how participatory planning becomes an engine for reorganization: each consultation stage layered new voices, services, and ecological considerations onto the inherited garden city fabric. Rather than pursuing a single development trajectory, the vision deliberately embraced plural futures, where cultural heritage, ecological resilience, and service innovation coexist as complementary dimensions of a diversified settlement.

Strategic activities for diversification. As part of its strategic activities, the LAG 'Green Neighbourhood' implemented projects aimed at strengthening social capital, supporting entrepreneurship, protecting the environment, and developing culture. Examples include the development of tourism and the promotion of local products, the creation of educational programmes for young people and seniors, as well as innovative projects such as 'Podkowa Leśna = Human Smart Town' and participation in European research projects (PoliRural, 2022; SHERPA, 2023). All activities are in line with the objectives of the European Green Deal and the concept of sustainable development based on services and cross-sectoral cooperation (LSR, 2024, pp. 7–8).

The strategic activities of the LAG 'Green Neighbourhood' confirm the thesis that local partnerships are capable of combining traditional resources (cultural heritage, landscape) with modern technological and social solutions, which is confirmed in the literature on rural development (Dax & Oedl-Wieser, 2016).

The Local Development Strategy provides for measures to promote the development and strengthening of human and social capital. The implementation of this objective includes, among other things, the creation of publicly accessible, non-commercial cultural, recreational, tourist, and sports infrastructure adapted to the needs of different age groups, as well as the elimination of architectural barriers for people with special needs. Another important element is the development of the Smart Village concept, whose grassroots nature and cross-sector cooperation are intended to promote partnerships, the exchange of experiences, and the acquisition of new knowledge.

The development of social and human capital will also be supported through educational activities in the field of ecology, environmental protection, and cultural heritage, which in the long term may lead to the creation of organizations or associations actively working in these areas. The LDS also provides for workshops to develop the digital skills of middle-aged and older people, animations and festivals aimed at young people, as well as educational initiatives to raise residents' awareness of issues related to disability. All these activities are intended to strengthen social ties and activate the local community.

The strategy also includes projects related to the development of services for the population. Their implementation will contribute to the creation of new businesses and, thus, local jobs, which will reduce the need for economic migration to Warsaw. Services addressed to people in difficult situations will be a particular priority.

Reading through the diversification lens, these activities exemplify how local initiatives layer new functions onto inherited structures: tourism diversification builds on cultural heritage, smart technologies extend the garden city ethos into the digital era, and education fosters social resilience across generations. Rather than focusing narrowly on economic growth, the LAG's strategy multiplies pathways of development, starting from cultural, ecological and shifting to digital and social, thus forming a diversified service ecosystem that strengthens the settlement's adaptability in the post-urban context.

Living infrastructure and social realities. The area covered by the LAG 'Green Neighbourhood' is characterized by great social and economic diversity. On the one hand, its proximity to Warsaw provides residents with access to the labour market and services, while on the other hand, the unique character of garden cities such as Podkowa Leśna and Milanówek has been preserved. The social diagnosis points to the important role of migration—the area attracts new residents, which increases its demographic potential, but also creates a need for social integration (LSR, 2024, pp. 15–17).

The structure of the population includes both people who are professionally active in the service and knowledge-based economy sectors, as well as seniors and disadvantaged people. In this context, the development of social, educational, and health services is of key importance. The infrastructure includes both modern public and recreational facilities, as well as historic buildings of high cultural value. The place is characterized by its landscape values, cultural heritage, and strong civic traditions, which make it attractive to both residents and tourists. The literature emphasizes that such peri-urban areas can serve as laboratories for social innovation, combining rural heritage with urban dynamics (Woods, 2011).

Placed in the diversification context, the current reality of the 'Green Neighbourhood' illustrates how 'living infrastructure' emerges from the coexistence of diverse populations, built heritage, and ecological assets. Migration inflows, ageing residents, and micro-scale entrepreneurship create overlapping demands that cannot be met by uniform planning. Instead, diversification strategies respond by layering services, enabling adaptive reuse of cultural spaces, and integrating ecological and social infrastructures into a flexible settlement fabric that bridges urban and rural logics.

Lessons for cultivating diversified communities. Implementing the local development strategies based on the LEADER approach brings a number of benefits. The most important of these are greater participation of residents in decision-making on the direction of the area's development, intensified cooperation between entities involved in the implementation of the strategy, and increased knowledge and competence in the management of the local territory. The structure of the LDS objectives is conducive to the creation of innovative and complementary projects that support harmonious and comprehensive development. Importantly, the LEADER approach enables the implementation of activities that are not available under other funds and promotes the implementation of complementary projects involving several local government units.

The experience of the LAG 'Green Neighbourhood' shows that the key to the success of such initiatives is strong roots in the local community, broad participation of residents, and flexibility in adapting to changing socio-economic conditions. It is also important to build tri-sector partnerships and take advantage of the opportunities offered by international cooperation projects. The literature emphasizes that the ability to combine technological innovation with traditional local values is a factor for success (Marsden, 2016).

Several elements that have been incorporated into the local development planning process can be identified. These are primarily the principles of transparency and co-decision-making, investing in human capital through education and training, developing nature-inspired infrastructure that supports the symbiosis between work and everyday life, and strengthening local entrepreneurship based on a service model and social innovation. The LAG 'Green Neighbourhood' shows that this approach allows for the building of sustainable and resilient local communities, and that residents, through participatory methods in shaping local development strategies, have the opportunity to influence the promotion of business that is not burdensome to the environment and residents. It is also an example of an institutional learning process (Navarro et al., 2016; Furmankiewicz et al., 2010), where participation and opening up the planning process to residents allowed for the identification and inclusion of the economic, social, and environmental development potential of the area (Kabisch et al., 2017).

In diversification terms, these lessons underline how sustainability emerges not from single-sector interventions but from the *layering of functions, actors, and values.* The 'Green Neighbourhood' demonstrates that diversification requires both structural tools, i.e., like participatory governance and cross-sector partnerships, and cultural capacities, such as civic trust and openness to innovation. Its experience shows how peri-urban settlements can serve as *learning laboratories* for the post-urban condition: places where ecological, social, and economic trajectories converge into a resilient, diversified fabric.

References

Albrecht, G. A. (2019). *Earth emotions: New words for a new world.* Cornell University Press. https://doi.org/10.1515/9781501715242

Allen, A. (2003). Environmental planning and management of the Peri-urban interface: Perspectives on an emerging field. *Environment and Urbanization, 15*(1), 135–148. https://doi.org/10.1177/095624780301500103

Bai, X., Roberts, B., & Chen, J. (2010). Urban sustainability experiments in Asia: Patterns and pathways. *Environmental Science & Policy, 13*(4), 312–325. https://doi.org/10.1016/j.envsci.2010.03.011

Baltic Seaside. (2025). *Lithuanian Sea Museum.* Retrieved March 14, 2025, https://www.balticseaside.lt/en/entertainment/lithuanian-sea-museum-2338/

Banister, D. (2008). The sustainable mobility paradigm. *Transport Policy, 15*(2), 73–80. https://doi.org/10.1016/j.tranpol.2007.10.005

Berkes, F., & Ross, H. (2013). Community resilience: Toward an integrated approach. *Society & Natural Resources, 26*(1), 5–20. https://doi.org/10.1080/08941920.2012.736605

Bock, B. B. (2016). Rural marginalisation and the role of social innovation: A turn towards nexogenous development and rural reconnection. *Sociologia Ruralis, 56*(4), 552–573. https://doi.org/10.1111/soru.12119

Brenner, N. (2016). *Critique of urbanization: Selected essays.* Birkhäuser.

Brunori, G. (2006). Post-rural processes in wealthy rural areas: Hybrid networks and symbolic capital. In *Between the local and the global* (pp. 121–145). Emerald Group Publishing Limited.

Bulkeley, H., & Betsill, M. M. (2013). *Cities and climate change: Urban sustainability and global environmental governance.* Routledge. https://doi.org/10.4324/9780203077207

Causeway Coast and Glens Borough Council. (2025). *Small settlements regeneration.* Retrieved March 14, 2025, from https://causewaycoastandglens.gov.uk/work/strategic-projects/regeneration-projects/regeneration-news/small-settlements-regeneration

Communications Regulatory Authority of Lithuania. (2023). Broadband internet coverage and development in Lithuania. https://www.rrt.lt.
Conn, S. (2024). Sub-urban or post-rural: Suburban development as a two-way street in the mid-twentieth century. *Journal of American Studies, 58*(1), 124–142.
Covenant of Mayors-Europe. (2022). About the initiative. https://www.covenantofmayors.eu.
Dax, T., & Oedl-Wieser, T. (2016). Rural innovation activities as a means for changing development perspectives: An assessment of more than two decades of promoting LEADER initiatives across the European Union. *Journal of Rural Studies, 46*, 141–152. https://doi.org/10.1016/j.jrurstud.2016.04.003
Druskininkai Municipality. (2022). Druskininkai 2022–2028 Strategic Development Plan. [In Lithuanian].
Druskininkai Rural LAG Strategy. (2023). Local development strategy for Druskininkai rural area 2023–2027. http://www.dvvg.lt/wp-content/uploads/2023/06/Druskininku-VPS-2023-2027-2025-05-29-patvirtinta.pdf.
Druskininkai Strategic Plan 2021–2029. Druskininkų savivaldybės 2021–2029 metų strateginis plėtros planas. https://druskininkusavivaldybe.lt/uploads/structure/docs/2023-08/2f835ec4a29b7e647dae39e56d190fa2e5057385bf8779abbfd04c0f6e299940.pdf.
Escobar, A. (2018). *Designs for the Pluriverse: Radical interdependence, autonomy, and the making of worlds.* Duke University Press.
Esparcia, J. (2014). Innovation and networks in rural areas: An analysis from European innovative projects. *European Planning Studies, 22*(11), 2097–2116. https://doi.org/10.1080/09654313.2013.819838
EU Tourism Platform (2024). Pledge formulated by Druskininkai Municipality Administration. https://transition-pathways.europa.eu/pledges/pledge-formulated-druskininkai-municipality-administration
European Commission. (2021). New EU urban mobility framework. https://transport.ec.europa.eu.
European Commission: Directorate-General for Environment. (2019). *Introducing the EU's green city tool: Compendium.* Publications Office. https://data.europa.eu/doi/10.2779/257141
European Commission: Executive Agency for Small and Medium-sized Enterprises. (2020). *Nature-based solutions: Horizon 2020 NBS research projects tackle the climate and biodiversity crisis.* Publications Office of the European Union. https://data.europa.eu/doi/10.2826/055643
Folke, C., Hahn, T., Olsson, P., & Norberg, J. (2005). Adaptive governance of social-ecological systems. *Annual Review of Environment and Resources, 30*, 441–473.

Furmankiewicz, M., Thompson, N., & Zielińska, M. (2010). Area-based partnerships in rural Poland: The post-accession experience. *Journal of Rural Studies, 26*(1), 52–62. https://doi.org/10.1016/j.jrurstud.2009.05.001
GEN Europe. (2023). What is an ecovillage?. https://gen-europe.org.
GPSmyCity. (2025). *Lithuanian Sea Museum*. Retrieved May 23, 2025, from https://www.gpsmycity.com/attractions/lithuanian-sea-museum-62948.html
Gutierrez-Velez, V. H., Gilbert, M. R., Kinsey, D., & Behm, J. E. (2022). Beyond the 'urban' and the 'rural': Conceptualizing a new generation of infrastructure systems to enable rural–urban sustainability. *Current Opinion in Environmental Sustainability, 56*, 101177.
Haraway, D. (2016). *Staying with the trouble: Making kin in the Chthulucene*. Duke University Press.
Harvey, D. (2012). *Rebel cities: From the right to the City to the urban revolution*. Verso. https://doi.org/10.1016/j.envsci.2010.03.011
Kabisch, N., Frantzeskaki, N., Pauleit, S., Naumann, S., Davis, M., Artmann, M., et al. (2017). Nature-based solutions to climate change mitigation and adaptation in urban areas: Perspectives on indicators, knowledge gaps, barriers, and opportunities for action. *Ecology and Society, 22*(2), 50. https://doi.org/10.5751/ES-09405-220250
Kędzierski, M. (2022). *Od idei miast-ogrodów do ruchu partyzantki ogrodniczej: Społeczne i kulturowe aspekty postaw proekologicznych miasta*. Wydawnictwo Rys.
Kreivinienė, B. (2019). Dolphin assisted therapy No. LLI-352. Vilnius University. https://atviri.emokymai.vu.lt/pluginfile.php/6071/mod_folder/content/0/Dolphin_assisted.pdf
Kreivinienė, B., & Perttula, J. (2012). Delfinų terapija Lietuvoje: Lūkesčiai šeimų, auginančių vaikus, turinčius kompleksinę negalią. *Socialinis darbas, 11*(1), 93–101. Retrieved from https://www.lituanistika.lt/content/45000
Latour, B. (2018). *Down to earth: Politics in the new climatic regime*. Polity Press.
Lefebvre, H. (1996). *Writings on cities*. Blackwell.
Lithuanian Municipal Environmental Rating. (2022). (In Lithuanian). https://am.lrv.lt/lt/lietuvos-savivaldybiu-aplinkosaugos-reitingas-puslapis/lietuvos-savivaldybiu-aplinkosaugos-reitingas/
Lithuanian Sea Museum. (2025a). *Dolphin assisted therapy centre*. Retrieved April 9, 2025, from https://old.muziejus.lt/en/paslaugos/dolphin-assisted-therapy-centre
Lithuanian Sea Museum. (2025b). *Services*. Retrieved March 14, 2025, from https://muziejus.lt/en/services-0
Lithuanian Tourism Department. (2022). Druskininkai: Lithuania's premier wellness destination. https://www.lithuania.travel
LKS Act (2015). Ustawa z dnia 20 lutego 2015 r. o rozwoju lokalnym kierowanym przez społeczność [Act on community-led local development, RLKS]. Dz.U. 2015 poz. 378 (Poland).

Mang, P., & Reed, B. (2012). Designing from place: A regenerative framework and methodology. *Building Research & Information, 40*(1), 23–38.
Marsden, T. (2016). Exploring the rural eco-economy: Beyond neoliberalism. *Sociologia Ruralis, 56*(4), 597–615. https://doi.org/10.1111/soru.12135
Ministry of Environment of the Republic of Lithuania. (2021a). National Climate Change Management Agenda 2021–2030. https://am.lrv.lt/en/
Ministry of Environment of the Republic of Lithuania. (2021b). Sustainable urban development guidelines. https://am.lrv.lt.
National Land Service. (2020). *Real estate co-ownership and management in Lithuania: Legal and administrative framework*. https://nzt.lt
Navarro, F., Woods, M., & Cejudo, E. (2016). The LEADER initiative has been a victim of its own success. *Sociologia Ruralis, 56*(2), 135–155. https://doi.org/10.1111/soru.12080
OECD. (2025). Mind shift, green lift: Six behavioural science trends for environmental policy. OECD Public Governance Policy Papers. https://www.oecd.org/content/dam/oecd/en/publications/reports/2025/01/mind-shift-green-lift_bf6d61a2/162c5a27-en.pdf
PoliRural. (2022). Future-oriented collaborative policy development for rural areas and people (Horizon 2020 Project No. 818496). https://polirural.eu/
Ray, C. (2006). Neo-endogenous rural development in the EU. In P. Cloke, T. Marsden, & P. Mooney (Eds.), *Handbook of rural studies* (pp. 278–291). Sage.
Raymond, C. M., Frantzeskaki, N., Kabisch, N., Berry, P., Breil, M., Nita, M. R., et al. (2017). A framework for assessing and implementing the co-benefits of nature-based solutions in urban areas. *Environmental Science & Policy, 77*, 15–24. https://doi.org/10.1016/j.envsci.2017.07.008
Regional Action Plan/ Study the possibility of extending existing car sharing solutions to resort remote areas Birštonas town and Druskininkai town (Lithuania). (2020). https://keep.eu/api/project-attachment/43469/get_file/
SHERPA. (2023). Sustainable Hub to Engage into Rural Policies with Actors (Horizon 2020 Project No. 862448). https://rural-interfaces.eu/
Short, J. R. (2015). City marketing. In J. D. Wright (Ed.), *International encyclopedia of the social and behavioral sciences* (2nd ed., pp. 662–668). Elsevier. https://doi.org/10.1016/B978-0-08-097086-8.74006-2
Shucksmith, M. (2000). Endogenous development, social capital and social inclusion: Perspectives from LEADER in the UK. *Sociologia Ruralis, 40*(2), 208–218. https://doi.org/10.1111/1467-9523.00143
Skindarienė, D. (2006). *Administration of active labour market measures in Druskininkai municipality*. Master Thesis. Mykolas Romeris University. Lithuanian Academic Libraries Network (LABT)/Mykolas Romeris University.
Smeds, E., & Acuto, M. (2018). Networking cities after Paris: Weighing the ambition of urban climate change experimentation. *Global Policy, 9*(4), 549–559. https://doi.org/10.1111/1758-5899.12587

Smiltynė. (2025). In *Wikipedia*. Retrieved May 23, 2025, from https://en.wikipedia.org/wiki/Smiltyn%C4%97

Sørensen, E., & Torfing, J. (2019). Designing for interactive governance: Insights from design theory. *Public Management Review, 21*(9), 1231–1250. https://doi.org/10.1080/14719037.2018.1544272

Stavrides, S. (2016). *Common space: The city as commons*. Zed Books.

State Data Agency. Statistics Lithuania. (2022). https://osp.stat.gov.lt/statistiniu-rodikliu-analize#/

Stowarzyszenie Lokalna Grupa Działania "Zielone Sąsiedztwo". (2024). Strategia rozwoju lokalnego kierowanego przez społeczność (LSR) wdrażana przez Stowarzyszenie Lokalna Grupa Działania "Zielone Sąsiedztwo": Brwinów, Milanówek, Podkowa Leśna.

UNESCO World Heritage Centre. (2025). *Curonian spit*. Retrieved May 23, 2025, from https://whc.unesco.org/en/list/994/.

URBACT (2023). *Integrated Action Plan: Druskininkai*. https://urbact.eu/sites/default/files/2023-01/TFC_IAP%20DRUSKININKAI.pdf

Westlund, H. (2014). Urban futures in planning, policy and regional science: Are we entering a post-urban world? *Built Environment, 40*(4), 447–457.

Westlund, H. (2017). Urban-rural relations in the post-urban world. In *In the post-urban world* (pp. 70–81). Routledge.

Westlund, H., & Borseková, K. (2025). The post-urban hypothesis. *Global Challenges & Regional Science, 1*, 100005. https://doi.org/10.1016/j.gcrs.2025.100005

Westlund, H., & Haas, T. (2018). In the post-urban world: An introduction. In *The post-urban world: innovative transformations in Global City regions* (pp. 1–12). Routledge.

Woods, M. (2011). *Rural (key ideas in geography)*. Routledge.

CHAPTER 8

Collaboration Strategy: Global Ecovillage Network—Open Innovations for Settlements

Rasa Melnikienė

In a post-industrial society, collaboration has become a key driver of societal development. Recent scientific literature highlights a shift in institutional relationships, with formal structures being replaced by network-based ones (Castells, 1996; Camarinha-Matos & Afsarmanesh, 2005). The way in which members of modern collaboration networks organize their relationships and initiate the diversity of activities doesn't fit into the framework established by traditional institutions. A network is a new form of organizing human relationships that differs significantly from traditional institutions and, due to its differences, provides additional benefits to network members.

The first collaboration networks were established to develop organizational structures that would better manage the key resource of the post-industrial economy—knowledge. These structures would facilitate faster and more extensive exchange of data, information, and experience, as well as the sharing of opinions, with an aim to create new value through joint, coordinated actions. However, it is important to note that they were quickly adopted by other areas of social life (Vidickienė et al., 2021). According to Roberto Camagni and Roberta Capello (2004), 'we speak

D. Vidickienė et al., *Human Settlement in the Service Economy Era*, Palgrave Advances in Bioeconomy: Economics and Policies,
https://doi.org/10.1007/978-3-032-19390-2_8

about network firms, network society and network economy; in an explicitly spatial context, we speak about network cities, city networks'.

Collaboration can be used as a tool for implementing innovative solutions in settlements, as the importance of network effects is particularly emphasized in the creation and implementation of innovations (De Noni et al., 2018). Scientific research indicates that the development of settlements is closely related to the predominant model of production in society. In post-industrial societies dominated by the service economy, new forms of work and leisure are becoming increasingly popular, residents are raising new expectations on the infrastructure of settlements, and the concept of what constitutes a high-quality place to live is changing. The post-industrial service-based economy has the potential to drive significant changes in current lifestyles and necessitate the development of a new vision for human settlement (Vidickienė et al., 2024).

The ecovillage movement and Global Ecovillage Network (GEN) have played a significant role in shaping a new lifestyle and adapting living conditions to this. GEN formulated a vision of alternative settlements based on an environmentally friendly lifestyle and successfully implemented this vision. The ecovillage movement was established in response to the environmental challenges posed by the industrial economy. Its primary objective was to transition from a predominant industrial production model to a less polluting and more sustainable alternative. The post-industrial economy, in which the service sector plays an important role, met the requirements of ecovillages (Vidickienė et al., 2024).

Research conducted by scientists specializing in ecovillages has highlighted the considerable impact of such initiatives on the transformation of regions across environmental, social, cultural, and economic domains (Manent, 2017; Accioly Dias et al., 2017; Fonseca et al., 2017). Most of the research on ecovillages is based on case studies of specific ecovillages, analysing ecovillage practices and identifying opportunities to apply them in other areas (Wagner, 2012).

When examining eco-settlements from this perspective, the question remains: what determined the success of eco-settlements, which led to their ideas being accepted on a global scale? There were several ecological movements in the 1970s, but many of them were unable to achieve a significant breakthrough in implementing their ideas. Whereas the ecovillage movement has proven its viability and has become a successful project for implementing a social initiative to create a new type of settlement, due to the collaboration tools developed by GEN. The success of GEN in the twenty-first century was determined by the foresight of its organizers and their ability to use the wave of technological, economic, and social change to develop their organization's activities. Therefore, this study does not focus on individual ecovillages, but rather on the innovative collaboration tools they employ.

A Brief History of GEN: From Ideas to Practice

GEN was established in the late 1990s. Research indicates that the concept of ecovillages emerged from the environmental social movements of the 1960s and 1970s, which advocated for the establishment of a new kind of intentional community that promoted sustainable living (Mare, 2000; Dawson, 2013; Farkas, 2017; Roysen et al., 2021). According to Christopher Mare (2000), 'sparked by a deep dissatisfaction with the prevailing institutions of economic materialism and global domination, responsive people took off in droves to create a better, purer lifestyle for themselves in the refuge of the countryside'.

The GEN organization was created by eco-communities that had been operating successfully for many years (Jackson & Jackson, 2004) and were in different regions, primarily in Europe and North America. Operating individually, they failed to achieve rapid dissemination of their ideas, and new villages established following their example faced challenges in community building, with some of these projects ending in failure (Mare, 2000; Garden, 2006).

The formal beginning of the ecovillage movement can be dated back to 1991, when the Gaia Trust, a charitable organization, commissioned Diane and Robert Gilman to conduct a global survey of the best examples of ecovillages. In their report *Ecovillages and Sustainable Communities*, they proposed a definition of an ecovillage as 'a human-scale, full-featured settlement, in which human activities are harmlessly integrated into the natural world, in a way that is supportive of healthy human development and can be successfully continued into the indefinite future' (Gilman & Gilman, 1991; Jackson, 1998).

The ecovillage movement gained momentum in Scandinavian countries and actively sought like-minded individuals not only in Europe but also across other continents. To change the world—make it more socially responsible, friendlier to nature, and more rational in its use of resources—it was necessary to join forces. From the very beginning, collaboration was a key idea in the ecovillage movement. To achieve fundamental changes in society, an organization was needed to speak on behalf of everyone. GEN was established in 1995, following the Findhorn Community's organization of the conference *Ecovillages and Sustainable Communities for the twenty-first Century*, which attracted 400 attendees from 40 countries (Forster and Wilhelmus, 2005; Jackson, 2006). Following the meeting, twenty ecovillage members decided to formally establish the Global Ecovillage Network (GEN). It consists of three regional networks, with administrative centres at The Farm (USA), Lebensgarten (Germany), and Crystal Waters (Australia). There is also an international coordinating office at GEN (Global Ecovillage Network, 2007a, archived).

The GEN collaboration strategy focused on the needs and opportunities of large systems at the macro level, presenting a vision for the development of innovative, environmentally friendly lifestyle at regional, national, continental, and even global levels. One of the most important goals of GEN in its initial phase was 'to support and encourage the evolution of sustainable settlements across the world, through Internal and External Communications services, facilitating the flow and exchange of information about ecovillages and demonstration sites' (Global Ecovillage Network, 2007a, archived).

Gradually, the GEN network expanded its activities to all continents. In 2025, GEN consisted of five regional networks: GEN Europe, North America (GENNA), GEN Africa, Latin America (CASA), Global Ecovillage Network of Oceania and Asia (GENOE). In the third decade of the twenty-first century, GEN presents itself as 'a global confederation of people and communities that meet and share their ideas, exchange technologies, develop cultural and educational exchanges, directories and newsletters, and are dedicated to restoring the land and living "sustainable plus" lives by putting more back into the environment than we take out' (Global Ecovillage Network, 2025).

Tools for Implementing the GEN Collaboration Strategy

Since its establishment, GEN has implemented innovative solutions to maximize eco-friendly engagement and collaboration, taking advantage of the benefits offered by the service economy. Studies on the evolution of collaboration models show that a successful collaboration model in a service economy is based on certain paradigmatic innovations: (1) the pursuit of competitive advantage shifts to the creation of mutual symbiosis between participants in the business ecosystem; (2) institutionalized collaboration is replaced by networked connections; (3) collaboration between participants with similar interests is shifting towards multi-actors partnerships; (4) the market economy is being replaced by the platform economy (Vidickienė et al., 2024). An analysis of GEN activities shows that the following tools for organizing activities have become key factors in the success of the eco-movement:

- An organizational structure based on networked connections and open membership
- Fostering multi-actors' partnerships
- Developing symbiotic relationships between network members
- Use of platforms to establish collaboration links

An Organizational Structure Based on Network Connections and Open Membership

The initiators of the ecovillage movement created GEN by taking advantage of the opportunities offered by networking as a new form of collaboration, made possible by the development of information technology. Researchers studying networks have found that networking as a way of organizing collaboration offers many advantages when an organizational network seeks to find like-minded individuals, disseminate knowledge, and share experiences (Forzati et al., 2010; Ye & Kankanhalli, 2013a; Ter Wal et al., 2016). Open collaboration is particularly useful in creating innovation because it generates a continuous innovation process by utilizing the ideas of network participants.

At the beginning of the movement, GEN developers had to decide on decision-making methods and the degree of openness in membership. According to Jackson and Jackson (2004), 'GEN members in the early days often discussed the question of whether there should be a qualification for membership in any given network and for the right to vote, or whether membership should simply be open to all on an equal basis. If the former, what criteria should be used? Should GEN play the role of judging whether a given project could justify the word "ecovillage" in its name? One result was a decision to keep membership open. The major result of these early discussions was the evolution of a voluntary audit system that an individual ecovillage can use to judge how far it has come relative to the ideal'. The decision to create GEN as an open network opened up opportunities not only for permanent members of the network, but also for those who are casually interested in the issue to participate in the network and propose innovative solutions based on their expertise and experience. This decision created significant potential for the network's growth.

After establishing GEN, the movement's initiators began looking for ways to quickly expand the network of villages—not only in regions where sustainable lifestyle ideas were already widely supported, such as the Nordic countries, but also by introducing them to new regions. The GEN Europe Annual Report (2003) stated: 'We need to stay connected to the ground and to each other, and to enhance more contacts and support between national networks. We need more input to the newsletter from the eco-villages to use the media better and improve the flow of information from eco-villages to the office'. GEN's main aim is to support and encourage the evolution of sustainable settlements across the world through the following:

- Internal and External Communications services; facilitating the flow and exchange of information about ecovillages and demonstration sites
- Networking and project coordination in fields related to sustainable settlements
- Global collaboration/Partnerships (UN Best Practices, EU Phare, EYFA, Ecosoc) (Global ecovillage network, 2016a, archived; Global ecovillage Network, 2025)

Five years after its founding in 2000, GEN comprised 100 members (individuals, communities, and organizations) in GEN Europe and Africa, 80 members in GEN Oceania, and hundreds of identified ecovillages in the Americas (although, admittedly, most of these were 'intentional communities' that have not yet reached 'village' scale). GEN had sprouted a new sub-regional office in South Asia that communicated with 40 ecovillages and included the Sarvodaya movement in Sri Lanka with 10,000 member villages (Mare, 2000).

GEN called upon individuals interested in sustainable living to join the network as active participants. In return, GEN offered them the benefits of an established global network—comprising ecovillages, individuals, organizations, educational institutions, and NGOs—and invited them to contribute to expanding GEN's contact base and outreach (Global ecovillage network, 2007a, archived).

Network members were expected to support GEN by sharing information through their publications and materials, mentioning GEN at conferences and public events, introducing the organization within their professional networks, and distributing GEN materials at relevant public meetings. The ecovillage network was structured across three levels:

- Regional—promoting the creation and development of national and regional networks.
- Demographic—to reflect on the role of youth in the Global Ecovillage Movement.
- Professional—by creating opportunities for professionals working in the field of sustainable development (consultants, scientists, educators, information content creators, etc.) to get involved in the network's activities.

In 2012, two regional networks, CASA (in Latin America) and GEN Africa, joined GEN, and GEN became a global network (Global ecovillage network, 2014, archived).

The decision to establish Next GEN, a youth organization within the Global Ecovillage Network, was made at the GEN+10 conference in 2005. The initiative was proposed by young people already involved in GEN activities, leading to the formation of the GEN Youth Council during the conference. As a result, NextGEN was officially founded as GEN's youth wing and has since expanded its activities to all GEN regions worldwide (Global Ecovillage Network, 2007a, archived). As of 2025, NextGEN comprised youth networks in Europe (NextGEN Europe), North America (NextGENNA), Latin America (CASA Jóvenes), and Africa (NextGEN Africa) (Global Ecovillage Network, 2025).

GEN's efforts to expand the ecovillage network in a short period of time were implemented as the public became aware of the importance of knowledge and information as a driving force for change. Therefore, from the very beginning, GEN's creators attached great importance to educational services and the dissemination of ideas about sustainable living as a means of building the network. Networks are usually created between existing members, but the uniqueness of GEN's activities lies in the fact that it coordinated a network of newly established members who adhered to certain innovative operating principles. This approach required the exchange of knowledge and experience between existing villages and those in the process of being established.

To achieve this goal, GEN summarized the knowledge accumulated in successfully operating ecovillages and developed training infrastructure and programmes. GEN actively applied the Living and Learning principle in its training. Living and Learning Centres became a core component of GEN's strategy for promoting sustainability and education (Snyder, 2013). Community-based demonstration and teaching centres were established in Europe, America, and Oceania, offering people the opportunity to come and learn about sustainable living through practical experiences that can be replicated throughout the world. These centres serve as 'local planetary models' and can be powerful catalysts for change. In Europe, such centres operated at The Findhorn Foundation, Scotland, ZEGG, Germany, Damanhur, Italy, Centre for Alternative Technology (CAT), Wales (Global ecovillage network, 2007a, archived).

GEN received a significant boost in 2005 with the launch of the Gaia Education programme initiated, by the Gaia Trust (Gaia Trust, 2025), which was expanded in 2016 into GEN Education and Consultancy. GEN has placed particular emphasis on promoting sustainable lifestyles among young people. In 2005, GEN partner Gaia began implementing a holistic introduction to designing sustainable settlements called *Ecovillage Design Education* (EDE), based on the GEN's Living and Learning principle (Gaia Education, 2025). Also, Gaia University offers a unique approach to higher education by providing students—referred to as Associates—with access to accredited bachelor's and master's degrees, as well as Graduate Diplomas, while they actively engage in both personal and planetary transformation (Gaia Trust, 2025). NextGEN helped attract new members by organizing youth training through a Mentor Programme with GEN Elders, conducting 'Training of Trainers' courses for the ecovillage and sustainability movement, and establishing regional coordination centres focused on education and training for young adults.

The partnership helped establish effective communication channels between villages, as well as national and regional networks, to ensure that knowledge about ecovillage creation practices would be accessible to individuals interested in sustainable living worldwide. GEN began providing an integrated sustainable systems consultation service for assistance in key areas of sustainability design and project development. The topics of consultation covered a wide range of issues related to the establishment of ecovillages, including ecological landscape design and land use planning;

village, neighbourhood and urban design; social ecology and decision-making; organizational development, management, and transformation (Global Ecovillage Network, 2007a, archived).

To attract as many members as possible to GEN activities, the training was adapted to both existing and newly established villages and offered solutions to ecovillages operating in rural areas and urban suburbs. Five programmes were implemented as part of the initiative: Ecovillage Incubator, Ecovillage Development/Transition, Greening School, EmerGENcies, and Urban Ecovillage (Global Ecovillage Network Annual Report, 2019).

GEN effectively utilized information technology to maintain regular communication with network members and to attract new participants. For example, GEN Europe created the Ecovillage Online Forum, which, according to Forum statistics in 2007, had 1670 registered participants. The GEN-Europe online Forum is a bulletin board featuring topics for public and GEN-Europe members. It contains a board for general discussions of GEN-Europe, a space for ecovillage advertisements, and an internal area designated for GEN members working groups (Global Ecovillage Network, 2007b, archived).

GEN and its regional networks have effectively used social networks (Facebook, Instagram, Twitter, YouTube, LinkedIn) to disseminate information about the network's activities. The growing number of followers indicates increasing interest in GEN's ideas. Annual reports have noted increasing traffic to the GEN website and a growing number of subscribers to its newsletters (Global Ecovillage Network Annual Report, 2021).

Distance learning has become another important tool for strengthening networks and disseminating ideas. This approach to training, which became popular worldwide during the Covid-19 pandemic, helped overcome the physical distance between educators and learners, enabled access to a wider audience, and reduced training costs for both providers and participants. According to researchers studying learning networks, networked learning environments can be used to encourage new connections between students, between students and teachers, and between students and learning resources (Schreurs et al., 2019).

The 2021 GEN Annual Report announced that 42 Established Networks and 30 Emerging Networks are participating in GEN activities, covering 116 countries and 7500 communities collaborating with GEN, with nearly 300 ambassadors promoting GEN activities to the public. It should also be noted that GEN has been actively involved in the creation of other European and global networks. Many of the partners listed on the GEN website are networks dedicated to advancing the sustainable development goals (United Nations, 2015), across various dimensions: social, environmental, cultural, and economic. They promote sustainable lifestyles, encourage permaculture and regenerative agriculture, and community activities that help mitigate climate change (Global ecovillage network, 2007a, archived).

Multi-Actors' Partnerships

The objectives of GEN's activities, aimed at achieving rapid change in the regions and globally, depended on how quickly the number of network members could be increased. From the outset, GEN decided on the openness of the network and the diversity of its members. In establishing multi-actor partnerships, GEN drew on collaborative models typical of the service economy. Recent studies on how servitization is transforming the business ecosystem of companies and regions also reveal large-scale collaboration involving multiple actors with diverse interests participating in different ways (Huikkola et al., 2020; Zhang et al., 2021; Kohtamäki et al., 2022). Collaborative activities involve not only formal members of organizations with regulated relationships, but also a variety of other participants—such as customers, business partners, employees, local authorities, and NGOs. By harnessing the power of its contributors, the network provides benefits and connects all parties in diverse and innovative ways. GEN can be defined as a multilateral network that brings together ecovillages, local communities, various NGOs, researchers, and government institutions. These are networks are typical of innovation ecosystems (see Fig. 8.1).

Partnership among ecovillages. GEN's multi-actor partnerships were shaped by the diversity of the ecovillages themselves. Both long-established and newly formed villages have participated in the ecovillage movement. They differed in terms of their legal community structures and the degree of shared ownership. These included Nonprofit Corporations, Cooperatives, Land Trusts, Limited Liability Companies (LLCs), and Community Land Trusts (Bluesmith, 2023). Ecovillages varied significantly in size—from a few members to a thousand residents—and in the age structure of their populations, which in turn influenced their organization and management. The residents of ecovillages were engaged in various income-generating activities, such as organic farming, ecotourism,

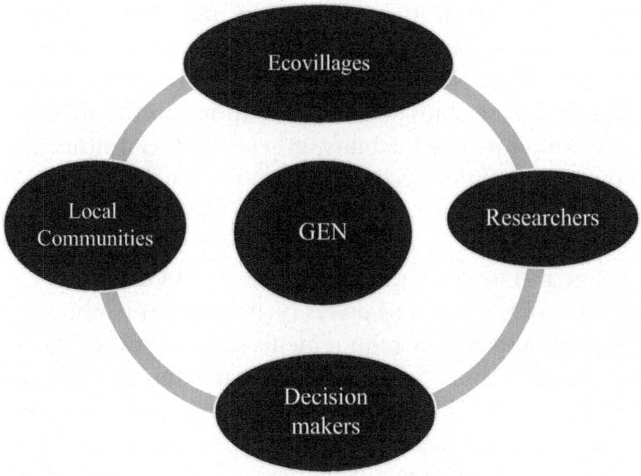

Fig. 8.1 GEN multi-actor partnerships. (Source: Author's figure)

personal development education, and social and consulting services (Vidickienė et al., 2013; Temesgen, 2024).

Although ecovillages shared a common vision for a sustainable future, individual communities varied in their degree of ecological awareness and in the strategies they employed to address environmental, economic, political, and social challenges. Behind the creation of ecovillages there are various counter-narratives to mainstream views based on extrinsic values—market economy, capitalism, statehood, traditional education, and historical religions. Ecovillages are caught in the middle between global and local, traditional and new, with broad social and political value systems (Bakó et al., 2021).

Researchers seeking to identify the ideal ecovillage and establish strict criteria for its definition have concluded that no single model of an ecovillage exists. They highlight the inherent heterogeneity of ecovillages, reflecting their diverse origins in spiritual, environmental, cohousing, and back-to-the-land movements (Fölke Günther, 1989; Dawson, 2013; Ashlock, 2010; Dias et al., 2017).

Since its inception, GEN has invited both private members and organizations to collaborate. By inviting individual members to join the network, GEN extended its reach to regions without existing ecovillages and established connections that could facilitate the development of national networks in the future. In its initial version, the GEN platform allowed individual members to assume roles as 'networkers', volunteers, or sponsors (Global Ecovillage Network, 2007a, archived). In its current mission, GEN welcomes partnerships with organizations and individuals actively engaged in community sustainability, green business ventures, renewable energy, ecological building, ecological production (food or other), ecotourism, and related educational initiatives (Global Ecovillage Network, 2007a, archived). These partners are encouraged not only to share their experience, but also to become active members of GEN.

In our view, GEN promoted diversity among its members through its open membership policy. The requirements set for network members joining regional organizations were aimed at ensuring that all participants contributed actively to the organization's stated goals (Garden, 2006). The GEN collaboration target groups were the following: Eco Citizens, Eco Projects, Eco/Green Schools, Eco Communities, Eco Neighbourhoods, Eco Cities, Eco Regions (Global Ecovillage Network Annual Report, 2019, 2021).

Partnership with researchers. Scientists have been involved in the network's activities from the outset; indeed, they participated in its establishment. In May 2004, Hildur and Ross Jackson wrote in their article 'Global Ecovillage Network History 1990–2004' that '… the Nordic Alternative Campaign of the 1980s initiated by Norwegian Eric Damman … linked 100 Nordic grass roots movements with the best of the scientific community in order to create a vision of how to tackle global social and environmental problems' (Jackson & Jackson, 2004).

Collaboration with the scientific community became one of GEN's strategic goals. To establish ongoing communication with scientists, the GEN Research Group—focused on the power of participatory action research—was established within the GEN organizational structure. This group sought opportunities to utilize 'existing platforms in the academic world for integrating ecovillage research in one place and disseminating information widely' (Global Ecovillage Network Annual Report, 2015).

By developing partnerships with scientists, GEN has established ongoing and long-term relationships. To support these collaborations, GEN created a dedicated webpage with information for researchers, an active mailing list, and regular online meetings (Global Ecovillage Network, 2016b, archived). During the GEN +20 Summit, open sessions on academic research on ecovillages were organized. GEN collected a database with profiles and publications (Global Ecovillage Network Annual Report,

2015) and created the Code of Conduct (CoC), which is designed to facilitate ethical, respectful, and mutually beneficial collaboration between researchers and ecovillagers/community members.

The activities of GEN and its regional networks were organized on a project basis, and the successful outcomes of these projects relied heavily on the diverse competencies of the project team. Partnership links were developed not only in the case of GEN or regional networks, but the ecovillages themselves also actively collaborated with both scientists and scientific institutions (Kroik, 2014). According to Rozália Klára Bakó et al. (2021), ecovillages are studied not only by academic investigations, but also by peer organizations and communities. These initiatives pay special attention to each other's strategies and successes in solving issues related to environmental sustainability.

Partnership with local communities. For a long time, collaboration between ecovillages and local communities was more fragmented than their cooperation with other network participants, as it occurred at the local level and was therefore shaped by social and cultural contexts as well as mutual understanding between the actors involved (Roysen & Schwab, 2021; Singh et al., 2020; Schwab, 2021; Singh et al., 2020). Local communities' interest in ecovillage practices was driven by the challenges they faced. Their efforts to address environmental issues reflect the bottom-up approach characteristic of ecovillages, combining practical aspect with the application of accumulated theoretical knowledge (Waerther, 2014). According to the adopted premises, communal territorial innovations, as exemplified by ecovillage practices, may broaden the range of solutions available for addressing contemporary, interconnected crises (Fonseca et al., 2022). The joint activities of individual ecovillages with local educational institutions and non-profit organizations, as well as activities in nearby communities, can be described as networked connections (Roysen & Schwab, 2021).

Communities are becoming increasingly active participants in the ecovillage network because GEN, together with its partners and with the participation of regional ecovillage networks, has begun to implement community-led initiatives. GEN joined the steering committee behind the UN Commission on Human Settlements (UNCHS) Best Practices Database and Local Leadership Programme (Global Ecovillage Network, 2007a, archived). GEN took part in promoting the dissemination, sharing and exchange of lessons learned from the many best practices, and facilitated the transfer of the knowledge, experience, and expertise associated with best practices in improving the living environment through cooperation on a north-north, north-south, and south-south basis. GEN participated in implementation projects related to sustainability of local communities: The Communities for Local Green Deals project, Community Learning Incubator for Sustainability (CLIPS), Energy Citizenship and Energy Communities for a Clean-Energy Transition (GEN Europe, 2025).

Partnership with decision-makers. The ecovillage movement began as a civic initiative grounded in the belief that environmental and social transformation requires the active involvement of all communities. According to Ross Jackson, one of the founders of GEN, the initiators of the movement should not have expected governments or other powerful institutions to implement the change important to the ecovillage agenda. He argued that 'the problems associated with sustainable living are too complex and diverse to be solved by a traditional "top-down" approach' (Jackson, 2000).

However, the leaders of the ecovillage movement understood from the outset that without political support, the movement's impact would be local and limited. Therefore, they sought to establish connections with national governments and international organizations, to gain support for the movement's projects. Acting as an international network, GEN focused its efforts on building relationships with policymakers and decision-makers within global institutions (Avelino et al., 2015; Dias et al., 2017). The United Nations and its agencies have become important partners in the development of GEN's activities (in 2000, GEN became a member of the UN Economic and Social Council Non-Governmental Organizations Committee and a partner of UN Institution for Training and Research (UNITAR)). Various activities carried out of GEN and its members were funded by international and national institutions, which encouraged diversity and partner engagement. The implementation of projects involved universities, public sector organizations, ecovillages, their national networks, local communities, and associated organizations. This multilateral partnership provided mutual benefits to all participants within the network (Global Ecovillage Network Annual report, 2015, 2021).

Symbiotic Relationships between Network Participants

GEN has successfully established multifaceted, beneficial connections between network participants. Ecosystem theory provides a new perspective on collaboration and the analysis of complex adaptive business environments. James F. Moore (1996, p. 26), who first introduced the concept of a business ecosystem, defined it as 'an economic community supported by interacting organisations and individuals – organisms in the business world'. This and subsequent definitions of business ecosystems proposed by scholars primarily emphasize interconnections between economic actors and the fact that their success and survival are interdependent (Den Hartigh & Van Asseldonk, 2004).

An ecosystem is a model of an economic system that can also be used to explain the cooperative relationships within GENs, both between ecovillages and beyond the boundaries of their collaborative networks. From the perspective of the innovation market, ecovillages create and offer a range of economic, environmental, and social innovations to society (Nogueira et al., 2024). Ecovillages are active participants in the service market. Nearly all ecovillages promote tourism (Van Schyndel Kasper, 2008) and attract regular visitors (Litfin, 2014) who engage in non-formal education activities, as the goal is to 'demonstrate' a more sustainable way of life. In some cases, visitors and guests voluntarily participate in internal activities as students (Brombin, 2015).

Eco-friendly collaboration is a multidirectional process in which eco-friendly companies not only create value for their partners but also benefit from the collaboration. By promoting alternative modes of production, lifestyles, and social relations, these companies seek partners who would contribute to the development of innovative solutions. They cultivate symbiotic relationships with various institutions to better understand societal needs for ecological and social innovation, identify the most effective channels for disseminating ideas, leverage the resources of other institutions to generate knowledge, and influence political processes. GEN has created an ecosystem built on symbiotic relationships with ecovillages, scientists, local communities, and international organizations.

Symbiotic relationships among ecovillages. As mentioned earlier, GEN coordinated a network of members who were establishing themselves and adhering to innovative operating principles. This approach required the exchange of knowledge and experience between existing villages (Jackson,

1998; Jackson & Jackson, 2004). Ecovillages sought to join the network to minimize the risk of making unsuccessful decisions (Wagner, 2012).

The biggest challenges faced by ecovillages during their establishment involved creating infrastructure for the settlements. Implementing the principle of harmony with nature was particularly difficult in towns and cities developed during the industrial era, where green spaces were scarce and the social structure was already established. Consequently, many settlements were founded in remote areas, where there were fewer economic and legal obstacles (Van Schyndel Kasper, 2008; Ergas, 2010, Litfin, 2014). Ecovillages also aimed for a certain level of self-sufficiency—primarily in food and energy production—which requires substantial physical space and access to natural resources. Establishing an ecovillage involved finding a new place to live, acquiring land, and securing appropriate buildings. In the early stages, ecovillage communities were typically small, and their long-term success depends on whether they could attract and retain minimum number of residents necessary to develop and sustain the required infrastructure (Gilman, 1991).

Living conditions, such as water supply, sewage systems, electricity, and heating, had a significant impact on residents' decisions to settle in an ecovillage. Researchers studying the establishment of ecovillages have noted that 'all too often, people try to form ecovillages without a solid understanding of the legal and technical issues associated with large numbers of people living on the same piece of land together. They find a large lot for sale out in the middle of the countryside, buy it, and start to make plans for communal living without first making sure that what they have in mind is even possible' (Hallsmith, 2012).

Eco-settlements established in suburban areas found it easier to develop, as they could take advantage of existing urban infrastructure. In contrast, those founded in remote locations further away from cities faced greater challenges, as they were built entirely from scratch as new, independent entities, e.g. the family homesteads established according to the 'Anastasija' ecovillage model (Vidickienė, 2013).Villages established as new cooperatives in rural farming areas required not only funding for new investments but also the implementation of green infrastructure and innovative technologies (Palojärvi et al., 2013).

No settlement can function without a reliable water supply and systems for human waste treatment. According to regulations, any water system serving more than 15 connections or 25 people for at least 60 days per year is classified as a public water supply. Implementing such infrastructure was often very costly due to strict environmental requirements (Hallsmith, 2012). Rural planning required a solid understanding of local Zoning and Subdivision Regulations. Community building also involved selecting an appropriate legal entity or ownership structure, such as a cooperative or non-governmental organization, an addressing issue related to land and home ownership (Roth, 2012). Additional key structural components of an ecovillage may include farming agreements, business models, design guidelines, decision-making protocols, conflict resolution processes, membership criteria, joining procedures, financial responsibilities, and insurance policies—the list goes on. Despite efforts towards self-sufficiency, most contemporary ecovillage residents still need to go to a larger village, town, city, or into cyberspace, to meet some of their essential needs (Hallsmith, 2012).

Ecovillages have experimented and developed new, environmentally friendly technological solutions in various areas, including planning and design of village layouts, construction using renewable materials, composting, recycling, ecological consumption, food production, transportation, communication, household and community energy systems, and wastewater management (Haxeltine & Seyfang, 2009; Palojärvi et al., 2013). They functioned as creative laboratories where innovations were developed and implemented, such as harnessing natural environmental factors and using local materials to create green infrastructure for the settlement.

Using eco-friendly resources to create and adapt infrastructure required agreement on solutions and the avoidance of conflict among residents. Ecovillage residents developed new methods of self-management based on the involvement of all community members in decision-making (Vidickienė, 2013; Blahovestova et al., 2020).

GEN and regional networks were used to disseminate green infrastructure solutions developed and already implemented by ecovillages, so that newly established ecovillages could benefit from tried and tested solutions. It should be noted that at the beginning of the activity, GEN had rather limited opportunities to reach potential ecovillage developers, as there were no possibilities to use online platforms or social networks for information dissemination. The seminars were held in person, and participants had to be invited to a specific location. This greatly limited the number of participants and required resources for organizing seminars (rental of premises and equipment, travel, etc.). Thanks to support from private donors and public organizations, educational programmes were developed, and a series of seminars was organized in various regions in a short period of time, which increased awareness of GEN and encouraged more participants to join the network (Gaia education, 2025). Seminars, study visits, lectures, and experience sharing were actively organized. Knowledge was exchanged between ecovillages in order to increase the value created for all network participants.

Symbiotic relationships between ecovillages and the academic community. Scientific institutions and researchers are an important part of the innovation system (Smith et al., 2014). Since its inception, the ecovillage movement has been based on the insights of researchers and has received active support from the academic community. The alternative lifestyle promoted in ecovillages manifested itself in various aspects: technological, social, economic, cultural, and environmental, with new ideas being put into practice. Therefore, from the very beginning of the network's creation, ecovillages established symbiotic relationships with the scientific community and became the subject of interdisciplinary research (Wagner, 2012). The collaboration created added value for both sides. Ecovillages introduced a new lifestyle concept to society. The main benefits of grassroots innovations for sustainable development are that they create space for new ideas and practices to be developed, experimented with, and achieve tangible results in improving sustainability, albeit on a small scale (Seyfang & Haxeltine, 2012).

The aim of the researchers collaborating with the ecovillages was to investigate the experimental practices of the ecovillages, summarize the accumulated knowledge, and find ways to apply innovative solutions. The ecovillages were open to the researchers' interests and actively shared information (Global Ecovillage Network, 2016b, archived). The authenticity of the research was enhanced by the fact that some of the researchers were residents of the ecovillages. At the same time, the ecovillages used the results of the research to spread ideas about ecological lifestyles, using them for consultations and training, and to exert political influence.

Innovative solutions in ecovillages led to a variety of scientific interests. Research in ecovillages covered several scientific disciplines: (a) examinations of the perspectives of individuals, (b) sociological investigations, and (c) ethnological and cultural investigations. Studies from the natural science perspective focused on areas of ecological sustainability, such as energy consumption, energy supply, additional aspects of production, and ecological footprints (Wagner, 2012).

In 2024, GEN created the E-community Research Platform (E-community Research Platform, 2025). This platform was the result of the ReGEN4All project, implemented by GEN Europe with EU funding. ReGEN4All 'aimed to make the knowledge gained within and through ecovillages more accessible both for academic research and to help inform policy decisions on sustainable lifestyle and regenerative practices'. The E-community Library, developed during the Regen4All project, curates a database as a comprehensive library, focusing on ecovillages and related subjects. This platform contains articles, reports and other types of materials on ecovillages and ecovillage-related topics (E-community Research Platform, 2025).

To strengthen collaboration between researchers studying ecovillages, the GEN Research Group and ReGEN4all organized a series of colloquiums and developed a new and innovative format in which not only researchers but also practitioners were invited to present and reflect on topics relevant to research. This activity sought to provide a space for interaction and constructive dialogue among community-led initiatives, universities, and academics. (E-community Research Platform, 2025).

Ecovillages' symbiotic relationships with local communities. Scientific literature contains many studies of ecovillages that demonstrate mutually beneficial relationships between ecovillages and local communities, showing that collaboration took place in the areas of environmental protection, economics, and social issues, and that collaboration was characterized by a wide variety of methods (Van Schyndel Kasper, 2008, Vidickienė et al., 2013; Martin et al., 2015; Roysen & Schwab, 2021). Ecovillages offered local communities' elements of the sharing economy (car, book, and clothes sharing), invited them to participate in the implementation of permaculture projects, and in the organization of community-based agriculture, which distributes the risk involved in agricultural production among consumers in the community and supports local small-scale agricultural producers (Dawson, 2006). They also shared their experience of renovating houses using ecological materials and installing solar power systems on the roofs of houses (Roysen & Schwab, 2021). In other words, consumer interest in eco-friendly lifestyles has encouraged ecovillages to offer local consumers services based on the practices applied in ecovillages in different dimensions of daily life: the social dimension (e.g. collective organization of daily tasks), the cultural dimension (e.g. spiritual practices), the ecological dimension (e.g. sustainable construction), and the economic dimension (e.g. sharing resources) (Boyer et al., 2016; Pisters et al., 2020; Roysen & Schwab, 2021).

Many ecovillages have begun to organize courses, lectures, seminars, internship programmes, and conferences for local communities on topics related to their ideas, such as permaculture, bioconstruction, communication and conflict resolution methods, child education, personal growth, etc. (Litfin, 2014, Fonseca et al., 2022).

Ecovillages actively participated in community (local) currency systems because these were consistent with the goals of ecovillages. Local currency systems aimed to improve community participation and social ties among users increase the confidence of local businesses and consumers, and develop and strengthen networking (Sanz, 2016). Some ecovillages, such as Filhorn (East, 2018) and Damanhur (Vidickienė et al., 2013), created and implemented their own local currency systems, while others supported projects implemented by local authorities (Seyfang & Longhurst, 2013). Studies show that local currency systems have helped to increase the use of local goods and services, reduce unemployment, and increase economic sustainability in the community (Kichiji & Nishibe, 2008).

Ecovillages created businesses, employed local residents, and thus helped to solve employment problems. In cases where villages were located in remote areas with few job opportunities, this support was very important for the local community (Dal Borgo & Gambazza, 2017). Ecovillages participated in local cultural life, organized concerts, and invited local residents to celebrate holidays. Ecovillages encouraged local residents to take a more active role in politics by representing their interest and in the decision-making processes of local authorities. In areas where ecovillages were established, local authorities paid increased attention to environmental issues (Dias et al., 2017; Roysen & Schwab, 2021).

Symbiotic relationships with international organizations. The global changes sought by GEN required an international platform. The founders of ecovillages understood that it was necessary not only to educate the public but also to change politicians' attitudes towards social development, climate challenges, and ways of addressing social and environmental problems—encouraging them to support the changes initiated by ecovillages.

The emergence of the ecovillage movement coincided with a period when governments around the world began to pay more attention to issues of nature conservation and the efficient use of natural resources. In 1986, the United Nations (UN) published the Brundtland Report, *Our*

Common Future, in which the authors formulated the goals and principles of sustainable development.

The ecovillage movement not only endorsed these goals but also put them into practice by creating models of sustainable living in communities. In 1998, the contribution of the ecovillage movement was recognized at the political level: ecovillages were first officially named among the United Nations' 'top 100 listing' of best practices as outstanding models of sustainable living (Jackson & Jackson, 2004).

The UN provided GEN with a platform for disseminating its ideas at the global political level, while ecovillages provided the UN with evidence that ecological lifestyle concepts can be applied in practice. At the meeting of the UN Economic and Social Council's Committee on Non-Governmental Organizations in June 2000, GEN was approved as an official UN NGO with Special Consultative Status.

Assessing GEN's collaboration with the UN, Maria Accioly Dias et al. (2017) stated, '… the institutional path of partnership with the UN has its limitations, considering that the international entity follows a logic that does not seek the structural transformation of society (such as the economic or political-institutional order)'. However, in our opinion, these were mutually beneficial symbiotic relationships that generated value for both institutions—UN and GEN, while also fostering social and technological transformations in various regions around the world (Avelino et al., 2015). According to GEN, this status gave GEN direct access to the UN system and the opportunity to join in the work of various committees relevant to their mission of promoting sustainable communities and practices worldwide. As mentioned earlier, GEN also became a partner of UNITAR (UN Institution for Training and Research) (Global Ecovillage Network, 2016a, archived).

Thanks to its collaboration with UN committees, GEN has grown from an organization seeking transformation in local communities into a global player capable of presenting its ideas to international experts and representatives of national governments, and participating in discussions on global policy changes in addressing climate change, higher standards of living, full employment, conditions of economic and social progress and development, human rights, and other issues. GEN has adapted the ideas of UN institutions by modernizing its strategic goals.

In September 2015, leaders from 150 countries gathered in New York (USA) and adopted Transforming our world: the 2030 Agenda for Sustainable Development (United Nations, 2015) which sets out 17

Sustainable Development Goals. GEN renewed its activities in line with these international commitments and collaborated with researchers and ecovillages from around the world to create a new Ecovillage Impact Assessment tool for communities, groups, and individuals to map, analyse, and showcase their work for participatory cultural, social, ecological, and economic regeneration (Global Ecovillage Network Annual Report, 2015, 2021).

By cooperating with UN institutions, GEN has strengthened its political influence, advocacy, and organizational capacities. At the same time, GEN has become a platform promoting the Sustainable Development Goals (SDGs) announced by the UN and contributing to their implementation in local communities. GEN's activities span all continents. As of early 2025, the GEN website featured information on 1240 eco-communities and national networks in 120 countries across all continents, with more than 1500 projects implemented by GEN regional organizations. GEN has integrated the UN's 17 Sustainable Development Goals into its activities, providing information on its contribution to their implementation in official reports (Global Ecovillage Network Annual Report, 2021).

Use of Platforms to Establish Collaboration Links

Another paradigmatic innovation in the service economy that the ecovillage movement has employed is the use of digital platforms to establish connections between market participants. Research on multilateral networks has shown that they operate much more effectively when coordinated by a so-called platform (Eloranta & Turunen, 2016; Muzellec et al., 2015; Ritala et al., 2014; Aarikka-Stenroos & Ritala, 2017; Schmidlechner et al., 2017). Recent studies on multistakeholder networks suggest that platforms not only shape how participants interact within the network but also foster integration by creating links that integrate diverse and semi-independent activities into an interactive system (Ansell & Gash, 2018; Ardolino et al., 2020). In addition, platform managers are responsible for creating synergies by coordinating collaborative activities. They achieve this, on the one hand, by encouraging parallel and semi-autonomous forms of organization, and on the other, by aggregating and coordinating these organizational efforts (Vidickienė et al., 2024).

The founders of GEN recognized the importance of digital platforms for network building early on. At the 1995 Conference *'Ecovillages and sustainable communities for the 21st century'*, organized by the Findhorn community—where GEN was established—it was decided to create a website. In its 2003 annual report, GEN Europe stated: 'We need to stay connected to the ground and to each other, and to enhance more contacts and support between national networks. We need more input to the newsletter from the eco-villages in order to use the media better and improve the flow of information from eco-villages to the office' (Global Ecovillage Network Annual Report, 2003).

Our analysis of the current and historical websites of GEN and its regional organizations reveals that specific objectives of the online platform can be identified. These objectives have informed both the website's structural design and the models used for information management and market engagement. In our view, three primary functions of the platform can be distinguished:

1. The digital platform facilitates collaboration and information exchange among GEN members and serves as a tool for coordinating network development activities.
2. It serves as a channel for disseminating information about GEN and eco-friendly initiatives to the public, local communities, NGOs, and academic institutions.
3. The digital platform incorporates features typical of service-oriented platforms, enabling GEN members and partners to offer consulting services, training, publications, eco-tourism, and related products to both local communities and a global audience.

The first website of the ecovillage movement—www.gaia.org—was established with support from the Gaia Trust charity. This website publishes information from Gaia Education about its programmes, as well as details of seminars and other events organized by ecovillages. It also features descriptions of successful ecovillages initiatives (Global Ecovillage Network Annual Report, 1996).

As the number of eco-labels increased, the available information became insufficient, and feedback from network participants became necessary. Consequently, the GEN digital platform, developed later, served not only as a tool for disseminating information, such as GEN's history, regional networks, events, and resources, but also fulfilled additional functions. Notably, the platform includes a feature that enables visitors to contact

GEN or its regional networks and to join the ecovillage movement as volunteers, sponsors, partners, or network participants.

Thus, the GEN platform also functioned as a tool for network expansion. It is important to note that changes to the digital platform were closely aligned with GEN's evolving needs and emerging opportunities, as well as the increasingly widespread use of digital platforms across various sectors of society (Beverungen et al., 2022).

To assess the impact of the GEN platform on the ecovillage movement, it is necessary to analyse its relationship with the regional networks. As integral components of GEN, these regional networks also developed their own digital platforms. In the early stages of the movement, the GEN Europe platform was comparable to the main GEN platform in terms of both the richness of information and its influence on network development (Global Ecovillage Network, 2007a, archived). For example, the GEN Europe online forum functioned as a bulletin board featuring topics for both the public and GEN Europe members. According to the forum statistics from 2007, 1670 participants were registered. The forum included board for general discussions related to GEN Europe, a space for ecovillage advertisements, and an internal section for working groups composed of GEN members (Global Ecovillage Network, 2007b, archived). The GEN platform included links to the websites of regional networks. These regional platforms played a crucial role in coordinating activities among specific network members. For example, in the initial version of the GEN platform, the section inviting individuals to join GEN provided guidance directing potential partners and volunteers to the appropriate regional organizations (Global Ecovillage Network, 2007a, archived).

Gradually, the GEN platform is acquiring more characteristics typical of the service economy. In addition to information about GEN's history, activities, and annual reports, which is typical for any organization, GEN publishes information about services provided by its members and partners, such as consultations, seminars, study visits, tourist trips, and books (Global Ecovillage Network, 2014, archived). With the rise in popularity of distance learning following the Covid-19 pandemic, GEN has also taken advantage of this opportunity. Some events are now organized remotely, with filmed material used for training purposes. New methods of disseminating knowledge have significantly increased the effectiveness of educational activities. GEN has also provided a platform for ecovillages to inform consumers about the services and projects they offer. Many ecovillages are involved in tourism, attracting visitors and generating additional income. By advertising their services on the GEN platform, this information becomes visible to a wide range of potential visitors (Global Ecovillage Network, 2025).

GEN has been responsible for facilitating communication and networking among ecovillages on a global scale since its establishment. Its activities have ranged from developing an active website and publishing newsletters, organizing regional and international programmes related to sustainable living.

Collaboration for Development of Ecovillages: Concluding Remarks on GEN

In a post-industrial society, collaboration is a key driver of change. This study examines the partnerships formed among ecovillages to implement a shared vision of alternative settlements based on environmentally sustainable lifestyles. The GEN was established to facilitate and support collaboration among ecovillages. From the perspective of settlement evolution, the case of GEN represents a unique example of self-regulation among ecovillages as organizational entities. It illustrates how innovative organizations employed collaborative strategy to implement a shared vision from the outset of their activities. GEN has evolved into a platform that facilitates collaboration, enabling ecovillages to pursue and achieve the goals of lower-level strategies developed within an evolution-based framework. By bringing together like-minded individuals across diverse locations, GEN has supported the realization of a unified vision. This has been accomplished through the promotion of new settlement creation and by attracting new residents to existing ecovillages. Through this collaborative approach, GEN has effectively enhanced the capacity and impact of its strategic efforts.

The study demonstrated that GEN's success was largely determined by its ability to leverage technological, economic, and social changes to develop its organizational activities. The ecovillage movement has played an instrumental role in driving social change, while simultaneously being shaped by broader processes of social transformation. GEN consistently capitalized on the advantages of networking as an innovative form of collaboration, establishing a multilateral network and integrating into other similar networks. Its adoption of an open membership policy further contributed to its rapid global expansion, resulting in the emergence of a widespread international community.

GEN has been developed as an ecosystem of open innovation, aimed at better adapting settlements to the evolving needs of residents. It has fostered mutually beneficial relationships among network participants and created opportunities for them to contribute to the generation of new value in various ways. GEN members demonstrated a high level of proficiency in implementing paradigm-shifting innovations, including networking, multi-actor partnerships, symbiotic relationships among participants, and the use of IT platforms in developing organizational solutions. The GEN experience offers a valuable model for the development of other open innovation systems.

References

Aarikka-Stenroos, L., & Ritala, P. (2017). Network management in the era of ecosystems: Systematic review and management framework. *Industrial Marketing Management, 67*, 23–36. https://doi.org/10.1016/j.indmarman.2017.08.010

Ansell, C., & Gash, A. (2018). Collaborative platforms as a governance strategy. *Journal of Public Administration Research and Theory, 28*(1), 16–32. https://doi.org/10.1093/jopart/mux030

Ardolino, M., Saccani, N., Adrodegari, F., & Perona, M. (2020). A business model framework to characterize digital multisided platforms. *Journal of Open Innovation: Technology, Market, and Complexity, 6*(1), 10. https://doi.org/10.3390/joitmc6010010

Ashlock, C. R. (2010). Lessons learned from the ecovillage movement: A global analysis focusing on francophone countries. .

Avelino, F., Dumitru, A., Longhurst, N., Wittmayer, J., Hielscher, S., Weaver, P., ... & Haxeltine, A. (2015). Transitions towards new economies. A transformative social innovation perspective [Working Paper n° 3].

Bakó, R. K., Hubbes, L. A., & Tamás, D. (2021). Eco-discourses in a virtual rural community. *Sustainability, 13*(6), 3082. https://doi.org/10.3390/su13063082

Beverungen, D., Hess, T., Köster, A., et al. (2022). From private digital platforms to public data spaces: Implications for the digital transformation. *Electronic Markets, 32*, 493–501. https://doi.org/10.1007/s12525-022-00553-z

Blahovestova, O. O., Pechertsev, O. O., & Dansheva, S. O. (2020). The basic principles of ecovillage design. IOP Conference Series: Materials Science and Engineering, 907, No. 1.

Bluesmith, K. (2023). Ecovillages as a solution to global challenges. Master's thesis, Harvard University.

Boyer, R. H., Peterson, N. D., Arora, P., & Caldwell, K. (2016). Five approaches to social sustainability and an integrated way forward. *Sustainability, 8*(9), 878. https://doi.org/10.3390/su8090878

Brombin, A. (2015). Faces of sustainability in Italian ecovillages: Food as 'contact zone'. *International Journal of Consumer Studies, 39*(5), 468–477. https://doi.org/10.1111/ijcs.12225

Camagni, R., & Capello, R. (2004). The city network paradigm: Theory and empirical evidence. *Contributions to Economic Analysis, 266*, 495–529. https://doi.org/10.1016/S0573-8555(04)66016-0

Camarinha-Matos, L. M., & Afsarmanesh, H. (2005). Collaborative networks: A new scientific discipline. *Journal of Intelligent Manufacturing, 16*(4), 439–452. https://doi.org/10.1007/s10845-005-1656-3

Castells, M (1996). The rise of the network society. The information age. *Economy, society and culture*, I. Blackwell. Print ISBN: 9781405196864. Online ISBN: 9781444319514.

Dal Borgo, A. G., & Gambazza, G. (2017). From abandoned village to ecovillage: A sustainable tourism experience by the community of Torri Superiore. *Bulletin-Société Géographique De Liège, 69*, 63–79.

Dawson, J. (2006). How ecovillages can grow sustainable local economies. *Communities, 133*, 56–61.

Dawson, J. (2013). *From islands to networks: A history of the ecovillage movement. Environmental anthropology engaging ecotopia: Bioregionalism, permaculture, and ecovillages for a sustainable future*. Berghahn Books.

De Noni, I., Orsi, L., & Belussi, F. (2018). The role of collaborative networks in supporting the innovation performances of lagging-behind European regions. *Research Policy, 47*(1), 1–13. https://doi.org/10.1016/j.respol.2017.09.006

Dias, M. A., Loureiro, C. F. B., Chevitarese, L., & Souza, C. D. M. E. (2017). The meaning and relevance of ecovillages for the construction of sustainable societal alternatives. *Ambiente & Sociedade, 20*, 79–96. https://doi.org/10.1590/1809-4422ASOC0083V2032017

East, M. (2018). Current thinking on sustainable human habitat: The Findhorn ecovillage case. *Ecocycles, 4*(1), 68–72. https://doi.org/10.19040/ecocycles.v4i1.107

E-community Research Platform. (2025). Retrieved July 16, 2025, from https://ecommunity.gen-europe.org/

Eloranta, V., & Turunen, T. (2016). Platforms in service-driven manufacturing: Leveraging complexity by connecting, sharing, and integrating. *Industrial Marketing Management, 55*, 178–186. https://doi.org/10.1016/j.indmarman.2015.10.003

Ergas, C. (2010). A model of sustainable living: Collective identity in an urban ecovillage. *Organization & Environment, 23*(1), 32–54. https://doi.org/10.1177/1086026609360324

Farkas, J. (2017). 'Very little heroes' history and roots of the eco-village movement. *Acta Ethnographica Hungarica, 62*(1), 69–87. https://doi.org/10.1556/022.2017.62.1.4

Fölke, G. (1989). *Ekobyar: ekologiskt anpassad och resurssnål bebyggelse.* GEN.

Fonseca, B. P., Fernandes, E., & Fonseca, M. V. (2017). Collaboration in science and technology organizations of the public sector: A network perspective. *Science and Public Policy, 44*(1), 37–49. https://doi.org/10.1093/scipol/scw013

Fonseca, R. A. A., Irving, M. A., Nasri, Y. X. G., & Ferreira, G. F. (2022). Sustainability and social transformation: The role of ecovillages in confluence with the pluriverse of community-led alternatives. *Climate Action, 1*, 23. https://doi.org/10.1007/s44168-022-00022-5

Forster, P. M., & Wilhelmus, M. (2005). The role of individuals in community change within the Findhorn intentional community. *Contemporary Justice Review, 8*(4), 367–379. https://doi.org/10.1080/10282580500334221

Forzati, M., Larsen, C. P., & Mattsson C. (2010). Open access networks, the Swedish experience. In *12th international conference on transparent optical networks*, Munich, Germany, pp. 1–4. https://doi.org/10.1109/ICTON.2010.5549139.

Gaia education. (2025). Gaia education. Retrieved July 16, 2025, from https://www.gaiaeducation.org/

Gaia Trust. (2025). Gaia Trust. Retrieved July 16, 2025, from www.gaia.org

Garden, M. (2006). The eco-village movement: Divorced from reality. *The International Journal of INCLUSIVE DEMOCRACY, 2*(3), 1–5.

GEN Europe. GEN Europe Annual Report (2003). https://web.archive.org/web/20070630041303fw_/http://gen.ecovillage.org/about/index.html

GEN Europe. (2025). GEN Europe. Retrieved July 15, 2025, from https://gen-europe.org/

Gilman, R. (1991). The eco-village challenge. *Context, 29*(10), 10–15.

Gilman, R., & Gilman, D. (1991). *Ecovillages and sustainable communities: A report of Gaia Trust.* Context Institute.

Global ecovillage network. Global ecovillage network Annual Report. (1996). https://web.archive.org/web/20070630041303fw_/http://gen.ecovillage.org/about/index.html

Global ecovillage network. Global ecovillage network Annual Report (2003). https://web.archive.org/web/20070630035125/http://gen.ecovillage.org/

Global ecovillage network. (2007a). Global ecovillage network [Archived version]. Archived Jule 30, 2007. Retrieved July 15, 2025, from https://web.archive.org/web/20070630035125/http://gen.ecovillage.org/

Global ecovillage network. (2007b). Global ecovillage network [Archived version]. Archived October 6, 2007. Retrieved July 15, 2025, from https://web.archive.org/web/20071006031528/http://forum.gen-europe.org/YaBB.pl

Global ecovillage network. (2014). Global ecovillage network [Archived version]. Archived June 25, 2014.Retrieved July 15, 2025, from https://web.archive.org/web/20140625105107/http://ecovillage.org/en/ecotourism

Global ecovillage network. Global ecovillage network Annual Report (2015). https://ecovillage.org/about/about-gen/reports/

Global ecovillage network. (2016a). Global ecovillage network [Archived version]. Archived February 19, 2016. Retrieved July 15, 2025, from https://web.archive.org/web/20160219050241/http://ecovillage.org/en/page/un-advocacy

Global ecovillage network. (2016b). Global ecovillage network [Archived version]. Archived October 31, 2016. Retrieved July 15, 2025, https://web.archive.org/web/20161031013329/http://ecovillage.org/en/page/research-ecovillages

Global ecovillage network. Global ecovillage network Annual Report (2019). https://ecovillage.org/about/about-gen/reports/

Global ecovillage network. Global ecovillage network Annual Report (2021). https://ecovillage.org/about/about-gen/reports/

Global ecovillage network (2025). Global ecovillage network. Retrieved July 15, 2025, from https://ecovillage.org/

Hallsmith, G. (2012). Ecovillage infrastructure: The skeleton of community. *Communities, 156*, 22.

Hartigh, E. D., & Asseldonk, T. V. (2004). Business ecosystems: A research framework for investigating the relation between network structure, firm strategy, and the pattern of innovation diffusion. In *ECCON 2004 annual meeting: Co-jumping on a trampoline*.

Haxeltine, A., & Seyfang, G. (2009). Transitions for the People: Theory and Practice of 'transition' and 'resilience' in the UK's Transition Movement (pp. 1–24). Tyndall Centre.

Huikkola, T., Rabetino, R., Kohtamäki, M., & Gebauer, H. (2020). Firm boundaries in servitization: Interplay and repositioning practices. *Industrial Marketing Management, 90*, 90–105. https://doi.org/10.1016/j.indmarman.2020.06.014

Jackson, H. (1998). What is an ecovillage. In *Gaia Trust Education Seminar*. https://habiter-autrement.org/05.eco-village/contributions-05/What-is-an-Ecovillage-Hildur-Jackson.pdf.

Jackson, H., & Jackson, R. (2004). Global ecovillage network history 1990–2004. https://gaia.org/wp-content/uploads/2016/07/HJackson_GEN-History.pdf.

Jackson, M. O. (2006). The Economics of Social Networks. *Econometric Society Monographs, 41*, 1.
Jackson, R. (2000). And we are doing it; Building an ecovillage future. Robert D. Reed Publishers.
Kichiji, N., & Nishibe, M. (2008). Network analyses of the circulation flow of community currency. *Evolutionary and Institutional Economics Review, 4*, 267–300. https://doi.org/10.14441/eier.4.267
Kohtamäki, M., Rabetino, R., Parida, V., Sjödin, D., & Henneberg, S. (2022). Managing digital servitization toward smart solutions: Framing the connections between technologies, business models, and ecosystems. *Industrial Marketing Management, 105*, 253–267. https://doi.org/10.1016/j.indmarman.2022.06.010
Kroik, P. (2014). Kiernan, Denise. The Girls of Atomic City: The Untold Story of the Women Who Helped Win World War II. New York: Touchstone, 2013. 373 pp. Working USA, 17: 135–140. https://doi.org/10.1111/wusa.12102_2
Litfin, K. T. (2014). *Ecovillages: Lessons for sustainable community.* John Wiley & Sons.
Manent, L. (2017). Realising Utopia: Contemporary Ecovillages as demonstration sites of sustainability in practice. Retrieved from July 20, 2025, from https://www.academia.edu/40677656/Realising_Utopia_Contemporary_Ecovillages_as_demonstration_sites_of_sustainability_in_practice
Mare, E. C. (2000). *A concise history of the global ecovillage movement.* Village Design Institute.
Martin, C. J., Upham, P., & Budd, L. (2015). Commercial orientation in grassroots social innovation: Insights from the sharing economy. *Ecological Economics, 118*, 240–251. https://doi.org/10.1016/j.ecolecon.2015.08.001
Moore, J. F. (1996). *The death of competition: Leadership and strategy in the age of business ecosystem.* HarperCollins.
Muzellec, L., Ronteau, S., & Lambkin, M. (2015). Two-sided internet platforms: A business model lifecycle perspective. *Industrial Marketing Management, 45*, 139–150. https://doi.org/10.1016/j.indmarman.2015.02.012
NextGEN Ecovillage Youth Network. (2025). NextGEN Ecovillage Youth Network. Retrieved Jule 20, 2025, from https://nextgen-ecovillage.org/
Nogueira, C., Marques, J. F., & Pinto, H. (2024). Intentional sustainable communities and sustainable development goals: From micro-scale implementation to scalability of innovative practices. *Journal of Environmental Planning and Management, 67*(1), 175–196. https://doi.org/10.1080/09640568.2022.2106553
Palojärvi, A., Pyysiäinenas, J., & Saloranta, M. (eds.) (2013). Įkvepiančios istorijos iš ekokaimų patirties: ekotechnologijų taikymo praktikoje pavyzdžiai. Vilnius, BMK Leidykla, 120 p. ISBN 978–609-8080-78-0.

Pisters, S. R., Vihinen, H., & Figueiredo, E. (2020). Inner change and sustainability initiatives: Exploring the narratives from eco-villagers through a place-based transformative learning approach. *Sustainability Science, 15*, 395–409. https://doi.org/10.1007/s11625-019-00775-9

Ritala, P., Golnam, A., & Wegmann, A. (2014). Coopetition-based business models: The case of Amazon.com. *Industrial Marketing Management, 43*(2), 236–249. https://doi.org/10.1016/j.indmarman.2013.11.005

Roth, C. (2012). An ecovillage future. *Communities, 156*, 11.

Roysen, R., Martins Arruda, B., Ferreira, R., Fonseca , R. A. A., Alvarenga, M. A. A., & Duarte, L. G. M. F. (2021). Zonas de Agroecologia e Ecovilas: Uma proposta para os planos diretores municipais. *Sustentabilidade: Diálogos Interdisciplinares, 2*, 1–15. https://doi.org/10.24220/2675-7885v2e2021a5527

Roysen, R., & Schwab, A. K. (2021). The potential of ecovillages for transitions in rural areas: A comparison of ecovillages in Germany and Brazil. In *Climate adaptation: Accounts of resilience, self-sufficiency and systems change* (pp. 231–249). Arkbound Foundation.

Sanz, E. O. (2016). Community currency (CCs) in Spain: An empirical study of their social effects. *Ecological Economics, 121*, 20–27. https://doi.org/10.1016/j.ecolecon.2015.11.008

Schmidlechner, L., Peruffo, E., Contreras, R. R., & Molinuevo, D. (2017). Coordination by platforms: Literature review. Working Paper. Eurofound.

Schreurs, B., Cornelissen, F., & De Laat, M. (2019). How do online learning networks emerge? A review study of self-organizing network effects in the field of networked learning. *Education Sciences, 9*(4), 289. https://doi.org/10.3390/educsci9040289

Schwab, K. (2021). *Stakeholder capitalism: A global economy that works for progress, people and planet.* John Wiley & Sons.

Seyfang, G., & Haxeltine, A. (2012). Growing grassroots innovations: Exploring the role of community-based initiatives in governing sustainable energy transitions. *Environment and Planning C: Government and Policy, 30*(3), 381–400. https://doi.org/10.1068/c10222

Seyfang, G., & Longhurst, N. (2013). Growing green money? Mapping community currencies for sustainable development. *Ecological Economics, 86*, 65–77. https://doi.org/10.1016/j.ecolecon.2012.11.003

Singh, B., Shrestha, M., Bajracharya, S. B., & Keitsch, M. M. (2020). Revisiting ecovillage as a sustainable settlement from a system's perspective—A case of Bandipur. *Nepal. Journal of the Institute of Engineering, 15*(3), 326–333. https://doi.org/10.3126/jie.v15i3.32213

Smith, A., Fressoli, M., & Thomas, H. (2014). Grassroots innovation movements: Challenges and contributions. *Journal of Cleaner Production, 63*, 114–124. https://doi.org/10.1016/j.jclepro.2012.12.025

Snyder, Ph., Living and learning canters. (2013). Retrieved July 15, 2025, from https://web.archive.org/web/20130514180133/http://gen.ecovillage.org/

Temesgen, A. K. (2024). Ecovillage scale-up and its well-being challenges: A case study from Norway. *Sustainability: Science, Practice and Policy, 20*(1). https://doi.org/10.1080/15487733.2024.2393912

Ter Wal, A. L. J., Alexy, O., Block, J., & Sandner, P. G. (2016). The best of both worlds: The benefits of open-specialized and closed-diverse syndication networks for new ventures' success. *Administrative Science Quarterly, 61*(3), 393–432. https://doi.org/10.1177/0001839216637849

United Nations. (2015). Transforming our world: The 2030 agenda for sustainable development. United Nations. https://docs.un.org/en/A/RES/70/1.

Van Schyndel Kasper, D. (2008). Redefining community in the ecovillage. *Human Ecology Review, 15*(1), 12–24. http://www.jstor.org/stable/24707480

Vidickienė, D. (Ed.). (2013). Kaip susikurti harmoningą gyvenimą? Įkvepiančios istorijos iš ekokaimų patirties. BMK leidykla, 124 p., ISBN 978-609-8080-32-2.

Vidickienė, D., Gedminaitė-Raudonė, Ž., Melnikienė, R., Simonaitytė, V., Lankauskienė, R. (2021). Bendradarbiavimo tinklų ir jų platformų vaidmuo servitizuojant kaimiškųjų regionų ekonomiką. Monografija. Lietuvos socialinių mokslų centro Ekonomikos ir kaimo vystymo institutas. 145 p.: iliustr., santr. angl. (online) ISBN 987-609-96239-1-7.

Vidickienė, D. Lankauskienė, R., Melnikienė, R., Gedminaitė-Raudonė, Ž., Simonaitytė, V. (2024). Rural transformation through servitization. A qualitative structure approach. Palgrave Macmillan. Hardcover ISBN 978–3–031-47185-8. Softcover ISBN 978–3–031-47188-9. eBook ISBN 978–3–031-47186-5. 387 p. https://doi.org/10.1007/978-3-031-47186

Vidickienė, D., Melnikienė, R., & Gedminaitė-Raudonė, Ž. (2013). Inovacijų diegimo Lietuvos ūkininkų ūkiuose motyvai ir barjerai. *Management theory and studies for rural business and infrastructure development, 35*(1), 140–149.

Waerther, S. (2014). Sustainability in ecovillages—A reconceptualization. *International Journal of Management and Applied Research, 1*(1), 1–16. https://doi.org/10.18646/2056.11.14-001

Wagner, F. (2012). Ecovillage research review. In M. Andreas & F. Wagner (Eds.), *Realizing Utopia: Ecovillage endeavors and academic approaches* (pp. 81–94). Rachel Carson Center for Environment and Society.

Ye, H., & Kankanhalli, A. (2013). Leveraging crowdsourcing for organizational value co-creation. *Communications of the Association for Information Systems, 33*, 13. https://doi.org/10.17705/1CAIS.03313

Ye, J., & Kankanhalli, A. (2013). Exploring innovation through open networks: A review and initial research questions. *IIMB Management Review, 25*(2), 69–82. https://doi.org/10.1016/j.iimb.2013.02.002

Zhang, K., Feng, L., Wang, J., Lin, K., & Li, Q. (2021). Servitization in business ecosystem: A systematic review and implications for business-to-business servitization research. *Technology Analysis & Strategic Management, 35*, 1480–1496. https://doi.org/10.1080/09537325.2021.2010698

CHAPTER 9

Conclusions: Symbiosis as a Key Trajectory in the Formation of the Post-Industrial Settlement Vision

Dalia Vidickienė

For the last two centuries, the management and development of human settlements have been guided by the industrial paradigm. This mechanistic and reductionist worldview has dominated science, education, and, especially, socio-economic thought since the Industrial Revolution. In the twenty-first century, there is a need for new modes of theorizing human settlement design and evolution beyond the industrial paradigm as society enters the post-industrial era. Following earlier agrarian and industrial 'revolutions', postindustrialism suggests yet another revolution that would again transform how societies are organized (Hoey, 2015). The transformation of society's organizational model is based on the concept of servitization and occurs through a shift from a product-oriented business model to a service-oriented business model. The servitization of the economy is leading to the development of a post-industrial society, shaping new lifestyles adapted to new livelihoods.

One of the fundamental objectives of this exploration was to gain insight into how the shift to the post-industrial livelihoods-based global economic system is transforming the vision of the high-quality human settlement model developed during the industrial era. However, there are several significant obstacles to orienting thinking towards the realities of

D. Vidickienė et al., *Human Settlement in the Service Economy Era*, Palgrave Advances in Bioeconomy: Economics and Policies, https://doi.org/10.1007/978-3-032-19390-2_9

the post-industrial world. Any paradigm shift necessitates a fundamental alteration in fundamental concepts and experimental practices. We cannot solve problems by using the same kind of thinking that created them, as using the same thinking patterns leads to stagnation and hinders progress.

A lack of a holistic approach is a primary obstacle to understanding and managing fundamental changes in the human settlement system. To explain how the industrial economic system works, the Cartesian mode of thought is perfect. This reductionist mode of thought posits that the universe is composed of fundamental building blocks. Such a way of thinking gives us the impression that we can understand the world by analysing each block and controlling and managing processes by manipulating these simple pieces with their simple rules (Grosholz, 1991). The management theory developed during the industrial era also emphasizes specialized roles and expertise within the organization to ensure the development of high-quality products, as the industrial product-oriented business model is based on the division of labour, with each worker responsible for a particular building block of the production process or a product. However, at the end of the industrial era, many problems arose in managing relationships between the basic building blocks of the economic system, and business society is learning to build and manage socio-economic processes in a new way.

To identify fundamental transformations, we must consider that not only do services differ significantly from products, but the human actions and relationships within a service-driven business model also need to be organized differently from those within a product-driven business model. Success in service relationships is based on symbiotic thinking, which focuses on the mutual benefits of the service provider and the clients. The symbiotic approach emphasizes the collaboration of actors and integration of diverse elements to achieve comprehensive results. Involved in a service-driven business, people learn to apply a symbiotic approach in various situations. As a result, the shift to a service-driven economic system is transforming not only the business model oriented to manufacturing but also all aspects of humanity's life organization.

The manifestations of the symbiotic approach involve breaking down the barriers between the structural blocks of the human life organization model that are perceived as separate within the traditional mindset of the industrial era. In the context of human settlements' evolution, innovative thinking should be oriented to a symbiosis between the following structural parts of human life developed by the industrial socio-economic system:

1. Traditional occupations
2. Work and leisure
3. Human and natural habitats

Symbiosis between the Traditional Occupations of the Industrial Era

Occupations are generally defined as categories of work containing similar tasks within the division of labour (Martin-Caughey, 2021). Occupations are also conceptualized as status groupings, generating a hierarchy of prestige across the occupational structure (Siegel, 1971; Penn, 1975; Treiman, 2013). While the division of labour was a hallmark of the industrial era, the traditional occupational structure played a significant role in all spheres of social life. Human settlement design and development are no exception, as occupation strongly influences interests, opinions, behavioral orientations, and the requirements for good living conditions. Occupation in manufacturing entails a significantly different lifestyle compared to an occupation in agriculture. In the industrial economy era, clear boundaries were established between the agriculture and manufacturing sectors. The urban population was mainly employed in the manufacturing sector, while the rural population worked in agriculture. In manufacturing, the division of labour has been recognized as a key principle of economic organization, which can enhance efficiency and effectiveness.

Successfully providing services requires a creative approach to job division. The post-industrial service economy offers mixed versions of job organization. Traditional job boundaries are less defined, and workers and farmers involved in service provision must adapt to new roles and acquire new skills in areas such as retail, marketing, education, hospitality, and other activities traditionally classified as part of the tertiary sector of the economy.

Blurring lines between traditional occupations blurs the requirements for high-quality urban and rural settlements. The conventional layout of industrial towns and cities, designed according to the lifestyle of workers, is considered outdated and uncomfortable by high-skilled service providers. In search of alternatives, they are increasingly looking for residential locations in rural areas. Over the last few decades, the countryside has become increasingly attractive to former urban inhabitants, including IT specialists and software developers, e-commerce and other online service providers, lawyers, marketers, financial advisors, designers, and artists.

However, the experience of the ecovillage movement demonstrates that high-skilled and creative newcomers have special requirements for rural areas as a place to live. It is a clear sign that a symbiosis between traditional occupations alters lifestyles and prompts a re-evaluation of the conventional rural-urban dichotomy as a basis for organizing the human settlement system.

Symbiosis between Work and Leisure

The shift to post-industrial society involves a shift away from a traditional mindset of 'life + work', as in the industrial era, life was organized into two different periods: work and leisure. Many people have the impression that they 'live' only during leisure time and that working time is heavy duty. Empirical studies indicate that attitudes towards the organization of work and leisure are undergoing significant changes (Yushkevich, 2021; Rashmi & Kataria, 2022; Gillette, 2023; Wong et al., 2023; Adrjan et al., 2025). Three trends that foster a symbiosis between work and leisure, as well as work and private life, are visible and have the potential to shape the future of the human settlement system. All mentioned trends in new ways of organizing work and generating income for households require making human settlements better adapted to the emerging symbiosis between the lower and upper needs of human beings.

Trend 1: Flexible Work Arrangement

Providing services requires a mobile, flexible, and spontaneous lifestyle; consequently, opposing views on the factory or office mode of organizing the working day are growing. Flexible working hours, also commonly referred to as 'flexitime' or 'flexi hours', are an increasingly popular way of working. Flexitime refers to a type of work schedule that allows employees more flexibility over standard working hours, whether due to personal preference or family commitments, particularly those related to childcare.

Over the last few decades, digitization has enabled practices such as telework and remote work (Kurkland & Bailey, 1999; Markus et al., 2000; Gurstein, 2001; Bailey & Kurland, 2002; Köffer et al., 2015). Working from home, which is offered on either a combined basis (splitting time between the home and office) or on a permanent basis (100% remote working), is very suitable for employees who perform desktop-related work, such as lawyers, marketers, and financial advisors. The COVID-19 pandemic further strengthened the trend, as governments worldwide mandated that people work from home to prevent the spread of the virus. It led to severe job changes for employees and managers, for whom distance work and distance management became compulsory. Studies indicate that an increasing portion of the workforce will continue to work from home after the pandemic (Silver, 2023; Adrjan et al., 2025). Increased productivity, not having to commute, and the opportunity to work even while traveling are just a few advantages of an innovative job organization. For example, some remote employees, known as digital nomads, opt for a nomadic lifestyle, which enables them to travel the world while working full-time for an employer. Employees are free to work from wherever they want as long as they meet these requirements.

Transitioning to new work organization practices proved advantageous to both employers and employees (Hajjami & Crocco, 2023; Fatima et al., 2024). First, the flexible working hours and remote work can lead to increased productivity for many employees. Studies and surveys indicate that a significant portion of remote workers achieve higher or comparable productivity levels compared to their in-office counterparts (Apollo, 2022; Criscuolo et al., 2021; Straus et al., 2023). Secondly, for many employees, the ability to achieve a desirable work-life balance ranks highly on their list of what they want from a workplace (Ferrara et al., 2022; Emanuel & Harrington, 2024; Faruque et al., 2024; Rustan et al., 2024).

The popularity of remote work has led commentators to predict a significant decrease in city business activity and tax revenues. At the same time, the dramatic rise of remote work poses a threat to the traditional source of urban growth, the unique ability of dense cities to provide a setting in which firms and employees share productive resources, match needs with skills, and transmit knowledge at low cost (Gillette, 2023).

Trend 2: Lifestyle Entrepreneurship

An increasing number of people are opting to leave a paid job to start building lifestyle businesses (Ivanycheva et al., 2024). One of the drivers of lifestyle entrepreneurship is the emergence of a service-driven business model, which offers more opportunities for this type of entrepreneurship compared to a product-driven business model. Moreover, experience in service provision develops managerial skills necessary for business, in contrast to industrial-age organizations, where formal hierarchies assigned specific roles to employees. In the service economy, many managerial functions are shifted to service providers, and previously highly specialized workers must carry out multiple tasks related to various business functions. In this way, they learn and gain self-confidence in their ability to navigate the challenges and opportunities of running a successful business.

The shift to the service economy allows people to combine activities needed for survival with the creation of new values, realizing and fulfilling one's potential by blurring the boundaries between lower and upper needs of human beings (Cahyani et al., 2024). Industrial workers had few opportunities to achieve the symbiosis of physiological human needs with self-expression and self-actualization. Becoming a lifestyle entrepreneur means that individuals build a career around the lifestyle they desire, focusing on their passions or hobbies, with the aim of personal satisfaction over profit. Earnings from passion present new opportunities for personal growth, autonomy, and freedom to create.

With the rise in popularity of a service-driven business model, a lifestyle business has become more accessible and is increasingly viewed as a popular option for employment. Young people appear to be less motivated to find a job and work hard to develop a career (Rosenberger, 2017; Li, 2020). Compared to older generations, the importance of work as a key part of personal identity is believed to be declining, as millennials have a reputation for job-hopping. Unattached to organizations and institutions, people from the Millennial generation, born between 1980 and 1996, are said to move freely from company to company, more so than any other generation (Hauw & Vos, 2010). The largest transformation approaching the workforce agenda is expected to be brought by the very recent Generation Z (Yushkevich, 2021; Swan, 2021; Kılıç, 2022; Hidayat, 2024).

The trend to build lifestyle businesses demonstrates that the service-driven business model offers numerous opportunities to integrate work and leisure, allowing entrepreneurial people to avoid dividing their lives into time for subsistence and free time. This means that it is blurring the boundaries between livelihoods and lifestyle.

Trend 3: Neo-Nomadism

It has become almost cliché to suggest that we live in a fast-changing world, yet we continue to cling to ideas of permanence. However, the combination of service-driven business models with the opportunities offered by digital technologies is shaping a neo-nomadic world, which requires an innovative approach to organizing human settlements.

Neo-nomadism is a lifestyle of continuous mobility, driven by the pursuit of freedom and a countercultural life, where individuals work and live in various locations rather than being tied to a permanent 'home base'.

Academic literature mainly examines digital nomadism, an emerging lifestyle based on remote work, digital technology, and leisure travels, which has evolved from a marginal phenomenon concerning isolated individuals in the early 2000s to a flourishing movement in less than two decades. In the post-COVID-19 context of mainstream remote work, the number of digital nomads has risen sharply (Bozzi, 2024) as the COVID-19 pandemic represented for many workers the opportunity to try this lifestyle (de Almeida et al., 2021). The term 'neo-nomad' is broader than the most often used term 'digital nomad'. Neo-nomadism is a relatively recent and still evolving concept that emphasizes a nomadic lifestyle without requiring a digital work component; that is, they do not necessarily engage in online work. Opposed to digital nomads, neo-nomads may or may not work while they 'wander'. An artist, retiree, or person taking a mid-career break who adopts a nomadic lifestyle is an example of a neo-nomad who is not categorized as a digital nomad.

The biggest challenge of neo-nomadism is not so much about mobility or traveling. It is about the need for responses to an increasingly widespread nomadic lifestyle. Neo-nomadism challenges the assumption that a high-quality human settlement system must be oriented towards a permanent place of living. A neo-nomad is a person who values freedom, mobility, and exploration, pursuing prolonged immersive travel or a transient lifestyle away from their 'home base' city or country. Neo-nomads are considered counter-cultural, seeking to live their lives in a very different context from the historical norm. However, their transnationally mobile lifestyle is not only an individual choice but is embedded in political and economic structures that both enable and limit their actions (Korpela, 2019). Consequently, the design of the human settlement system in the future must include places where neo-nomads can discover their work-life balance.

Symbiosis between Natural and Human Habitats

Over the last several decades, the most widely discussed issue in the development of humanity and its habitats has been the environmental dimension, as the outcomes of industrial livelihood activities and human needs-oriented urban development have greatly damaged the natural environment. However, despite numerous political initiatives aimed at solving environmental problems caused by human activities, progress has been minimal.

One of the key obstacles to reducing humans' negative impact on the planet is that most efforts are still based on dualistic thinking, which views human and natural habitats as two distinct structural parts of the world. This traditional mindset led to the next logical step, which contrasts eco-centric and anthropocentric (human-centered) attitudes towards the natural environment. Anthropocentrism posits that humans are separate from and superior to nature, holding that only humans possess intrinsic value, while other beings are valuable only in how they serve human purposes. In response to the unprecedented exploitation and destruction of nature, the ecocentric movement emerged and gained significant momentum in the latter half of the twentieth century. Ecocentrism emphasizes that problems of natural environment degradation are caused by the overexploitation of natural resources, and humanity's moral duty towards nature is to protect the natural environment. The members of this movement believe that conservation is a key solution to our environmental crisis and strive to achieve global conservation goals.

The rise of ecocentrism, an attitude that values nature for its own sake, presented a radical challenge to the long-standing and deeply rooted anthropocentric attitudes prevalent in the culture, science, and politics of the industrial era. The ecocentric approach remains popular, but doubts about its ontological belief and practical effectiveness are growing. The negative attitude towards any exploitation of nature and the division of the world into two parts, focusing on protected versus non-protected natural areas, can be defined as two major weaknesses of the ecocentric movement. It is being increasingly recognized by natural and social sciences that: (i) protected areas cannot function in a vacuum, isolated from the surrounding human-modified areas; (ii) exploitation plays a special role in the establishment of symbioses and the later evolution of mutual benefit.

The twenty-first century is a time when humans are beginning to recognize the synergistic interconnectedness among species as a necessity for sustaining the conditions that support life on Earth. The service economy is a primary contributor to the fundamental shift in our relationships with nature. As the service-oriented business model is based on collaboration for a symbiotic relationship, the industrial-style mindset of human/non-human benefits is also gradually shifting towards innovative ecological thinking, based on the concept of symbiosis (the term is derived from the

Greek word meaning 'living together' or 'companionship'). As ecocentric thinking focuses on a less exploitative attitude towards nature, it does not suggest companionship as a union in which partners have mutual consent and equality, because the care of nature is managed according to the 'sick care' model. Nature is treated as a creature in need of constant care, and people are presented as powerful protectors of natural areas. The 'sick care' mental model is based on a reactive approach to the care of nature and is very expensive, and, to some degree, ineffective.

As pointed out by Albrecht (2016, p. 13), 'the next era in human history should be named the Symbiocene (from the Greek *sumbiosis*, or companionship)'. Collaboration between the natural and social sciences, focused on the research of symbiosis phenomena, led to the creation of many new solutions and even the emergence of specialized fields of activity focused on symbiotic relationships as an innovative approach (symbiotic architecture, natural farming, symbiotic economics, etc.). All symbiotic approach-oriented solutions are based on a philosophy of working with nature and are referred to as 'transformative eco-innovations'. 'Eco-innovation encompasses various innovative practices which enhance resource efficiency by combining economic value with environmental performance' (Levidow et al., 2016, p. 55). By combining environmental and economic goals, eco-innovation is widely seen as 'enabling win-win synergies' (OECD, 2012). Symbiosis-oriented approach encourages a shift from the 'sick care' model advocated by the ecocentric movement to a proactive approach that enables the care of nature by solving problems before they escalate.

The experiments of newly established ecovillages and transition towns, based on a symbiotic approach to human settlement design and exploitation, offer a hope that reorganizing relationships between humans and non-humans through transformative eco-innovations will alter the situation by suggesting innovative ways to generate positive or at least neutral synergistic effects in human-nature relationships.

Symbiotic processes between (1) traditional occupations, (2) work and leisure, and (3) human and natural habitats call people to create an innovative vision of high-quality human settlement. However, the vision of post-industrial human settlement cannot be designed as a new combination of the same structural parts. We cannot merely put together the structural parts of human life organization, which were created according to the rules of the industrial economic system. Symbiotic processes must generate a synergistic effect, and a straightforward addition of elements cannot achieve this. Synergy refers to a combined effect that is greater than the sum of individual parts. It implies a non-linear interaction where the whole is more powerful than the individual components working separately.

The foundation for this understanding and practical implementation by strategic solutions is based on the theory of Qualitative Structure, which allows us to design human settlements by transforming structural components that are independent of the dominant economic system. The structure, which remains constant in each cycle of human settlement evolution, consists of three interrelated components: inhabitants, place, and infrastructure (see The Qualitative Structure of a Human Settlement in Chap. 2). This Qualitative Structure is appropriate for all types of human settlements. The primary challenge is to understand how the transition from an industrial to a post-industrial economic system transforms lifestyles and to highlight the key characteristics of each component relevant to a post-industrial lifestyle.

The literature review and case studies, organized according to an evolutionary approach based on the theory of Qualitative Structure, helped to provide some insights into how service-oriented livelihoods and lifestyles gradually transform the typical industrial settlement model and influence the three components of the qualitative structure of human settlements.

The new characteristics of key components of the qualitative structure of post-industrial human settlements at the stage of innovation strategy can be briefly described as follows.

Component A: Inhabitants as Organizers

Post-industrial people are oriented to service-oriented livelihoods. The shift from a product-driven to a service-driven business model implies a transition from the Producer's lifestyle to an Organizer's lifestyle. (*According to the Cambridge Dictionary, an organizer is a person or group that plans and arranges an event or activity. Synonyms for ORGANIZER: manager, planner, designer, arranger, plotter, schemer, originator, director, formulator, leader.*)

The key specific characteristics of organizers in the post-industrial era are the following:

- *Creativity.* In contrast to maximally standardized processes of industrial production and supply chain management, the service economy requires creativity at each step. Consequently, a group of people with well-developed organizational skills grow. Organizers trained in the provision of services view executing in uncertain and complex situations as expected and are willing to respond creatively to new situations. They demonstrate innovative thinking that is different from traditional patterns.

- *Focus on relationships.* As the production of things and their exchange do not dominate, servitization is the power to switch humanity from a 'world of things' to a 'world of relationships' (Vidickienė, 2023, p. 77). Skills for building service relationships in business can be applied in all areas of life, including creating a thriving community within a settlement. Focusing on building and nurturing relationships between inhabitants is crucial for community well-being.
- *Willingness to collaborate.* Competition among producers is a key success factor in the industrial economic system. In the service economy, collaboration is becoming a fundamental success factor, rather than competition. Moreover, in many cases, competing is impossible because comparing services tailored to individual customer requirements is not feasible. The shift to a service-driven business model requires the establishment of a new kind of relationship, one that emphasizes value co-creation for the mutual benefit of all parties involved. It means that people learn new ways to live together.

A new generation of human settlements oriented to post-industrial reality, especially newly established ecovillages, are designed and built by groups of people with strong characteristics of the above. They are the active force of the innovation strategy, which has the capacity to make a new generation of human settlements epicentres of human potential, enabling innovation, creativity, and societal progress.

The activities of this group of people cannot be classified into sectors based on the specialization of the work in the industrial era. Their creativity, knowledge, and skills are focused on outcomes that integrate agriculture, manufacturing, and natural resource extraction through service-driven business models. Such orientation allows them to practice different lifestyles, which are various versions of the compilation of lifestyles dominated during the pre-agrarian, agrarian, and industrial eras. For example, neo-nomads embrace a lifestyle characterized by high mobility and a sense of freedom, often rejecting traditional notions of fixed residence and seeking experiences and a sense of belonging in various locations. At the same time, most of them are workers of large companies who perform their job duties remotely, using the internet and digital tools.

Component B: Place Relevant for Symbiotic Life Organization

The several decades of experience accumulated by the ecovillage movement demonstrate that there is no one-size-fits-all definition of a place relevant for symbiotic life organization, as each community has distinct requirements and opportunities to realize them in densely populated regions. In contrast to the villages of the agrarian era, which were strongly oriented to the availability of land for farming, or industrial towns oriented to the needs of manufacturing plants, there are no clearly defined requirements for a place most relevant to post-industrial settlement.

In the past, people often associated relocations to the countryside or smaller towns with post-retirement periods, when they were no longer interested in the professional opportunities that cities, as employment centres, provided. Now, many providers of high-quality services do not need to wait for retirement to move to live close to nature. However, the desire to live in a location with ample green space, proximity to forests, rivers, or other natural elements does not mean that all other characteristics of the chosen place are relevant to individuals oriented towards the Organizer's lifestyle.

The Organizers seek to be 'embedded in nature', but for them, it means being an integral part of the natural world. Contrary to the public perception that the term 'eco' is a synonym for 'nature', most activists in the ecovillage movement give the term 'eco-village' a much broader meaning. Originating from the ancient Greek οἶκος (oîkos), the word 'eco' does not mean 'nature'; it means 'home, house, household'. The leaders of the ecovillage movement seek to reframe the dualistic distinction between human and nonhuman habitats. They emphasize that it is unrealistic to divide a space into human and natural habitats and experiment with projects based on the concept of a 'common home' for human beings and other inhabitants of the Earth. This approach suggests viewing all components of the environment as inhabitants embedded in the place.

The experience of the Global Ecovillage Network, accumulated over the last three decades, shows that newly established villages can be located in a wide variety of places. It means that a community of Organizers does not have many special requirements for the primary characteristics of the component 'place'. Inhabitants oriented towards the Organizer's lifestyle are ready to transform mere locations into lived-in environments for both human and nonhuman inhabitants. The transformations are centred on all available knowledge of where and how landscapes and wildlife intersect with the needs of the community. There are numerous examples of new ecovillage establishments that initiate healing transformations of the natural environment, aiming to regenerate the land and benefit wildlife (see the case studies of Amatciems and Kardokai ecovillages in Chap. 4, Resonansia ecovillages in Chap. 5, and the Tamera ecovillage in Chap. 6).

Component C: Living Infrastructure

For a long time, the creation of infrastructure facilities mainly depended on engineering ideas, knowledge, and skills. During the industrial era, grey infrastructure expanded in both urban and rural landscapes, with a focus on large-scale structures. Contemporary infrastructure building usually comes with high costs to communities and the environment. Moreover, rigid, artificial design makes infrastructure facilities hardly adaptable to changing socio-economic and environmental conditions. Today, the built infrastructure of the industrial era is often referred to as 'grey' (human-made; anthropogenic). Growing awareness of the harmful effects of infrastructure has driven social movements and communities to criticize 'grey' infrastructure and offer an alternative 'green' (natural, living) infrastructure.

Many studies and policy programs on urban development still consider this new trend a simple supplementation of grey infrastructure with some natural elements, such as parks, urban gardens, green roofs, and bioswales. At the same time, they emphasize the necessity to shift to green technologies, building infrastructure with minimal environmental harm. This includes renewable energy sources, energy-efficient buildings, smart waste management, and green transportation.

Initially, the same approach to infrastructure building was used by the creators of the innovative eco-settlement vision. They described the eco-settlement's infrastructure as a component being designed with environmentally friendly technologies that aim to reduce negative impacts on the environment. However, post-industrial reality demands a more complex approach to rethinking and remodelling industrial human settlements. This approach calls for a paradigm shift in how we perceive the role and functions of infrastructure in a society where most people are oriented to service-driven business and lifestyle.

According to the industrial era paradigm, the infrastructure facilities should help control nature. Proponents of a new paradigm strive to work in closer partnership with the living world. However, efforts to collaborate with nature for the creation of 'living infrastructure' differ from a simple combination of grey and green. Living infrastructure designers and practitioners seek to expand consideration to both human and non-human communities, recognizing the importance of hydrological cycles, soil quality, and the necessity of other species for healthy ecosystem function. Ultimately, these practitioners have broadened traditional definitions of infrastructure by blurring the division between man-made and natural infrastructure. For instance, in 2016, California began to recognize source watersheds as integral components of California's water infrastructure (Barrett, 2016). Their efforts reflect a broad and growing commitment to living infrastructure, which can be understood as a practice that respects and facilitates the dynamic processes that are at the heart of all life. Especially active in this process is a new generation of urban morphologists and architects, who have concluded their PhD over the last decade (Oliveira, 2024). They often use the term 'nature-inspired' to describe their efforts to understand, synthesize, and imitate natural objects or phenomena, which enables us to gain improved insights into nature. Such inspiration can come through materials, processes, or designs we see in the natural world. Nature-based solutions are often higher quality, lower cost, more resilient, and more beneficial to society than maintaining, repairing, or replacing grey infrastructure.

Most efforts to create a living infrastructure are still focused on integrating natural and man-made elements without involving social infrastructure. Affected by a long tradition of examining human life as distinct from life in the natural world, the integration of social aspects with physical environment remains poor in living infrastructure creation practices. However, some ecovillages go beyond the goal of organizing their living place with physical infrastructure. Lessons learned from the experience of the ecovillage movement, summarized by Global Ecovillage Network, highlighted that living infrastructure must integrate built, natural, and social systems, blurring the boundaries between them. Designing eco-settlements infrastructure holistically, the perception of industrial social infrastructure should be transformed. First, maintaining and developing a symbiotic approach in relationships with the natural environment requires a reorganized education system (see case study on Kardokai Nature School in Chap. 5) and the application of more symbiotic co-living practices that enable collective decision-making, shared responsibility, and trust-building among inhabitants (see case study on Sociocracy in Chap. 5). Employing a symbiotic approach to human and natural life, the healthcare system can also be transformed (see case studies on the regeneration of Smiltynė by such transformative services as dolphin-assisted therapy in Chap. 7 and the Rozkalni ecovillage, developing a friendly approach to individuals with developmental disabilities in Chap. 6).

The described characteristics of the three components provide a general vision of post-industrial settlement at the stage of innovation strategy, as most of the pilot projects aimed at creating a post-industrial settlement are still in the initial stage of their development. However, some ecovillages have been in existence and operating successfully for over three decades. They have already passed some stages on the evolutionary path and can advise on the most critical challenges and how to overcome them. It enabled us to highlight some new challenges to the post-industrial paradigm-developing strategies that comprise the evolutionary framework, as defined by the Qualitative Structure theory (see Chap. 2). Understanding challenges to the following stages of evolution provides actionable insights for newly established eco-communities to focus on key strategic actions that can help to increase the quality of their settlement, and policymakers involved in the regeneration of industrial towns.

In summary, the findings presented in the monograph highlight that from the perspective of human settlement evolution, the application of service-driven business and consuming models encourages a symbiotic approach to integrating the key structural parts of human life that were developed by the industrial economic system. The latest scientific discoveries made about symbiosis also prove its centrality in maintaining life. Understanding symbiosis is the main condition for moving from the historical period known as the Anthropocene (Chua & Fair, 2019) into a new era (Everard & Everard, 2016; Mead et al., 2023; Skubała & Ochwat, 2023). According to the main direction of changes, the post-industrial period may be called the Symbiocene.

The book presents only the first step in applying the Qualitative Structure Method, which has a wide range of possibilities, to research on human settlements. Further research is needed to examine the future trends and multi-factorial impacts on the evolution of habitation in the post-industrial era. More in-depth studies devoted to the analysis and construction of each strategic model, adapted to the specific characteristics of a particular country or region and the current issues of the period under study, may reveal many new aspects that are important for the development of service economy-oriented human settlements.

Application of the Qualitative Structure Method and other similar holistic and evolutionary approaches is particularly relevant at this time because the industrial paradigm and its allied mental models are stubbornly resistant to change. As pointed out by Duffy (2009), creating a paradigm shift is like converting an entire religious community to a new religion. The holistic and evolutionary character of the Qualitative Structure Method helps to mitigate the confrontation between innovators oriented to the Service era thinking and advocates of the industrial paradigm. First, the evolutionary approach emphasizes that all previous known eras in the history of humanity are not discarded. On the contrary, the best features of the human settlements system developed during each era continue to be used in combination with the human settlement model developed during the following new era. Secondly, we live in a time of paradigm shifts, and the future will require new ways of thinking based on metaknowledge elaborated by the integration of different disciplines. The holistic approach enables refocusing discussions between industrialists and post-industrialists from such dichotomies as rural and urban settlements, the built and natural environments, and human and non-human habitats towards key paradigm innovations necessary for exiting the Anthropocene and entering the Symbiocene.

The monograph is an invitation to both researchers and practitioners to extend the ideas proposed. Although according to the theory of evolution, it is impossible to skip to a higher stage of evolution without passing through the preceding ones, a theoretical understanding of all stages of the evolutionary cycle can accelerate the process of evolution.

References

Adrjan, P., Ciminelli, G., Judes, A., Koelle, M., Schwellnus, C., & Sinclair, T. M. (2025). Working from home after COVID-19: Evidence from job postings in 20 countries. *Labour Economics, 96*, 102751. https://doi.org/10.1016/j.labeco.2025.102751

Albrecht, G. A. (2016). Exiting the Anthropocene and entering the Symbiocene. *Minding Nature, 9*(2), 12–16.

Apollo. (2022). *Surprising Working From Home Productivity Statistics.* Retrieved August 18, 2025, from https://www.apollotechnical.com/working-from-home-productivity-statistics/

Bailey, D. E., & Kurland, N. B. (2002). A review of telework research: Findings, new directions, and lessons for the study of modern work. *Journal of Organizational Behavior: The International Journal of Industrial, Occupational and Organizational Psychology and Behavior, 23*(4), 383–400.

Barrett K. (2016). New California law recognizes meadows, streams as "green infrastructure", eligible for public works funding. https://www.ecosystem-marketplace.com/articles/california-peru-part-global-trend-recognizing-forests-rivers-infrastructure/.

Bozzi, A. (2024). Digital nomadism from the perspective of places and mobilities: A literature review. *European Transport Research Review, 16*(1), 1–15. https://doi.org/10.1186/s12544-024-00663-z

Cahyani, R. R., Riani, A. L., Harsono, M., & Sunaryo, S. (2024). The impact of entrepreneurial lifestyle on business success: A systematic literature review. *Journal of Ecohumanism, 3*(4), 3395–3405.

Chua, L., & Fair, H. (2019). Anthropocene. In F. Stein, S. Lazar, M. Candea, H. Diemberger, J. Robbins, A. Sanchez, & R. Stasch (Eds.), *Cambridge encyclopedia of anthropology.* https://doi.org/10.29164/19anthro

Criscuolo, C., Gal, P., Leidecker, L., Losma, F., & Nicoletti, G. (2021). The role of telework for productivity during and post-COVID-19: Results from an OECD survey among managers and workers. OECD productivity working papers, 2021–31, OECD Publishing, Paris.

De Almeida, M. A., Correia, A., Schneider, D., & de Souza, J. M. (2021). COVID-19 as opportunity to test digital nomad lifestyle. In *2021 IEEE 24th international conference on computer supported cooperative work in design (CSCWD)*, pp. 1209–1214. https://doi.org/10.1109/CSCWD49262.2021.9437685.

Duffy, F. M. (2009). Paradigms, mental models, and mindsets: Triple barriers to transformational change in school systems. *International Journal of Educational Leadership Preparation, 4*(3), 1–23.

Emanuel, N., & Harrington, E. (2024). Working remotely? Selection, treatment, and the market for remote work. *American Economic Journal: Applied Economics, 16*(4), 528–559.

Everard, M., & Everard, M. (2016). Co-creating the Symbiocene. In *The ecosystems revolution* (pp. 139–153). Palgrave Macmillan.

Faruque, M. O., Talukder, T., Pranto, M. N., Debnath, A., & Sultana, S. (2024). The rise of remote work and its impact on small businesses. *American Journal of Industrial and Business Management, 14*(6), 869–890.

Fatima, H., Javaid, Z. K., Arshad, Z., Ashraf, M., & Batool, H. (2024). A systematic review on the impact of remote work on employee engagement. *Bulletin of Business and Economics (BBE), 13*(2), 117–126.

Ferrara, B., Pansini, M., De Vincenzi, C., Buonomo, I., & Benevene, P. (2022). Investigating the role of remote working on employees' performance and well-being: An evidence-based systematic review. *International Journal of Environmental Research and Public Health, 19*(19), 12373. https://doi.org/10.3390/ijerph191912373

Gillette, C. P. (2023). Remote work and City decline: Lessons from the Garment District. *Journal of Legal Analysis, 15*(1), 201–234. https://doi.org/10.1093/jla/laad004

Grosholz, E. R. (1991). Cartesian method and the problem of reduction. Oxford University Press. https://doi.org/10.1093/acprof:oso/9780198242505.001.0001.

Gurstein, P. (2001). *Wired to the world, Chained to the Home: Telework in Daily Life.* UBC Press.

Hajjami, O., & Crocco, O. S. (2023). Evolving approaches to employee engagement: Comparing antecedents in remote work and traditional workplaces. *European Journal of Training and Development, 48*(3/4), 375–392. https://doi.org/10.1108/ejtd-10-2022-0103

Hauw, S. D., & Vos, A. D. (2010). Millennials' career perspective and psychological contract expectations: Does the recession Lead to lowered expectations? *On JSTOR. Journal of Business and Psychology, 293*, 40605787.

Hidayat, A. I. (2024). The future of employment: How generation z is reshaping entrepreneurship through education? *Edu Spectrum: Journal of Multidimensional Education, 1*(1), 28–37.

Hoey, B. A. (2015). Postindustrial Societies. In J. Wright (Ed.), *International encyclopedia of the Social & Behavioral Sciences* (2nd ed., pp. 663–669). Elsevier.

Ivanycheva, D., Schulze, W. S., Lundmark, E., & Chirico, F. (2024). Lifestyle entrepreneurship: Literature review and future research agenda. *Journal of Management Studies, 61*(5), 2251–2286.

Kılıç, F. (2022). The relationship among entrepreneurship tendency, income level and life satisfaction of future business people: Generation Z. *International Business Research, 15*(3), 1–12.

Köffer, S., Anlauf, L., Ortbach, K., & Niehaves, B. (2015). The intensified blurring of boundaries between work and private life through IT consumerisation. ECIS 2015 completed research papers. Paper 108. http://aisel.aisnet.org/ecis2015_cr/108

Korpela, M. (2019). Searching for a countercultural life abroad: Neo-nomadism, lifestyle mobility or bohemian lifestyle migration? *Journal of Ethnic and Migration Studies, 46*(15), 3352–3369. https://doi.org/10.1080/1369183X.2019.1569505

Kurkland, N. B., & Bailey, D. E. (1999). The advantages and challenges of working here, there anywhere, and anytime. *Organizational Dynamics, 28*(2), 53–68. https://doi.org/10.1016/S0090-2616(00)80016-9

Levidow, L., Lindgaard-Jørgensen, P., Nilsson, Å., Skenhall, S. A., & Assimacopoulos, D. (2016). Process eco-innovation: Assessing meso-level eco-efficiency in industrial water-service systems. *Journal of Cleaner Production, 110*, 54–65. https://doi.org/10.1016/j.jclepro.2014.12.086

Li, H. (2020, December). Low motivation of youth in 21st century: A case study of the US, China, and Japan. In *2020 3rd International Conference on Humanities Education and Social Sciences (ICHESS 2020)* (pp. 272–276). Atlantis Press.

Markus, M. L., Manville, B., & Agres, C. E. (2000). What makes a virtual organization work? *MIT Sloan Management Review, 42*(1), 13.

Martin-Caughey, A. (2021). What's in an occupation? Investigating within-occupation variation and gender segregation using job titles and task descriptions. *American Sociological Review, 86*(5), 960–999. https://doi.org/10.1177/00031224211042053

Mead, J., Gibbs, K., Fisher, Z., & Kemp, A. H. (2023). What's next for wellbeing science? Moving from the Anthropocene to the Symbiocene. *Frontiers in Psychology, 14*, 1087078.

OECD. (2012). The future of eco-innovation: The role of business models in green transformation. .

Oliveira, V. (2024). The present and future of human settlements, urban morphology and ISUF. In *ISUF, Urban morphology and human settlements: Advances and prospects* (pp. 257–274).

Penn, R. (1975). Occupational prestige hierarchies: A great empirical invariant? *Social Forces, 54*(2), 352–364.

Rashmi, K., & Kataria, A. (2022). Work–life balance: A systematic literature review and bibliometric analysis. *International Journal of Sociology and Social Policy, 42*(11/12), 1028–1065.

Rosenberger, N. (2017). Young organic farmers in Japan: Betting on lifestyle, locality, and livelihood. *Contemporary Japan, 29*(1), 14–30.

Rustan, A. F., Rahayu, M. K. P., & Surwanti, A. (2024). A review of work-life balance trends in remote work. *International Research Journal of Multidisciplinary Scope, 5*(4), 316–330.

Siegel, P. M. (1971). Prestige in the American occupational structure (Doctoral dissertation, The University of Chicago).

Silver, H. (2023). Working from home: Before and after the pandemic. *Contexts (Berkeley, Calif.), 22*(1), 66. https://doi.org/10.1177/15365042221142839

Skubała, P., & Ochwat, M. (2023). On the role of symbiotic thinking in the age of the Anthropocene. *Dialogue and Universalism, 33*(2), 37–60.

Straus, E., Uhlig, L., Kühnel, J., & Korunka, C. (2023). Remote workers' well-being, perceived productivity, and engagement: Which resources should HRM improve during COVID-19? A longitudinal diary study. *The International Journal of Human Resource Management, 34*(15), 2960–2990.

Swan, P. (2021). *Entrepreneurship and generation Z: The behavioural characteristics of generation Z entrepreneurs in Wales.* University of South Wales.

Treiman, D. J. (2013). *Occupational prestige in comparative perspective.* Elsevier.

Vidickienė, D. (2023). Innovative business model 'product plus service'as paradigm innovation in farming. In *Rural transformation through Servitization: A qualitative structure approach* (pp. 69–90). Springer International Publishing.

Wong, K. P., Teh, P. L., & Chan, A. H. S. (2023). Seeing the forest and the trees: A scoping review of empirical research on work-life balance. *Sustainability, 15*(4), 2875.

Yushkevich, N. (2021). How approaches to work and leisure have changed in recent years—The experience of Gen Z. Startup Jedi. https://startupjedi.vc/content/how-approaches-work-and-leisure-have-changed-recent-years-experience-gen-z

Index[1]

[1] Note: Page numbers followed by 'n' refer to notes.

D. Vidickienė et al., *Human Settlement in the Service Economy Era*, Palgrave Advances in Bioeconomy: Economics and Policies, https://doi.org/10.1007/978-3-032-19390-2

The manufacturer's authorised representative in the EU is Springer Nature Customer Service Centre GmbH, Europaplatz 3, 69115 Heidelberg, Germany. If you have any concerns regarding our products, please contact ProductSafety@springernature.com

Printed and bound by CPI Group (UK) Ltd, Croydon, CR0 4YY
17/09/2026
02218454-0012